Time Out Guides Limited
Universal House
251 Tottenham Court Road
London W1T 7AB
Tel + 44 (0)20 7813 3000
Fax + 44 (0)20 7813 6001
Email guides@timeout.com
www.timeout.com

Editorial

Editor Tom Lamont
Deputy Editors Simon Coppock, Sarah Thorowgood
Listings checkers Cathy Limb, Gemma Pritchard, Fiona Shield
Proofreader Tamsin Shelton
Indexer Jackie Brind

Managing Director Peter Fiennes
Editorial Director Sarah Guy
Series Editor Cath Phillips
Business Manager Daniel Allen
Editorial Manager Holly Pick
Assistant Management Accountant Ija Krasnikova

Design

Art Director Scott Moore
Art Editor Pinelope Kourmouzoglou
Senior Designer Henry Elphick
Graphic Designers Kei Ishimaru. Nicola Wilson
Advertising Designer Jodi Sher

Picture Desk

Picture Editor Jael Marschner
Deputy Picture Editor Lynn Chambers
Picture Researcher Gemma Walters
Picture Desk Assistant Ben Rowe

Advertising

Commercial Director Mark Phillips
Sales Manager Alison Wallen
Advertising Sales Ben Holt, Jason Trotman
Copy Controller Alison Bourke

Marketing

Senior Publishing Brand Manager Luthfa Begum
Art Director Anthony Huggins
Circulation & Distribution Manager Dan Collins
Marketing Intern Alana Benton

Production

Group Production Director Mark Lamond
Production Manager Brendan McKeown
Production Controller Damian Bennett

Time Out Group

Chairman Tony Elliott
Chief Executive Officer David King
Group Financial Director Paul Rakkar
Group General Manager/Director
Nichola Coulthard
Time Out Communications Ltd MD David Pepper
Time Out International Ltd MD Cathy Runciman
Time Out Magazine Ltd Publisher/MD Mark Elliott
Group IT Director Simon Chappell
Marketing & Circulation Director Catherine Demajo

Contributors Geoff Andrew, Ismay Atkins, Simone Baird, Hal Brown, Matt Brown, Martin Coomer, Simon Coppock, diamond geezer, Guy Dimond, Alexi Duggins, Malcolm Eggs, Jessica Eveleigh, Will Fulford-Jones, Sarah Guy, Ronnie Haydon, Malcolm Hays, Phil Harriss, Matt Haynes, Emma Howarth, Joshua Heller, Stuart Husband, David Jenkins, Tom Lamont, John Lewis, Cathy Limb, Jennifer Lipman, Stuart McGurk, Dean Moston, Lisa Mullens, Paul Murphy, Anna Norman, Cathy Phillips, Monique Rivalland, Nicholas Royle, Paul Sentobe, Fiona Shield, Andrew Shields, Vid Simoniti, Alice Stanners, Gabriel Tate, Sarah Thorowgood, Peter Watts, Tyler Wetherall, Andy Woolgar.

Interviews by Fiona Shield, except Jacqueline Wilson (Ronnie Haydon) and Cerys Matthews (Eddy Lawrence).

The Editor would like to thank all contributors to *Time Out* guides and *Time Out* magazine (whose work forms the basis for parts of this book), as well as the following for suggestions and assistance: Krista Booker, Maggie Davies, Paul Fairclough, Ruth Jarvis, Abigail Lelliott, Kate Miller, Emma Perry, Lisa Ritchie, Kate Riordan, Chris Salmon, Dan Starza-Smith, Christina Thiesen, Elizabeth Winding.

Front and back cover Heloise Bergman; Andrew Brackenbury; Michael Franke; Rob Greig; Britta Jaschinski; Hadley Kincade; Mockford and Bonetti; Jonathan Perugia; Gordon Rainsford; Olivia Rutherford; Alys Tomlinson; Muir Vidler; Anthony Webb.

Illustrations by Ian Keltie – IKCA – www.iankeltie.com

Photography by Britta Jaschinski, except: pages 5 (top left), 7 (bottom right), 97 Haris Artemis; pages 5 (bottom centre), 302 Troy Bailey; pages 5 (top centre and bottom right) 10, 15, 66, 67, 89, 90, 124, 125, 127, 130, 137, 165, 168, 177, 187, 210, 240, 275, 280, 306 Andrew Brackenbury; pages 5 (top right), 7 (bottom left), 18, 23, 76, 87, 129, 163, 185, 227, 250 Alys Tomlinson; pages 7 (bottom centre), 201, 202 Michael Franke; pages 7 (top right), 13, 39, 47, 81, 82, 117, 147, 150, 155, 247, 248 Rob Greig; page 9 (bottom) Matt Carr; pages 9 (centre), 170, 284 Scott Wishart; page 30 Angelo Cavalli/Getty Images; pages 32/33 Jael Marschner; page 59 Claire Greenway; page 59, 246 Michelle Grant; page 60 Emma Wood; pages 69, 237 Leon Chew; pages 70, 144, 241 Jonathan Perugia; page 79 Laura Mtungwazi; pages 83, 195 Paula Glassman; pages 105, 286, 287 Nigel Tradewell; pages 112, 158, 294 Rogan Macdonald; pages 119, 133, 164, 223, 257, 279 Heloise Bergman; pages 121, 122 Oliver Knight; page 147 (top right) Liane Harris; page 153 Abigail Lelliot; pages 175, 206 Olivia Rutherford; page 178 Arcaid/Alamy; page 190 Timothy Allen/Axiom; pages 193, 255, 266, 273 Ming Tang Evans; page 204, 268, 290 Agnese Sanvito; page 218 Christina Theisen; page 225 Aine Donovan; page 230 Geoffrey Lipscombe/Fotolibra; page 239 Tricia de Courcy Ling; page 245 Ben Murphy; pages 259, 260, 261, 262 Alexander Shields and William Eckersley; page 270 Barry Lewis/Corbis; page 277 Belinda Lawley; pages 296, 297 Ed Marshall; page 303 www.simonleigh.com.
The following images were provided by the featured establishments/artists: pages 29, 33, 101, 102, 107, 109, 215, 246, 265, 288, 303, 307.

Contents

LONDON'S
MOST WANTED
CHICAGO
THE MUSICAL
CHICAGOTHEMUSICAL.CO.UK See 0844 412 4652
CAMBRIDGE THEATRE LONDON WC2

About the guide

Telephone numbers

All phone numbers listed in this guide assume you are calling from within London. From elsewhere in the UK, prefix each number with 020. From abroad, dial your international access code, then 44 for the UK, and then 20 for London.

Disclaimer

While every effort has been made to ensure the accuracy of information within this guide, the publishers cannot accept responsibility for any errors it may contain. Businesses can change their arrangements at any time so, before you go out of your way, we strongly advise you to phone ahead to check opening times and other particulars.

Advertisers

The recommendations in *1000 Things to do in London* are based on the experiences of Time Out journalists. No payment or PR invitation of any kind has secured inclusion or influenced content. The editors select which London activities are listed in this guide, and the list of 1,000 was compiled before any advertising space was sold. Advertising has no effect on editorial content.

Let us know what you think

Did we miss anything? We welcome tips for 'things' you consider we should include in future editions and take note of your criticism of our choices. You can email us at guides@timeout.com.

Introduction

We began by posing a question. If a friend, an out-of-towner, arrived in the capital for an afternoon, what would we show them? They wouldn't have long before leaving, a few hours at most. At the expense of a spin on the 'Eye or a neck-wrench at the gates of Buckingham Palace, what secret corner of the city would we unveil to reveal how much London meant to us?

We went further. If *we* were forced to leave London – at short notice, dragged biting and thrashing, no doubt, our claw-marks left in a riverside bench on the South Bank – where would we go to sop up the best of the city in our final afternoon?

We put the question to our team of writers, die-hard Londoners to the last. Food critics, arts experts, shopaholics, drink connoisseurs, kids specialists, fitness fanatics, museum fiends, niche enthusiasts, capital know-it-alls, slathering London eccentrics. Their every answer was different. *1000 Things to do in London* was born.

This guide does not rank, nor does it alphabetise or categorise. Number one does not represent the capital's best, nor number 1,000 its worst. We have not sought to do the impossible: put London into order. Instead, our suggestions come at you rather like this great city itself: suddenly, without easy arrangement or arbitrary pigeon-holing, but with London's particular immediacy and disorder. (Of course, if order's your thing, there's also a handy thematic index on *p315*.)

The end result is a book that can be read in the comfort of an armchair at home, enjoyed as a series of ardent odes to the city we love, or – our chief hope – kept on your person at all times: as an indispensable guide to the city's foremost 1,000 unmissables, as necessary to the Londoner as an *A-Z*, a spur for those times when inspiration just won't come. Not sure what to do on your lazy Saturday afternoon? For your celebratory night out? With your out-of-town friend who's in the capital for a few hours at most? Plop open the book. Have a flick. Let something catch your eye. Fall for London all over again – 1,000 times.

Tom Lamont, Editor

1 Take in the view from Tower Bridge

When Londoners want a great view of the capital's mighty river, they often head to either Waterloo Bridge or the London Eye – and both are worthy vantage points (see, respectively, p290 and p132). For the best Thames panorama, however, we reckon Tower Bridge can't be beaten. Here – from up high on the walkways – you get an unequalled sense of the river's awesome breadth and its ceaseless activity. Truly breathtaking.

2 Swim outdoors... in the middle of town

The Oasis Sports Centre's 25-metre outdoor swimming pool – with a sun deck and even the odd potted palm tree – is a central London gem. It is open all year round, come rain or shine, and in the winter months steam rises off the warm blue waters (maintained at between 25°C and 28.5°C). All for just £3.90 a swim.
Oasis Sports Centre *32 Endell Street, WC2H 9AG (7831 1804/www.gll.com).*

3 Eat in the pie room at the Newman Arms

Despite a modest spruce-up in the poky but historic downstairs bar, the main draw at the Newman Arms (23 Rathbone Street, W1T 1NG, 7636 1127, www.newmanarms.co.uk) is the 'Famous Pie Room' upstairs. Duvet-sized puffs of pastry envelop such special fillings as mutton with apple and cider; there are also seven standards always on offer (beef and Guinness, steak and kidney, and so on). Names of new pies are splashed across the side of the pub along the narrow alleyway between Rathbone and Newman Streets. It gets very busy here, so be sure to book ahead.

4 Cruise from Tate to Tate

If you want to travel in style between London's two Tates, there's only one way to go – take the dedicated, super-smooth catamaran service operated by Thames Clippers (7887 8888, www.tate.org.uk/tatetotate). As you might expect, even the design of the Tate-to-Tate service merits respect: the interior and exterior of one of the boats used is decked out in Damien Hirst's coloured spots and, at the Tate Britain end, it leaves from the striking steel Millbank pier, designed by architects David Marks and Julia Barfield (also responsible for the London Eye). Buy tickets at either Tate, online, by phone or (subject to availability) onboard. You'll get a third off with your Travelcard, making a single just £3.85 (£5 without).

5 Toast the town from the 42nd floor

Check in at reception, pass through X-ray machines and metal detectors, and then take a neon-illuminated express lift to top-floor champagne bar Vertigo 42. The whole operation feels like the security checks before a flight, but once you've made it to your destination you'll be rewarded with staggering 360° views of London. The decor, once a little too reminiscent of an airport executive lounge may have been revamped with a soothing purple and green colour scheme, but it's the sight of London spread beneath you through floor-to-ceiling windows that will really blow your mind. Expect to pay £12.75 for a glass of champagne.
Vertigo 42 *25 Old Broad Street, EC2N 1HQ (7877 7842/www.vertigo42.co.uk).*

6 Pop in to the Photographers' Gallery

Entry is still free to this marvellous little gallery, with exhibitions of still photography, film and installations. Its compact size means it isn't as daunting as larger exhibition spaces – you can nip in on your lunch break.
Photographers' Gallery *18 Ramillies Street, W1F 7LW (7831 1772/www.photonet.org.uk).*

7 Try on a bearskin at the Guards' Museum

The bearskin boys of the Guards are one of London's most distinctive sights – a must-see for fans of AA Milne. At the Guards' Museum, as well as trying on the famous hat, you can learn the history of the Grenadier, Coldstream, Scots, Irish and Welsh Guards who, along with two regiments of Household Cavalry, have the responsibility of guarding Brenda and her kin. At 11am every day (from May to July, and every other day for the rest of the year), the Guards form up outside the museum in preparation for the Changing of the Guard.
Guards' Museum *Wellington Barracks, Birdcage Walk, SW1A 6HQ (7414 3271).*

8 Pay homage to Dr Johnson

Hidden away in a grand court of Georgian townhouses, once home to many writerly sorts, is the stately home of Dr Samuel Johnson, one of the 18th century's greatest men of letters and author of perhaps the most important English dictionary. The museum has creaky floors and Queen Anne furniture; you can almost feel the old wit's presence. Johnson, though, didn't always love his job: 'To make dictionaries is dull work,' he wrote in his definition of the word 'dull'. To get an image of the man, stop by his statue in the churchyard of St Clement Dane, nearby on the Strand. Where once he worshipped, now he stands, book in hand. 'When a man is tired of London, he is tired of life; for there is in London all that life can afford.' Amen, Dr Johnson, amen to that.

Dr Johnson's House *17 Gough Square, off Fleet Street, EC4A 3DE (7353 3745/www.dr johnsonshouse.org).*

9 Keep bees

Who would have thought that being a beekeeper in the capital is likely to earn you a higher honey yield than your equivalent in the country? Talk to North London Beekeepers (www.beekeeping.org.uk/nl) for information and advice on how to become an urban beekeeper, and tap into the rich nectar resources of London's many parks and gardens. The organisation offers beginners' classes, a supervised 'adopt a hive' scheme and plenty of sound advice – such as stressing the importance, when it comes to neighbourly relations, of keeping good-tempered bees.

10 Wave a silk hanky at the veteran car rally

If you can haul yourself out of bed at the crack of dawn in early November, you can see off this parade of around 500 vintage motors. The cars (none of which exceed 20mph) set off on the long run to Brighton from Hyde Park between 7.30am and 9am, aiming to reach the seaside by late afternoon. Sleepyheads can get up later and join the crowds further along the route. The handsome, buffed-up vehicles are on Regent Street to be admired the previous day. For exact dates, check the website (www.lbvcr.com).

11-14 *Climb London walls*

London's mountains are notable by their absence, but that needn't dampen your enthusiasm for climbing in the capital. In the face of Mother Nature's oversight, Mother Necessity has conceived a worthy alternative: the indoor climbing wall.

Arguably the best climbing wall in London is the Castle (Green Lanes, N4 2HA, 8211 7000, www.castle-climbing. co.uk). Set inside an imposing Victorian folly, it has a huge range of top-roped climbs, as well as excellent crash-matted bouldering walls and a cave with a fully climbable roof.

Operating out of an old pipe-bending factory, the Mile End Climbing Wall (Haverfield Road, E3 5BE (8980 0289, www.mileendwall.org.uk) is run by serious climbers, with the average route presenting a tougher climb than at most of its competitors. Mile End is the most informal and atmospheric of London's 'big three' walls – owing largely to the fact that it's the oldest. The Monkey Room is our favourite: four walls and a sloping ceiling of holds that never stops being challenging. Still, climbers of all abilities will find courses to suit them.

At the Westway Sports Centre (1 Crowthorne Road, W10 6RP, 8969 0992, www.westwaysports centre.org.uk), 50 new routes and 50 new boulder problems are devised every month. Oddities here include a towering 'totem pole' and a bouldering wall with strange freestanding obelisks.

Since 2007, the Mile End and Westway centres have been pooling their resources for East Meets West, a climbing competition held over two consecutive weekends in November at both venues. Entry is open to all climbers for an admission fee of £12, and all participating climbers' results are pooled to determine whether east or west has the better climbers.

Finally, for something a little cooler, the Ellis Brigham gear shop in Covent Garden (3-11 Southampton Street, WC2E 7HA, 7395 1010, www.ellis-brigham.com) contains an indoor ice-climbing wall. Refrigerated to -15ºC, it's perfect for those who want a taste of vertical Alpine thrills without having to touch the void.

15 Watch the Village Cricket Final at Lord's

Lord's isn't just used for England matches and Middlesex games, but also for dozens of 'minor' games – like the National Village Cricket Final. Last year's finalists Findon of Sussex and Woodhouse Grange from Yorkshire, reached the final after a tournament that involves around 430 different local teams. This is cricket as Dickens wrote about it, slightly shambolic and hugely enthusiastic, with a good-natured, partisan crowd that numbers a few hundred fuelled with alcohol and roaring on their local heroes – husbands, dads and brothers. Very, very English.

16 Get your hands on the latest Apple gadget

The Apple Store is a glass-staired mecca to Mac design. All that shiny chrome and cool white looks so good that after a minute or two your palms will be sweating with the urge to touch but also to reach into your pocket and drop a month's salary on the latest bit of Apple wizardry. Fortunately, friendly staff are happy for you to do the former without the latter.
Apple Store *235 Regent Street, W1B 2EL (7153 9000/www.apple.co.uk).*

17 Visit the Freud Museum

Sigmund's last home is preserved as it was when he died, and as his previous house was when he fled Vienna in 1938 (he had the position of everything in his study written down, so it could be exactly recreated in London). Yes, the couch is here, but no, you can't lie on it to unburden yourself of troubles.
Freud Museum *20 Maresfield Gardens, NW3 5SX (7435 2002/www.freud.org.uk).*

18 Float

Set up back in 1984 as the first of its kind in the UK, the London Float Centre (South London Natural Health Centre, 7A Clapham Common Southside, SW4 7AA, 7720 4952, www.london floatcentre.com) has been providing relaxation, hallucinations, even hangover cures for two decades. It boasts four spacious flotation tanks – complete with individual showers and Neal's Yard toiletries – each with a large pool of warm, Epsom-salted water. As well as helping with back problems, arthritis and insomnia, this treatment – it is claimed – promotes accelerated learning and can reduce high blood pressure. A single float costs £45; three introductory sessions cost £90.

19 Beadle about Burlington Arcade

Long before Londoners were browsing high-spec concept shops, superstores and suburban malls, the city's consummate consumers flocked to the select tailors, corsetières and jewellers around Piccadilly. It was here that the city's first shopping centres were built, in the form of genteel and architecturally elegant arcades. Opened in 1819, skylit Burlington Arcade (off Piccadilly, between Old Bond Street and the Royal Academy of Arts) is the most famous of these arcades. It is also the most traditional.

According to archaic laws still on the books, it is illegal to sing, whistle, carry large parcels, open umbrellas or hurry in the arcade – and beadles were stationed to prevent any such misbehaviour. Three of these top-hatted, frock-coated men ('the smallest private police force in existence', according to the Arcade) are employed to this day.

20 Learn to mix a Martini

Dirty, naked, smoky, muddy – not a hike through a Laotian jungle, but the range of Martinis you'll learn how to mix at master-classes held once a month at Christopher's (18 Wellington Street, WC2E 7DD, 7240 4222, www.christophersgrill.com, check website for times). The hour-long sessions cost £12.

21 Watch the Great Gorilla Run

Once a year, hundreds of primates take over London's streets for the Great Gorilla Run (www.gorillas.org/greatgorillarun), an annual charity event that features people dressed up as monkeys. The 7km run is organised to raise money to protect the endangered gorillas of Rwanda. Previous runs have been a great success and a tremendous spectacle, with the hairy-suited athletes zooming past Tate Modern and over Tower Bridge. Still undecided about taking part? Remember that once the event is over, you get to keep the gorilla suit.

22 Have dinner in a converted power station

There can be few more unusual spots to eat out in the capital than Wapping Food, housed in a former hydraulic power station. The dramatic conversion of this vast space into a restaurant – and associated gallery/performance space – makes no effort to hide the building's industrial origins, with rusting and peeling pumps, chains and giant hooks still firmly in place. Set against the fading mint-green paint of the industrial equipment, the trendy orange plastic chairs, silver chandeliers and crisp white linen of the restaurant achieve a quite stunning brand of industrial chic. The menu changes daily: you might be offered smoked eel and pork belly with cauliflower purée infused with herbs; succulent Brecon lamb with a dollop of harisa-like tomato relish; or courgette flowers stuffed to bursting with goat's cheese. After pudding (balsamic ice-cream with strawberries anyone?), wander next door for an art exhibition or to enjoy some modern dance and complete a truly extraordinary dining experience.

Wapping Food *Wapping Hydraulic Power Station, Wapping Wall, E1W 3ST (7680 2080/ www.thewappingproject.com).*

23 Chomp a steak at Gaucho

This expanding mini-chain goes from strength to strength. The meat served – rump, sirloin, fillet, ribeye and churrasco de lomo (a speciality cut of fillet) – is so tender you might cut it with a spoon (no steak knives are even offered). You'll find Gauchos at Bank (1 Bell Inn Yard, off Gracechurch Street, EC3V 0BL, 7626 5180), Broadgate (5 Finsbury Avenue, EC2M 2PG, 7392 7652), Canary Wharf (29 Westferry Circus, Canary Riverside, E14 8RR, 7987 9494), Chelsea (89 Sloane Avenue, SW3 3DX, 7584 9901), Hampstead (64 Heath Street, NW3 1DN, 7431 8222), the O2 (Peninsula Square, SE10 0DX, 8858 7711), Richmond (The Towpath, TW10 6UJ, 8948 4030) and the flagship in Piccadilly (25 Swallow Street, W1B 4QR, 7734 4040). Check the website (www.gauchorestaurants.co.uk) for new openings.

24-33 Get to know London's city farms

Ronnie Haydon, *editor of* **Time Out London for Children,** *enjoys the whiff of manure without setting foot in the country.*

The old urbs vs rus debate is thriving down on the city farm. Hard-core urbanites will say there is no place for an all-mooing, all-bleating, rural idyll in the heart of the city – children in London are better off learning about free running than free-range eggs. The more bucolically inclined counter that city kids need to see cows, pigs, chickens and sheep, not least because they should know where their burgers, bacon, nuggets and kebabs come from. We just think there's something rather poetic about seeing sheep safely graze in the shadow of Canary Wharf (as at Mudchute City Farm in Docklands) and being assailed by the unmistakeable farmyard byre aroma as you get off the train at Vauxhall (you've Vauxhall City Farm to thank for that).

The apotheosis of urban agriculture, Mudchute City Farm was the venue back in 2005 for a big party to celebrate 25 years of the Federation of City Farms & Community Gardens (FCFCG) – we're not sure if these farming folk had a barn dance or hoedown, but the federation certainly deserves a big glass of scrumpy. As the representative body for the 64 city farms, 1,000 community gardens and 70 school farms in the UK, it has its work cut out, helping us hopeless urban cases – particularly the younger ones – make the connection between, say, cows and milk, sheep and chops, turkeys and twizzlers.

The 16 London farms overseen by the Federation include the 32-acre Mudchute (that's an awful lot of Docklands to be keeping out of the hands of property developers) and some real East End characters, like Stepney's appealingly scruffy Stepping Stones, with its railway carriages full of staw bales and full complement of donkeys, pigs, sheep, poultry and rabbits, all rubbing along together very nicely in the shadow of the Norman church. In Hackney, the multitude of middle-class parents toting tow-haired toddlers has given the cobbled farmyard at Goldsmiths Row a Cath Kidston vibe, and the lovely Frizzante Café on the farm (*see p240*) is a right bunfight for Sunday lunch. Craft classes and Indian head massage are typically Hackney add-ons, but most people just love to lean over the gate enclosing Bella the saddleback pig's pen, and scratch the old sow behind the ears. Larry the donkey is another minor celebrity round here. Down on Surrey Docks Farm, an airy place on the riverbank, you can get rather closer to the animals than you might want. A motley crew of badly behaved goats mobs you when you enter the gated yard with a bag of food (you buy this at the café; we've never forgiven one for nicking the KitKat out of our rucksack. That's another advantage of city farms: the animals are such superstars they tend to get cocky. The shadow of the slaughterhouse is seldom cast over these pampered beasts, so this is farming at its cuddliest.

Deen City Farm *39 Windsor Avenue, SW19 2RR (8543 5300/www.deencityfarm.co.uk).*
Freightliners City Farm *Paradise Park, Sheringham Road, off Liverpool Road, N7 8PF (7609 0467/www.freightlinersfarm.org.uk).*
Hackney City Farm *1A Goldsmiths Row, E2 8QA (7729 6381/www.hackneycityfarm.co.uk).*
Kentish Town City Farm *1 Cressfield Close, off Grafton Road, NW5 4BN (7916 5421/ www.ktcityfarm.org.uk).*
Mudchute City Farm *Pier Street, E14 3HP (7515 5901/www.mudchute.org).*
Newham City Farm *Stansfeld Road, E6 5LT (7474 4960/www.newham.gov.uk).*
Spitalfields City Farm *Pedley Street, entrance on Buxton Street, E1 5AR (7247 8762/www.spitalfields cityfarm.org).*
Stepping Stones Farm *Stepney Way, junction with Stepney High Street, E1 3DG (7790 8204).*
Surrey Docks Farm *Rotherhithe Street, SE16 5ET (7231 1010/www.surreydocksfarm.org.uk).*
Vauxhall City Farm *165 Tyers Street, SE11 5HL (7582 4204/www.vauxhallcityfarm.org.uk).*

Inn the know

Stuart Husband explores a little-known enclave of quiet courtyards and bustling lawyers, right in the middle of the city.

The Inns of Court – four self-contained precincts where barristers traditionally train and practise – are an oasis of calm in the middle of the city. With their tranquil quads and lawns, dominated by majestic plane trees, and their Grade I-listed medieval chapels and Tudor-style libraries and dining halls, they resemble hushed and venerable Oxbridge campuses. Yet few Londoners realise that the grounds of the Inns are open to the public, and fewer still take advantage of the opportunities to bask or picnic in their gardens, or simply wander aimlessly along their pathways. 'I've met people who've lived in London all their lives,' says Molly Rumbelow, a historian who leads guided walking tours through the Inns, 'and they've no idea that the Inns are here. In some ways, they're London's best-kept secret.'

The Inns – Lincoln's Inn, Gray's Inn, Inner Temple, Middle Temple – meander in a broad zig-zag from Holborn down through Chancery Lane to Blackfriars and the Embankment. They trace their history back to the 14th century, when the old manor house belonging to Sir Reginald de Grey, Chief Justice of Chester, was converted into a 'hostelry' for law students

fleeing the disarray of King Edward's court (hence Inns). They then spread to incorporate land owned by the medieval Christian military order of the Knights Templar (hence Temples). By the 1600s they had become independent societies: the Temples remain 'liberties' of the City of London, which means they're within the historic boundaries of the City but operate as their own local authorities; the Inns are under the more prosaic jurisdiction of Camden council. And while the Inns no longer accommodate students, judges (or 'benchers', to use Inn parlance) are still entitled to stay overnight in advantageously apportioned apartments, though they rarely do in practice (it's 'a security nightmare', according to those in the know).

The first thing anyone attempting to penetrate the enclosures of the Inns (whose portals consist of unheralded and unadorned wooden gates, which are emphatically locked as soon as the last tenant leaves the premises) will notice is that they're rather off-putting. Signs purporting to issue from such splendidly Dickensian bureaucrats as the 'Master of the Walks' or the 'Sarjeant-at-Arms' authorise the immediate removal of anyone 'constituting a

'I've met people who've lived in London all their lives with no idea that the Inns are here.'

nuisance'. (The best of these can be found at the entrance to Staple Inn, just by Chancery Lane station, which expressly mandates the non-admittance of 'old clothesmen' and 'rude children'). Anyone daring to venture further, however, will find immaculately suited barristers disappearing through hidden archways and bustling purposefully through paved courtyards dominated by tinkling fountains. (This is probably the closest London has to offer to the disorienting *Don't Look Now*-style Venetian experience of getting definitively lost, with horsehair wigs standing in for red duffel-coats.) Eventually, these give way to impressive swards like Gray's Inn Gardens or the rolling fields of Lincoln's Inn, where you can join the m'luds as they kick off their Lobbs and loosen their Chanels for alfresco lunches (don't get too horizontal: the gardens are generally open to the public noon to 2.30pm only).

As you might imagine, the Inns are steeped in history. The huge Tudor Hall dominating Lincoln's Inn (a 19th-century facsimile of the 15th-century original) was one of the settings for *Bleak House*; Dickens's first job was actually as a clerk in Gray's Inn, and the recent BBC adaptation of his novel was just the latest period drama (after *Wilde* and *Pride & Prejudice*, among others) to have the Inns serving as a kind of all-purpose Olde London backdrop. Shakespeare, meanwhile, personally supervised the first production of *Twelfth Night* at Middle Temple Hall, where Elizabeth I was a frequent guest. The redoubtable Halls, with their august stained glass and old-buffer wood panelling (and, in the case of Middle Temple Hall, genuine minstrels' gallery), aren't open to the public unless you group-book ahead, and even then – unless you can be admitted on a barrister's coat-tails – you're strictly forbidden to disturb the Inns' most sacred ritual: dining.

The rec tables and comfort food – stews and custards, essentially – are defiantly retrograde, as are the arcane rites: students have to consume 12 dinners before they can be called to the Bar (a medieval prototype for the Caffè Nero-style loyalty card, perhaps), and no one is permitted to leave Gray's Hall – however much they've drunk and need bladder relief – until 'Mr Junior' (the diner closest to the exit) applies to 'Mr Senior' (the barrister of greatest authority at high table) for 'permission to smoke'. 'Permission' is never refused.

The Inns also have their own places of worship, generally open to the public 11am to noon and 1pm to 4pm, outside of special services. John Donne, the 17th-century poet and later Dean of St Paul's, once presided over the Gothic chapel at Lincoln's Inn, whose campanologists may have inspired him to write 'never send to know for whom the bell tolls; it tolls for thee': to this day, the bells are rung to alert the Inn's denizens to the death of a bencher. The Inner Temple Church was built on the site of a 12th-century Knights Templar church and graveyard; effigies of some crusty old knights are on display inside, while a diminutive Nicola Hicks sculpture of a pair of knights on a scrawny horse – representing their supposed piety and poverty – is perched on a plinth in the adjacent square. Inner Temple Church is one of the multitude of ecclesiastical sites with walk-on parts in *The Da Vinci Code*: it's worth catching a Friday lecture by the current 'Master' of the church, Robin Griffith-Jones, who specialises in forensic debunking of Dan Brown's 'research'.

But you don't have to have a PhD in Lucrative Conspiracy Theories or even be a hardline Dickens nut or medievalist to enjoy the singular ambience of the Inns. Simple perambulation through these secret gardens – through archways, down cobbled lanes, past rose gardens – is reward in itself, especially on a bright day. And if you stop on one of the generously sized benches to watch the genuine gas lamps being lit as dusk falls, and squint just enough to blur out the modern appurtenances – the Maseratis in the bencher parking slots, the iPod of a passing junior clerk – you can imagine yourself in a palimpsest of the modern, frenetic city that lies outside the gates; a London that's more tranquil, more civilised and, somehow, more mysterious.

35 Take afternoon tea at the Wolseley

Dinner at the Wolseley is a certainly a big-budget affair, but never fear – you can get an affordable taster of the splendour and elegance of this landmark venue by opting instead for afternoon tea. For less than a tenner, indulge in a plate of freshly baked scones, complete with own-made jam, clotted cream and a pot of tea. We've tried afternoon teas all over London and rate the Wolseley's one of the best (you even get an hour-glass timer to ensure your tea brews for the correct length of time). Renowned pastry chef Claire Clark left her post here in 2005, but her legacy lives on in the superlative mix of English cakes and French pâtisserie on offer. From homely victoria sponges to fondant-topped coffee éclairs, moist rum babas and creamy fruit tartlets, this place makes stylish cakes with flair, commitment and impeccably good taste. On our last visit, we tucked into a mouth-watering pastry tart, filled with a deep layer of rich chocolate mousse and topped with the sharp bite of whole raspberries – a match made in heaven. Next time, we'll plump for the vanilla cheese-cake, which has a big reputation among London's cake aficionados.

The Wolseley *160 Piccadilly, W1J 9EB (7499 6996/www.thewolseley.com).*

The Wolseley

36 Watch – but don't join in – the competition for the Peter Pan cup

Every Christmas morning members of the Serpentine Swimming Club bravely take a plunge into the frosty waters of Hyde Park's pond for the Peter Pan Cup Christmas Morning Handicap Swim. To compete, each swimmer must be a club member, have competed in a series of competitions… and be wearing a Santa hat. With average temperatures rarely exceeding 4°C, the club requires participants to endure several months of winter training to help the body acclimatise to the extreme conditions. Still, it's great fun to watch from the bank, wearing nice warm clothes. The race begins at 9am on 25 December each year, on the south bank of the lake.

37 Stay late in the museum

If your social schedule is getting in the way of cultural pursuits, combine both by attending an evening event at a museum or gallery. The framework is pretty well established – late opening of the current blockbuster show with extra entertainment – but the contents can be impressively unexpected.

Our favourite series is Late at Tate. Held at Tate Britain (Millbank, SW1P 4RG, 7887 8000, www.tate.org.uk) on the first Friday of every month, Late at Tate is often avant-garde and always fun. Previous late visitors here have been treated to the Gothic Nightmares show of supernatural paintings by Blake and Fuseli, then regaled in a side gallery by a modern shamen snorting a mysterious South American hallucinogenic before commencing a convulsive rant about the interconnectedness of all life. Compelling stuff. Other events have seen slideshows of record cover art to a soundtrack DJed by Jerry Dammers. The Victoria & Albert Museum (Cromwell Road, SW7 2RL, 7942 2000, www.vam.ac.uk) holds a similarly edgy evening on the last Friday of the month: Friday Lates feature guest DJs, live performances and the all-important pay bar.

The British Museum (Great Russell Street, WC1B 3DG, 7323 8783, www.thebritish museum.ac.uk) offers a double bill of late shows: Thursday nights are high brow – a talk or debate centred around an exhibition (a recent lecture chose the lure of the forest in Indian Culture as its topic) – and Fridays more about entertainment (there's usually a film showing related to one of the current exhibitions).

Like the British Museum, the National Portrait Gallery (St Martin's Place, WC2H 0HE, 7306 0055, www.npg.org.uk) splits its late events between serious (Thursday talks) and sensual (music on Friday). Highlights in the past have included talks by historian David Cannadine, film director Michael Apted and author Jeanette Winterson. Musical Friday nights have seen an acoustic Pet Shop Boys evening by classical cellist Nick Squires and a night of underground tango.

38 Sing-along to the Sound of Music

Once a month (usually on the last Friday), the Prince Charles Cinema (Leicester Place, WC2 7BY, 7494 3654, www.princecharlescinema. com) hosts 'Sing-a-Long-a Sound of Music', a special showing of the classic film specially designed for those people who are unable to resist belting out 'Maria' or 'Lonely Goatherd' at the top of their lungs – often while enjoying the equally dubious pleasure of fancy dress. Women (and, of course, men) dressed as nuns lustily deliver the title tune, entire contingents of Von Trapps sing out their favourite things and plenty of bemused first-timers sit at the back, enjoying the spectacle. Full marks to those who do show up in costume, but we have to wonder: did they ride the tube like that? There is a bar, lest you fear singing in public when cold sober. Book tickets online at www. singalonga.net (prices vary).

39 Explore the flavours of Sichuan

While the world's other major cuisines have their regional cooking well represented in London, the Chinese food in our city is virtually a monoculture of Cantonese dishes. Yet the cooking of China's other regions is as distinct from Cantonese as Swedish food is from Spanish. Sichuan food – spicy, colourful dishes from the humid, lush, south-western province – is one of China's great regional cuisines, and popular right across China, yet it is only reaching our shores now.

Bar Shu (28 Frith Street, W1D 5LF, 7287 6688, www.bar-shu.co.uk) isn't London's first Sichuan restaurant, but it's the first to do things so thoroughly – with five chefs from Sichuan – and in such style. In the newly refurbished surrounds of the smart three-storey site in Soho try 'dongpo pork knuckle', dry-fried green beans with minced pork and preserved mustard greens, or steamed scallops in a fragrant chili sauce.

Longer-standing is Belgravia's Hunan (51 Pimlico Road, SW1W 8NE, 7730 5712, www.hunanlondon.com). The best approach here is to give free reign to the waiters and let them offer up a succession of small dishes (the plates keep on coming, though, so tell them when you've had enough or the bill might be be a shock). Highlights include the delectable bamboo cups containing guinea fowl, chicken, pork and egg white in a gingery stock. A set meal can cost up to £150 per person, depending on how hungry you are.

40 Visit Shri Swaminarayan temple

The gleaming pinnacles and pillars of the Shri Swaminarayan Mandir would be a truly extraordinary sight anywhere – but rising out of suburban Neasden, with nothing more remarkable than the North Circular and IKEA for neighbours, they're particularly special. A vast but incredibly intricate vision in limestone and marble, this Hindu temple ('mandir') is the biggest in the western hemisphere. Some 2,820 tonnes of Bulgarian limestone and 2,000 tonnes of carrara marble from Italy were carved in India by hundreds of craftsmen, before the parts were shipped to London and assembled over the course of three years; the building was finished in 1995. Dress respectfully to enter.

Shri Swaminarayan Mandir
105-119 Brentfield Road, Neasden, NW10 8LD (8965 2651/www.mandir.org).

41 Pray in a floating church

Docked right by Canary Wharf, St Peter's Barge (West India Quay, E14 4AL, 7093 1212, www.stpetersbarge.org) is London's only waterborne church. The Dutch freight barge was bought in 2003 and made its way across the North Sea to the UK later that year – under its own steam. It has a full-time Church of England minister and holds a service at 4pm and 6.30pm every Sunday.

42 Spin the globe at Stanfords

With three floors stacked full of travel guides, travel writing, road and wall maps (some imported), as well as illustrated books covering all continents, atlases, globes, magazines and accessories, the flagship branch of Stanfords is a vital stop for anyone planning that big trip – or just a weekend break. Brit-map junkies will thrill at the full range of Ordnance Survey maps in the basement. Get plotting.

Stanfords *12-14 Long Acre, WC2E 9LP (7836 1321/www.stanfords.co.uk).*

43 Heli-tour the skies over London

Get a dramatically different view of London with a Cabair heli-tour flight. Departing from Elstree Aerodrome in north London (Borehamwood, WD6 3AW, 8953 4411, www.cabairhelicopters.com), the five-seater Twin Squirrel helicopter flies you at a height of 1,000 feet over all the classic sights – Kew Gardens, Buckingham Palace, the Houses of Parliament and along the Thames as far east as the Barrier. Flights last 30 minutes and cost £150 per person; a commentary is given. Don't forget your camera or camcorder, and remember to bring ID bearing your photo and address or you won't be permitted to fly. A stockpile of appropriate quotes cribbed from Vietnam war films is optional.

44 Shop for vintage phones at Radio Days

The choice of reconditioned retro radios at vintage favourite Radio Days (87 Lower Marsh, SE1 7AB, 7928 0800) is pretty good, but it's only one facet of a laid-back and reasonably priced emporium. Old-fashioned phones are a highlight, with lots of Bakelite beauties dating from the 1930s onwards. You can pick up vintage magazines and advertising, plus there's a great range of '40s glad rags.

45 Play London skittles

Try to knock down nine pins with a 10lb 'cheese' (more of a wedge than a ball) in as few throws as possible. A rare 'floorer' is the apogee, when all the pins are downed with one throw. Three floorers on the trot will earn you a place in London skittles history (17 were recorded in 1934, but the feat hasn't been managed since 1960). Sadly, this historic London game is nearing extinction, but there is an alley at the Freemasons Arms (32 Downshire Hill, NW3 1NT, 7433 6811). Play it to save it!

46 Don't stop till you get enough

It seems that the rivers of vomit that some predicted our capital's streets were to be washed with have – happily – not materialised. In fact it's also true that, half a decade on from the much-talked-about extension to alcohol licencing hours, it can even be a stuggle to find somewhere to drop in for drink come 3am. Here, notwithstanding, are a few of our favourite late-night London establishments – places that usually get started during the small hours, power through the night and often headlong into the next day.

Egg (200 York Way, N7 9AP, 7609 8364, www.egglondon.net) is vital bolt-hole should you find yourself turfed out of somewhere at 3am with your legs still jiggling. As well as three floors of epic sound-systems thumping out techno, house and electro, there's a grand outdoor space that can make for a welcome respite from it all. On Sunday monrnings, Breakfast at Egg opens at 5am and keeps going late into the day – one for those with only the hardest of cores.

While predominantly a gay club, visitors to Fire (38-42 Parry St, SW8 1RT, 7820 0550/ www.fireclub.co.uk) are really only interested in dancing their faces off throughout Friday night and all the way through until late on Sunday afternoon. Taking full advantage of their 24-hour licence, Fire relentlessly pounds down house and techno to people who simply refuse to let the night end.

When most clubbers are queuing for the nightbus home, Redlight (Club Aquarium, 256-264 Old Street, EC1V 9DD, 7253 3558, www.redlight.co.uk) is just opening. From 3am until 9am, the party offers banging techno, dirty electro and deep house to a polysexual crowd. Leave your inhibitions at home – locked in a box.

Arguably London's most unusual venue, Public Life (82A Commercial Street, E1 6LY, 7375 1631, www.publiclife.org.uk) is a late club located in an old public toilet under Commercial Street. With a reputation for playing some of the best techno in the Capital and a capacity of only 100 people, it's a pressure cooker of dance energy; this is the real London underground.

47 Discover Bloomberg Space

Instead of simply leasing or buying art to enhance its European headquarters, the financial news and media provider Bloomberg decided in 2002 that it would dedicate a space within its London premises to art. Never a company to do things by halves, the firm recruited respected art-world figures to curate an ongoing exhibition programme of contemporary pieces. Any difficulties with the corporate architecture of the space have been overcome by the excellent quality of the exhibitions: recent highlights have included new work by Peter Liversidge and DJ Simpson. **Bloomberg Space** *50 Finsbury Square, EC2A 1HD (7330 7959).*

48 Get back in to the Young Vic theatre

Built on a bombsite in under a year, the Young Vic opened on The Cut in 1970 and has always operated on egalitarian principles, with a remit to nurture young talent among aspiring directors of all backgrounds. But by the millennium the cheaply knocked-together building and shabby industrial stage – originally intended to last only five years – were beginning to look a bit crumpled so the theatre promptly booked itself in for a comprehensive makeover (helped in no small part by the fund raising of Young Vic alumnus Jude Law).

David Lan, the theatre's artistic director since 2000, also oversaw its relaunch in 2006 and has been a strong hand at the helm since. The new space is a RIBA award-winning building with two new theatres (the 80-seater Clare and 160-seater Maria) on the all-new strip that is The Cut these days. Recent hits have included the claustrophobic *Kursk* – almost certainly theatre's only play set in a submarine and a collaboration between the Sound & Fury theatre company and playwright Bryony Lavery. **Young Vic** *66 The Cut, SE1 8LZ (7922 2922/ www.youngvic.org).*

wagamama

1000 things to do in london
slurp noodles at wagamama!

delicious noodles | rice dishes | freshly squeezed juices
wine | sake | japanese beers

positive eating + positive living

wagamama.com

uk | ireland | holland | australia | dubai | antwerp | auckland | copenhagen | istanbul

49 Get yourself a proper shave

The shaving ritual at Geo F Trumper could put the precisions of the tea ceremony to shame. This venerable institution, established in Curzon Street in 1875, has 'served the needs of London gentlemen and members of the Royal Court for over 125 years' and is still run by a Trumper. The process entails getting your face doused in 'skin food', wrapped in hot towels, cut-throat shave, cold towels, face massage and moisturiser. There's also a shaving school here, at which gentlemen are taught shaving techniques one-to-one.
Geo F Trumper *9 Curzon Street, W1J 5HQ (7499 1850/www.trumpers.com).*

50 Eat your way round Alan Yau

Start at Wagamama, founded by Yau in 1992. Yau is no longer associated with the chain, but the business stays close to his original ethos, providing wholesome noodle dishes at a fair price; see www.wagamama.com for a list of London's branches. Next, head to Busaba Eathai, operating since 1999. Style is king at this Thai mini-chain (three outlets in central London, see www.busaba.com), where Yau's hand is evident in the streamlined interior. People share chunky wooden tables and the tasty dishes (think intriguing ingredients like wing beans and rose apple) arrive in a trice. Yau's flagship – and, ever since it opened in 2001, the jewel in his crown – is Hakkasan: all lattice black screens, misty blue glass and spotlit tables and superlative Chinese dishes. The quality of the food is beyond reproach; as a cheaper alternative, the dim sum (*see p132*) is also excellent. Yau's dim sum restaurant Yauatcha, which opened in Soho 2004, remains a smash hit with the fashionable; the upstairs tea room (*see p276*) is a particular treat. His most recent two ventures – upscale Japanese diner Saké no Hana on St James's Street, and the modern noodle house mini-chain Cha Cha Moon (with branches on Ganton Street and Queensway) – are the latest in Yau's impressive and, we hope, still growing portfolio.

A few of my favourite things

51-57

Nicholas Royle, author

I love to eat an American Hot and drink cold beer in the jazz room downstairs at Pizza Express Jazz Club (10 Dean Street, W1D 3RW, 7437 9595, www. pizzaexpress.com/ jazz). Because chilled bottles of Peroni, jazz and Pizza Express pizzas are a few of my favourite things.
I love to follow the New River Walk from St Paul's Road to Canonbury Road, N1. It feels like a secret known only to a few.
I love to go to Hatton Cross tube station, where the planes coming in to land at Heathrow are so low you can feel your bones vibrate. It's a visceral experience.
I love to walk from Centre Point to Marble Arch without once setting foot on the hideousness that is Oxford Street. You feel like you've cheated death.
I used to love drinking the cocktails mixed by the incomparable Salvatore Calabrese in the Library Bar (Lanesborough Hotel, Hyde Park Corner, W1J 7JZ, 7259 5599, www.lanesborough.com). Salvatore doesn't work there anymore, but the bar is still a fine one.
I love to walk to my destination and get there faster than the idiots stuck on the tube or, even worse, the bus. Or, worse still, paying through the nose for a cab.
I love to buy CDs in Harold Moores Records (2 Great Marlborough Street, W1F 7HQ, 7437 1576, www.hmrecords.co.uk). It's a wonderful old shop where they know what they're talking about. It's the Rough Trade of classical music.

Nicholas Royle's latest book, Mortality, *is published by Serpent's Tail.*

58

Worth every penny of the £2 fee, these green and white icons are enticingly laid out in spring and summer.

59 Hike along a railway on the Parkland Walk

At the west end of Finsbury Park just above the tennis courts, the bridge across the current railway morphs into the disused railway track that is the Parkland Walk. Formerly part of the London and North Eastern Railway's line from Finsbury Park to Edgware, the railway was closed in 1970. In 1984 the tracks were removed and Parkland Walk was opened. The 4.5 mile trail runs all the way to Alexandra Palace, past the abandoned Crouch End platform and Highgate station.

Stepping up (or down) onto Parkland Walk is a transformative experience. The trees lining the path are thick and tall and so even though there are busy roads just metres away, they are completely hidden from view – you could almost, with a little imagination, be on a woodland path deep in the heart of the countryside.

The sign at the Highgate end lists the flora and fauna to be seen. A thriving community of foxes makes sense, but the colony of slow-worms, muntjac deer and over 60 species of birds are more of a surprise – as is the rich list of trees that the sharp eyed may spot: apple, ash, birch, cherry, field maple, hawthorn, hazel, holly, oak, poplar (Italian and white), rowan, sycamore and yew.

60 Spend a Sunday with the French at Ciné Lumière

Launched by Catherine Deneuve in 1998, this plush cinema puts on some excellent seasons – and not all with a French focus. But if you do fancy something Gallic, pop along at 2pm on a Sunday for its screenings of classic French films: anything from a Godard to cutting-edge contemporary masterpieces. Either way, you have a high chance of catching some arty angles and emotionally charged tobacco consumption. Tickets cost £9, £7 concessions. **Ciné Lumière** *Institut Français, 17 Queensberry Place, SW7 2DT (7073 1350/www.institut-francais.org.uk).*

61 Play softball in Regent's Park

Had softball – a close relation of baseball that isn't, whatever you might have expected, played with a soft ball – not been removed from the 2012 Olympics programme, Regent's Park would have hosted the games. Home to the London Softball Federation, the park has 17 softball pitches available for use by members of the public (May-Aug). They are hugely popular, though, so if you want to play you'll have to book months in advance (7486 7905).

62 Reflect on a crime of passion over a pint

Ruth Ellis, the last woman to be hanged in Britain, shot David Blakely here on Easter Day in 1955, and two weathered bullet holes on the front wall outside (plus framed press cuttings) mark the event. Today, the Magdala (2A South Hill Park, NW3 2SB, 7435 2503) is a sedate spot for a pint of London Pride or Greene King IPA.

63 Gamble on art

During its yearly 'Secret' fundraiser, international stars are invited by the Royal College of Art (www.rca.ac.uk) to create postcard-size works of art that go on sale for £35 each. The catch is that the identity of the artist isn't revealed until after the work has been purchased. Although half of the fun is in trying to spot the Damien Hirst, be wary of work that seems readily identifiable; the well-known artists tend to enter into the spirit of the event by disguising their handiwork. To take part in the sale you have to register in advance at one of the viewing days or by emailing secret@rca.ac.uk. The viewing days happen mid- to late November each year.

64-67 Book your place at a literary night out

Apples and Snakes

London's foremost performance poetry production house puts on spoken word gigs (from hip hop-inspired poetry slams to more traditional readings from poets all over the world) on a fortnightly basis. Emerging talents rub shoulders with master wordsmiths such as Jean Binta Breeze and John Hegley and draw in a crowd of devoted personal fans and poetry aficionados. Ticket prices vary from free to £8, depending on the venue (www.applesandsnakes.org).

Book Slam

Thanks to its popularity, this now-legendary monthly musical-literary club night recently found yet another new home (it keeps outgrowing venues) at the Tabernacle (34-35 Powis Square, W11 2AY, 7221 9700, www.bookslam.com), where it takes place on the last Thursday of the month. Tickets are £6 in advance (£8 on the door), but get in there early as it often sells out. Recent highlights have included MC Speech Debelle and David Simon, creator of *The Wire*.

The First Tuesday Poetry Club

Running since 2005, this small poetry club is now firmly established at ace Clerkenwell boozer the Three Kings (7 Clerkenwell Close, EC1R 0DY, 7253 0483). It's fascinating – and it's free.

Foyles

Foyles' (113-119 Charing Cross Road, WC2H 0EB, 7437 5660, www.foyles.co.uk) venerable tradition of bringing authors together with their readers goes back to 1930 when Christina Foyle, the bookshop's legendary managing director, organised her first literary luncheon. Since then, Foyles' literary events have attracted giants of the publishing world like Enid Blyton and Doris Lessing. These days the luncheons have been mostly replaced by intimate soirées with best-selling authors. Entrance is free.

68-72 *Find your fetish*

Although Soho hangs on to its reputation as centre of the capital's sex trade, and fetish designers continue to colonise Holloway Road, London's fetish shops are scattered far and wide. Those wishing to – cough – plug into the growing scene should start by contacting Coffee, Cake & Kink (7419 2996 www.coffee cakeandkink.com), where you can pick up a copy of the London Fetish Map. For whips, canes, floggers and paddles, Holloway Road still delivers the goods: try Fettered Pleasures (No.90, N7 8JG, 7619 9333, www.fettered pleasures.com), which also sells chain and rope by the metre. In Waterloo, Honour (86 Lower Marsh, SE1 7AB, 7401 8219, www.honour. co.uk) has an upstairs 'bondage attic' for sex toys, cuffs and clamps, while Myla (with branches accross London, see www.myla.com), does a saucy line in upmarket accessories and toys. But the coolest kink of all has to be in Covent Garden at Liberation (49 Shelton Street, WC2H 9HE, 7836 5894, www.libidex. com). Its fetish antiques are unique: why settle for cookie-cutter modern paraphernalia when you could be spicing up a role play with a Victorian bridle and spurs or an antique holy communion set?

73 *Get alongside London's ghosts*

If you believe the spookologists, London is crawling with ghostly visitors. Among them is the theatrical ghost of Covent Garden tube, a tall spectre in a grey suit, tight trousers and a homburg hat who has been spotted rattling the door of the ticket office. A seance discerned this was the ghost of actor William Terris, murdered by a fellow thesp outside the Adelphi Theatre in 1897. He used to frequent the baker's that stood on the site, proving that even in death, a man needs his buns.

The more scenic location of St James's Park is the stamping ground of the headless Lady of the Lake, who is sometimes to be seen emerging from the lake, drifting on to land and then breaking into a frantic run. She was the wife of a sergeant of the guards, who decapitated her, buried the head and flung the body in the lake. In 1972 a driver swerved to avoid her and crashed into a lamp-post. When the history of the haunting was brought up in court, the driver was acquitted of dangerous driving.

If ghost-spotting with a pint in hand is more your style, stop by the riverside Morpeth Arms (58 Millbank, SW1P 4RW, 7834 6442), allegedly one of the most haunted pubs in London. As well as being the place where real-life spooks go for a snifter after a hard day's spying at the Secret Intelligence Service HQ (formerly MI6) across the Thames, the pub is on the site of the 19th-century Millbank penitentiary. There's said to be a vast network of tunnels beneath, frequented by the spectre of an escaping prisoner who never found his way out.

Soho's John Snow boozer (39 Broadwick Street, W1F 9QJ, 7437 1344) was named after the doctor who discovered that cholera was a water-borne disease, tracing an outbreak to a water pump near here. The pub is haunted by a shadowy figure who sits in a dark corner, his face twisted into a terrible grimace and with ghastly red glowing eyes – he is believed to be a victim of the cholera epidemic.

If you want expert guidance in such matters, London ghost authority Richard Jones runs regular Ghost Walks (www.london-ghost-walk. co.uk) that take you through alleyways and graveyards at night for maximum chill factor.

74 *Drop anchor at the Museum in Docklands*

Nowhere else in the capital gives you a better sense of the importance of the Thames to the evolution of London than this museum, set in a Georgian warehouse. The Roman, Danish and Saxon history of the river is presented via exhibits and a series of videos narrated by Tony Robinson, before the museum takes on the birth of the docks and the lives of those who worked there. The Sailortown section recreates the sounds and smells of an alley in 19th-century Wapping, and there's a brilliant model of Old London Bridge.

Museum in Docklands *No.1 Warehouse, West India Quay, Hertsmere Road, E14 4AL (7001 9844/www.museumindocklands.org.uk).*

75 Play with swords

If you're searching for a martial art with real cut and thrust (or simply want to hit people with sticks), Marcello Zizzari's battodo Japanese sword class is the activity for you. Beginners are welcome at all three venues (see www.battodo-fudokan.co.uk for details), where the skill of swinging a heavy sword, stance, sheathing and cutting movements are first practised with wooden weapons and poles. Then it's on to the real thing. Classes costs £10 for an introduction, then £50 for six weeks.

76

Drive dodgems on the South Bank

The South Bank's not all about high art and pedestrianised zones: less sophisticated pleasures of a four-wheel variety are on offer at Namco Station (County Hall, Westminster Bridge Road, SE1 7PB, 7967 1067, www.namco experience.com). Its indoor bumper cars are a fine way to release artistic tension – and it stays open until midnight. Two quid a go.

77

Make yourself part of the Critical Mass

Critical Mass London is less about taking a pleasant spin round the capital than reclaiming the roads through cycling. But you get to take a pleasant spin in any case. Although, as the website puts it, 'There are probably as many aims of CM as there are participants', few would disagree with the general principle that 'more bikes means less cars'. By cycling en masse Critical Mass (www.criticalmass london.org.uk) forces the motorised traffic to give way to the pedalled variety. The regular group ride takes place on the first Friday of every month, starting at 6.30pm from under Waterloo Bridge on the South Bank. If you want to join in, just bring along a bike.

78

Eat breakfast over the market at Roast

Breakfast here – Borough Market's first proper dining establishment, aptly dedicated to British food – is a satisfyingly indulgent start to the day, thanks to crisp linen and a nice quiet restaurant. Go for the Full Borough (£15), featuring Ayrshire smoked streaky bacon, cumberland sausages, fried bread, black pudding, grilled tomatoes, field mushrooms and eggs. From the mezzanine level you can look down and watch the market come to life. **Roast** *The Floral Hall, Borough Market, Stoney Street, SE1 1TL (0845 034 7300/ www.roast-restaurant.com).*

79

Play 18 holes – without the walk outdoors

If you don't fancy trekking out into the suburbs for your game of golf, Urban Golf (33 Great Pulteney Street, W1F 9NW, 7434 4300, www.urbangolf.co.uk) lets you play a full round without stepping beyond the bounds of Soho. Its high-tech simulators let you play 40 of the world's most famous courses without ever leaving London. There are lessons on offer, plus food and drink served in the 'clubhouse' bar, which comes complete with a PlayStation console and games. Prices range from £20-£50 per hour, per simulator (up to 8 people can play together) depending when you want to play.

80-81

Chill, big-style

At the risk of drawing some seriously nasty jinx down upon their heads, we're going to say it: child-friendly festival organisers turned nightlife barons Big Chill (www.bigchill.net) can do no wrong. Since starting a club night at Islington's Union Chapel over 15 years ago, and hosting a small festival in Wales the following year, Katrina Larkin and Pete Lawrence have steadily expanded the Big Chill empire. Their festival in Eastnor, Herefordshire, attracts 35,000 smiling folk each August and sells out faster every year, there are now Big Chill events around the globe and there's even a successful record label.

In late 2005 the Big Chill Bar (Old Truman Brewery, off Brick Lane, E1 6QL, 7392 9180) took a grey steel bunker of a room and turned it into a super-friendly and vibrant DJ bar. It's been busy ever since, which is no mean feat on the famously competitive East End nightlife scene. Then came along the Big Chill House (257-259 Pentonville Road, N1 9NL, 7427 2540) in 2006. The venue has four floors, each independently themed, and a suntrap of a south-facing terrace with its own cocktail bar – pretty much bringing all the attractions of the festival under a single roof.

82 Heal with the homeopaths

Ernst Louis Ambrecht opened Nelsons Pharmacy, the first homeopathic pharmacy in London, in 1860; after three decades, it relocated to Duke Street in Mayfair. Since then this has been the physical and spiritual home of homeopathic medicine. In the 1930s Dr Edward Bach began to sell his Bach Original Flower Remedies here. Apothecary bottles with handwritten labels still line the counter but, nowadays, the pharmacy responds to requests from all over the world, using its vast 'potency bank' of more than 2,000 remedies. There's a peaceful clinic, too, where you can book an in-depth consultation.
Nelsons Pharmacy *73 Duke Street, W1K 5BY (7629 3118/www.nelsonspharmacy.com).*

83 Play carrom

Andrew Shields introduces an all-action board game that's sliding back from obscurity.

If you wandered through Spitalfields Market on a Sunday a few years back, you might have noticed groups of players flicking black and white objects into pockets at the corners of a beautifully decorated board. They were among the first of a now growing number of Londoners who discovered the addictive qualities of carrom – a board game with some similarities to pool, snooker and billards, but without the cues, smoke-filled dives and dodgy reliance on outdated formal wear.

The game is at least two centuries old, but the basic concept of shooting objects into holes quicker than someone else has been around for thousands of years. Its origins are hotly contested, though the word *carrom* comes from Timor in south-east Asia. From there the term travelled with the Portuguese, who used it to describe the Malabar coast of India and applied it to a type of fruit. By the late 18th century the English-speaking world was familiar with the word in the context of 'carrom billiards', a game that was played on a table without pockets. Later, it came to mean 'hitting one thing on to another' – and was soon corrupted to 'cannon', the term that is still used in cue sports.

Either two people or four people can play the game at one time. Their aim is to be the first to pocket nine white or black 'men', plus the red 'queen', using a 'striker' that you flick with your index finger 'Subbuteo'-style. Skill and determination are vital, but a little bit of luck never goes amiss.

The rules of carrom are comparatively simple and the board, being only 29 inches square, requires far less space than, say, a pool table – factors that have helped carrom move beyond the market and into some of the capital's coolest clubs. You can play at the Vibe Bar (Truman Brewery, Brick Lane, E1 6QL, www.vibe-bar.co.uk, call or check website for details of when games are being played – although it's usually on Monday evenings from April to September), at Ginglik (1 Shepherd's Bush Green, W12 8PH, 07944 303749, www.ginglik.co.uk) and, of course, every Sunday, 10am to 5pm, at Sunday UpMarket (The Old Truman Brewery, Brick Lane, E1 6QL, www.sundayupmarket.co.uk). The website www.carromshop.co.uk has further information about the game and some lovely boards for sale. A complete set costs £44.95.

The UK Carrom Club was set up in 1986, and now organises tournaments and leagues in London, Croydon, Kent, Crawley and further afield; it costs £6 a year to join. First, though, why not give it a try for free at a club night? It's finger-flickin' good.

84-92 *Folk about*

Start your folk odyssey at Cecil Sharp House (2 Regent's Park Road, NW1 7AY, 7485 2206, www.efdss.org), home to the English Folk Dance and Song Society, where a variety of events are staged in somewhat ascetic surroundings; check online for details of its barn dances, ceilidhs and folk-dance classes.

Then there's the antifolk circuit, a loose collective of like-minded songwriters, rebels and general mischief-makers convening regularly at the Blang nights at the 12 Bar Club (26 Denmark Street, WC2H 8NL, 7240 2622, www.blang.co.uk). Amid these fashionable new folkies, the old-school folk scene has rather slipped between the cracks. But it's still there, defiantly maintained by a clutch of old-timers and an increasing number of younger converts. As well as this, there are also occasional genuinely old-school folk shows at the 12 Bar Club – check the website for details.

The Green Note in Camden (106 Parkway, NW1 7AN, 7485 9899, www.greennote.co.uk) is also a lively venue which books its fair share of traditional artists, along with blues musicians and singer-sonwriters. And there's further folky fare at London's other weekly folk clubs, which are dotted around the capital and scattered through the week. Among the best are the often irreverent Islington Folk Club, held on Thursdays (except in the summer) at 8pm at the Horseshoe in Clerkenwell (24 Clerkwenwell Close, EC1R 0AG, 7253 6068, www.islingtonfolkclub.co.uk); the largely traditional Cellar Upstairs, which takes place each Saturday at 8.15pm at Euston's Exmouth Arms (1 Starcross Street, NW1 2HR, 7281 7700, www.cellarupstairs.org.uk); 'folk and spooky country' night Soft Focus, held on monthly Saturdays at the Three Kings of Clerkenwell (7 Clerkenwell Close, EC1R 0DY, jeremy@clerkenwellmusic.co.uk); and the eclectic Walthamstow Folk Club, which is staged at 7.30pm every Sunday, Sept-Jun, at the Plough Inn (173 Wood Street, E17 3NU, 8503 7419, www.walthamstowfolk.co.uk). All-comers are welcome, with membership always available on the door.

Finally, the Magpie's Nest, is the best of a new breed of folk clubs, putting on up-and-comers as well as revered old hands. In addition to their mid-monthly Wednesday night gigs at Islington's Old Queen's Head (44 Essex Road, N1 8LN, 7354 9993), they throw one-off bashes at bigger venues such as Cargo.

93 *Watch the penguins being fed at London Zoo*

Daily at 1.30pm.
London Zoo *Regent's Park, NW1 4RY (7722 3333/www.zsl.org/london-zoo).*

Close
knīt

Sarah Guy sees the fashionistas catch on to her favourite hobby.

Knitting is fashionable again, which means it's never been easier to make the pastime a social event. It's been clicking its way back into popularity for a few years now, as a DIY pursuit, as a feature of the catwalk (check out the knitwear sold at Weardowney Get-Up Boutique, for example, where woollen boob tubes and catsuits sit alongside yarns, knitting kits and info about classes) and as a respected craft (the Crafts Council's intriguing Knit2Tog exhibition was visited by 14,000 people – a record for one of its exhibitions). Knitting clubs have sprung up in pubs, cafés, schools and even south London florist and café You Don't Bring Me Flowers, where there's an informal Tuesday club. A quick glance at www.iknit.org.uk shows just how many styles of knitting group there are in London: queer knitting, knitting in a cinema and men-only sessions are just a few of the ones on offer. Indeed, once you get online there's a seemingly endless trail of sites and blogs and patterns for you to follow – for starters, have a look at www.stitchnbitch.co.uk, www.castoff.info and www.vam.ac.uk/collections/fashion/features/knitting for an idea of the different approaches.

Of course, for many people, knitting never went away, with the haberdashery departments at John Lewis or Liberty and various old-school wool shops in the suburbs keeping the faith through the fallow years. But now a clutch of modish yarn shops has opened in London. Loop, an alluring wool shop in Islington, tells you all you need to know about the current resurgence in popularity. It looks pleasingly boho, in an altogether un-English kind of way, so it's no surprise to find that the owner, Susan Cropper, is American. Like most wool shops (including the department stores), Loop runs a range of knitting classes. They include ones for beginners, children's half-term workshops, crochet classes, even one in experimental knitting, and they offer a mix of instruction and socialising that's hard to beat. All are very popular and get booked up fast; tea and cakes are served. There's also a drop-in SOS clinic

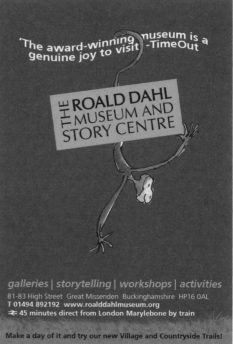

once a month or, if the shop isn't busy, a member of staff can probably help you out – all are proficient knitters.

Simply looking at the wools on sale here is enough to tempt anyone into picking up their needles – yarns come from Europe (especially Italy and Germany), Japan, New Zealand and the US. We asked Susan why she thought knitting had become so popular again, and she agreed that it was partly because 'the yarns are so gorgeous', with many having been hand-spun and hand-dyed, and partly because patterns had caught up with the times. What's more, she feels that a backlash against the uniformity of the high street means that more and more people are feeling the thrill of being able to make something unique. She also thinks that the craft skipped a generation – younger women don't seem to be as worried as their mothers about appearing interested in domestic activities. And then there's the sense of community knitting offers.

That's something that's apparent in other wool shops around London. They may reflect the areas they're based in – neat, bright Stash Yarns in Putney, the very proper Patricia Roberts Knitting in Knightsbridge and the laid-back I Knit in Vauxhall – but all of them are friendly and inclusive in a way that seems to be typical of the craft. The vibe is pretty much summed up by the mission statement of I Knit London: 'A shop, a sanctuary and a place to learn and be inspired – share ideas, share experience and share your needles.'

Loop

I Knit *106 Lower Marsh, SE1 7AB (7261 1338/www.iknit.org.uk).*
John Lewis *278-306 Oxford Street, W1A 1EX (7629 7711/www.johnlewis.co.uk).*
Liberty *Regent Street, W1B 5AH (7734 1234/ www.liberty.co.uk).*
Loop *41 Cross Street, N1 2BB (7288 1160/ www.loopknitting.com).*
Patricia Roberts Knitting *60 Kinnerton Street, SW1X 8ES (7235 4742/www.patricia roberts.co.uk).*
Stash Yarns *213 Upper Richmond Road, SW15 6SQ (8246 6666/www.stashyarns.co.uk).*
Weardowney Get-Up Boutique *47 Kendal Street, W2 2BU (7402 8892/www.wear downey.com).*
You Don't Bring Me Flowers *15 Staplehurst Road, SE13 5ND (8297 2333/www.youdont bringmeflowers.co.uk).*

95-97 *Take a bat walk*

Bat walks are booming. These late-night strolls – some of them accompanied by ultrasonic detectors that make bat chirps discernible by humans, others that rely on nothing more than the keen eyes and ears of a guide – are becoming more and more popular. Do you want to be able to distinguish your Myotis daubentonii from your Pelcotus auritis? Look out for walks at sunset or late at night in Highgate Woods, the WWT Wetland Centre and Tower Hamlets Cemetery Park. The London Bat Group (www.londonbats.org.uk) lists all the bat walks taking place in the city.

98 *Gird your loins at Rigby & Peller*

The corsetier to the Queen is still at the top of its game in terms of accurate measuring and fitting. Indeed, women (and men) have much for which to thank Mrs Rigby and Mrs Peller, who established this shop in 1939. Those in the know (thank you, ma'am) consider it one of life's greatest pleasures to have your undergarments snugly fitted here.
Rigby & Peller *22A Conduit Street, W1S 2XT (7491 2200/www.rigbyandpeller.com).*

99 *Orienteer*

A sport that has been likened to tackling *The Times* crossword while enjoying a jog, orienteering is the art of navigating round a course in the shortest possible time using a map and compass. If the navigation bit worries you, don't be deterred – it's sociable and family-friendly. Beginners are welcome at regular club events, which are colour-coded to suit different skill levels. There are also permanent courses in London and the south-east: you buy a map and information pack from a local sales point, then head off the beaten track at a time that's convenient for you. The British Orienteering Federation (01629 734042, www.british orienteering.org.uk) has a list of courses.

100 *Comb the shore for historical loot*

It's primal, gut-level fun – and there's the potential for economic reward. On the shores of the Thames, fragments of the city's great sprawl of history are churned up day after day, quite literally by the skipload, and they're yours to make of exactly what you will. A pair of hiking or wellington boots is strongly recommended for messing about by the river, and you'll want to avoid wearing your best clobber – this is an activity justly known as 'mudlarking'. You'll need a plastic bag to keep your treasures in, and a little trowel can come in handy for prodding and levering. Also, in order to squeeze the most out of an hour or two's potter along the foreshore, you'll need a Port of London Authority (PLA) tide chart to spot the monthly lows (see www.portoflondon.co.uk for details).

Because the river is continually disturbing the mud and depositing new objects on the beach, the same stretch of foreshore can contain totally different artefacts from one day to the next. Metal detectors aren't much use because of the sheer volume of metal waste and nails, so it's more a case of scanning for anything odd and then digging it up for a better look.

There are some restrictions: anything of potential archaeological value should be reported to the Museum of London, digging should go down to a maximum depth of only three inches and holes should be filled back in. Finds from our recent trips include nails from old ships, old bottles, iron shoes and clay pipes (complete pipes can sell on eBay for £15), a cow's tooth dating back more than 3,000 years, and a piece of Roman roof. According to marine archaeologist and expert beachcomber Mike Webber, walks from St Paul's and Bankside are the best for finds that you can take home with you. Alternatively, try Canary Wharf: it was here ships once docked after voyages to the New World and Australia. Who knows what goodies might be hidden in that sludge?

101-107

Jacqueline Wilson, children's author

I love the little details in Battersea Park Children's Zoo (*see p237*), like the plastic viewing bubbles in the meerkat enclosure. I also like the way they place the various species – the barn owl's in an enclosure done up to look like a barn.
If I'm meeting someone in London, I often choose the (now recently renovated) Royal Academy of Arts restaurant (Burlington House, W1J 0BD, 7300 8000, www.royalacademy.org.uk) where there's lots of choice and no one minds if you sit talking for a long time. I adore the lovely Victorian Hotel Russell (1-8 Russell Square, WC1B 5BE) and all its Bloomsbury connections. It's a hoot there, with its Viriginia Woolf burgers – it even hosts an antiquarian book fair each month. **In fact, I love book shopping in London. My favourite shops are Lion & Unicorn (19 King Street, Richmond, Surrey TW9 1ND, 8940 0483, www.lionunicornbooks. co.uk) and the Children's Bookshop (29 Fortis Green Road, N10 3HP, 8444 5500).** As far as big tourist sites are concerned, the Tower of London is a big thrill. I was delighted to be taken around the Crown Jewels – heaven for someone like me who's wedded to flashy jewellery. **I enjoy going to the theatre. I very much like Bloomsbury's Peacock Theatre (Portugal Street, WC2A 2HT, 0844 412 4319) and the wonderful Unicorn Theatre for Children (147 Tooley Street, SE1 2HZ, 0870 053 4534, www.unicorntheatre.com).** London is a wonderful place for walking. I like to go to Hampstead Heath or, a little more local for me, Richmond Park. One thing I keep meaning to do is visit one of the lidos (*see p126*), such as the ones at Tooting Bec or Brockwell. I'm going to wait for a really hot day this summer. *Jacqueline Wilson's most recent book is* Hetty Feather. *She was Children's Laureate from 2005-2007.*

108

Learn to make shoes

Aspiring Manolo Blahniks can test their potential by enrolling in a two-day shoemaking course for beginners (£266-£313, including shoe components and refreshments) at training school Prescott & Mackay (52 Warren Street, W1T 5NJ, 7388 4547), founded by Black Truffle shoe shop owner Melissa Needham. You come away with an own-made pair of women's mules.

109

Keep your eyes peeled for internationally renowned street artists on Leake Street

Underneath Waterloo Station, in a tunnel connecting York Street and Lower Marsh, lies Leake Street, a 200-metre stretch of dank underpass brightened considerably by a constant stream of new works by inspiring street artists. In 2008 the street became London's largest 'legal wall' when Banksy organised his very own 'Cans' festival, sanctioned by Lambeth Council. Groups of graffiti artists from around the world descended on the then derelict tunnel and covered it with their colourful and imaginative stencilwork. Cans 2 soon followed, encouraging more freehand artwork, and a year down the line the tunnel is now daubed with myriad styles from the likes of Blek, 3D and others. Despite the tedious textbook graffiti tags that also surface here, the ingenuity of other artists who still use the space manages to keep things remarkably fresh – as evidenced by the recent invasion of the tunnel by a group of underground knitting specialists – 'gritters' if you will – who covered the tunnel in a spooky, woolly spider's web.

110 Ride the DLR in the front carriage

Push the kids out the way and pretend that you're the driver. Because kids don't know how to drive trains.

111-124 *Eat pie and mash*

As London's white working-class communities continue to sell up and shift out to the outlying boroughs, the eateries that nourished them must transform, relocate or die. The city's boozers have in the main trodden the transformation route, making the most of their Victorian interiors, yet jettisoning their pickled eggs for parma ham, their Ben Truman for Bourgogne aligoté.

No such compromise has been – perhaps can be – made by London's time-honoured caterers to the workers: the pie and mash shops. They resolutely stick to providing food that has altered little since the shops appeared in the middle of the 19th century: potatoes (a wedge of glutinous mash), pies (minced beef and gravy in a watertight crust), eels (jellied and cold or warm and stewed) and a ladleful of liquor (an unfathomable lubricant

loosely based on parsley sauce). Escalating eel prices have meant many places only serve pie and mash these days. Vinegar and pepper are the preferred condiments, a fork and spoon the tools of choice, and expect to order in multiples: one pie, two mash; two pies, three mash…

A choice bunch of these establishments remains – resplendent with tiled interiors, marble-topped tables and worn wooden benches. The oldest and most beautiful is M Manze's on Tower Bridge Road, established in 1902, though F Cooke of Broadway Market, the Kellys and the Harrington's all date from the early 20th century. Visit these family-run businesses while you can, for each year another one closes, and with it vanishes a slice of old London. Relish the food, the surroundings, the prices (you'll rarely pay more than a fiver) and also your dining companions: Londoners to the core, not yet seduced by the trashy allure of the international burger chains.

WJ Arment *7 & 9 Westmoreland Road, SE17 2AX (7703 4974).*
Castle's *229 Royal College Street, NW1 9LT (7485 2196).*
Clark's *46 Exmouth Market, EC1R 4QE (7837 1974).*
Cockneys Pie & Mash *314 Portobello Road, W10 5RU (8960 9409).*
F Cooke *9 Broadway Market, E8 4PH (7254 6458).*
F Cooke *150 Hoxton Street, N1 6SH (7729 7718).*
AJ Goddard *203 Deptford High Street, SE8 3NT (8692 3601).*
Harrington's *3 Selkirk Road, SW17 0ER (8672 1877).*
G Kelly *414 Bethnal Green Road, E2 0DJ (7739 3603).*
S&R Kelly *284 Bethnal Green Road, E2 0AG (7739 8676).*
AA Manzes *204 Deptford High Street SE8 3PR (8692 2375).*
L Manze *76 Walthamstow High Street, E17 7LD (8520 2855).*
L Manze *74 Chapel Market, N1 9ER (7837 5270).*
M Manze's *87 Tower Bridge Road, SE1 4TW (7407 2985/www.manze.co.uk).*

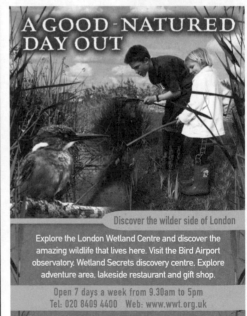

125 Do the Duck Tour

There is something inherently comical about chugging down Whitehall and past the ritzy shops of Piccadilly in a yellow amphibious vehicle dating back to World War II; some 21,000 such vehicles were used to transport supplies from sea directly on to dry land. The real excitement comes, however, when the vehicle launches – with surprisingly dramatic speed – into the Thames next to SIS (formerly MI6) at Vauxhall; the odd splashed passenger at the back only adds to the excitement. Unlike most of the major river tour boats, the 'Ducks' sit entertainingly low in the water, giving the experience an extra edge of pleasure. The 75-minute tour takes in the big sights of Westminster – Big Ben, Trafalgar Square, St James's Palace, Green Park, Buckingham Palace (from behind) and Tate Britain – and the quick-fire live commentary is chirpy (for the kids) and packed with quirky facts about London (for the grown-ups). Tours starting at Chicheley Street behind the London Eye run daily and cost £20; call to check times.
London Duck Tours *55 York Road, Waterloo, SE1 7NJ (7928 3132/www.londonducktours.co.uk).*

126 Reacquaint yourself with the Roundhouse

One of London's greatest counter-culture venues, the Roundhouse reopened in 2006 after a lengthy refit, and has now firmly re-established itself as one of the capital's coolest gig venues. Built in Camden in 1847 as an engineering shed for trains, the Roundhouse became a performance venue in the 1960s, and on 15 October 1966 achieved legendary status as party host for the underground newspaper *International Times*. It's more mainstream now, but still hugely creative, holding events as diverse as book readings by *Thick Of It* genius Armando Iannucci to genre-defying vaudeville act La Clique. Bold, unusual and original.
Roundhouse *Chalk Farm Road, NW1 8EH (0844 482 8008/www.roundhouse.org.uk).*

127

Learn how to be a blacksmith
The smithy classes run by Kevin Boys at Surrey Docks Farm (South Wharf, Rotherhithe Street, SE16 5ET, 07984 416 269) teach you how to get to grips with hammer, anvil and tongs to shape things out of metal, starting with a simple hook. A course of four sessions costs £80.

128 Smoke... while you still can

Smoking in enclosed public spaces may be well and truely a thing of the past, but you can – for the moment at least – still destroy your lungs at home. So why not do it in style by shopping at G Smith & Sons (74 Charing Cross Road, WC2H 0BG, 7836 7422)? Established back in 1869, it was the first shop on Charing Cross Road and holds a 'condition of lease' stating its site can only ever house a tobacconist. Not great for the anti-smoking lobby, but good news for all cigarette, pipe and cigar buffs out there, many of whom travel for miles, even from abroad, to visit this unique spot. Basically unchanged since it opened, G Smith is a place where you can buy Marlboro Lights if you must, but with the quality and rarity of products on offer, you'd be wasting a lung for nothing.

129 Be a basket case at Nike Midnight Madness

Games at this annual search for Britain's top basketball talent tip off at 8pm and continue until the small hours. The ten ballers who amass the most points in the qualifiers (late July/early August) join ten of Britain's elite players in a showcase final at Crystal Palace National Sports Centre (mid August). Previous years have seen guest appearances from Chicago Bulls star Luol Deng and former LA Laker Steve Bucknall, one of the few Brits to make it in the NBA. Entry is free whether you want to play or just hang out, but online registration (www.midnight-madness.com) is essential, and you need to be uder 23 to enter.

130 See double at the Riverside Studios

Better known for dance and theatre events, Riverside Studios also screens intelligently selected repertory double bills. Ticket prices are friendly (£7.50), coming in at less than the cost of a single bill at a West End cinema.
Riverside Studios *Crisp Road, W6 9RL (8237 1111/www.riversidestudios.co.uk).*

131-132 Get inside artists' studios

Open studio weekends, when artists and artisans throw open the doors of their private work spaces, provide a great opportunity to get your finger on London's creative pulse. Most venues hold open studio weekends twice a year, typically in early December and late spring or early summer. Studios tend to be in former factories, with sweet factories seeming a particular favourite. You're more likely to see paintings than toffees, but the good news is that it's all for sale. However, the real value of open studios – for artists and visitors alike – is the opportunity to make contact with an eye to future commissions. That could be anything from a bespoke hat to a vast painting.

Arts Unwrapped (www.artsunwrapped.com) organises Europe's biggest open studios event, which involves over 1,000 London artists and designers from 40 studios, over three weekends (one in May, two in June). To encourage visitors, a free shuttle service ferries you between premises. Also check out Hidden Art (7729 3800, www.hiddenart.com), a not-for-profit organisation that supports designer-makers working on a small or large scale. It holds open studio events in a series of locations around Holborn and Clerkenwell. The websites for each organisation have details of future events.

133 Browse the Petrie Museum with a torch

This museum, set up in 1892 by eccentric traveller and diarist Amelia Edwards, is named after Flinders Petrie, one of the indefatigable excavators of ancient Egyptian treasures. Where the British Museum's Egyptology collection is strong on the big stuff, the Petrie (pronounced 'pee-tree') focuses on the minutiae of ancient life. Its aged wooden cabinets are filled with shards of pottery, grooming accessories, jewellery and primitive tools. The fact that some corners of this small museum are so gloomy staff offer torches only adds to the fun.
Petrie Museum of Egyptian Archaeology
University College London, Malet Place, WC1E 6BT (7679 2884/www.petrie.ucl.ac.uk).

134

Jump London

London's growing army of traceurs (the name for those who practise parkour, or free running) is an increasingly vocal and visible presence – in stark contrast to their French counterparts, who advocate a circle of near secrecy that is in keeping with the 'actions rather than words' attitude of the sport's founder David Belle. You may well have seen some of them in action – leaping between metal stairwells on east London housing estates, or teetering along impossibly precarious concrete ledges at the Barbican – but chances are you passed them up as just another bunch of kids making trouble.

In fact, *le parkour* (literally 'the art of moving') is urban sport at its most unadulterated, and while arguments rage as to whether it's a form of martial art or urban performance theatre, few would deny the beauty inherent in its transformation of decrepit urban landscapes into arenas for physical expression, or the jaw-dropping simplicity of its purpose: to pass obstacles in the fastest and most direct manner possible, whether this means jumping, climbing, crawling or some improvisational combination of them all.

Following a sudden boom in parkour's popularity in the early noughties – largely inspired by the Channel 4 documentary *Jump London* and a particularly stomach-churning BBC ident featuring David Belle himself – Paul Corkery established Urban Freeflow (www.urbanfreeflow.com) to promote the safe practice of parkour at a time when copycat kids were launching themselves between the roofs of multi-storey car parks with wild abandon. As such, Corkery and co run an Urban Freeflow Academy offering two-hour classes on Monday and Thursday nights (£5 per session) at the Moberley Sports and Education Centre (101 Kilburn Lane, W10 4AH, 7641 4807), and a range of more advanced outdoor classes (£8 per session) that take place at a variety of spots throughout the capital, and are offered on a first-come, first-served basis.

135-139
Centre yourself with tai chi

Tai chi chuan, a meditative martial art that originated around 1,000 years ago in China, comprises a sequence of deceptively simple postures, performed very slowly and with great care. The calm, deep breathing helps distractions to evaporate, developing a sense of 'centredness', energy and self-awareness in regular practitioners. Don't expect quick results – tai chi is an art of gradual improvement, but a year of practice should be sufficient to enable you to master the basic set of movements that is known as the 'form'.

Tai chi is taught in many gyms and fitness clubs in London, although these classes may concentrate on the physical aspects of the art and not address thoroughly its principles, philosophy or applications. If you're hoping for a deeper involvement, it's better to seek out classes at one of London's dedicated tai chi centres. Tai Chi Finder (8819 2767, www.taichifinder.co.uk) and the Tai Chi Union for Great Britain (www.taichiunion. com) list classes by area.

We recommend the London School of Tai Chi Chuan (8566 1677, www.londontaichi. org.uk), founded in 1979 and holding regular classes for all standards in Soho and Marylebone. Try Hall of Energy (07896 210 860, www.hallofenergy.co.uk) for Barnes and Mortlake; James Drewe (07836 710 281, www.taiji.co.uk) in various locations in central London and the City; the John Ding Academy (7780 1818, www.johndingacademy.com) in Docklands; and Wu's Tai Chi Chuan Academy (7033 3993, www.wustyle-europe.com) in Bethnal Green. Most centres offer beginners' courses and private tuition, as well as weekend workshops. You may feel a little silly the first time you attend a class, but tai chi soon feels like the most natural thing on earth.

140
Get up early to see the deer in Richmond Park

The park opens at 7am (7.30am in winter). See www.royalparks.gov.uk for more on the deer.

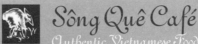

141-145
Eat fine Vietnamese food

Huong-Viet (An Viet House, 12-14 Englefield Road, N1 4LS, 7249 0877) was one of London's first Vietnamese eateries. Tucked behind the nondescript doors of the An-Viet Foundation, a charity devoted to giving practical help to Vietnamese refugees, the canteen has been serving good-value Vietnamese food since the early 1990s. It seems to get ever better with age, remaining one of the capital's best spots to sample fresh and fragrant Vietnamese food. The menu offers a huge selection of salads, stir-fries, grills, noodle soups and spring rolls, and the food more than lives up to its reputation – think spare ribs in bite-sized morsels, encrusted with chilli, ginger and lemongrass, or crispy Vietnamese pancake, stuffed with beansprouts, onions and tender prawns, and served with a divine sweet dip.

Other top picks for Vietnamese fare in east London include budget stalwart Sông Quê (134 Kingsland Road, E2 8DY, 7613 3222), which has an extremely extensive menu and faded kitsch decor; Namo (178 Victoria Park Road, E9 7HD, 8533 0639), which goes for a trendy look, imaginative Vietnamese dishes and zippy service; elegant Que Viet (102 Kingsland Road, E2 8DP, 7033 0588); and Mien Tray (122 Kingsland Road, E2 8DS, 7729 3074), which specialises in the fresh, sweet flavours of southern Vietnam.

146
Check out the Christmas show at Chickenshed

Every year, the renowned Chickenshed Theatre in Southgate stages a Christmas show. The 2009/10 production, *Pinocchio*, looked set to wow audiences with its 200-strong cast as this book went to press. Critics have described previous shows as 'the opposite of the traditional panto, mutating into a darker, stranger, braver beast'. Each production is a manifestation of the inclusive ethos of Chickenshed, so you can expect to see large numbers of child actors (the theatre has a thriving youth programme) and sign language deftly incorporated into the choreography, as well as feeling a vibrant buzz around the proceedings.

Chickenshed Theatre *Chase Side (at junction with Bramley Road), N14 4PE (8351 6161/ www.chickenshed.org.uk).*

147-149
Get a table without booking

Forgotten to book a table on a busy Friday night? Left Valentine's Day treat until the last minute? Head to global tapas bar the Tapa Room (109 Marylebone High Street, W1U 4RX, 7935 6175), on the ground floor below the restaurant Providores; it runs a no-reservations policy. Excellently placed in Marylebone, it's saved us from our lack of forethought a number of times. Further west, the Bibendum Oyster Bar (Michelin House, 81 Fulham Road, SW3 6RD, 7589 1480) doesn't take bookings either: go there for excellent seafood in pared-down surroundings. Lastly, the bar at justifiably popular St John (26 St John Street, EC1M 4AY, 7251 0848) is first-come, first-served; it offers a shorter but equally extraordinary version of the restaurant's menu of British food.

Chickenshed

150

Forage for mushrooms

Foraging for fungi requires patience, a keen eye and curiosity. There's an art to it. When London-based Andy Overall, co-founder of the Fungi To Be With mushroom club and forage leader, discovered mushrooms growing in his north London back garden in the early 1990s, he drew off previous knowledge gleaned from a love of nature. He picked, identified and then fried the horse mushrooms with garlic and butter – and never looked back. Now working on a book about urban fungi, Andy runs autumn and spring forays and workshops on Hampstead Heath to share his passion (see www.fungitobewith.org for more information).

The secret for success is making use of good identification books, cross-referencing photos with illustrations to get a positive ID, and putting in enough time and effort. 'Fungi are fascinating and ecologically crucial,' he says. 'Most mushrooms have a relationship with trees so knowing some of them is a key way to learn about fungi. You'll then start to get a feel for where things may appear.'

Look for oak, beech and silver birch trees and their companions – the edible cep or porcini and the bay bolete. Wild food springs up in the most unexpected places, and morels – another prize edible mushroom – have sprouted on bark-chip mulch used in gardens in Edmonton, in south London and around the Dome.

In spring, expect to see some seasonal specials: St George's mushrooms, found in unimproved grassland, appear around the patron saint's day and last well into May. Known and savoured as the mousseron in France, it is tasty cooked with butter, spices and yoghurt and used as a soufflé or flan filling. A word of warning, though: some mushrooms can cause gastric upsets, sickness, even death. The fly agaric, the fairytale favourite, with its distinct red cap and white spots is toxic, and the infamous death cap is lethal. If you're in doubt, leave it out of the pan.

151-157

Tick off London's essential clubs

Egg

King's Cross mainstay Egg attracts a consistently excellent line-up of DJs who play some of the filthiest electro and the bangingest techno around on its three floors (each with an equally impressive sound system). But perhaps it's the massive chill-out area/garden that really makes this club stand out: much of it is tented and the abundant bean bags are ideal for flopping on when you need a break from the hard pace of the dancefloors. Open until 6am, Egg deserves to be your plan A while also making for a fantastic plan B.

Egg *200 York Way, N7 9AP (7906 8364/ www.egglondon.net).*

Dalston Superstore

Conceived by the people behind Disco Bloodbath and Trailer Trash, the Superstore is the standard bearer for 'Dalston chic' in every way. Supposedly inspired by the ultra-hip 1980s disco clubs of New York and Chicago, this camp stamping ground is a favourite among local hipsters as well as those filled with Soho club ennui. The two-tiered café-cum-night-time-pleasure-pen, all concrete walls and steel pipes, is plastered with local artwork (for sale), kitsch fairy lights and graffiti-style murals. In the daytime drop by for some reasonably priced café fare, or some notably scrumptious cakes. After sunset, however (the downstairs opens at 10pm), expect to see anything from drag queens to barn dances, but whatever happens to be on, the chances are that it'll be eccentric, artistic and 'du jour'. The drinks menu is basic (there is no wine or draught beer) and the music styles vary depending on the night, but local talent spinning disco, house and electro seems to be a predominant theme. Visit the club's Facebook page for details of who's playing and what's on.

Dalston Superstore *117 Kingsland High Street, E8 2PB (7254 2273).*

Fabric

Big Daddy Fabric is the most popular club in London – despite being more than ten years old. Its problems are obvious – cost, tourists and space to move – yet while the price of the drinks may knock you off your feet, the tourists still come because the music is relentlessly good and, if you search for it, you can find space to dance. The systems are exquisite and the line-up will always be rammed with heavy-hitters and the next big thing. Expect to queue on a Friday.

Fabric *77A Charterhouse Street, EC1M 3HN (7336 8898/www.fabriclondon.com).*

Dalston Superstore

Fire

At the heart of Vauxhall's clubbing district, Fire is one of the city's most notorious 24-hour licensees. The lights have won awards and the hard electronic beats are exquisite. While the crowd is predominantly gay, there is still a variety of genders and sexualities strutting their stuff here, most of them interested in nothing but dancing from early in the morning until early the next morning.

Fire *38-42 Parry Street, SW8 1RT (7820 0550/www.myspace.com/firelondon).*

Matter

Run by Fabric's people, this new space in the Millenium Dome offers outstandingly good sound and a purpose-built design with a good balance of spaces. Hospitality and Ram are two of the biggest drum 'n' bass residencies on the planet – no self-respecting drum 'n' bass head would dream of missing them. OK, we admit that this is not the easiest venue to get to, but with sound this good, does that Matter?

Matter *O2, Peninsula Square, SE10 ODY (7549 6686/www.matterlondon.com).*

Plastic People

A laid back and friendly vibe amid the posing and pretence of Shoreditch, Plastic People also has an immensely powerful sound system considering the relatively small venue (capacity 200). Don't miss FWD>>, London's flagship weekly (Sundays) dubstep night; it's perfectly suited to this relaxed and intimate club.

Plastic People *147-149 Curtain Road, EC2A 3QE (7739 6471/www.plasticpeople.co.uk).*

Shunt

Offering an endlessly varied clubbing experience, each weekend at this cavernous space under the brick arches of London Bridge station is 'curated' by a different group of artists. Expect short plays, strange live music and arty films alongside some serious DJs spinning everything from house to disco to funk. Surely one of the most enlightening club nights in the capital, Shunt may have moved venue by the time you read this – check the website for details of eagerly awaited developments.

Shunt *20 Stainer Street, SE1 9RL (7378 7776/ www.shunt.co.uk).*

Matter

158 Peruse the eggheads at the Clowns' Church

Holy Trinity Church in Dalston (Beechwood Road, E8 3DY, 7608 0312 office hours only, www.clownsinternational.com) hosts a yearly Grimaldi Service on the First Sunday in February in remembrance of the godfather of modern clowning Joseph Grimaldi. Clowns from all over the country turn up in full 'motley and slap' to worship on this day, but the Church also holds a fascinating collection of memorabilia relating to the man: there are photos (including one of him out of costume), a History of Clowning archive in the crypt, even a stained glass window in his honour. Perhaps the strangest exhibits of all, though, are the 'egg faces' that clowns used to paint to keep as a record of their own clown make up and thus avoid duplication with any other performer.

159 Learn ceroc dancing

This fusion of jive and salsa comes from France and is the fastest growing style of partner dance this side of the Channel. All ceroc nights start with a 45-minute beginners' class, followed by a session for intermediates, culminating in 90 minutes of uninterrupted dance for everyone to practise their skills. After one evening you should be able to string together a routine. Contact Ceroc UK (8969 4401, www.ceroc london.com) for a directory of classes in London.

160 Scuba dive

The London School of Diving (11 Power Road, W4 5PT, 8995 0002, www.londonschoolof diving.com), with its on-site pool, is London's only purpose-built dive centre. The school runs a number of courses for children as young as ten and has its own adult diving club, which organises dive trips both in the UK and abroad; courses cost from £25. For other diving clubs (there are a surprising amount, given London's distinct lack of, y'know, sea), contact the British Sub-Aqua Club (0151 350 6200, www.bsac.com).

161 Zip along the Thames in a speedboat

Until recently, if you wanted to explore London by boat, you could expect a pretty sedate experience. Charlie Matheson's slick RIB (rigid inflatable boat) operation has changed all that. You can book by phone or online or turn up at Waterloo Millennium Pier on spec. Arrive 20 minutes before the off to be kitted out with a waterproof jacket (you're unlikely to get wet unless it's actually raining, but you might be glad of the extra warmth) and a life jacket.

The experience starts calmly enough, with a Thames Waterman providing a commentary about the bridges and buildings in central London. Then, once you're past Tower Bridge, the skipper on the 12-seater RIB opens up the engine and heads for Greenwich: wait until you experience how exhilarating it can be to swoop along the Thames at almost 30 knots, leaving the lumbering traditional river cruisers far behind. Trips are daily on the hour in summer from 11am until 5pm and cost £32.50-£45 (£19.50-£28 for children). **London RIB Voyages** *7928 2350/7401 8834/ www.londonribvoyages.com.*

162 Go to a plant sale at the Garden Museum

Occupying a prime site in a former church beside the Thames and just across from the Houses of Parliament, the Garden Museum (Tradescant Trust, St Mary at Lambeth, Lambeth Palace Road, SE1 7LB, 7401 8865, www.museumgardenhistory.org) exists to enhance the appreciation of gardens and garden history. Throughout the year the museum plays host to fantastic plant fairs – traditionally held in spring, autumn and winter. Entrance to the fairs is £6; check the website for exact dates.

Camera action

Wars, wolves, ghosts and getaways: London's streets have seen some spectacular cinematic moments. **David Jenkins** *and* **Simon Coppock** *tour the city's blockbuster sites.*

Can the flat shared by Hugh Grant and Rhys Ifans in Roger Michell's *Notting Hill* (1999) really be the same one as earlier occupied by Jean-Pierre Léaud in Finnish miserabilist Aki Kaurismäki's *I Hired a Contract Killer* (1990)? Can the Strand's disused tube stop, Aldwych station – a hub of filmmaking activity – truly have hosted both the horrors of Dave Stewart's *Honest* (2000) and the deeply affecting horror of Gary Sherman's subterranean cannibal flick *Death Line* (1972)? Familiarity and contempt. London is the world's third busiest city for filming production after Los Angeles and New York – that's 12,600 shooting days a year, or an average of almost 35 crews busy in the capital every single day – which means selectivity is the key when you begin a survey of London's walk-on roles.

The idle or unadventurous can get flick kicks without going beyond the cast-iron tourist hotspots. The clichés are most economically delivered in the classic establishing scene from the live-action version of *101 Dalmatians* (1996). Using only a pair of dog-walkers for notional continuity, director Stephen Herek manages to squeeze in every essential London sight – Battersea Park, St Paul's Cathedral, Big Ben, Hampstead Heath, Trafalgar Square, 10 Downing Street, the BT Tower, Battersea Power Station, Wembley, Walthamstow dog track, Southall Market... Less than four minutes of celluloid time producing hours of potential photo-op fodder.

Bridget Jones's Diary (Sharon Maguire, 2001) showed a little more London savvy in situating Renée Zellweger's flat above Borough Market's Globe pub (8 Bedale Street, SE1 9AL, 7407 0043), but what has taken the role left vacant when the Routemaster was axed and London's friendly bobbies took to wearing submachineguns at the hip? The shorthand for 21st-century London is evidently Tate Modern:

witness *Enduring Love* (Roger Michell, 2004),
The Constant Gardener (Fernando Meirelles,
2005) and *Match Point* (Woody Allen, 2005)
for starters. In truth, we're more taken with
Richard Loncraine's cheeky use in *Richard III*
(1995) of Bankside power station, as it was
before Tate Modern arrived. He makes it and
two other modernist masterpieces – Battersea
Power Station and St Pancras – stand duty
as the architectural icons of an imagined
1930s Fascist Britain, complete with Ian
McKellen as tyrant.

Anyone who manages to dig out Kevin
Brownlow and Andrew Mollo's *It Happened
Here* (1963) can see what Nazi-occupied Britain
might have looked like in 1944: swastikas
adorn Nelson's Column and the SS visit St
Paul's. Jules Dassin's accomplished Brit noir
Night and the City (1950) also makes use of
St Paul's, with Richard Widmark on the run
in the shadow of Wren's mighty cathedral.

Other chunks of Old London that get solid
film roles include the Church of St Bartholomew
the Great, beside Smithfield Market, where
Joseph Fiennes's Shakespeare mourns the
murdered Kit Marlowe in John Madden's
Shakespeare in Love (1998); nearby Postman's
Park, off Aldersgate Street, EC1, which is a
key location in the film adaptation of Patrick
Marber's *Closer* (2004), starring Jude Law and
Julia Roberts; and the Painted Hall of the Royal
Naval College in Greenwich, where the royal
family endures a bell concert in Nicholas
Hytner's *The Madness of King George* (1994).

A historical artefact of a different order
is exquisitely dated spook movie *The Ipcress
File* (Sidney J Furie, 1965); marvel at the soot-
black exteriors around the south side of now
pedestrianised Trafalgar Square or peer up
at the very window from which Michael Caine
looks, Nelson's Column reflected in his plate-
glass specs, during a dressing down by Ross

(it's above the Tesco). On a grander scale, the whole of Whitehall stars in *V for Vendetta* (2005): it was closed overnight so that James McTeigue could stage an attack by soldiers, tanks and masked revolutionaries that used around 1,000 people.

One refreshing alternative – what London might be like if there were less bloody people in it – forms the bravura opening of *28 Days Later…* (2002). Danny Boyle combined frighteningly early mornings for his cast with cheap and convenient DV technology to depict an entirely deserted city – decidedly spooky for anyone used to the commuter mess of a Monday morning.

Indeed, many of the starring roles allotted to London are dystopic. John Landis's horror comedy *An American Werewolf in London* (1981) contrives a fine advert for the NHS in the comely form of Jenny Agutter's nurse, but the film is more memorable for its finale – in which Piccadilly Circus gets wrecked – and an earlier scene in which a dapper City gent gets savaged in Tottenham Court Road station. In *Hellraiser* (1987) the mouth of hell opens in a residential suburb in the north-west: 187 Dollis Hill Lane, renamed 66 Lodovico Street perhaps in deference to local house prices. At least a stroll around Bishop's Park, just off the end of Putney Bridge, is better fun for set-jetters than it was for the cleric in Richard Donner's *The Omen* (1976): he was impaled when a lightning rod fell from the nearby church.

Fans of high-grade psychodrama might well care to take an aimless wander in the vicinity of Brompton Road, SW1, where Catherine Deneuve's sanity so expressively unravels in Polanski's *Repulsion* (1965). Would-be suitor John Fraser takes her out for a fish and chip supper – fish and chips? That's Catherine Deneuve! – at Dino's (1-3 Pelham Street, SW7 2ND, 7589 3511).

Further sites of celluloid sadism can be visited in the northern subway beneath the huge circular advertising installation on Trinity Road in Wandsworth. This is where droogs attack an old tramp in Stanley Kubrick's *A Clockwork Orange* (1971). The tramp's later revenge on the reprogrammed, docile and thoroughly vulnerable Alex occurs under the Albert Bridge. We also recommend visiting the key site in Michael Powell's provocative and disturbing masterpiece

It's difficult to imagine Tom Cruise ordering a pint of real ale in a dimpled pint pot, yet the oft-duped super-spy can be seen sharing a cheeky half with sidekick Ving Rhames in the Anchor Pub.

Peeping Tom (1960). Newman Passage, which runs adjacent to the Newman Arms on Newman Street, is where voyeuristic psychopath Mark Lewis commits his first murder: of a prostitute played by Brenda Bruce. The door from which she turns to camera leads straight into the little main bar – no sexual misadventures are sold here, but you can invest in some decent ale and a pie (*see p12*).

It's not all beatings and elaborately obscene murder in celluloid London. You could join the chess aficionados of Gillies Mackinnon's *The Grass Arena* (1991) at the tea rooms in Hampstead's South End Green, NW3, or feel the brawl from mod classic *Quadrophenia* (Franc Roddam, 1979) in situ at Alfredo's classic caff in Islington, now serving sausage and mash as an S&M Café (4-8 Essex Road, N1 8LN, 7359 5361). And while you'd be hard put to recreate the terrific helicopter shot that opens Hitchcock's 1972 thriller *Frenzy* by sweeping under Tower Bridge (you could try to prevail on the nice people at Cabair, *see p26*), everybody can sup a pint in Covent Garden: both the Globe (37 Bow Street, WC2E 7AU, 7379 0154) and the Nell of Old Drury (29 Catherine Street, WC2B 5JS, 7836 5328) are still there, although spivvy murderer and stallholder Barry Foster would hardly recognise the market itself – back then it still flogged fruit and veg. For something more luxurious, the Hyde Park Hilton plays the Coburg Hotel, to which Dick Blaney (Jon Finch) takes Babs Milligan (Anna Massey) in the film.

The unavoidable cinematic pub pilgrimage is, of course, to one-time Mother Black Cap (41 Tavistock Cresent, W11 1AD, 7727 9250). The pub featured in seminal booze movie *Withnail & I* (Bruce Robinson, 1986), with our hapless dandies managing to forestall a beating from an Irish hard man. (The pub itself, currently boarded up, was renamed in honour of the film.) In such cases, life follows art, but art and life are sometimes barely on speaking terms. It's difficult to imagine Tom Cruise ordering a pint of real ale in a dimpled pint pot. Yet *Mission: Impossible* (Brian De Palma, 1996) does indeed feature such a scene in the Anchor Pub (34 Park Street, SE1 9EF, 7407 1577), where the oft-duped super spy can be seen sharing a cheeky half with Ving Rhames. Further unreality can be had in Clerkenwell's bar-restaurant Vic Naylor (40 St John Street), owned by Sting in Guy Ritchie's mockney classic *Lock, Stock & Two Smoking Barrels* (1998).

More believable is the boozer-turned-zombie fortress in Edgar Wright's rom-zom-com *Shaun of the Dead* (2004). Renamed 'The Winchester Arms' for the film, it's actually the Duke of Albany (39 Monson Road, SE14 5EQ, 7639 6409). You won't be able to get a drink: the pub was boarded up and all the interiors shot in the studio. Perhaps we could suggest the Five Bells (155 New Cross Road, SE14 5DJ, SE14 5DJ) instead? Here Gary Oldman's dad used to prop up the bar – hence its appearance in Oldman Jnr's none-more-grim *Nil by Mouth* (1997). But, for those who like to do their cinematic boozing properly, we nominate the Salisbury (1 Grand Parade, Green Lanes, N4 1JX, 8800 9617). In *The Long Good Friday* (John MacKenzie, 1979) this is where Bob Hoskins's sidekick Colin conducts shady dealings with the IRA.

Tired of sitting down? Take a wander around King's Cross. Ealing classic *The Ladykillers* (Alexander Mackendrick, 1955) is based around St Pancras and you can still see – without the inestimable charms of Frankie Howerd's cockney barrow-boy – the view from the old lady's house (Argyle Street in King's Cross), although the house itself was specially built on nearby Frederica Street, so it could back on to the railway tracks. King's Cross is also the essential backdrop for *Mona Lisa* (Neil Jordan, 1986), albeit with the scuzziness so perfectly captured by the film rapidly disappearing in the face of the area's Eurostar-led redevelopment.

One Notting Hill location has also effectively disappeared: Hugh Grant's blue-doored house from *Notting Hill* (Roger Michell, 1999) drew so many tourists the owners changed the doorframe and painted the door black. No point visiting 280 Westbourne Park Road, then, so why not head off the beaten track to Lambeth? One exquisite Ealing comedy, *Passport to Pimlico* (Henry Cornelius, 1949), was shot here on a Blitz bombsite. Despite extensive redevelopment, you'll recognise the railway arches if you look in the direction of the river from Lambeth Road between Kennington Road and Hercules Road.

London's transport system has played some significant film roles. The biggest – if we pass over Hitchcock's blown-up Routemaster in *Sabotage* (1936) – is as the lucky/unlucky tube train of *Sliding Doors* (Peter Howitt, 1998). Gwyneth Paltrow exits and enters Embankment station, even though the fateful doors belong to a bright and shiny Waterloo & City train at Waterloo station rather than a dull, workaday carriage on the District line. Some protagonists eschew even the Waterloo & City: in *The World is Not Enough* (Michael Apted, 1999) James Bond bursts through the wall of the MI6 (now the Secret Intelligence Service) headquarters in a speedboat. Re-enact his high-speed chase along the Thames without Apted's awesome budget by taking an RIB speedboat trip (*see p61*).

We reckon the city's greatest and most inexplicably romantic scene is the moment in Michael Winterbottom's *Wonderland* (1999) when Gina McKee sits weeping on the back seat of a night bus, having been turned down by a potential suitor. She's on the top floor of one of the now defunct Routemasters, so make do with an atmospheric early hours stroll down Old Compton Street. She won't be working in her café there – but you never know who else's story you might stumble into.

188 Recoil at the contents of the Hunterian Museum

This is a museum whose bottled specimens would test the sturdiest constitution. How about a look at the brain of mathematician Charles Babbage? Or Churchill's dentures? Located in the dignified HQ of the Royal College of Surgeons of England, the museum reopened in 2005 after a two-year, £3 million renovation. It's now as stylish as you'll be squeamish, with the weird glass jars on clean glass shelves.

Hunterian Museum *Royal College of Surgeons, 35-43 Lincoln's Inn Fields, WC2A 3PE (7869 6560/ www.rcseng.ac.uk/museums).*

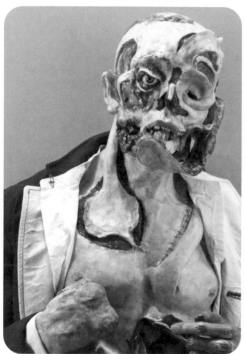

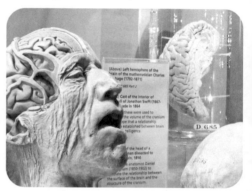

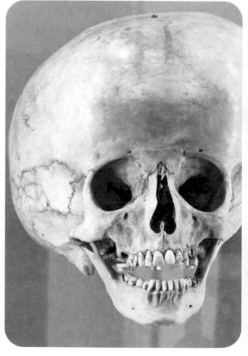

189 Savour bone marrow on toast at St John

There's nowhere better to tuck into the parts of an animal that others eschew than at Fergus Henderson's stark white temple to new-Brit cooking. Occupying a former smokehouse, conveniently located just around the corner from the Smithfield meat market, St John comprises a first-floor restaurant and ground-floor bar. It is on the snacky bar menu that you're likely to encounter bone marrow on toast (although the list changes daily), along with such delicacies as oysters, welsh rarebit, or a little bun filled with ox heart and pickled walnut. The offal adventure continues in the pricier restaurant (rolled pig's spleen and bacon, anyone?), yet fish-eaters and vegetarians aren't forgotten and even those of a delicate cast of mind will relish the desserts (steamed hazelnut and treacle sponge, for instance). Many a connoisseur counts this their favourite restaurant in London.

St John *26 St John Street, EC1M 4AY (7251 0848/www.stjohnrestaurant.com).*

190 Watch a Bollywood film at the Boleyn cinema

A beacon of charm amid fast food shops on Barking Road, this ornate three-screen cinema screens a strict diet of Indian Bollywood films.
Boleyn Cinema *7-11 Barking Road, E6 1PN (8471 4884/www.bolyncinema.co.uk).*

191 Jam into the Jerusalem

The indecently cosy Jerusalem Tavern (55 Britton Street, EC1M 5UQ, 7490 4281, www.stpetersbrewery.co.uk) may be cramped, but it's the only London boozer associated with the excellent Suffolk-based St Peter's Brewery. You could try Old-Style Porter, Golden Ale or a seasonal beer – or all of the above. The woody, slightly wonky, interior (behind a façade that was added in 1810) fairly heaves with beer lovers young and old, male and female, from home and abroad. Who can blame them?

192 Raise a glass to the bad boys of French letters

It's '73 and a scruffy pair of bohemian lovers are after digs in Camden Town. Same old, same old. Except it's 1873 and the couple are authors in the process of rewriting the rules of modern poetry. A simple plaque on the wall of 8 Royal College Street offers the bald facts: 'The French poets Paul Verlaine and Arthur Rimbaud lived here May-July 1873.' Which leaves out the booze- and drug-fuelled rows, sometimes involving razor blades, that filled their attic room. And the farcical end to their residence: the precocious Rimbaud shouts from the window that brutally hungover Verlaine, returning from market with the breakfast kippers, has *l'air con*. Verlaine runs upstairs, hits him in the face with one of the fish and packs for France. Take a flask of absinthe and a good British kipper to salute departed genius – then thank your lucky stars you were never their landlord.

193 Listen to an oration at Speakers' Corner

This London curiosity grew out of revolt, when Edmund Beales led the Reform League to Hyde Park in 1866 to complain about the lack of a vote for working men. The marchers were blocked from entering the park by police and there was a minor riot. The Reform League continued to meet at Marble Arch to test their right to hold public meetings in the park. In 1872 the government relented and granted the right to assembly and free speech in the north-east corner of Hyde Park. The Met promptly responded by turning Marble Arch into a tiny police station to keep an eye on the rabble below. Head on down to watch the efforts of a loudmouth with a complex, rattling off rehearsed patter before the derision and heckles of a crowd. You'd have to pay money to see the same in a comedy club.

194-199
Get backstage at the theatre

'Who wants a squeeze of my big juicy oranges?' shouts the woman on the steps of London's oldest theatre. A bloke from across the street volunteers his services, but he's out of luck because this is Nell of Drury Lane, orange seller and King's mistress, and she's being played by an actress as part of a tour of the Theatre Royal Drury Lane (tours 2.15pm & 4.15pm Mon, Tue, Thur, Fri; 10.15am & noon Wed, Sat; £11.50, £9 concessions). A vital but often overlooked element of the city's theatre scene is the magnificent architecture in which the performances take place.

Many theatres offer daytime tours. At the Theatre Royal you get to see underground tunnels that once connected the building to the Thames, explore under the largest stage in London and sit in the Royal Room, its walls decorated in 24-carat gold leaf.

'The audience would be drinking, shouting and chatting, and prostitutes would be "doing business" in the upper circle, all during a performance,' according to Shakespeare's Globe guide (tours every 15-30mins 9.30am-5pm daily Oct-Apr and 9.30-12.30 Apr-Oct; £10.50). Eating and drinking are still allowed during shows, he continues, although lobbing vegetables at the actors is now frowned on.

A tour of the National Theatre (six times daily, phone 7452 3400 for more details; £5.90, £4.90 concessions) offers an excellent insight into how major productions are developed – plus you find out what Laurence Olivier's favourite colour was. You'll also have to go on a tour to appreciate just how vast is the Royal Opera House in Covent Garden (tours 10.30am, 12.30pm & 2.30pm Mon-Fri, on the half-hour 10.30am-1.30pm Sat; £9, £7-£8 concessions). Visitors are led up and down some of the eight floors and get to nose around the workshops that produce the masses of costumes required for each production. The 10.30am tour also includes ten minutes spent watching the ballerinas in rehearsal.

Other worthwhile tours include the Old Vic (7981 0909 for details of times and prices), where you can peek into Kevin Spacey's warm-up room, and Soho's Prince Edward (0844 482 5122 for details), which was the home of *Jersey Boys* at the time of going to press.

National Theatre

200

*Take in the view
from Parliament Hill...*
**This extraordinary panorama
encompasses the highs of the
capital – the Gherkin, the
London Eye, the Houses of
Parliament, St Paul's – and
many harder-to-spot highlights.**

201-209

...or admire the city from another of London's stunning summits

Brixton Hill, SW2

Technically, this is the half-mile of the A23 that links Brixton with Streatham Hill. It follows the line of the old Roman road, with Rush Common – common land protected by an 1811 Act of Parliament – to the east. It was a riot of trams and horse-buses in the late 19th century.

Cornhill, EC3

The highest hill in the City, named after a medieval grain market. It boasted a prison (the Tun), stocks and a pillory in which the novelist Daniel Defoe spent a day in 1703 for publishing a seditious pamphlet.

Denmark Hill, SE5

Formerly Dulwich Hill, it was rechristened in honour of Queen Anne, wife of Prince George of Denmark, who lived on the east side. The Fox on the Hill pub stands on the site of the 'Fox under the Hill', the only building in the area shown on John Cary's 1786 map.

Forest Hill, SE23

When the Croydon Canal closed, it was bought by the London & Croydon Railway Company. The opening of its line in 1839 transformed the aptly named Forest Hill into a thriving suburb.

Herne Hill, SE24

The road itself connects the former 'Heron's Hill' (named for the birds who gathered here) to neighbouring Denmark Hill. According to the English Place Name Society, the first reference to Herne Hill appears in 1789: the River Effra, down which King Canute is said to have rowed, ran along the foot of it.

Muswell Hill, N10

Muswell Hill, the site of a spring ('Mossy Well') thought to have healing properties, was a place of pilgrimage in medieval times. Its impressive views over the Thames and Lea Valleys made it a popular rural retreat, until – back in 1896 – key estates were bought by developer James Edmondson, who built new houses and shopping arcades, effectively creating a London suburb from scratch.

Primrose Hill, NW3

A former hunting ground for Henry VIII and his courtiers, this hill to the north of Regent's Park was opened up to the public only in 1842. Once a popular spot for duellists, it is now the stamping ground of idiotic celebrities. War trivia buffs might be interested to know that anti-aircraft guns were sited on the 207-foot-tall summit in 1939.

Shooters Hill, SE18

The highest point in south London (reaching 433 feet), Shooters Hill was a favourite with archers during the Middle Ages and with highwaymen in the 17th century: it was the route of the mail coaches that ran between London and Dover. There was a gallows at the bottom, and the bodies of the hanged were displayed on a gibbet at the summit, close to where the Victorian gothic water tower now stands. The triangular folly Severndroog Castle was designed by Richard Jupp in 1784 and is occasionally opened up to the public during Open House Weekends.

Tower Hill, EC3

There was a Bronze Age settlement here, then a Roman village, then (in the 7th century) the church of All Hallows-by-the-Tower, an original arch of which survives. More than 70 Tower prisoners were executed here, including Richard II's tutor Sir Simon Burley (the first, in 1388) and Sir Thomas More in 1535. The dispatch in 1780 of two prostitutes and a one-armed soldier marked the end of a bloody era.

210 Shop for vintage clothes at The Girl Can't Help It

Deep in the heart of Alfies Antique Market, a Hawaiian shirt swings from a hanger and cocktail glasses brazenly display their pin-up girl motifs. Nearby, exquisite 1950s bikinis, frou-frou summer frocks and Mexican skirts all jostle for space. 'It's about more, more, more!' enthuses co-owner Sparkle Moore, an exuberant, busty New Yorker with a flowing platinum mane and scarlet lips. Even the menswear and home accessories, provided by her dapper Dutch partner Jasja (pronounced Jasha) Bolelhouwer, are bold, a little brash and suave as can be.

The Girl Can't Help It *Alfies Antique Market, 13-25 Church Street, NW8 8DT (7724 8984/ www.thegirlcanthelpit.com).*

211 Browse Daunt Books

An original Edwardian shop, packed to the rafters with travel tomes. These are housed in the beautiful oak-galleried area at the back of the premises, with its viridian walls and stained-glass window.

Daunt Books *83 Marylebone High Street, W1U 4QW (7224 2295/www.dauntbooks.co.uk).*

212 Get a table at the Ivy

The Ivy allegedly has a two-track booking system: one for favoured customers and celebrities, the other for the rest of us. So unless you're AA Gill, an A-list (or B-list) celebrity, or a high-spending regular, you'll have to submit to ordeal by automated phone response or book through the website. Don't despair though: if you are prepared to eat lunch at 2.30pm, or want to brighten up a dreary Monday (when bookings are usually easier to come by anyway), you may get lucky with just a few hours' notice. And as every luvvie knows, lunch is the only way to do the Ivy.

The Ivy *1 West Street, WC2H 9NQ (7836 4751/ www.the-ivy.co.uk).*

213 Get to know the old folk at Age Exchange

It's said that old people are slowly disappearing from London, scared out of town by the bustle and perceived crime, retreating to the 'burbs where things happen at a slower pace, if at all. But not in Blackheath, where the Age Exchange centre (11 Blackheath Village, SE3 9LA, 8318 9105, www.age-exchange.org.uk) offers a place for south-east London's senior citizens to meet, chat and generally reminisce pleasantly about the old days. The Age Exhange also features an area decked out like a well-stocked 1930s shop, features regular exhibitions and often invites in schoolchildren to learn about the past. Oh, and there's a café if all you fancy is a nice cup of tea.

214 Take part in the Great Spitalfields Pancake Race

The pancake race is said to date back 500 years to a woman who was cooking at home when she heard the church bells calling people to confession and ran out of her hovel, still holding the frying pan. Flash forward to the present, and there are a number of races held in the capital every Shrove Tuesday to mark this historic (possibly completely imagined) event. Among the best of which is the Great Spitalfields race: the traditional tomfoolery starts at about midday on Brick Lane, and requires teams of four in fancy dress who must bring their own pan for the relay race. There are awards of an engraved frying pan for the race winners and the best dressed. See the website (www.alternativearts.co.uk/events/ pancake_race) for exact times.

215 Visit Little Ben

Given to London by the French at a time of fine cross-channel relations in 1892, Little Ben is a little (not that little, at 30 feet tall) brother to our grandest timepiece, Big Ben. Unlike its Westminster sibling, Little Ben sits rather sadly on a traffic island on Victoria Street, SW1.

Know more.
Do more.

Subscribe to Time Out Magazine today

WHY SUBSCRIBE TO TIME OUT?

- **The most comprehensive guide to what's on in London**
- **Insider tips on the latest hotspots, shows and deals**
- **Fast, free delivery to your door, every week**
- **No obligation – cancel anytime and pay nothing more**
- **Save even more – on Time Out Guides plus regular offers and freebies**

" Time Out will always mean London to me **"**
Dame Helen Mirren

216 *Look out over Buckingham Palace from the bridge in St James's Park*

217-225

Skate outdoors...

The grand 18th-century courtyard at Somerset House is where the trend for seasonal outdoor skating started, and it still provides one of the most impressive backdrops in town. The ice rink (www.somersethouseicerink.org.uk) opens in mid November and runs until the end of January; and there's a skating school that offers lessons and taster sessions for beginners. Whatever your level of expertise, be sure to invest in a cup of hot chocolate with marshmallows afterwards.

Other temporary ice rinks spring up all over town as Christmas approaches, with new ones popping up every year. Look out for them in Broadgate Circle (www.broadgateice.co.uk), Canary Wharf (www.canarywharficerink.com), Shepherd's Bush (www.shepherdsbushfestival. com), Hampstead Heath (www.hampsteadheath icerink.com), Hampton Court Palace (www. hamptoncourtpalaceicerink.com), Kew Gardens (www.kewgardensicerink.com), the Natural History Museum (www.nhmskating.com) and the Tower of London (www.towerof londonicerink.com).

226-230

...or indoors

Can't wait for the winter? There are a clutch of year-round indoor ice rinks in the capital. Queens Ice Bowl (17 Queensway, W2 4QP, 7229 0172, www.queensiceandbowl.com) is the most famous: countless top skaters have learned their moves here. The international-size rink at Alexandra Palace (Alexandra Palace Way, N22 7AY, 8365 4386, www. alexandrapalace.com) was where Robbie Williams filmed his Torvill and Dean-esque video for 'She's the One'. Elsewhere, there's Lee Valley Ice Centre (Lea Bridge Road, E10 7QL, 8533 3154, www.leevalleypark.org.uk), Sobell Leisure Centre (Hornsey Road, N7 7NY, 7609 2166, www.aquaterra.org) and Streatham Ice Arena (386 Streatham High Road, SW16 6HT, 8769 7771, www.streathamicearena.co.uk).

231 — Eat your way around Selfridges

It may not have the cutesy appeal of Fortnum & Mason's food hall, but Selfridges Foodhall has an outstanding collection of enlightening edibles. You'll find the very best of fresh and cooked meat, fish, cheese, fruit, freshly baked pretzels, pies from the Square Pie Company, caviar from Caviar Kaspia, plus the wonderfully extravagant Moët champagne and oyster bar. Given the surrounding razzle-dazzle of 'It bags' and luxe labels, we hardly need warn you that this grocery store won't beat anyone on price – in fact, it proudly launched the 'World's Most Expensive Sandwich' at a farcical £85 in 2006. But since most foodstuffs are charged by weight, a sample-sized portion of one of the delicacies will be affordable. And there isn't anything – beyond mild embarrassment – to stop you asking for free tasters.

Selfridges Foodhall *400 Oxford Street, W1A 1AB (0800 123 400/www.selfridges.com).*

232-235

Belly dance yourself healthy

Belly dancing (*raq sharqui*, or 'Eastern dance', to use its original Egyptian name) is a form of self-expression for women of all ages. The dance can be soft and sensual, controlled and commanding, or passionate and powerful, and provides a brilliant workout for hips, waist and legs. Jacqueline Chapman (8300 7616, www.bellydancer.org.uk) runs classes and workshops around London, or you could learn to belly dance at the following dance centres: Basement Dance Studio (Basement Units, York House, 400 York Way, N7 9LR, 7700 7722, www.jumpanddance.com), Danceworks (16 Balderton Street, W1K 6TN, 7629 6183, www.danceworks.net) and Greenwich Dance Agency (Borough Hall, Royal Hill, SE10 8RE, 8923 9741, ww.greenwichdance.org.uk).

It won't do your fitness levels any good, but if you'd rather keep your belly hidden and watch a pro doing the jiggle instead, you can book a table for the evening performance at Lebanese restaurant Maroush V (4 Vere Street, W1G 0DH, 7493 5050, www.maroush.com) or Levant (Jason Court, 76 Wigmore Street, W1U 2SJ, 7224 1111, www.levant.co.uk). And hidden behind a heavily carved wooden door, Pasha (1 Gloucester Road, SW7 4PP, 7589 7969, www.pasha-restaurant.co.uk), is a superbly heady, opulent and gastronomic environment in which to expand your own belly while watching the talented gyrations of someone else's.

236

Lift a gold bar at the Bank of England Museum

Attached to the Bank of England itself (Bartholomew Lane, EC2R 8AH, 7601 5545, www.bankofengland.co.uk), this museum is housed in a replica of the original bank interior designed by Sir John Soane. Test the weight of a real-life gold bar as part of the exhibition, or you could check out the complete set of NatWest piggy banks, circa 1983.

A few of my favourite things

237-241

Sarah Waters, author

Shopping on Lower Marsh is some of the best in London. It's got everything you could want: retro clothes, a fetishwear shop, brilliant bookshop Crockatt & Powell (119-120 Lower Marsh, SE1 7AE, 7928 0234), a library, jewellery, wholefoods and, in Scooterworks Cafe (132 Lower Marsh, SE1 7AE, 7620 1421), fabulous Italian coffee and a few resident cats. **Hampstead Ladies' Bathing Pond (Hampstead Heath, NW5 1QR, 7485 4491, see p126) is a great place to go for a sunbathe or a dip on a sweltering London day. Hugely popular with ladies of all stripes, but especially lesbians. Worth visiting for the satisfaction of being able to pass smugly through the gate marked 'No Men Allowed Beyond this Point'.** Islington has lost a little bit of its individuality lately, but Candid Café (3 Torrens Street, EC1V 1NQ, 7837 4237, see p132) is a wonderful place to escape to when you've had enough of the chain coffee shops and smart delis of Upper Street. It's tucked away down an atmospheric alley, the food is good, the chairs are comfy and the camp decor – velvet, candelabra and naked ladies – makes you want to stay all day. **Crystal Palace Park (Thicket Road, SE20 8DT, see p90) is not by any means the most handsome park in London, but the life-size dinosaur models really make it worth a visit. They were built in the 1850s, and are both sinister and quaint. Glimpsed through a mist on an autumn day they can actually seem quite scary.** I wish my own house looked like Sir John Soane's Museum (13 Lincoln's Inn Fields, WC2A 3BP, 7405 2107, see p309). It's the most eccentric in London, packed to the rafters with a higgledy-piggledy collection of wonderful things from all over the world: paintings, casts, models, statues and an Egyptian sarcophagus or two.

CENTRE STAGE FOR THE WORLD'S LEADING CLASSICAL MUSIC PERFORMERS

OVER 400 CONCERTS EVERY YEAR

CONCERTS EVERY EVENING, MONDAY LUNCHTIME AND SUNDAY MORNING

HOME OF THE BEST CLASSICAL CHAMBER, INSTRUMENTAL AND VOCAL MUSIC

Only a 5 minute walk from Oxford Circus

Box Office 020 7935 2141

www.wigmore-hall.org.uk

The Wigmore Hall Trust. Registered charity No. 1024838. Wigmore Hall 36 Wigmore Street London W1U 2BP Director: John Gilhooly

242-246

Visit London's aquariums

Horniman Museum
100 London Road, SE23 3PQ (8699 1872/
www.horniman.ac.uk).
Reopened in July 2006 after a £1.5 million refurbishment. Tickle stingrays or watch the sharks being fed. Admission free.

London Zoo Aquarium
Regent's Park, NW1 4RY (7722 3333/www.zsl.org).
Part of London Zoo since 1924, the aquarium hosts such oddities as Banggai Cardinal fish, Egyptian tortoises and Moon jellyfish. Zoo admission is £18.50, children cost £15.

Palm House, Kew Gardens
Royal Botanic Gardens, Kew, Richmond,
Surrey TW9 3AB (8332 5655/www.kew.org).

Recreated here are the four most significant marine habitats: coral reefs, estuaries and salt marshes, rocky shorelines and mangrove swamps. Admission £11-£13, under-17s free.

Sea Life London Aquarium
County Hall, Westminster Bridge Rd, SE1 7PB
(0871 663 1678/www.sealife.co.uk/london).
After a multi-million pound redevelopment, this is undeniably the daddy with its glass tunnel walkways and over 400 species of fish. Admission £16, children (3-14-year-olds) £11.

Yauatcha
15-17 Broadwick Street, W1F 0DL (7494 8888).
This Soho dim sum restaurant has an enormous fish tank bar. Admire with cocktail in hand.

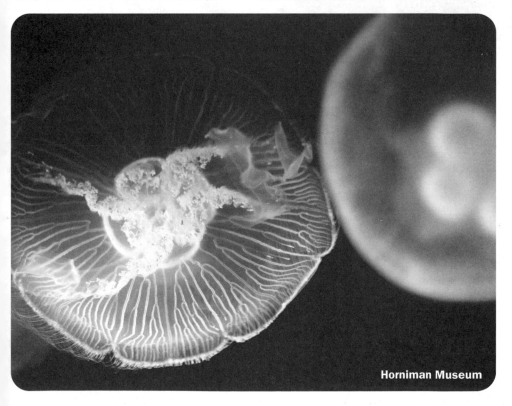

Horniman Museum

Mucking about

Peter Watts braves giraffe dung and bloodthirsty tigers – all in a day's shift at London Zoo.

'That's why they tell you to never shake hands with a zookeeper,' whispers Emma, the London Zoo press officer, as we stand aside watching zookeeper Jane pull apart a piece of giraffe poo and have a good whiff of what's inside. Animal excrement, Jane explains with noted enthusiasm, is a recurring motif in a zookeeper's life; all of a sudden, knee deep in urine-soaked straw and confronted with a dung-sniffing maniac, those of us who are taking part in the zoo's 'Be A Keeper For The Day' scheme (£165 for half a day or £260 for a full day) can't help but wonder what exactly we've let ourselves in for.

Fortunately, Jane proves to be excellent company, an ebullient guide to the mysteries of animal husbandry, and not in the least bit bats. She started work at the zoo six years ago while studying psychology, and has been a full-time keeper since 2003. She wasn't much of an animal lover before, but now owns two cats, two gerbils, seven dormice, one snake and two bird-eating spiders. And twice a week she takes

a break from looking after small mammals to help members of the public spend a day pretending to be zookeepers.

We meet at 9am, when the zoo's human bustle is superseded by the howls of monkeys, chirping of birds and harrumphs of excitement from neophyte zookeepers. There are four of us taking part in the scheme today: Pete and Louise each received their zookeeping day as a present; I'm here because it's my job; and Emma has been corralled from the press office to act as my minder.

The London Zoological Society was founded in 1826 by Sir Stamford Raffles, who hoped for a 'zoological collection which should interest and amuse the public'. Previously, this role had fallen to the Royal Menagerie at the Tower, which started in 1235 when King Henry III was given three leopards by the Holy Roman Emperor and simply had nowhere else to put them. (You can read the story of the Royal collection, which was closed down in 1832, in Daniel Lahm's *The Tower Menagerie*,

Obaysch was just one of a number of famous animal residents: Jumbo the elephant was acquired in 1865 (along with Alice, who lost a foot off her trunk in an ugly incident one bank holiday); a black bear called Winnie the Pooh joined the zoo in 1914; Guy the Gorilla appeared in 1947. The quagga (a type of zebra) and thylacine (a Tasmanian tiger), both now extinct, were exhibited here. The zoo survived the Blitz and a financial/ethical crisis in the 1980s and has since prospered: recently being voted Best Tourist Attraction by *Time Out* readers.

Our day's work begins at the giraffe pen. Giraffes first arrived here in 1836, prompting a fashion for giraffe-print dresses among the more impressionable members of polite society. Clad rather less strikingly in green boiler suits, we set to clearing out the shitty straw and replacing it with clean straw that the giraffes will soon be making shitty again. It's not quite the Augean stable, but there is something

'Knee deep in urine-soaked straw, we wonder what we've let ourselves in for.'

which describes monkey rooms, drunken elephants, and fights between lions and tigers.) In Victorian times London also had exotic pet shops such as Cross's in Charing Cross where elephants, tigers and monkeys were kept and from which they sometimes escaped.

London Zoo opened back in 1828 with 200 animals and was a hit from the very start, drawing 100,000 visitors in its first year (and pulling in more than 900,000 people a year by 1876): men had to leave their whips at the gate while women were allowed to keep their parasols but were asked not to poke them through the bars. The first reptile house in the world was added in 1843 (the keeper tried to charm a cobra but was bitten between the eyes and died), followed by the first aquarium in 1853 (it was drained during World War II and some of the edible species were, well, eaten). When Obaysch the hippo (who later had an obituary in *The Times*) arrived in 1850, he was the first seen in Europe since the days of the Roman Empire.

Sisyphean about our task. As we sift, the stench of ammonia is eye-watering; the giraffes look bemused. 'How often do you have to do this?' I ask the giraffe-keeper. 'Once a week, on "Be A Keeper For The Day" day,' she replies. Through sweat and tears, I think I detect a smirk.

When the stable is eventually clean, we are given bananas and pieces of bread, which we feed to the giraffes, their leathery tongues snaking out and snagging the food. After all that hard work, the simple pleasure of feeding the animals is genuinely rewarding, and it's this opportunity – getting up close to unusual creatures – that makes the scheme so enjoyable.

From the giraffe pen, we trot to the penguin pool, pausing only to sling a stinking sheep's stomach at the African hunting dogs. The penguins have been moved from Lubetkin's pool – a classic example of 1930s modernist architecture and one of 13 listed buildings at the zoo – to a new home they seem to prefer. Most of the penguins are of the black-footed variety and sceptical of human company (a penguin peck can really smart), but there's a rockhopper called Roxy with a cute punk hairdo happily waddling after us as we get busy cleaning poo off rocks. If you've ever wanted to stroke a penguin (and to be honest, who hasn't?), this is the only legal way you'll get the chance.

I'd heard rumours of lesbian penguins, but Emma is unconvinced: 'We've had the odd male pair who team up for a short while and then waddle off to find a female, but not lesbians. It could be that we named them wrongly – you can't tell the sex of a penguin until they've got adult feathers. We've got a couple called Stan and Stewart who had babies last month.' Nonetheless, back in September 2005, the zoo hosted its first Gay Day, with drag queens, cocktails and a debate on animal sexuality. It proved so popular that the happy day has been repeated every year since. (Gays aren't the only minority to be celebrated at the zoo – in 2004 they held Ginger Sunday, inviting redheads to visit for half price in honour of the birth of redhead Laa Laa the Francois Langur.)

Intentionally or otherwise, the 'Be A Keeper' scheme drives home the amount of thought and care that goes into looking after the animals. The area where we prepare food for the bearded pigs is hung with giant blackboards, one for each species, listing the different ways in which the life of that animal can be 'enriched'.

So, for instance, one hippo likes to put things on its head, so the keepers are recommended to find things it can do this with. Similarly, in the tigers' cage, we're given perfume to smear on trees – the smells stimulate the tigers,

encouraging them to leave their own scent. The zoo's intention is to keep the animals content while retaining their natural instincts. No wonder Jane looks aghast when fellow keeper-for-a-day Pete asks whether the parrots can talk.

The exception is the animals used in performances, and it's here we head to meet skunks (de-stinked, soft fur), coatis (playful mammals from Central America) and kinkajou (cute regal mammals), who clamber all over us and stick their noses in our ears. By now, Jane has dropped all pretence of making us work: this is fun, pure and simple. Many of these animals were pets brought to the zoo after their owners got tired of looking after them, hence they are comfortable being around humans.

After chopping fruit and veg for the monkeys, we move on to the tigers, who've been enticed from a spacious paddock to a caged sleeping area while we run around hiding lumps of meat in tree trunks. As we file back out, the two Sumatran tigers can smell meat on our hands. They prowl back and forth, growling, bashing the bars and rearing up on hind legs, while Matt the languid big cat keeper regales us with stories of zookeepers from around the world who have been mauled by big cats. It's entertainment, of sorts.

And that's it. We leave the tigers to their tea and change back into civvies. Pete – a burly maintainence engineer in his fifties, and certainly no soft touch – admits, 'I've been smiling so much since I got here that my face is starting to hurt.' It has been a memorable day.

London Zoo *Regent's Park, NW1 4RY (7722 3333/www.zsl.org/shop/keeper-for-a-day).*

248

Visit the Ragged School Museum

Ragged schools were an early experiment in public education: they provided tuition as well as food and clothing for destitute children. The Copperfield Road Ragged School was the largest in London, and it was here that the famous Dr Barnardo taught. It's now a fascinating museum that contains a complete mock-up of a ragged classroom, in which historical re-enactments are staged for schoolchildren, as well as an Edwardian kitchen. Admission is free.

Ragged School Museum *50 Copperfield Road, E3 4RR (8980 6405/www.raggedschoolmuseum.org.uk).*

249

Take a trip down a real-life Diagon Alley

One for Harry Potter fans everywhere. In 1996, Walthamstow-born psychic Julia Laverne was asked to design a major psychic centre after giving a client reading. She 'saw' the location of the site as being in some way connected to the Queensway ice rink during the reading, and so Psychic Mews, located in Queensway Market (23-25 Queensway, W2 4QL, 7221 8049) a few doors down from Queensway ice skating rink, found its home. The centre itself is located directly above the rink (Julia's vision was impressively accurate) but sadly you can't enlist her help in finding it as she's based in Islington Green. So you'll just have to wander around the hotch-potch market, selling everything from cheap computers to Russian sweetmeats, until you stumble across it. The impressively authentic recreation of a Victorian street has seven individually themed houses and a gypsy caravan at the end of it. All of them are filled with psychics plying their trade and selling clairvoyancy-related wares.

250
Model in the nude

Get your kit off for cold, hard cash. And art! The Bare Facts workshop is designed for aspiring life models. Trot along to the drop-in classes on Wednesday evenings at Islington Arts Factory (2 Parkhurst Road, N7 0SF, 7607 0561, www.islingtonartsfactory.org) where you'll get assessed for basic aptitude, blush factor and the like. If you are deemed to be up to scratch (most are), you can pay a nominal fee to join as a life model, after which the cash comes in as quickly as the clothes come off.

251 *Flash mob*

You may have seen an impromptu pillow fight outside Tate Modern or a rabble descending en masse on a major railway station for a mammoth dancing session. Flash mobs had their moment in the sun a few years back now, but London's mobs go manfully on, coming up with new and intriguing spins on the 'turn up in large numbers and do something silly' format. It's an exhilarating experience to watch or take part in; visit www.geocities.com/londonmobs to see what they are planning next.

252 *Have a cuppa with a cabbie*

You may have spotted green garden sheds in apparently random spots around London (Embankment, Russell Square, Warwick Avenue…) and wondered what they were for. Well, the long queue of black cabs on the streets outside should be a clue. These Cabman's Shelters were set up by a Victorian philanthropist as a place where cabbies could get a spot of tea and sympathy without having to disappear to the nearest pub. Many have been demolished, but there are just over a dozen extant in London. If you ask nicely, they might even let you inside for a mug of rosie and some hair-raising banter about ex-Mayor Ken Livingstone. A London institution.

253

Drop by 19 Princelet Street

Fragile and consequently rarely open, this 'museum of immigration' is an intriguing oddity among London's cultural offerings. Housed in an 18th-century Georgian family home, 19 Princelet Street has been home to Huguenot weavers and a Polish synagogue. It is sporadically open for tours and exhibitions; check the website for dates.
19 Princelet Street *E1 6QH (7247 5352/ www.19princeletstreet.org.uk).*

254 *Visit Tyburn Convent... shhhh!*

This Catholic retreat on the Bayswater Road in the centre of London is a truly remarkable, if spooky, place. In the ground-floor chapel a handful of devout Londoners pray in silence, joining one of the 25 resident nuns who take it in turns to maintain a continuous contemplation before the cross, a commitment that has been observed since 1903. Sisters are available for guided tours daily at 10.30am, 3.30pm and 5.30pm. These tours take in a frankly terrifying crypt below the convent: as well as an altar piece modelled on the Tyburn gallows from which criminals were once hanged 20 at a time (a grand total of 50,000 between 1197 and 1783), there are wall-mounted cases containing the fingernails, bone splinters, hair and skin (yes, skin) of hanged Catholic martyrs. Dead scary and utterly fascinating.
Tyburn Convent *8 Hyde Park Place, W2 2LJ (www.tyburnconvent.org.uk).*

255 *Blow glass*

Contemporary British glass artist Adam Aaronson's Aaronson Noon Studio (7610 1900, www.adamaaronson.com) in west London gives excellent classes for beginner glass-blowers. The half-day Saturday course costs £175 per person, and at the end of the day you will have made several solid and blown glass pieces for your mantelpiece.

256 *Eat dessert at Maze*

Maze is notable for its Asian-influenced French 'tasting dishes' – but a special note went in our book for its tantalising desserts. The peanut butter and cherry jam sandwich (with tonka – aka vanilla – bean cream and cherries) is, without a shadow of doubt, the most unexpectedly lovely pudding this reviewer has ever had. Ever. Ever. Ever.
Maze *Marriot Hotel, 10-13 Grosvenor Square, W1K 6JP (7107 0000/www.gordonramsay.com).*

257-260 *Learn burlesque dancing*

Fancy yourself as the next Dita Von Teese? Time Out*'s Social Club editor* Simone Baird *on the most seductive way to shape up.*

As the trend for all things vintage continues and the previously long-lost art of burlesque shimmies back to take its place centre stage, there's been an influx of dedicated evenings, clubs and salons springing up all over town in the last few years.

It follows that, even as we are stunned into slack-jawed submission by someone's dazzling routine, there may be those among us who think: 'I can do that'. It's one thing to decide to learn the lambada after a night in the theatre watching *Dirty Dancing*, but where do you go to learn tassel-twirling and hip thrusts?

All burlesque roads in London lead to Jo King. She's been a burlesque striptease artist for 30 years, and back in 2000 became the first person in the UK and Europe to offer classes. Running the London School of Striptease (www.london schoolofstriptease.co.uk), she gives even nervous beginners the chance to become budding burlesque queens. The Teasemaids, Miss Polly Rae and the Hurly Burly Girlys are just some of the well-known London performers who started with her.

'Women love glamour, and burlesque is a way for them to be sexy in a way that isn't threatening,' says King. 'It's seen as a tease and highly sexual, but it isn't dangerous.' She continues: 'Burlesque isn't just about striptease. Someone could do a really cute dance in a sweet little outfit, or a balloon act, or a balloon act on rollerskates. Striptease can be part of it, but it doesn't have to be. A burlesque class is just about dancing – no clothes come off!'

King's burlesque classes featured in the Workers School of Excellence at the Bethnal Green Working Men's Club (42-44 Pollard Row, E2 6NB, see p295), which also offered classes in chorus, tap and pole-dancing. King also teaches Burlesque Buzz, a month-long series of weekly performance classes for beginners, at Danceworks (16 Balderton Street, W1 6TN, 7629 6183, www.danceworks.net) as well as four-hour workshops at LA Fitness in Golders Green (152-154 Golders Green Road W11 8HE, 8731 7312, www.lafitness.co.uk).

So what are the fitness benefits of this most flamboyant of dance crazes? 'It's not aerobics,' says King, 'but you don't just stand there and take your clothes off. Girls at the end are always saying "ooh, my legs, my bum, my waist." It's very good for toning.'

The most important thing that burlesque classes – and performing a burlesque routine – can offer, says journalist and dancer Natalie Blenford, is confidence. 'Burlesque routines require certain movements that you would never do unless you were drunk in a club, such as hip thrusts and sexy figure of eights,' explains Blenford. 'If you're not the kind of woman who oozes sexiness on a day-to-day basis, the idea is probably terrifying.'

In a two-hour class you can expect to pick up the traditional burlesque movements, including shimmying your bottom and breasts, burlesque crossover steps, high kicks and bumping your hips. King's Burlesque Buzz course is geared towards those who want to put a performance together (if only for their boyfriend). It covers all the basics, from physical theatre and prop-work to learning about putting on a persona and characterisation. Twirling of nipple tassels isn't included, though – that's a stand-alone class for bolder pupils who are ready for some striptease lessons.

If you've ever spent a entire dance class frustrated and two steps behind everyone else, you'll appreciate the lack of formality associated with learning burlesque. The emphasis isn't on ensuring that your arm is in a perfect line with your shoulder; developing a routine is all about you and what you can bring to it, which means that exaggerating a move is quite all right. In fact, it's actively encouraged.

261 Eat ice-cream at Gelateria Danieli

This hole-in-the-wall ice-cream parlour makes all its own ices using fresh fruit and the minimum of additives. We think they're just about the best-tasting ice-creams in London, eclipsing better-known brands and working out cheaper too, at £1.50 per generous scoop. The 30 flavours of ices include pistacchio, fig and mandarin; the ones we tried were silky-textured, not sickly sweet, and had vibrant fruit or nut flavours. The dairy ices are also lower fat than usual, at 6 per cent. There are non-dairy ices and sorbets as well, and rice cones for those on gluten-free diets. On our visit, there was a queue out the door as people strolled over to adjacent Richmond Green in the sunshine. The only drawback is that you can't sit in – there's just not enough room.

Gelateria Danieli *16 Brewers Lane, Richmond, Surrey TW9 1HH (8439 9807).*

262-265

Get yourself a pair of bespoke shoes

John Lobb is one of London's finest old establishments. The original Lobb made his name as a cobbler during the reign of Queen Victoria, when he shod the Prince of Wales, who later became King Edward VII. Today, the firm (9 St James's Street, SW1A 1EF, 7930 3664, www.johnlobbltd.co.uk) remains testament to the old adage that quality never goes out of fashion, and John Lobb's is the first name out of the hat when the subject of custom-made shoes comes up. Unfortunately, anyone lacking royal pedigree will find the £2,000-plus price tag difficult to muster. Of course, a peek at the beautifully old-fashioned, wood-panelled interior costs nothing.

For a cheaper bespoke shoe experience – albeit, as with anything bespoke, certainly not cheap – visit George Cleverley (13 The Royal Arcade, 28 Old Bond Street, W1S 4SL, 7493 0443, www.gjcleverley.co.uk, from £1,900) or Tricker's (67 Jermyn Street, SW1Y 6NY, 7930 6395, www.trickers.com, from £850). Caroline Groves (37 Chiltern Street, W1U 7PW, 7935 2329, www.carolinegroves.co.uk, from £1,200) specialises in some exquisitely nostalgic styles for ladies.

266

Tour the City Livery Halls

Few Londoners know much about London's livery companies, but these ancient institutions played a crucial part in the development of the City. Many were formed in the Middle Ages, essentially as trade guilds. Some accumulated much wealth and exerted powerful influence over the governance of the City. Organisations such as the Worshipful Company of Drapers based at Drapers' Hall (Throgmorton Avenue EC2N 2DQ) – can trace their roots back to 1361 and built impressive halls after the devestation of the Great Fire in 1666. Tours can sometimes be arranged (although it obviously helps if you know a member), alternatively, several throw open their doors on Open House day (*see p126*).

267

Ignore the show-courts at Wimbledon

Get a basic entry ticket for the summer tournament and you can watch matches on the minor courts. Indeed, if you get seats right at the back of Court Three, you can stand and see over the fence in to Court Two where there are plenty of high-profile matches during the competition's busy first week.

All England Lawn Tennis Club *Church Road, SW19 5AE (8946 2244/www.wimbledon.org).*

268

Wonder at the Wallace Collection

The fourth Marquess of Hertford and his illegitimate son Sir Richard Wallace were largely responsible for this impressive collection of *objets*. Open to the public since 1900, room after room of the handsome Hertford House on Manchester Square contains an embarrassment of Louis XIV and XV furnishings, priceless porcelain, paintings by Titian, Velázquez and Gainsborough (to name just a few) – even grand suits of armour.

Wallace Collection *Hertford House, Manchester Square W1U 3BN (7935 0687/ www.wallacecollection.org). Admission free.*

269

Test recipes at Books for Cooks

The lovely smells that emanate from this traditional-looking bookshop ensure its continued popularity: every day, staff in the smart test kitchen at the back set about cooking up treats from the limitless supply of recipes at hand. Amid the thousands of recipe books covering every type of cuisine, the shop's own publications are worth a look. There are titles on nutrition and culinary history, as well as biographies of celebrated chefs. Cookery workshops take place upstairs.

Books for Cooks *4 Blenheim Crescent, W11 1NN (7221 1992/www.booksforcooks.com).*

270-274
Treat yourself to a posh cinema ticket

The movies have always prided themselves on being a democratic art form – a modern medium of mass entertainment that makes all people equal in the dark theatre. In the niche-friendly noughties, though, the trend is for the luxury ambience of exclusive movie dens, free from the sickly waft of munched popcorn and irritating chatter of the hoi polloi. Of course, the arts crowd has always been able to huddle at firmly alternative cinemas such as the Renoir, ICA and the Other Cinema, but those willing to pay a premium for an elite experience will find that London now hosts a handful of defiantly first-class picture palaces.

Charlotte Street Hotel
15-17 Charlotte Street, W1T 1RJ (7806 2000/ www.firmdale.com).
Visit on a Sunday night to combine a three-course set meal with watching a classic film in the mini-cinema; booking is advisable.

Covent Garden Hotel
10 Monmouth Street, WC2H 9HB (7806 1000/ www.firmdale.com).
This gilt-edged hotel has a snug 53-seater screening room.

Electric Cinema
191 Portobello Road, W11 2ED (7908 9696/ www.the-electric.co.uk).
One of London's oldest cinemas, and one of its most lavish, with leather armchairs and two-seater sofas.

Everyman Cinema Club
5 Hollybush Vale, NW3 6TX (0870 066 4777/ www.everymancinema.com).
The Everyman's two-seater 'club suites' come complete with foot stools, a wine cooler and plush upholstery.

One Aldwych
1 Aldwych, WC2B 4RH (7300 1000/ www.onealdwych.com).
This luxury hotel's intimate screening room has good-value dinner and movie packages.

Electric Cinema

275

Science always thinks it's right. Which makes it all the more satisfying when it gets things wrong. Opened in 1854, the Crystal Palace Dinosaur Court in Crystal Palace Park (Thicket Road, SE20) was the world's first attempt to recreate life-size models of the giant lizard-like creatures whose bones had recently been discovered. Sadly, the understanding of dinosaurs at the time fell short of modern standards and so the models are slightly lacking in anatomical correctness (thumb bones were mistaken for nose horns for example). Still, the big beasts are in great shape (and are now Grade II-listed) and kids love 'em.

276 *Learn aikido*

In this ancient Japanese martial art, holds, locks, throws and blows are used to subdue your attacker, employing spherical movements, designed to turn the aggressor's energy back on himself. At the London Aikido Club (60A Windus Road, N16 6UP, 8806 3219, www. londonaikidoclub.co.uk), ten-week courses cost from £70 and include free martial arts suits. So, it's like fighting – but in pyjamas.

277 *Pop in to Mayfair's tiny Postcard Teas*

A hobby tearoom in the heart of Mayfair, with only a trickle of customers paying a pittance for a cup of prime-quality tea, Postcard Teas is a gem. The teas cost £1.50 a large cup, which isn't bad for varieties of this excellence: black teas, green teas and oolong teas of many different styles. The owner, Timothy d'Offay, has even travelled abroad to visit many of the growers – for that added, personal touch.
Postcard Teas *9 Dering Street, W1S 1AG (7629 3654/www.postcardteas.com).*

278 *Watch Irish hurling in an Irish pub*

Hurling is Europe's oldest team game and the national pursuit of Ireland. The 15-a-side game is fast, furious and really quite violent... making it perfect pub telly fodder. The Corrib Rest (76-82 Salisbury Road, NW6 6PA, 7625 9585) in Queen's Park is one hurling-loving pub, the Crown & Cushion (133 Westminster Bridge Road, SE1 7HR, 7803 0573) another, but you can also visit just about every pub in Kentish Town and Kilburn and find it taking pride of place on the TV over the Premiership. The rules might take some explaining if you're not familiar with the game, but the Irish are legendary in their hospitality.

If you're looking to play yourself, websites www.londongaa.co.uk and www.gaa.ie have useful information to get you started. Brave soul.

279 *Actually use river transport*

Have a gander at any Olde London picture of the Thames and the first thing that'll strike you is the amount of river traffic there used to be. Many of the boats on the river are used by tourists – and perfectly nice they are too, taking you about the many sights of the Thames. But the river can also be used for everyday travel: London River Services (www.tfl.gov.uk) runs boats at 20 minute intervals from a variety of piers between Embankment and Woolwich, with prices cut by a third if you use already have a travelcard. An excellent way to get from east to west – or just to see the river's landmarks without a microphone commentary.

280 *Drink vodka in a Polish bar*

Other venues may nod towards a theme, bung a couple of Cyrillic letters into their name, stick a bowl of tapas into the microwave – but Bar Polski (11 Little Turnstile, WC1V 7DX, 7831 9679) is the real deal. From the Polish kitchen (churning out bigos, barszcz and kielbasa until 10pm) to the authentic Polish fridge, this sleek and simple alleyway bar doesn't do dilettante. Speaking of fridge: vodkas by the vatload, most at £2.50 a shot, are categorised into 'dry and interesting' or 'nice and sweet' to help the uninitiated. Think of them as meze – try a sweet caraway seed Kwinkowy, or an Orzechowka infused with unripe walnuts.

281 *Revisit the Royal Observatory*

The £15 million redevelopment of the Royal Observatory, Greenwich, culminated in the opening in 2007 of four new galleries and the whizzy, state of the art, copper-cladded Peter Harrison Planetarium. Once you've been unable to resist putting your feet in different hemispheres on either side of the meridian line (*see p165*) they are all worth a look.
Royal Observatory *Blackheath Avenue, SE10 8XJ (8312 6565/www.nmm.ac.uk).*

282 Sample first-class sushi in Ealing

Head west for the best of the Far East: Sushi-Hiro (1 Station Parade, Uxbridge Road, W5 3LD, 8896 3175) offers some of the finest sushi in London at a fraction of Mayfair's prices. The reason? The restaurant is in a prime location for intercepting hungry office workers on their way home from the tube to the Japanese expatriate enclaves of Ealing and hence attracts much Japanese custom. Behind an unpromising-looking frosted white shopfront, a friendly husband-and-wife team produces straightforward sushi made with fine ingredients and faultless technique. Try the ten-piece tokujo set meal, which includes startlingly fresh scallop and sweet prawn, plus melting chu-toro (tuna) and sea eel.

283 Celebrate Russian 'Old New Year'

The Russian Winter Festival takes place annually on the eve of 'Old New Year' – new year as based on the Julian calendar. Held in Trafalgar Square, the family-friendly event includes children's games and puppet performances, classical folk song and dance and stalls selling Russian crafts and food. Call event organisers on 7983 4100 for an exact date.

284 Sit in the Great Court at the British Museum

The largest enclosed courtyard in Europe, the British Museum's Great Court has all the benefits of a classical public square – grandeur, proportion, shops, restaurants, people, events, light, air – without any of the attendant meteorological risks. Designed by Foster & Partners with engineers Buro Happold, the Great Court is dominated by the undulating glass roof (made up of 3,300 separate triangles). At its centre is the former British Library reading room – once open to scholars only. Free to enter.
British Museum *Great Russell Street, WC1B 3DG (7323 8000/www.thebritishmuseum.ac.uk).*

285 Take a candlelit tour of Dennis Severs' House

The ten rooms of Dennis Severs' House on Folgate Street have been decked out to recreate, down to the smallest detail, snapshots of life in Spitalfields between 1724 and 1914. A tour through this compelling 'still-life drama', as creator Dennis Severs branded it, takes you through the cellar, kitchen, dining room, smoking room and upstairs to the bedroom. With hearth burning, smells lingering and objects scattered haphazardly, it is as if the inhabitants deserted the rooms just moments before. A tour of the house by candlelight, on Monday evenings (£12, book in advance), adds considerably to the atmosphere. Otherwise, visit on Sunday afternoons (£8), or at lunchtime on the Monday following the first and third Sunday of each month (£5).
Dennis Severs' House *18 Folgate Street, E1 6BX (7247 4013/www.dennissevershouse.co.uk).*

286 Cue up at London's snooker clubs

Some people are just too cool for pool. The smoke-filled halls of snooker's yesteryear may have gone, but pretty much everything else remains the same – including the splendidly louche image that the sport still seems to encourage (it's no surprise that Ronnie 'the Rocket' O'Sullivan is the sport's most popular ambassador) while at the same time demanding immense skill from its players. Anyone can sink a ball or two on a pool table after downing a few pints at the pub but snooker presents a far stiffer, and more sophisticated, challenge. If you feel up to it www.londonsnooker.co.uk lists many of the capital's best clubs. Membership is always required but can be paid for on the door at almost all places.

Mangal 1 **RESTAURANT**

10 Arcola Street • London • E8 2DJ
(off Stoke Newington Road)
Tel: 020 7275 8981 • www.mangal1.com

With its legendary reputation for grills, Mangal doesn't bother with frills. It has started producing a takeaway menu, but diners are asked to choose from the long list of kebabs above the counter before taking their seats (this can occasionally mean queuing). The interior is long, dominated on one side by the counter and the ocakbasi grill. Tiled walls feature traditional kilim mats preserved in frames of various dimensions. The functional tables have plain wooden tops and metal legs, like old school desks. More starters are now available, including lahmacun, houmous and cacik. That's all to the good, but it's the grills that have earned Mangal a hallowed status – and they're worthy of it. A long lamb beyti hung off the edges of our plate and came with chopped leaf salad and bread (both thick fresh pide and fine saç bread). Fresh herbs and spices could clearly be seen and tasted in the minced lamb after it had been sliced: excellent. The slow evolution of Mangal is commendable, but don't expect the chefs to stray too far from the grill. Nor should they.

Time Out Eating & Drinking Guide 2009

• Starters range
from £1.50 - £5.00 •

• Kebabs start
from £6.50 - £9.00 •

287 *Do the Camden Crawl*

London's celebrated indie festival-cum-endurance test takes place in mid-April, in venues around Camden over a Friday and Saturday (noon-4am both days). Previous Crawls have seen the likes of Madness, Kasabian, Little Boots and Idlewild wow the crowds. Check the website (www.thecamdencrawl.com) or *Time Out* magazine nearer the time for full line-ups of future events.

288 *Grab a 3am bagel at the Brick Lane Beigel Bake*

Famously open 24 hours a day, the Beigel Bake (159 Brick Lane, E1 6SB, 7729 0616) provides safe harbour for clubbers on the hoof, bleary-eyed nightshift workers and peckish insomniacs. Many punters call in for takeaways, though there are a few stools along a counter. Bagels have been baked here since the 1960s; cream cheese, smoked salmon or salt beef are the favoured fillings. Stupendously moreish cakes and buns are on display behind the counter. The breads aren't bad either.

289 *Make use of the library at the Royal Geographical Society*

Members of the public can access the collection of two million maps, books, photos, documents and objects spanning the past 500 years of geographical exploration. Users can research the lives of famous explorers such as Mary Kingsley or Livingstone, study 19th-century maps of Britain, Africa, Asia, the Caribbean and Europe, or use the collection of travel guides to research a holiday. The project, which was partly funded by the Heritage Lottery Fund, includes online access as well as personal visits to the Foyle Reading Room (take proof of identity to register as a new reader) and exhibitions plus educational events for school and adult groups. Use of the library costs £10 a day.
Royal Geographical Society *1 Kensington Gore, SW7 2AR (7591 3000/www.rgs.org).*

Brick Lane Beigel Bake

290-296
Pick your own fruit and veg

All around the outskirts of London, hundreds of pick-your-own farms offer an invigorating rural experience and a cheap way to stock up on fruit and veg. Remember that all crops are seasonal, so contact the farm in advance to check your chosen fruits and vegetables are available to pick before making a special journey.

Barn Yard Farm Shops & Gore Farm
Oak Lane, Upchurch, Sittingbourne, Kent ME9 7BE (01634 235059/www.the-barnyard.co.uk). For soft fruits.

Crockford Bridge Farm
New Haw Road, Addlestone, near Weybridge, Surrey KT15 2BU (01932 853886). For strawberries, raspberries, blackberries, marrows, beans, courgettes, peas and rhubarb.

Garsons Farm
Winterdown Road, Esher, Surrey KT10 8LS (01372 464389/www.garsons.co.uk). For soft fruits (including strawberries, raspberries and cherries), cabbages, broad beans, onions, sweetcorn and more.

Grays of Wokingham
Heathlands Road, Wokingham, Berks RG40 3AN (0118 978 5386/www.graysfarm.co.uk). For most soft fruits, broad beans, runner beans, broccoli, carrots, sweetcorn, potatoes and cabbage.

Grove Farm
Ivinghoe, Leighton Buzzard, Beds LU7 9DZ (01296 668175/www.grovefarmpyo.co.uk). For soft fruits, onions, potatoes, carrots, parsnips, broccoli, beetroot, peas, spinach, garlic, coriander, sweetcorn and chard.

Parkside Farm
Hadley Road, Enfield, Middx EN2 8LA (8367 2035/www.parksidefarmpyo.co.uk). For soft fruits, plums, tomatoes, onions, beans, spinach, sweetcorn and cucumbers.

Spencers Farm Shop
Wickham Fruit Farm, Wickham St Pauls, Halstead, Essex CO9 2PX (01787 269476/ www.spencersfarmshop.co.uk). For soft fruits, including (in season) plums and 18 varieties of apple.

297
Drink tequila

Those fond of the 'down the hatch' tequila technique may be surprised to hear that there are connoisseurs of the Mexican national tipple who appreciate the magic that can be made with a distillate of blue agave. Mexican-themed La Perla (28 Maiden Lane, WC2E 7JS, 7240 7400, www.cafepacifico-laperla.com) is the best place in London to drink it, serving a wide range, including blanco (young un-aged tequila), reposado (aged in oak for up to 12 months), añejo (aged for more than a year), plus top-of-the-range Premium tequilas. Try one of the 'tequila flights' for a thorough introduction.

Meanwhile, Shoreditch's Green & Red (51 Bethnal Green Road, E1 6LA, 7749 9670, www.greenred.co.uk) boasts an impressive 245 bottles of tequila, plus flights and a variety of well-prepared tequila-based cocktails – not to mention culinary specialities from Jalisco, Mexico's tequila region.

298 *Visit the Dulwich Picture Gallery*

Sir John Soane's neo-classical building in southeast London has been described as the most beautiful small art gallery in the world. The contents are worth a look too: Rubens, Van Dyck, Cuyp, Rembrandt, Gainsborough, Poussin, Raphael and Reynolds, among others.
Dulwich Picture Gallery *Gallery Road, SE21 7AD (8693 5254/www.dulwichpicturegallery.org.uk).*

299 *Swim in the Berkeley's rooftop pool*

The crowning glory of the Berkeley hotel, this rooftop pool – open to the elements in good weather – isn't huge but is rarely busy. There are loungers aplenty, plus a fridge stocked with freshly squeezed juices. A day pass, including access to the Berkeley Spa's gym, sauna and steam room as well as the pool, costs £65.
The Berkeley Spa *The Berkeley, Wilton Place, SW1X 7RL (7201 1699/www.the-berkeley.com).*

300 Bowl

*Tom Lamont **admires London's boutique bowling alleys.***

Bowling in London used to mean a retail park somewhere out in the suburbs that suppled blaring arcade machines, sticky floors and those fluorescent blue 'raspberry slushes'. The bowling of balls took a backseat to kids' birthday parties, chicken nuggets, and boy–girl groups of teens testing the waters of mixed-gender fraternity.

Happy days for some, but changes have rolled into town in the last few years. Perhaps influenced by the stateside success of 'boutique' bowling alleys – darker, less sticky, with bars, dining areas and no kids – Londoners have been enjoying an alternative to the retail parks in the forms of Bloomsbury Bowling Lanes (Basement of Tavistock Hotel, Bedford Way, WC1H 9EU, 7183 1979, www.bloomsburylanes.co.uk) and All Star Lanes (Victoria House, Bloomsbury Place, WC1B 4DA, 7025 2676, www.allstarlanes.co.uk).

Other successful outfits such as Bar Kick (for table football, *see p217*) have shown there's a market for gently accessible sports that anyone can enjoy, regardless of innate athletic talent or blood-to-alcohol ratio. Bowling has been waiting its turn for trendification. It's loud, destructive, but also sociable, and it taps into the sort of cool that runs through cult films such as *The Big Lebowski* and *Kingpin,* not to mention a much-loved episode of *The Simpsons.*

So what's the difference between the two Bloomsbury haunts? While both are geared towards adults rather than kids – think office parties or groups of students from the London universities – All Star Lanes is noticeably aimed at the richer end of the market. Their four bowling lanes (plus two private lanes upstairs) are only part of the set-up: All Star also has a pricey diner-style restaurant (steaks ring in at £17-£22.50) and an even pricier red-leather bar beyond (cocktails climb to £7 and there are no beers on tap). Still, the quality is high and, as long as you can afford it, the bar has buckets more atmosphere than its rival. And it's obviously been popular – the original was joined by a Bayswater branch (6 Porchester Gardens, W2 4DB, 7313 8363) and another outpost in the super-hip Old Truman Brewery (95 Brick Lane, E1 6QE, 7426 9200).

Bloomsbury Bowling wins out in other departments, however. With twice as many lanes and lower hire costs (£5.50 per game at peak time as opposed to All Star's £8.50), this is a less intimidating outfit. The low-key, intentionally scruffy decor is less flashy than at All Star Lanes, and the worn booths in the restaurant (burgers from £7.95) seem a more authentic representation of Americana than All Star's unspoiled shininess (although there's also now a flashy new 'Kingpin' Suite here to rival All Star's private lanes – with a DJ booth, games room and, er, karaoke machine, as well as bowling lanes). To top it all, bowling in the daytime (Mon-Wed before 4pm) only costs £3 per game – surely one of the best prices in London, retail park or not.

With capped scorelines, bowling will never be an Olympic discipline but as a fresh, flippant drink-side pursuit, it seems to be exactly what Londoners have been waiting for.

All Star Lanes

301-302

Size up London's weapon collection

Predictably, weapons feature predominantly at the National Army Museum (Royal Hospital Road, SW3 4HT, 7730 0717, www.national-army-museum.ac.uk). The 2,500 edged weapons, 200 pole arms and 1,850 firearms should keep bloodthirsty teenagers interested. Similarly well 'packed', the Royal Artillery Museum (Royal Arsenal, SE18 6ST, 8855 7755, www.firepower.org.uk), or Firepower as it's also known, covers the history of guns and gunpower from Ancient China to contemporary Iraq. The first floor mixes antique weaponry with informative history, while the ground floor is given over to some serious hardware. Look out for the mortar in the shape of a tiger.

303-304

Smash up cars – or just watch – at Wimbledon Stadium

Naturally, we're not talking about descending upon the car park with a set of keys and a baseball bat. On Sundays, Wimbledon Stadium (Plough Lane, SW17 0BL, 01252 322 920, www.spedeworth.net) offers the opportunity to race around its track in bangers. Be warned, they're not named after the noises their shonky engines make every time you put the pedal down – they are designed to bang into other racers. Probably best to let someone else drive home, though. If driving the things yourself doesn't appeal, you can pop along to the regular Sunday banger races and watch the experts smash their vehicles to pieces.

World of leather

*It's nearly 20 years since now-legendary fetish club the Torture Garden opened its dungeon to fans of body adornment, rubber and bondage. **Andy Woolgar** dared to enter.*

Nothing quite prepares you for the queue for the Torture Garden cloakroom. I'm not talking length, more the view you get from standing in it. The cloakroom is located on the top floor of the cavernous converted church that is Brixton's Mass. Which means that, once the cream of London's perverati have deposited their coats and outer layers, they're forced to walk back down past everyone else queueing on the stairs. Which makes this narrow spiral staircase the most spectacular and jaw-dropping catwalk on the planet.

In the queue all of 30 seconds and I'd already seen the following five sights troop past: a perfectly proportioned naked woman sprayed head to foot in gold paint; a middle-aged man wearing nothing but a metal thong and a stuffed eagle on his shoulder; a Caprice lookalike in Doc Martens and flimsy Agent Provocateur underwear; a man dressed in a forensic officer's paper suit with four dismembered toy dolls hanging from his chest; and a statuesque blonde whose leather bra contained a pair of gargantuan breasts (false), but whose transparent pants clearly contained a huge penis (real).

This went on for the next 15 minutes (the procession, not the transexual's huge passing penis) while I stood in line, nervously clutching my coat like an improvised protective shield.

Welcome to the world's largest fetish club – and its eclectic mix of clubbers, fashionistas and assorted pervs. Conceived in London in 1990 by promoters Alan Pelling and David Wood, the monthly Torture Garden has become renowned as much for its hedonistic party-goers as its cutting-edge dance music and performers.

It's also a thriving international business, having exported its unique brand of club pervery to the US, Russia, Japan, Croatia, Greece and beyond. In fact, with a range of CDs, DVDs, books and a fashion label to its name, this fetish institution is rapidly becoming a fetish corporation. Kink Inc, if you will.

But on a cold, October Saturday night in Brixton, this is the essential Torture Garden. A Halloween extravaganza where 1,400 TG disciples have flocked to a former church to dress bizarrely, dance madly and exercise their filthiest fantasies.

From the initial sights that pass the cloakroom queue, it's clear this is no run-of-the-mill Halloween party. For a start, there's not a pumpkin in sight. Unless you count your correspondent stuffed into a pair of leather trousers so dated even Jon Bon Jovi might declare them passé. In truth, among this outlandish crowd, I feel as hip as Boris Johnson. My female partner (also a fetish club virgin) fares no better. Attired outrageously, or so she thought, in a short kilt and sports bra, she looks so overdressed she might as well have worn hiking boots and a fleece top.

But be warned, the TG atmosphere is strangely infectious. As we near the cloakroom, my partner suddenly decides to nip to the loo only to emerge minutes later, minus her bra and with the words 'MEDIA WHORE' scrawled in lipstick across her naked chest. 'Bollocks to it,' she says, checking in her bra with her coat. 'Everyone was staring at me in that top so I might as well give them something to look at. Wait till you see what I've written where my knickers were!' And all this before we've even reached the bar. Something tells me this could be a long night.

Twenty minutes later and I'm beginning to wish I'd come here when I was 18. Because quite simply, until you've been to the Torture Garden, you can't claim to have been clubbing. A never-ending parade of barely decorated flesh, it's a visual extravaganza like no other. And if S&M isn't your bag, with five rooms spread across three floors, it's big enough for you not to see any. But if spanking and nipple tweaking is how you get your jollies, wild horses probably won't drag you from the dungeon playrooms. The music's damned good too. Loud enough to melt internal organs, it varies from disco punk to glamour trash and retro house – with a constant backbeat of the thwack of leather on buttock.

But more than anything, it's the diverse and welcoming crowd that makes TG what it is. Everyone dresses up to such a degree that the only people who feel conspicuous are those who haven't made much of an effort. Or have attempted to wing it in a bad pair of leather trousers. Yeah, sorry about that. The dress code is strictly enforced. As a rule of thumb, the club's organisers claim that if what you're wearing wouldn't get you stared at in the street, don't bother even queueing up to get in.

It all helps generate an atmosphere so electrifying, the air feels almost solid. And unlike most nightclubs, there's a complete

absence of threatening or intimidating behaviour. 'I go to run-of-the-mill nightclubs dressed really conservatively and I frequently get groped or hassled by guys,' said Kathy, a 24-year-old nurse wearing nothing but a fishnet body stocking. 'But I regularly come here dressed like this and I've never had anyone even attempt to feel me up. Unless I've asked them to! People are so much more respectful in fetish clubs. They may look like something out of your worst nightmare but you won't meet a more friendly and polite bunch of people.'

Indeed, this may be an environment that encourages the exploration of your sexuality but there are strict codes of conduct. Touching without permission is strictly forbidden. 'You'll notice stewards dotted around,' added Kathy, 'but I've never known them need to get involved. The punters have developed this habit of policing the club themselves – so if someone's making a nuisance of themselves, clubbers nearby will quickly turn on them and immediately sort it.'

It's this relaxed, friendly and safe environment that helps attract a host of celebrities to let off steam at TG. Notable regulars include Marilyn Manson, Boy George, Jean Paul Gaultier and Dita Von Teese. Alas, tonight I can only spot a Page Three legend and a rather lonely-looking TV magician (and no, it wasn't Daniels).

But who wants to star spot when there's so much more to feast your eyes on? In the dungeon playroom I'm drawn to a man demonstrating the art of Japanese rope bondage by tying his mature wife's breasts to a winch. To be honest, her bosoms looked like Christmas balloons in Februrary before hubby got to grips with them. But now, bound tightly, they look like a pair of engorged baubles, on the verge of popping. There's a murmur of approval from the gathered throng as he expertly adjusts his knotwork. It's like watching Ray Mears. If Ray Mears was ever inclined to swap his khaki shorts for a pair of backless chaps.

TG prides itself on staging a variety of cutting-edge performances throughout its nights. But in truth the punters are far more entertaining than anything occuring on the stages. I bump into an impossibly beautiful American lawyer who's travelled from Florida for this night. 'I heard such good reports of TG that I had to come and experience it for myself,' she says, eyeing my bad trousers disdainfully. 'So far it's a trip definitely worth making – I just need to find some cute English ass to amuse me,' she adds, lifting her ballgown to reveal a shapely pair of thighs topped by a fearsome-looking black strap-on.

Thankfully, my partner provides a timely distraction by introducing me to two women in their thirties dressed as X-rated Lara Crofts, but sounding more like Annabel Croft. 'We've come down from Hertfordshire for the weekend,' laughs Sandra, a mum of two. 'We never miss a TG. It's a chance for us to dress up and live out our wildest fantasies in a safe and accepting environment. We told our husbands that we were coming down to see a show. They've no idea we're into all this – they wouldn't understand it and would go mad if they knew we were here dressed like this. By the way, your friend the media whore is a filthy bitch.'

I look over her shoulder to see my partner brazenly groping and tongue-kissing the second Lara Croft. This is the power of TG. I've known her ten years and yet had no idea she was even remotely bi-curious. She pauses for breath to yell, 'Come on, we're all going back to their hotel. Get your coat, we've pulled!'

Told you it was going to be a long night.

Torture Garden *www.torturegarden.com*

306 Watch Tower Bridge opening

When unveiled in 1894, Tower Bridge represented a dazzlingly pioneering feat of engineering. To watch Tower Bridge in action is to see why London was once the most technologically advanced city in the world. Check the website to see when it's going to open and, for more history of the bridge, check out the Tower Bridge Exhibition, which lets you walk along the upper tier of the bridge for spectacular river views.
Tower Bridge *Tower Bridge Road, E1 2UP (7940 3985/www.towerbridge.org.uk).*

307 Bid at Christie's

Christie's was founded in London in 1766, and quickly became the centre of the international art trade (after Paris got distracted by a revolution). It's now the world's largest auction house, and while the average punter can't compete with the big bidders, there are auctions taking place every day that take in everything from teddy bear collections to rare wines. Catalogues are printed three weeks in advance and are also on the website (www.christies.com). You have to register as a bidder to take part and usually people are asked to hold up a paddle to indicate interest – if someone makes another gesture that seems to imply they are making a bid, the auctioneer will always ask them to confirm it.
Christie's *8 King Street, SW1Y 6QT (7839 9060); 85 Old Brompton Road, SW7 3LD (7930 6074).*

308 Salsa dance

This popular dance was developed in Cuba in the 1940s, drawing on local musical styles. Since then, jazz, traditional Puerto Rico rhythms and R&B have all gone into the mix. There are clubs offering beginners' lessons across the capital, many taking over upstairs rooms of pubs, including Salsamoves (www.salsamoves.co.uk) and Salsa UK (www.uksalsa.com).

309 Watch a hockey match

The country's elite hockey players are in action every weekend in the capital and admission to games is usually free, though you might be encouraged to buy a programme for £1 or so. Hampstead & Westminster, Old Loughtonians and Surbiton (who had seven players in the last England squad) are all in the men's Premier Division while Old Loughts are London's representatives in the women's top flight. For details of fixtures and venues see www.englandhockey.co.uk.

310 Learn lounge culture at the Geffrye

A quite marvellous physical history of the English interior, housed in a set of converted almshouses. It recreates typical English living rooms from the 17th century to the present, and has a series of lovely gardens designed on similar chronological lines. There's an airy restaurant and special exhibitions are mounted throughout the year in a purpose-built downstairs space.
Geffrye Museum *Kingsland Road, E2 8EA (7739 9893/www.geffrye-museum.org.uk).*

311 Impress your date at divinely decadent Loungelover

A wealth of extravagantly theatrical fixtures, fittings and accessories – fabulous chandeliers, a stuffed hippo's head, hot-house plants, a replica religious fresco adorning one wall, glass-topped tables, coloured Perspex lighting, red velveteen stools and faux Regency chairs, giant green coach lamps and candles – create a uniquely flamboyant look at Loungelover (1 Whitby Street, E1 6JU, 7012 1234, www.loungelover.co.uk). Mock croc-bound menus list cocktails such as Love Letter (elderflower cordial and raspberry vodka stirred with white cranberry and grape juice, served straight up in a martini glass); they're pricey (£8-£16) but are guaranteed to make a very good impression.

312-316

Play a board game in a pub

Every Wednesday night the popular Swiggers Games Club meets at the Shipwrights Arms (88 Tooley Street, SE1 2TF, 7378 1486) from around 5.30pm (to 11pm) to play board games such as Civilization, Diplomacy, Escape from Colditz, Family Business, History of the World, Settlers of Catan, Antike, Caylus, Louis XIV, Power Grid, Puerto Rico, Shadows over Camelot and Zepter von Zavandor. It's free and all are welcome. For more classic games like Scrabble and Monopoly, pop into pubs the Pig's Ear (35 Old Church Street, SW3 5BS, 08710 750953), the Westbourne (101 Westbourne Park Villas, W2 5ED, 7221 1332) or even Cargo (83 Rivington Street, EC2A 3AY, 7749 7844). Alternatively, kick back with the *Neighbours* game and the *EastEnders* game at the Skiddaw (46 Chippenham Road, W9 2AF, 7286 7815).

Skiddaw

317 *Learn to box...*

Enzo Giordano's excellent Boxing London operation (20 Hazelville Road, N19 3LP, 07956 293768, www.boxinglondon.co.uk) has something for everyone. Rocky Balboa wannabes will find (spit-)bucketfuls of seedy glamour by the ringside (think rickety weight machines and well-thumped bags); fitness fans will be taken to the limit; and those who want to learn the basics in a friendly, good-humoured environment will find out all they need to know from the one-time super-middleweight contender. Classes are busy with a lively assortment of punters of both sexes, from local child prodigies and seasoned boxers through to resting actors, out-of-shape journalists and East End wide boys. Classes cost £8, or £70 for a block of ten plus an annual membership fee of £50. Trials for non-members are £15.

318 *...or watch the pros knock lumps out of each other*

For a truly authentic taste of boxing, head to Bethnal Green's York Hall (5-15 Old Ford Road, E2 9PJ, 8980 2243). It's an old-school bear pit of a venue, with London geezers barracking the fighters, but in recent years it's attracted a more mixed crowd. It can host anything up to 15 fights on sparodic weekends; call for details.

319 *Get an allotment*

What better way to thwart the supremacy of the supermarkets than by growing your own fruit and vegetables? Getting a plot in London takes patience – waiting lists are often years-long – but otherwise relatively simple. Contact your local council or visit its website to find out your nearest plot and how long the wait will be. You could also try www.london allotments.net, a forum that lists spare plots as well as waiting-list times.

320 *Rent out a cinema instead of a DVD*

Shortwave (10 Bermondsey Square, SE1 3UN, 7357 6845, www.shortwavefilms.co.uk) is the latest welcome addition to the redeveloped Bermondsey Square. This 50-seater art house cinema has a varied programme of films which are shown from Thursday-Sunday each week. But we've also discovered that you can hire the whole cinema and screen whatever film takes your fancy (films are shown on a DVD projector). Call for further details of availability and prices.

321 *Go bellringing*

Ringing started in England in the early 17th century, and the way it is carried out has changed surprisingly little. The group activity, then as now, can be a remarkably rewarding and stimulating hobby – involving precision, team work and even a degree of physical exertion. Don't expect to be able to ring perfectly straight away, but there are plenty of practice sessions around London that welcome beginners. For more details, see www.mcaldg.org.uk/week. We particularly recommend St John at Hackney (Mondays, www.stjohn-at-hackneychurch.org.uk) and St Mary Abbots Kensington (Thursdays, www.stmaryabbotschurch.org).

322 *Tour the BBC*

Auntie Beeb'll be more than happy to open her televisual arms and take you on a tour of the world-famous BBC nerve centre on Wood Lane (0370 603 0304, www.bbc.co.uk/tours). Don't think your licence fee will get you a free tour of the building, though – it'll cost £9.50. Still, for that you get an award-winning tour that takes in the news desk, the TV studios and the Weather Centre. Advance booking is essential.

A few of my favourite things

323-329

Mark Thomas, comedian

The best Lido ever is on Tooting Common (Tooting Bec Lido, Tooting Bec Road, Tooting Bec Common, SW16 1RU, 8871 7198). In the summer after the kids finish school on Fridays the whole family heads up there to hang out. The place is big, brash, popular and full of south London charm. Mums carrying trays of chips rub shoulders with serious outdoor swimmers while kids kick footballs about before plunging in to the pool. Come winter it's left to the hardcore – but there is something beautiful about watching swimmers as the snow falls.

My son and I make the journey to Sister Ray (34-35 Berwick Street, W1F 0QF, 7734 3297, www.sisterray.co.uk) in Berwick Street on a Saturday morning as a treat. It's a great record shop – everything from '60s garage band the Sonics through to the McClusky offshoot Shooting at Unarmed Men (my son found that one). None of your overpriced stuff either, a record shop for people who like to flick through the CDs at leisure.

After this we go through to Lina Stores (18 Brewer Street, W1R 3FS, 7437 6482), one of the original Italian delis in Soho. The place smells like heaven should: of bread, olives and meat. We buy homemade pesto, fresh pumpkin pasta and salty reggiano.

Walking the Thames footpath (*see p256*) – from the Thames Barrier through to Tower Bridge – is beautiful and full of surprises: from the statue of Dr Salter and his daughter (the story of one of the first public health campaigners and his daughter is unbelievably sad) through to the gatherings of cormorants on the mud banks by the defunct Dome.

The Foundry (84-86 Great Eastern Street, EC2A 3JL, 7739 6900) is run by mates of mine and is a bar and art gallery. It has a certain squatter chic with odd chairs and grimy looking tables. They feature all sorts of art, the ethos being it costs nothing to exhibit but each artist must donate one of their works to the bar. Each Friday lunchtime they run a live radio show from the bar, featuring musicians, artists and assorted odd folk.

Every last Friday of the month cyclists meet up under Waterloo Bridge by the National Film Theatre, at sixish, for the Critical Mass bike ride (*see p37*). When a sufficient number of folk are ready the ride heads off across Waterloo Bridge into town. The rule is this: spread out, slow down and head to where the car traffic is worst. As there is no leader to the route each ride takes a different way around town. Folk dress up – especially in the summer – as fairies or dayglo fiends; some bring bubble racks and some bring sound systems. Everyone is there for their own different reasons, some want to protest climate change, some want more cycle lanes and some want to take part in an anarcho leaderless carnival of protest whereby each and every person on the ride becomes a spokesperson for themselves.

Under the Serious Organised Crime and Police Act passed by the government in 2005, anyone wishing to demonstrate within Parliament Square is now required to get prior permission from the police. As demonstrations are ill defined by law it means that even one person carrying one banner needs to get permission from the police. Lone Mass Demonstrations (www.markthomas.info.com) was my response to this: a plan to bury the police in paperwork by getting as many individuals as possible to demonstrate – on their own, en masse. The law is said to be under review, but it's still (at the time of writing) necessary to get permission to demonstrate here. So you can still do your bit for freedom of speech by organising your own demo. (You need to apply for permission to protest six days in advance.) Past demos have included 'Make children play in the rain', 'Free Palestine' and 'A demonstration to defend surrealism' (there was also a counter demo to smash surrealism – but that's realists for you). It's legal, it's fun and it's a bit annoying to the government and the police. Hurrah!

330-340

Travel back in time on north London's antiques row

Church Street off Lisson Grove has always held an attraction of one sort or another for Londoners. In 1832 you might have gone to the newly built Pavilion theatre to see 'crude melodrama and comic songs'. Or to Portman Market to stock up on hay and straw for your noble steed. By 1880 the street even had its own department store – Jordan's. You can still shop there and perhaps even buy a few of the Victorian goods once on sale, except that now Jordan's is Alfie's Antique Market (Nos.13-25, 7723 6066, www.alfiesantiques.com). Since Alfie's opened in 1976, other dealers have followed suit and the east end of Church Street is now almost entirely devoted to antiques shops, although antiques (technically objects over 100 years old) are slowly being replaced by shiny (and pricey) 20th-century furniture and lighting. But you can still find treasures here.

For starters, ace vintage clothes shop The Girl Can't Help It (*see p73*) is worth a look and don't miss Dodo Posters (7706 1545, www.dodoposters.com) on the first floor with a huge collection of ads from the 1920s and 1930s. For all things silver, stop off at Goldsmith & Perris (7724 7051, www.goldsmithandperris.com) on the ground floor – it's ideal for special gifts such as enamel-backed dressing table sets. There's also a rooftop café with views, which does a good line in toasted sandwiches.

Once refreshed head back on to Church Street for the individual shops. It's not chi-chi here – you'll see builders' caffs, drinkers' pubs and budget food shops. Walk west towards Edgware Road and it feels a bit like *EastEnders* with an ethnic flavour – the bustling market sells everything from cauliflowers to jilbabs.

Andrew Nebbett Antiques (Nos.35-37, 7723 2303, www.andrewnebbett.com) is the last antiques shop heading west on the strip. Nebbett has great taste, covering a range of time periods, and a penchant for large pieces with wow factor. Walk across the street to Cristobal (No.26, 7724 7230, www.cristobal.co.uk) for a completely different look: the shop is crammed with collectable costume jewellery by names such as Haskell and Hugler, and mirrored boudoir furniture. If you like the deco style here, then you'll love Susie Cooper Ceramics (No.18, 7723 1555, www.susiecooperceramics.com) further along. As well as the namesake ceramics, the shop glitters with 1930s and '40s mirrored dressing tables, cocktail trays and photograph frames.

Bloch & Angell Antiques (No.22, 7723 6575) offers large-scale, good-quality furniture and objects to impress even the most macho anti-shopper. Andrew Angell, who shares Bloch's space, specialises in vintage advertising signs and tins. At D&A Binder (No.34, 7723 0542, www.dandabinder.co.uk), catch a glimpse of what Alfie's might have looked like 100 years ago when it was a department store. Binder deals in lovely old shop fittings, from vast mahogany display cabinets down to individual hat stands; they now find a new life at smart stores seeking a retro look.

Other shops to dip into include North West Eight (No.36, 7723 9337, www.northwesteightantiques.com) for decorative antiques, and James Worrall (No.2, 7563 7181, www.jamesworrall.com) for furniture, leather chairs and kitchenalia. Head down Lisson Grove to the Facade (No.99, 7258 2017, www.thefacade.co.uk) for elegant-meets-kitsch gilded furniture, mirrors and chandeliers.

341

Go to the Proms, but not the last night

Tickets for the hilariously over-the-top Last Night, when normally well-behaved grown-ups act like schoolchildren, throwing paper darts and parping klaxons at inappropriate moments, are difficult to get hold of, but the event is over-hyped anyway. Instead, attend one of the other 70 or so orchestral concerts that are held in the Royal Albert Hall during the Proms season, which runs from the middle of July to the first week of September, or perhaps one of the matinée Proms of chamber music held in smaller London venues. The BBC also runs a series of talks, interviews, discussions and other events connected to the Proms. See www.bbc.co.uk/proms/whatson for details.

342-348

Take in a pint and a performance at a theatre pub

The barman rings the bell and a dozen or so people pick up their drinks, shuffle through a back door and take their seats for an evening of theatre. At the King's Head pub in Islington, this happens almost every night. And at pubs all over London too. Of course, the audience reappears at the interval to refresh their glasses: just one of the many cheap and convivial advantages to pub theatre-going.

The King's Head Theatre (115 Upper Street, N1 1QN, 7226 1916, www.kings headtheatre.org) was the original London pub theatre, and founded 35 years ago. Like most of the others set up in the years that followed, it has a small stage shoehorned into the pub premises, and an even smaller, more awkward budget (the theatre lost its Arts Council funding some years ago). But what history. A young Hugh Grant appeared here in *The Jockeys of Norfolk*, and the A-list of past performers goes on till the present day. The pub itself is a Victorian charmer, always with a crowd in ramshackle high spirits (there's live music here too).

The nearby Hen & Chickens (109 St Paul's Road, N1 2NA, 7704 2001, www.unrestricted view.co.uk), whose young artistic team favours new British and international writing, receives hundreds of scripts every year. Quality is high and variety is immense. Its black box theatre is so small that almost every seat is the best in the house, wonderfully close to every twitch and nuance on the actors' faces. Also in Islington are the Old Red Lion

Theatre (418 St John Street, EC1V 4NJ, 7837 7816, www.oldredliontheatre.co.uk), which finds a home in an old-man-and-his-dog, dusty velvet seat pub, and the Rosemary Branch (2 Shepperton Road, N1 3DT, 7704 6665, www.rosemary branch.co.uk); both show a good range of old and new plays.

One of the most innovative of the bunch is the Gate Theatre, above the Prince Albert pub (11 Pembridge Road, W11 3HQ, 7229 0706, www.gatetheatre.co.uk). Its emphasis is on new or under-championed international writing usually performed in translation and it's the only London theatre that's exclusively dedicated to this kind of work. The performing space feels a bit like a doll's house theatre, with rows of rickety wooden chairs (choose wisely) set before a tiny stage. Its former sister theatre at the cosy Latchmere pub (503 Battersea Park Road, SW11 3BW, 7978 7040) has been reorganised and rechristened Theatre 503. Housed in an old Victorian hotel, it stages the work of new playwrights.

Etcetera Theatre (www.etceteratheatre. com) admit that five people can 'feel like you've got a decent audience' in their tiny 42-seater pub space but the comany has also bagged some big-name premières like Ayckbourn's *Between the Lines* before now and is supportive of young actors and writers. The host pub is the Oxford Arms (265 Camden High Street, NW1 7BU, 7482 4857), a boozy local where on match nights you may have to squeeze through a crush of football fans to reach the theatre.

349

Have a laugh
Incredibly, there are several groups in London dedicated entirely to the art of laughter. For a gentle giggle – 'no jokes just natural joy' – meet with Laughter Yoga (Julie Whitehead, 07973 164369, www.laughteryoga.co.uk, various venues). Alternatively, laugh to get fit at Laughter Workout (The Meeting Rooms, Neal's Yard, WC2H 9DP, 07789 954972, www.laughingmatters.co.uk), where you'll do smiling exercises and a belly-muscle workout. Or, if you think it's your chuckle itself that needs a bit more work, try a Laughter Session (07904 334222, www.shinetime.co.uk, various venues), where they'll teach you how to laugh more for £10.

350 *Learn to butcher*

Fancy learning the delicate and intimate art of animal dismemberment? Then look no further than the Ginger Pig in Marylebone (8-10 Moxon Street, W1U 4EW, 7935 7788, www.learnbutchery.co.uk). Evening classes with Perry and Borut focus on various different butchery skills, you get to take home your own hacked-to-pieces handywork and they also throw in a meal and drinks after all the blood, sweat and tears. Classes cost £120.

351 *Try a posh scotch egg*

Oliver Peyton's flagship deli/bakery, situated in the old flower stall in Heal's department store, has a 1930s feel to it, in both the decor and the food. Nourishment is of the 'old-fashioned and honest' school, and our favourite by far (after all the gorgeous cakes, of course) are the jolly good scotch eggs. These über-eggs have hardly any jacket, in fact the white of the egg shows through in places. But what jacket there is contains clearly discernible strands of meat and is coated in very small breadcrumbs. Inside all this is a pale-yolked, hard-boiled egg. Smashing.
Peyton & Byrne *Heal's, 196 Tottenham Court Road, W1T 7LQ (7580 2522/ www.peytonandbyrne.com).*

352 *Visit the Fan Museum*

The world's only museum dedicated to fans. It's a tiny space that holds two rooms and a total collection of 4,000 antique fans, some of which date as far back as the 11th century. Look out for instructions on fan etiquette, and fans depicting patriotic battle scenes.
Fan Museum *12 Crooms Hill, SE10 8ER (8305 1441/www.fan-museum.org).*

Peyton & Byrne

353-357

Partake in pétanque

Near London Bridge the Balls Brothers wine bar (Hay's Galleria, Tooley Street, SE1 2HD, 7407 4301, www.ballsbrothers.co.uk) runs a free pétanque pitch in the middle of the smart Hay's Galleria shopping arcade. It's proved such a success that there's also an annual lunchtime pétanque tournament in summer. The game couldn't be more simple, requires no prior experience and can be played on equal terms by young and old, male and female, drunk and sober. (Although in France the players tend to be old, male and drunk.) In triples, each team has two boules each, which they must throw as near as possible to the golf ball-sized cochonnet. The player or team whose boule is closest to the cochonnet at the end of the frame wins a point. The first team to win 13 points wins the game.

You can also play pétanque in the newly completed Bermondsey Square (SE1), outside the Prince of Wales (48 Cleaver Square, SE11 4EA, 7735 9916) and the Surprise (16 Southville, SW8 2PP, 7622 4623) pubs, as well as on a pitch near the Chevening Road entrance to Queen's Park, NW6 (8969 5661).

358

Discover an unlikely collection of art

The Imperial War Museum (Lambeth Road, SE1 6HZ, 7416 5320, www.iwm.org.uk) is better known for its displays of the mechanics and artefacts of war, but it also contains some notable works of art. Most of these can be found in two galleries on the second floor that are dedicated to art from World War I and World War II. One of the most powerful paintings is John Singer Sargent's *Gassed* (housed in the Sargent Room), which depicts a line of blinded soldiers staggering through a battlefield. Many of the leading artists of the 20th century are represented in the collection, including Augustus John, Stanley Spencer, Paul Nash, Graham Sutherland, Percy Wyndham Lewis and Henry Moore. The works on display are changed at regular intervals.

359

Soak up a bit of pomp and ceremony

Routinely shunned by Londoners as little more than fodder for tourists, the Changing of the Guard is, in fact, a terrific spectacle. A regiment of Foot Guards dressed in a fetching scarlet coats and bearskin hats lines up in the forecourt of Wellington Barracks from 10.45am; at 11.27am the soldiers march, accompanied by their regimental band and mascot, to Buckingham Palace to relieve the sentries in the forecourt. The guard is mounted daily in spring and summer, and on alternate days in autumn and winter. The Household Cavalry stands guard from 10am to 4pm every day at Horse Guards on Whitehall; their change of guard begins at 10.28am (an hour earlier on a Sunday), with a gallop along the Mall to Horse Guards Parade from their barracks beside Hyde Park – the actual ceremony takes place at 11am (10am on Sundays) on Horse Guards Parade.

If this has whetted your appetite for London ceremonials, you can also watch the gun salutes that mark the arrival of dignitaries, a variety of royal birthdays and certain solemn occasions such as Remembrance Day. The King's Troop Royal Horse Artillery makes a mounted charge through Hyde Park, sets up the guns and fires a 41-gun salute (at noon, except on the occasion of the State Opening of Parliament) opposite the Dorchester Hotel; see www.royalparks.gov.uk/tourists/gun_salutes.cfm for the schedule. Keen not to be overshadowed, the Honourable Artillery Company fires a 62-gun salute at the Tower of London at 1pm, also to mark important state occasions.

However, the city's military showstopper is surely Trooping the Colours (Horse Guards Parade, Whitehall, SW1A 2AX, 7414 2479, www.trooping-the-colour.co.uk), which has honoured the monarch's birthday since 1805. The current Queen was born on 21 April, but her official birthday is 16 June; at 10.45am she makes the 15-minute carriage journey from Buckingham Palace to watch the meticulous manoeuvres of 200 horses and more than 1,400 soldiers, including 400 musicians.

✳ *Eltham Palace and Gardens*

Eltham Palace is a truly unique house – once a medieval royal palace where Henry VIII grew up – but also one of the finest Art Deco houses in the country. Located in Eltham, it's very easy to get to from Victoria or London Bridge station. Rediscovered after centuries of neglect by the ultra rich Courtaulds they built a glamorous show home around the original Tudor Great Hall in the 1930s! The whole house has now been beautifully restored and opened to the public by English Heritage.

You can imagine yourself living in these glamorous surroundings as you wander through the rooms of the house, from the ocean-liner style of the entrance hall, to the gold tiles and lion-head taps in Virginia Courtauld's bathroom. Then explore the 19 acres of beautiful gardens, crossing over London's oldest working bridge.

Eltham Palace & Gardens
Court Road, London, SE9 5QE
Open year round (except January) Sunday to Wednesday
020 8294 2548 / www.english-heritage.org.uk

✳ *Apsley House*

Apsley House has a commanding position at Hyde Park Corner – together with a commanding reputation as colloquially known as 'Number One' London! The original home of the first Duke of Wellington – who beat Napoleon at the Battle of Waterloo in 1815 – it is full of treasures including incomparable paintings from the Spanish Royal Collection including Velazquez, Rubens, Van Dyck and Goya. Explore the palatial Waterloo Gallery where the annual banquet took place to celebrate the Battle of Waterloo – the house is still free to the public on Waterloo Day (June 18th) every year! Discover unusual memorabilia including an original pair of "Wellington Boots" and the death masks for the Dukes of Wellington and Napoleon.

Apsley House
Hyde Park Corner, London, W1J 7NT
Open daily except Mondays
020 7499 5676 / www.english-heritage.org.uk

360

Drink Dutch

Plenty of bars these days can boast about the Lowland beers they've got on tap and their half fridge of bottled options. What they don't have is the century-long history of Dutch pub De Hems – and perpetual orange footie on the box. Once a refuge for homesick Dutch sailors, the then Macclesfield was taken over by a certain De Hems and became a rallying point for the Dutch Resistance during World War II. Today, this spruced-up dark-wood bar boasts towering beer pumps of Amstel and Oranjeboom, three types of Leffe and the rare draught option of Belle-Vue Kriek. Orval, Vedett and Kwak are among the multitude of Benelux bottles. The Dutch range of seasonal bar food features pannenkoeken (pancakes either savoury or sweet) and bitterballen (meatballs in breadcrumbs). The oyster bar upstairs was the setting for many a musicbiz payola exchange in the 1960s.

De Hems *11 Macclesfield Street, W1D 5BW (7437 2494).*

361 *Pick a bead*

Beads come in every colour, size and material imaginable at the Bead Shop (21A Tower Street, WC2H 9NS, 7240 0931, www.beadshop.co.uk). They're laid out like archaeological discoveries on sectioned tables, while the wall-mounted pigeonholes give the place the feel of an old-fashioned sweet shop. You even get a little basket to hold your selections as you browse. Individual beads cost from 5p up to a fiver.

362 *Ride London's last steam railway*

This miniature railway runs on Sundays between April and October at Kew Bridge Steam Museum (Green Dragon Lane, Middx TW8 0EN, 8568 4757, www.kbsm.org).

363 *Check out 1930s gadgets at Eltham Palace*

Eltham Palace was acquired by Edward II in 1305 and provided a home for kings and queens, including a young Henry VIII, until the royal party decamped to Greenwich in the 15th century. But nowadays the draw is the additions made to the palace in the 1930s, under commission from super-rich society couple Stephen and Virginia Courtauld who wanted a country residence to complement their Grosvenor Square townhouse. The Courtaulds took advantage of all the latest technology: a clock that received a time signal direct from Greenwich, loudspeakers that could pipe music through the whole ground floor and a centralised vacuum cleaner system. Decorative highlights include block-printed wallpaper featuring Kew Gardens in the master bedroom, the black-and-white lacquerwork in the art deco dining room and caged sleeping quarters decorated with bamboo forest murals for Mah-Jongg, the Courtauld's pet ring-tailed lemur, bought from Harrods.

Of the original royal building, the Great Hall, with stained glass and hammer-beam roof, remains. In the grounds there is also a beautiful 15th-century stone bridge over a moat, probably built by Edward IV, and further medieval ruins. The extensive grounds have been carefully restored to a 1930s design, complete with a sunken rose garden and rock garden with water cascades. The traditional tearoom and shop also have a 1930s flavour.

Eltham Palace *Court Yard, SE9 5QE (8294 2548/ www.elthampalace.org.uk).*

364

Go to a lunchtime gig in a record store

Instore gigs have become central to a band's marketing, so most of the retail giants regularly host free gigs. And independents like Rough Trade (www.roughtrade.com) and Pure Groove (www.puregroove.com) have seen many high-profile performers grace their premises in the past. Check websites for details.

365 *Visit Lambeth's secret garden...*

Lisa Mullen visits luscious urban retreat Roots & Shoots, formerly a patch of waste ground.

David Perkins, education and resources manager for Lambeth's Roots & Shoots community garden, is in Paradise Corner when I arrive, busy digging a hole. Along with student Wayne and two other members of staff, he's bringing exotic plants and a pond back to this sunny, south-facing spot, after a period during which it was used by some local builders working nearby. In some ways, this regeneration process typifies the whole story of Roots & Shoots, which began in 1982 with a large-scale leap of faith: the transformation of an acre of derelict wasteland into a beautiful, inspiring wildlife garden.

'Where you're standing at the moment – for most of the 20th century that was a toilet,' says Perkins, cheerily. 'Of course, from 1740 till 1904, these were gardens, quite posh ones. But then there was a warehouse factory here that was built in 1903. That was demolished in about 1979, but when Roots & Shoots came in 1982 it was just concrete floors, corrugated fences round it, broken glass, demolition debris generally. Linda [Phillips, manager of the project] cleared the site, brought topsoil in and laid it out as a community garden in about 1984.'

For a while, the plot was open to the public 24 hours a day, but problems with vandalism triggered a rethink, and now access is restricted to office hours (10am-4pm Mon-Fri) and staffed weekend and evening events (call for details); admission is free. 'If I become aware that we've got some teenagers in, like we did last week in half-term, I just discreetly wander over and say, "Are you all right?",' says Perkins. 'And if they're up to no good then they leave, because they can see they're being watched. But if they're genuinely interested then I'll give them a bit of my time and talk to them about frogs or whatever.'

Perkins, whose background is in education and natural history, is proud of the garden's wildlife. 'Some gardeners might think it's a bit untidy but because it's lovely and wild you get lots of insects. We've got 15 species of butterfly, seven species of bumblebee, 20 other species of bees, over 30 species of beetle, three species of grasshopper in the meadow and two rare crickets. They're amazing creatures. They just spotted this tiny patch of greenery and moved in.'

There are plenty of opportunities for visitors to learn about the resident invertebrates, birds, frogs and newts, from identification charts dotted around the garden to full-scale educational events, like the four seasonal open weekends featuring stalls selling fresh organic fruit and vegetables, honey from the London Beekeepers' Association and crafts by local people. The Roots & Shoots shop sells a seasonal range of produce all year round. 'You can't really buy nice organic fruit and vegetables round here,' Phillips points out. 'We've linked up with a farming co-operative in Norfolk, so we should be able to sell lots of lovely food. There will also be plant sales in May and June – we grow herbs and bedding plants to sell, as well as organic compost. We press our own apple juice in the apple barn in the autumn, and that sells really well.'

These commercial opportunities support the main purpose of Roots & Shoots, which is to provide vocational training – conducted in a newly constructed eco-building bristling with green features – for young people with special educational needs. 'We pick up the ones that no one else really wants,' says Phillips bluntly. 'But we have a very high success rate of people getting jobs. At the moment we have about 19 to 20 students at one time, doing a 40-week course.'

Funding for the community garden is always under threat, but Phillips is an old hand at winkling money out of government bodies; she likes to show bureaucrats round when the tea-roses are in flower and 'they take us to their hearts', she says. Maybe it isn't just rare crickets who appreciate a little patch of green from time to time.

Roots & Shoots *Walnut Tree Walk, off Kennington Road, SE11 6DN (7587 1131/ www.rootsandshoots.org).*

366-375 ...and lose yourself in the city's other secret gardens

Calthorpe Project

A popular garden with patients who want a chance to relax before visiting the nearby dental hospital, this community project also works closely with local schools.

Calthorpe Project *258-274 Gray's Inn Road, WC1X 8LH (7837 8019).*

Camley Street Natural Park

A rare spot of greenery in the industrial hinterland north of King's Cross station, this reclaimed site alongside Regent's Canal bursts with wildlife, especially water-loving species.

Camley Street Natural Park *12 Camley Street, NW1 0PW (7833 2311).*

Chelsea Physic Garden

Founded by the Society of Apothecaries as the Apothecaries' Garden in 1673, it features several acres of healing herbs, rare trees, dye plants, medicinal vegetables and such botanical superstars as *Filipendula ulmaria* (meadowsweet), the plant from which salicylic acid was derived. Unimpressed? It was from salicylic acid that aspirin was synthesised in 1899.

Chelsea Physic Garden *66 Royal Hospital Road, SW3 4HS (7352 5646/www.chelseaphysic garden.co.uk).*

Culpeper Community Garden

An Islington oasis just off the bustle of Upper Street, Culpeper is both an award-winning city park (including a lawn, ponds, rose pergolas, vegetable plots and a wildlife area) and a thriving environmental community project.

Culpeper Community Garden *1 Cloudesley Road, N1 0EG (7833 3951).*

Greenwich Peninsula Ecology Park

Once known as Greenwich Marsh, this once-industrial site is now home to a thriving wildlife population. It is a popular spot for birdwatchers. Phone for details of the numerous organised community events.

Greenwich Peninsula Ecology Park *John Harrison Way, SE10 0QZ (8293 1904).*

Gunnersbury Triangle

Local people fought hard to protect this slice of wild woodland from the developers, and it is now home to a lively ecosystem of plants and animals, with a pond, a marshy area and a meadow alongside the woodland.

Gunnersbury Triangle *Bollo Lane, W4 5LW (8747 3881).*

London Wildlife Garden Centre

An award-winning park that features a sustainable building with a living roof planted with herbs. The shop specialises in organically grown native plants.

London Wildlife Trust Centre *28 Marsden Road, SE15 4EE (7252 9186).*

Phoenix Garden

This wildlife garden is in an unlikely location between Shaftesbury Avenue and St Giles High Street. What was once a car park is now a delightful green surprise.

Phoenix Garden *21 Stacey Street, entrance on St Giles Passage, WC2H 8DG (7379 3187/ www.thephoenixgarden.ik.com).*

Roe Green Walled Garden

This secret garden was originally built back in 1899 by the Duchess of Sutherland. It's now open to the public every Tuesday, Thursday and Saturday, and features a children's area, model animals and butterflies that dance in and out of the abundant flora.

Roe Green Walled Garden *Roe Green Park, NW9 9HA (8206 0492).*

Tower Hamlets Cemetery Park

Closed for burials in 1966, the cemetery is now a designated nature reserve and a haven for wildlife (including 20 species of butterfly and 35 types of bird, woodpeckers among them) in an increasingly built-up area. During the day members of the public just wander in, but the 'friends' of the cemetery also organise special activity days through the year.

Tower Hamlets Cemetery Park *Southern Grove, E3 4PX (07904 186981/www.tower hamletscemetery.org).*

376 *Have the best cup of coffee in town*

Flat White (17 Berwick Street, W1F 0PT, 7734 0370, www.flat-white.co.uk) is a groovy, Australian-run 'espresso bar' that serves a great coffee courtesy of a La Marzocco machine (handmade in Florence), trained *baristas* and acclaimed Square Mile coffee (www.square milecoffee.com). The Monmouth Coffee Company's shops (27 Monmouth Street, WC2H 9EU, 7379 3516; 2 Park Street, SE1 9AB, 7645 3585; and Borough Market; www.monmouth coffee.co.uk) provide an equally punchy caffeine fix using their own magic coffee blends. The atmosphere is welcoming and warm in both places; the devotion to the bean is more single-minded at MCC, with more choice of coffee types but not much beyond classy pastries and bread and jam as accompaniment, whereas Flat White is more of a café (serving filled rolls, waffles and brownies alongside the Vegemite) and something of a hang-out for Antipodeans. Both are worthy of your custom.

377 *Work your way through the real ales at the Wenlock*

Built in 1835 and opened as a pub a year later, the Wenlock Arms narrowly escaped being bombed into oblivion a century on by the Luftwaffe, who took out the local brewery but missed the nearby munitions factory. Perhaps that explains its perpetually cheerful ambience and unfaltering popularity, despite being situated in a bit of a no-man's land. The big draw here is the bewildering (to the layman) variety of speciality ales on offer, many of them with picturesque names like Top Totty, Hebridean Berserker, Pictish Claymore and Dark Star Nut Brown Ale. Darts, an open fire and a list of football fixtures testify to the traditional, community-based nature of the place, as does the fact that locals aged from seven to 70 pack in on Sunday afternoons for a sing-song round the old joanna.
Wenlock Arms *26 Wenlock Road, N1 7TA (7608 3406/www.wenlock-arms.co.uk).*

Phoenix Garden

Stand and deliver

Intrepid first-time poet Fiona McAuslan learns from the pros – and takes to the stage herself.

'The first time I read in public I was so nervous that I had to put the piece of paper on the floor, lower the microphone and read it kneeling down so that no one could see how much I was shaking.'

I'm discussing the rigours of the spoken word with Niall O'Sullivan, poet, compère and organiser of the Poetry Unplugged evening at the Poetry Café, which has been running a now-legendary open mic night every Tuesday here for over a decade. Unplugged is an evening where amateurs and professionals take turns to read their poems aloud. It's a free-for-all with no restrictions – anyone can get up and have a bash. With some 50 poets and their families and friends crammed into a hot and sweaty Covent Garden basement, it can seem a daunting prospect – not least for me, as tonight I'm planning to take my turn alongside London's aspiring poets.

Unassuming and ordinary, the regulars at the Poetry Café might look an unlikely lot to be at the forefront of a trend, but the spoken word (many poets hate the term 'performance poetry') is breaking out all over town, from Deptford to WC2, and every day the Poetry Library adds a fistful of new events listings to its website (www.poetrylibrary.org.uk). When Camden bar At Proud opened in July 2006 one of the first events it held was a poetry recital, attracting a clutch of celebrities, including Sadie Frost and Lisa Moorish (who even read some of her lyrics, but don't let that put you off). Poets are also being booked in increasing numbers for festivals and cabaret nights across the capital. So what's going on?

'In entertainment terms, poetry has always been the limpy kid to comedy but ... there's been a definite upsurge in interest,' says Tim Wells, whose poetry collection *Boys' Night Out in the Afternoon* was nominated for the Forward Poetry Best First Collection prize in 2006. 'In the early '80s, spoken verse was all about political ranting, but now it's moved on to become a social night out. I think people are more interested in poetry than we give them credit for.'

Spoken word has a rich history in the capital. 'The progression has been quite fragmented,' says Nathan Penlington, an alternative poet who has written an MA thesis on the subject. 'Many modern poets are performing without realising all their influences.' Allen Ginsberg's electrifying reading at the Poetry Olympics at the Albert Hall in 1965 first awakened 1960s London to the drama and vitality of live poetry. The Liverpool Poets – among them Roger McGough and Brian Patten, who performed their poetry long before they ever secured a publishing deal – carried the mantle into the 1970s, when it was taken up by the likes of punk poet John Cooper Clarke and dub poet Linton Kwesi Johnson. John Hegley's mix of poetry, anecdote and song, which he used to perform at the Comedy Store and on John Peel sessions in the early 1980s, has proved inspirational, if unconsciously so, to today's poets – as has the arrival of Slam poetry from the United States, a performance format that pits poets against one another in competitive three-minute bouts.

While the crowd at Poetry Unplugged is largely composed of those visibly itching for their chance to read, it's a good place to go for a first taste of the scene. One early tip: sit near the exit if you plan to sneak off before the end – defectors are much more likely to be heckled than performers. An open-mic poetry night is as much a gamble as fringe theatre or a band playing an early gig – some poets appear to have cast a box of poetry fridge-magnets into the wind – but the good work outweighs the bad. On my visit I heard an elderly gentleman sporting a beige sports jacket – introduced by O'Sullivan as a Poetry Café virgin – blaze through a satirical number called 'War on Terror', while an enigmatic Dagenham boy with a burgeoning 'fro who went by the name of Requiem read a touching poem about a girl who could skim pebbles. The most raucous applause goes to those who use comedy or swear words – or, best of all, both. As I learn at an event a couple of nights later, while listening to a girl with a surfeit of lip gloss emote her way through poems on lost lovers (I can see why they've gone), humour is a defining factor in the success of the spoken word. O'Sullivan's own works, collected as *You're Not Singing Anymore*, are cases in point – funny and compassionate observations about disparate lives glimpsed on London street corners.

Growing out of the current popularity and seemingly unceasing demand for burlesque and cabaret, another type of performance poetry – mixing visuals and a soundtrack with the spoken

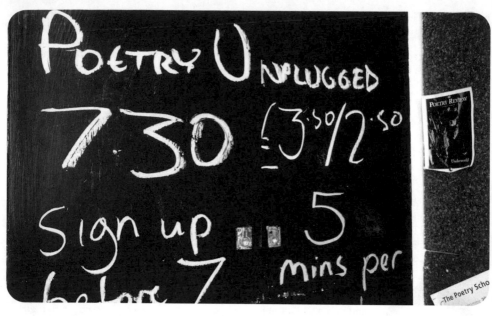

'Already the page is dissolving in an acid bath of hand sweat... nothing slashes your attention span like hyperventilation.'

word – looks set to dominate. Writer and director Suzanne Andrade mixes sensuality and perversion into her witty and dark epics about urban freaks. With impeccable choreography, kooky graphics and perfect timing, as well as her magnificent stage presence (black vintage dress, scarlet lips and a Louise Brooks bob). Similarly, Penlington's fusion of humour, storytelling and visuals has won plaudits and attention from critics.

Watching such accomplished performers makes me realise that I've got a long way to go with my own offering. Back at Poetry Unplugged, I'm rigid with fear. I've asked if

I can go on early, not least because if I leave it any later, I won't be able to read what I've written – already the page is starting to dissolve in an acid bath of hand sweat. In retrospect, it would have been better to wait until the crowd had warmed up – and drunk more. Virgins who go on towards the end of the evening are greeted by whoops and cheers. I get a polite smatter of claps. On the other hand, at least I'll be able to enjoy the rest of the evening's entertainment. Nothing slashes your attention span like hyperventilation.

There's no poetry faux pas greater than talking during someone else's recital, but frankly I would have welcomed the diversion. The level of concentration in the faces I can see as I stand at the front of the stage is extremely unnerving. I take a deep breath, project my voice and get started. Like all first times, it doesn't last long. Two minutes of garbled musings about a tree on a hill at the height of autumn (it's the spoken word – you had to be there) and it's all over. As applause washes over me, I'm strangely elated and, as I make my way back to my seat, I decide that I might do it again. If I can just find a backdrop, a few props and a wig, I could make a career out of this.

Poetry Café *22 Betterton Street, WC2H 9BX (7420 9887/www.poetrysociety.org.uk).*

379-380
Visit Bevis Marks synagogue, then eat in the restaurant

Bevis Marks (Bevis Marks, EC3A 5DQ) is London's oldest purpose-built synagogue – circa 1701, pub quizzers. Pay your respects, then settle down in the adjoining kosher restaurant (7283 2220, www.bevismarkstherestaurant.com): through the windows you can see the synagogue's chandeliers. Lunch is served in the courtyard or upstairs, where there's elegant napery and spot-lit modern art. The food can be erratic and the service lackadaisical, but plus points include an extensive wine list and unusually good desserts: the likes of pears and fresh figs served with rosewater or almond macaroons, cherry tarte tatin, and gooseberry crumble with a more than passable ice-'cream' (kosher rules dictate that dairy products cannot be served with meat).

381
Watch the Great River Race

A bit like the Oxford v Cambridge Boat Race but more fun, this annual race (www.great riverrace.co.uk) sees more than 300 'traditional' boats, from Chinese dragon boats and Hawaiian war canoes to Viking longboats, compete over a 22-mile course to become the UK Traditional Boat Champions. The early September event usually starts below Ham House in Richmond and runs to Island Gardens opposite Greenwich Pier (sometimes they race in the opposite direction, depending on the tides). The best viewing points are Richmond Bridge, along the South Bank, Hungerford Bridge and Tower Bridge. Take a trip on the passenger boat (£27, £12 concessions) to watch the action up close.

382
'Suffer the children' at the Foundling Museum

The Foundling Hospital, England's first hospital for abandoned children, was founded by Thomas Coram in 1739 and home to 27,000 children until its closure in 1953. This museum tells the story of the hospital and the children who lived here, and its 18th-century interiors also house an excellent art collection featuring works by Gainsborough, Reynolds and Hogarth, the latter being one of the hospital's original governors. The museum also has a copy of Handel's *Messiah* and other Handel memorabilia; the composer was involved in fundraising for the hospital during his lifetime: in 1750 he donated the chapel organ and from that year onwards the *Messiah* was performed here under his direction each year.
Foundling Museum *40 Brunswick Square, WC1N 1AZ (7841 3600/www.foundlingmuseum.org.uk).*

383
Play disc golf

The principle of disc golf (www.bdga.org.uk) is the same as the sport's more conservative version apart from – of course – replacing the ball with a Frisbee, which is thrown into specially designed baskets or natural objects such as trees. Croydon's Lloyd Park is became London's first basketed course in spring 2007 (www.croydondiscgolf.com). Elthorne Park in Boston Manor and Greenford's Ravenor Park are both also popular.

384
Eat a Chelsea bun

First made in Pimlico in the late 17th century and name-checked in the work of Jonathan Swift and Charles Dickens, these buns of coiled dough sprinkled with currants, sugar and cinnamon are quintessentially London (though not, oddly, quintessentially Chelsea). You can buy them in bakeries all over the place, but the pricier variety made by trendy bakers Flour Station are very, very tasty. Buy them for a quid each at Borough Market (Southwark Street, SE1 1TL, 7407 1002), Queen's Park Farmers' Market (Salusbury Primary School, opposite Hopefield Road, NW6 6RG) and Wimbledon Farmers' Market (Wimbledon Park First School, Havana Road, SW19 8EJ).

385-387 *Skate with the masses*

Roller Stroll, a communal skate each Sunday in Hyde Park, is one of London's best freebies. The route changes weekly but is usually circular and six to eight miles long; check in advance at www.rollerstroll.com. The race is open to any skater able to turn and stop effectively while going downhill (it's in your interest, believe us). Wear helmet, wrist, knee and elbow pads and meet on the east side of the Serpentine at 2pm. A portable sound system keeps spirits high.

The Roller Stroll isn't the only event in London for bladers. Other free skating events include the Urban Rites Friday Night Skate (www.lfns.co.uk), which starts most weeks at 8pm from the Duke of Wellington Arch (Hyde Park Corner tube, exit 2) and the Easy Peasy Skate (www.easypeasyskate.com) in Battersea Park. This last is aimed at children and beginners, convening every Saturday at 10.30am at the Peace Pagoda.

388-396

Take to the lidos for an outdoor swim

For those people who like their swimming to be on the bracing side of refreshment, a dive into one of London's open-air pools is like a rite of passage. The following lidos are open daily in summer; all have an entry charge of a few pounds, with reduced fees for children.

Brockwell Lido
Brockwell Park, Dulwich Road, SE24 0PA (7274 3088/www.brockwell-lido.com).

Charlton Lido
Shooters Hill Road, SE18 (8317 5000/www.gll.org).

Hampstead Heath Ponds
Hampstead Heath, NW5 1QR (7485 4491).

Hampton Heated Open Air Pool
Hampton Hill High Street, Hampton, Middx TW12 2ST (8255 1116/www.hamptonpool.co.uk).

London Fields Lido
London Fields Westside, E8 3EU (7254 9038/ www.hackney.gov.uk).

Park Road Pools
Park Road, N8 8JN (8341 3567/ www.haringey.gov.uk).

Parliament Hill Lido
Hampstead Heath, Gordon House Road, NW5 1QR (7485 5757/www.cityoflondon.gov.uk).

Serpentine Lido
Hyde Park, W2 2UH (7706 3422/ www.serpentinelido.com).

Tooting Bec Lido
Tooting Bec Road, Tooting Bec Common, SW16 1RU (8871 7198/www.wandsworth.gov.uk).

397
Be a nosy neighbour for Open House London

An annual event held around mid September that gives architecture lovers free access to more than 500 fascinating buildings all over the capital. An essential experience for the born snooper; see www.openhouselondon.org for exact dates and locations.

398
Take a date for oysters at Bibendum

Forget the rule about there being an 'r' in the month: oysters are available all year round at this seafood specialist on the ground floor of the lovely 1911 Michelin building. It's a great setting for an informal light lunch. You can sit in the foyer (which is a thoroughfare for customers to Bibendum restaurant above and the Conran Shop next door), in a room to one side, or at the front of the building, sandwiched between the oyster stall and flower stand – the best place for keeping an eye on the South Kensington street action. Tiled floor and walls (decorated with images of Bibendum, aka the Michelin Man) mean the clatter of dining can get pretty noisy. There's plenty of crustacea – crab salad, lobster mayonnaise, a fruits de mer platter for two – plus salads, daily specials and even oscietra caviar (a cool £87 for 30g). On our latest visit we ordered a half-dozen super-fresh mixed rock oysters, followed by high-quality gravadlax with pickled cucumber, and fabulously sweet-sour rollmop herrings with onion salad and crème fraîche.

Bibendum Oyster Bar *Michelin House, 81 Fulham Road, SW3 6RD (7589 1480/www.bibendum.co.uk).*

399
Get tickets for the Army v Navy rugby match

Some people would pay very good money to see sweaty men in uniform grappling for pleasure, and many of them will be at the annual Army v Navy rugby match at Twickenham. Described by the *Daily Telegraph* (who else?) as a 'glorious anachronism that gets bigger by the year', the match was first played at the Kennington Oval in 1878 but was established as an annual event in 1907, making the tradition over 100 years old. The Navy needs to buck its ideas up, though: it hasn't won since 2001.
www.armynavymatch.org

400 *Let the kids loose on HMS* Belfast

This 11,500-ton battlecruiser (Morgan's Lane, Tooley Street, SE1 2JH, 7940 6300, www.iwm. org.uk) is the last surviving big gun World War II ship in Europe and a floating branch of the Imperial War Museum. It makes an unlikely playground for children, who tear easily around its cramped complex of nine decks, boiler, engine rooms and gun turrets. The *Belfast* was built in 1938, provided cover for convoys to Russia and was instrumental in

the Normandy Landings. She also supported United Nations forces in Korea before being decommissioned in 1965; a special on-board exhibition looks at that 'forgotten war'. Guided tours take in the living quarters, explaining what life was like on board. The ship's guns, incidentally, are trained on London Gateway services on the M1 – a distance of 12.5 miles away. Anyone who's had a meal at a motorway service station might sympathise.

401 Tower over the city atop Westminster Cathedral

Often overlooked in favour of the more famous Westminster Abbey, Westminster Cathedral is spectacular in its own bizarre way. Part wedding cake, part sweet stick, this neo-Byzantine confection – finished in 1903 – has an incredible 360° view from its 273-foot bell tower. Access (by lift) costs £3.

Westminster Cathedral *Victoria Street, SW1P 1QW (7798 9055/www.westminster cathedral.org.uk).*

402 Lunch from a tray at Rasa Express

It's a strange irony that in a corner of London that's full of wealthy media companies, you'll also find one of the capital's best lunchtime deals. Rasa Express – a very small and very pink takeaway outlet on Rathbone Street, offers a fantastic Indian meal in a tray, including two curries (usually one with chicken and one with lentils), rice, a chapati, pickles and a small tub of rice pudding for just £3.50. Ignore the fact that it looks like an oven ready-meal, this is Keralan fast food at its finest. You can eat in or venture just around the corner to tiny Colville Place park, which is something of a local secret. Turn right out of Rasa Express, right down Percy Passage, walk left on Charlotte Street, and you'll find the park is down a paved passage on the right.

Rasa Express *5 Rathbone Street, W1T 1NX (0871 426 3470).*

403 Hold a wine tasting at home

If your knowledge of wine doesn't stretch far beyond the basics (small glass or large?), ask France in London (www.franceinlondon.com) to organise a tasting session in your own home. It seems pricey – £250 for six people – until you realise that that's just over £40 a head for dinner cooked by a top chef and an evening sipping three or fours wines with expert Isabelle Legeron.

404 Attend the Frost Fair

The whole tradition of holding Frost Fairs in London started in the winter of 1564, when the Thames froze over and Londoners set up stalls on the ice to sell their mulled wine, roast meats and all the other popular goodies of the day. Sadly, no ice can be expected during our warm wet modern winters (although outdoor ice rinks have made a welcome comeback in recent years, *see p76*), but the event maintains its strong community feel, with crafts, food and wine stalls set up on Bankside, SE1. It all makes for a good week's entertainment in the run up to Christmas.

405 Judge wildlife photography for yourself

Wildlife Photographer of the Year is an exhibition held at the Natural History Museum (Cromwell Road, SW7 5BD, 7942 5000) from October to April each year. The competition attracts submissions from around the world. The winning shots are invariably of an incredibly high standard, made all the more fascinating by the accompanying explanation of the conditions under which the photograph was taken. Contenders for the 2009 title included a dazzling portrait by Danish photographer Morten Hilmer called 'Hare Spat'. He captured two Arctic hares boxing in a sparkling snowscape. Tickets cost £6, concessions £3.50.

406 Celebrate Pride

See London drag up in style for Pride (www.pridelondon.org), the annual gay and lesbian festival attended by around a million people all camping it up in a carnival of cabaret, clubbing and comedy. Stretching across the last fortnight of June it culminates in Pride Day at the end of the month when there's a colourful and very noisy parade from Marble Arch through the centre of London. Other events include cabaret in Leicester Square and a chill-out area in Soho Square.

407-410

Take to the mic in a karaoke bar

Lucky Voice

It took London a while to hop on to the karaoke bandwagon, but there are now dozens of different venues suiting all styles and wallets. Those who prefer proper beer to expensive booths, irony and red velvet, will want to check out the Thursday and Friday night karaoke at the Duke of Sussex (23 Baylis Road, SE1 7AA, 7928 6814), an old-school pub in Waterloo where crooners belt out tracks loud enough to make the wallpaper peel. Far fancier (and offering the luxury of privacy) is Soho's Lucky Voice (52 Poland Street, W1F 7NQ, 7439 3660, www.luckyvoice.co.uk), a karaoke bar that has nine self-contained rooms, state-of-the-art technology and an expensive Japanese-themed cocktail menu. It's proved so popular that they've even opened a branch in Islington (173-174 Upper Street, N1 1RG, 7354 6280). Cut from a similar cloth are Murehis (102-108 Clerkenwell Road, EC1M 5SA, 7251 3783) and the booths at the Bloomsbury Bowling lanes (*see p97*) underneath the Tavistock Hotel.

411 *Fill up on the cheap at the legendary Stockpot*

It serves popular British and continental dishes at rock-bottom prices, yet it's situated in a prime central London location that you'd expect the big chains to gobble up. Just how does this old Soho favourite do it? Not by cutting corners with the food, in our experience; the dishes always pass muster. And we love the retro feel of the menu: maybe egg mayonnaise as a starter, vegetarian moussaka or gammon and pineapple (from 4.50) and jelly and cream for pudding. It might remind you of school dinners, but school didn't offer you a bottle of house wine for less than a tenner. Puddings, such as golden syrup and lashings of custard, cost a mere £1.95 – heck, you can barely buy a cappuccino for that little these days. For reliable, affordable food in the heart of London, the Stockpot has no peers.

The Stockpot *18 Old Compton Street, W1B 5BE (7287 1066).*

412

The Scoop at More London, to use its full name, is a pristine open-air amphitheatre on the South Bank (between London Bridge and Tower Bridge, www.morelondon.co.uk) that runs a free arts programme of films, concerts and plays from May to October every year. Check it out.

413

Do dim sum at Hakkasan

We love Hakkasan. It's still one of London's most glamorous restaurants, and the beauty of it can startle. The low-lighting, dark oriental screens (seemingly stretching into infinity), and general buzz of the big basement are like nothing else in town. The place is best for a weekday dim sum lunch, when it's quieter; there's rarely a need to book. Then you can explore the innovative dim sum menu, yet still spend a mere £15-20 per head on a meal that might comprise baked venison puffs, steamed dumplings topped with flying-fish roe, or perfectly slithery cheung fun.

Hakkasan *8 Hanway Place, W1T 1HD (7927 7000/ www.hakkasan.com).*

414 Ride the London Eye at night

Most people hold out for blue skies to take a spin on the London Eye, but the skyline looks just as spectacular – and considerably more romantic – at night.

London Eye *Riverside Building, County Hall, Westminster Bridge Road, SE1 7PB (0870 500 0600/www.londoneye.com).*

415 Play korfball

A mixed-sex sport, korfball has similarities to netball and basketball, and is set up so there is no advantage to being male or female, tall or short, stocky or slim – the only thing that matters is your ability to co-operate with your teammates. Fourteen clubs compete in the London regional league and all welcome beginners; contact the London & District Korfball Association (www.londonkorfball. co.uk) for details.

416 Take a twilight tour of Linley Sambourne House

Cartoonist Edward Linley Sambourne's house was built in 1870 and has almost all of its original fittings and furniture. Twilight tours (£20; see website for tour dates) focus on the seedier side of his artistic endeavours. Conducted by costumed actors, the tours last an hour and a half, at the time when preparations for dinner would have been under way in the Victorian household. Visitors are offered a glass of wine to help them enter into the spirit of the occasion.

Linley Sambourne House *18 Stafford Terrace, W8 7BH (7602 3316/www.rbkc.gov.uk/linley sambournehouse).*

417 Make a Romantic tryst

Ladies! Why wait for the next leap year to propose to your man? *Carpe diem…* and hie thee to the lovely gardens beside Old St Pancras Church (St Pancras Road, NW1 1UL, 7387 4193). Here, over the grave of her esteemed mother Mary Wollstonecraft, Mary Godwin declared her love for Percy Bysshe Shelley. The author of *Frankenstein* got her man, too – she eloped with the Romantic poet in 1814. A cautionary note, though: Shelley was at the time of their elopement already married to Harriet Westbrook.

418 Mingle with the arty types at Candid Arts Café

In a dark, attic-like room, with battered floorboards and what seems like 100 years' worth of wax drippings, north London's arty types lounge in red velvet chairs or sit and read at the stately communal table. Some rehearse plays over coffee, others whip out a drawing pad and sketch fellow customers while they eat. Candid is bohemian to a T. Sure, prices are a little steep and none too bohemian-friendly, but for the atmosphere it's worth digging deep.

Candid Arts Café *Candid Arts Trust, 3 Torrens Street, EC1V 1NQ (7837 4237/www.candidarts.com).*

Candid Arts Café

419 *Learn to rub brass*

The London Brass Rubbing Centre is sited in the crypt of St Martin-in-the-Fields Church (Trafalgar Square, WC2N 4JJ, 7766 1122, www.stmartin-in-the-fields.org) – an atmospheric location in which to learn the art of rubbing brass. There's a choice of 90 replica brasses, including medieval knights in armour, elaborately costumed ladies, St George and the Dragon, and William Shakespeare. Amenable staff provide all the specialist papers and metallic waxes needed, along with expert advice. The Centre is particularly popular with children, whose parents can grab a bite and a cuppa at the crypt's café.

420 *Watch the sprint cycling at Herne Hill Velodrome*

The last remaining venue still in use from the 1948 Olympics, the Velodrome is home to the Velo Club de Londres which holds cycle training sessions and races throughout the year. The track is 450m long and the steepest part of it banks at 30 degrees. Herne Hill has a special emphasis on youth cycling; 2004 Olympic champion Bradley Wiggins trained on the track as a child and it is hoped that the stars of London's 2012 games will be discovered here.

Herne Hill Velodrome *Burbage Road (entrance between Nos.102 and 106), SE24 9HE (www.hernehillvelodrome.com/www.vcl.org.uk).*

421 *Seek out some satire*

The Political Cartoon Gallery (32 Store Street, WC1E 7BS, 7580 1114, www.politicalcartoon.co.uk) is the world's only centre dedicated to political cartoons and caricature. Here you can discover the history of the genre in Britain, which dates back to the time of Hogarth. The gallery also holds regular exhibitions: 'Cameron in Caricature', an already sizable collection of visual digs at the leader of the Tory party, was showing as we went to press Original cartoons are for sale, including work by Steve Bell.

422-434

Get a taste of New York City in London

Automat
33 Dover Street, W1S 4NF (7499 3033/
www.automat-london.com).
Knowingly kitsch American comfort food
specialists, offering the likes of prawn cake,
creamed spinach and macaroni cheese.

B&K Salt Beef Bar
11 Lanson House, Whitchurch Lane, Edgware,
Middx HA8 6NL (8952 8204).
Reputed to have the best salt beef in town;
portions are huge, prices are low.

Cybercandy Sweet Shop
3 Garrick Street, WC2E 9BF (0845 838 0958/
www.cybercandy.co.uk).
American sweet shop selling Hershey Cookies
and Cream bars, Mountain Dew soda, Tootsie
Rolls and Twinkies.

Eagle Bar Diner
3-5 Rathbone Place, W1T 1HJ (7637 1418/
www.eaglebardiner.com).
New York-style bar and diner serving
American breakfasts, burgers, salads,
grills, shakes and malts. The menu also
lists little-seen Brooklyn Lager.

Goodman
26 Maddox Street, W1S 1HQ (7499 3776/
www.goodmansresaurant.com).
Dark wood panelling, leather booths and
a bar counter running the length of the
restaurant – steakhouse Goodman's misson
has been to bring Manhattan to Mayfair.

Harry Morgan's
29-31 St John's Wood High Street, NW8 7NH
(7722 1869/www.harryms.co.uk).
Harry Morgan's is well-liked for its chicken
soup and salt beef.

Hummingbird Bakery
133 Portobello Road, W11 2DY (7229 6446).
Home-style American bakery specialising in
New York-style cheesecake, brownies, cookies
and wholesome cakes.

Lower East Liquor Bar and Bistro
28 Westferry Circus, E14 8RR (7536 2862/
www.lowereast.co.uk).
A slice of downtown NYC in London's
financial district, Lower East Liquor Bar
and Bistro (promising a happy combination
of New York staple dishes and expertly mixed
cocktails) had just opened as we went to press.

Lucky 7
127 Westbourne Park Road, W2 5QL (7727 6771).
Tom Conran's take on a New York-style diner,
offering imaginative burgers, shakes and
sundaes. The fries are skinny and the must-try
milkshakes come in three levels of thickness.

Madison's Deli
11 Buckingham Parade, Stanmore, Middx HA7
4ED (8954 9998).
Try chopped liver with matzo crackers, gefilte
fish, cheesecake and lockshen pudding. The
reuben sandwiches (corned beef, cheese and
sauerkraut on rye) are also winners.

Panzer's
13-19 Circus Road, NW8 6PB (7722 8596/
www.panzers.co.uk).
Fabulous, family-run delicatessen with a great
American selection, including New York
flatbreads, sourdough pretzels, Hershey
bars and mini Oreos.

Platters
10 Halleswelle Parade, Finchley Road, NW11 0DL
(8455 7345).
Small but perfectly formed deli offering
organic spelt flour bagels, cocktail latkes,
salt beef brisket, garlic salami and pickled
yellow cucumber.

Rosslyn Delicatessen
56 Rosslyn Hill, NW3 1ND (7794 9210/
www.rosslyndeli.co.uk).
A Hampstead institution that's a veritable
shrine to American classics: Mezzetta kosher
dill pickles, Jose Goldstein garlic ketchup and
Harry's organic pretzels.

435 *Head inside the Coccoon*

Here, amid a vast and beautiful concrete chrysalis encased within steel and glass, you can learn all about the 22 million or so insects in the vast Natural History Museum collection – and talk to the scientists that look after them.
Darwin Centre *Natural History Museum, Cromwell Road, SW7 5BD (7942 5000/www.nhm.ac.uk).*

436

Enjoy a galette with a glass of cider

Since the closure of Marylebone's La Galette in 2005, galettes – savoury sibling to the crêpe, hearty Breton staple and Parisian equivalent to a post-pub kebab – have been hard to find in London. Fortunately, fans can still make a pilgrimmage to the charming Chez Lindsay (11 Hill Rise, Richmond, Surrey TW10 6UQ, 8948 7473, www.chez-lindsay.co.uk) which specialises in the thin buckwheat delights. Here you can enjoy decadent fillings such as onion and roquefort sauce, scallops and leek as well as classic varieties like cheese and ham. To accompany galettes, the drink of choice has to be one of the superior French sparkling ciders.

437-448

Upgrade your lifestyle on Cheshire Street

Once a mere overspill zone for Brick Lane's jumble of fruit and cheap electrical goods, in the past few years Cheshire Street (E2) has bloomed into a fully fledged shopping enclave. It's at its most lively on Sundays, when Spitalfields and Brick Lane markets, plus the Sunday (Up)Market, are in full flow.

At City 16 (No.1, 7613 5604), vinyl junkies can pick up Hawkwind's *Doremi Fasol Latido* or perhaps some early Jacques Brel. Next door is the Shop (No.3, 7739 5631), which sells a host of vintage clothing and china – you can even purchase an early Sindy wardrobe complete with contents. Mar Mar Co (No.16, 7729 1494, www.marmarco.com) adds some quality Scandinavian homewares to the mix, more Skandium than IKEA. Old-fashioned Labour and Wait (No.18, 7729 6253, www.labourand wait.co.uk) combines cool with homespun, selling high-quality household items such as brooms, twine and aprons, while at No.22 Comfort Station (7033 9099, www.comfort station.co.uk) displays unusual, highly covetable fashion accessories such as silk cuffs and belts with silver buckles. Yugoslavian designer Dragana Perisic (No.30, 7739 4484, www.draganaperisic.com) creates distinctive and deceptively simple garments in silk, cashmere and organza, as well as delicate fabric jewellery, belts and scarves.

Shelf (No.40, 7739 9444, www.helpyour shelf.co.uk) is an arty 'purveyor of gifts and fineries' and a great place to find individual items such as Katy Hackney's delicate silver jewellery and E Loveless's cloth-bound book *Gelati in Venice*. Also sold are delightful, regularly changing limited edition prints. Next door at Mimi (No.40, 7729 6699, www. mimiberry.com), an unusual collection of jewellery sits among well-priced handmade-to-order leather bags and belts in girly colours.

Alongside Ella Doran's (No.46, 7613 0782, www.elladoran.co.uk) trademark photographic tablemats you'll find cushions, espresso cups, fabrics, make-up bags – even plant pots and picnicware.

Finally, it's worth making special detours for a few more highly original shops: Luna & Curious (198 Brick Lane, 07977 440212, www.lunaand curious.com) and Laden (23 Bacon St, E2 6DY, 7613 3339) both showcase original and vintage (in the case of Luna and Curious) clothes designers; Bernstock/Speirs (234 Brick Lane, E2 7EB, 7739 7385, www.bernstockspeirs.com) make beautiful, and cool, hats.

449-450

Give and receive free books

On the first Monday of the month watch out for a bright purple lollipop outside some of London's busiest tube stations. Beside them you will find a pile of books to which you may help yourself – for free. Once you've finished reading, write your name in the front of the book, return it either in person (on the right Monday) or use the 'drop box' (for details see www.choosewhatyouread.com). The book – and any others from your shelves that you care to donate – simply slip back into circulation for another commuter to enjoy. Current distribution stations are: Liverpool Street, Westminster, King's Cross, Charing Cross, London Bridge and Tottenham Court Road.

451-452

Stroll – or float – down Regent's Canal

Opened in 1820 to provide a link between east and west London, Regent's Canal was opened to the public as a scenic path in 1968. The route's industrial trappings have been transformed over the decades since. Any stretch of the canal is worth a stroll, but the most popular patch is from Camden Lock west to Little Venice, passing Regent's Park and London Zoo. Narrowboat cruises travel the water in summer and on winter weekends. They depart from Camden Lock and cost around £6.50 for a single fare or £8.50 return. (Jason's Canal Boat Trip, 7286 3428; Jenny Wren, 7485 4433, www.walkersquay.com; and London Waterbus Company, 7482 2660, www.londonwaterbus.co.uk).

453 *Phone ahead at Milk and Honey*

With the cachet of a members' bar, but without the pretension of complete exclusivity, the London incarnation of Manhattan's legendary referral-only destination is quality stuff. It isn't just the 40-odd cocktails (although they are exquisitely concocted with just the right touch of egg white or Maraschino, say, and chilled with hand-cut jagged chunks of ice), it's the service too. Hunker down in your own snug booth, one of six in the main Red Room. Numbers are kept comfortable by the house policy of booking in a limited number of non-members, generally at the start of the week and always before 11pm, according to custom on any given evening – always phone ahead (before 5pm). Members (£350 for the year) have access to the private bar and games room upstairs.
Milk & Honey *61 Poland Street, W1F 7NU (7292 9949/0700 655 469/www.mlkhny.com).*

Regent's Canal

454

Enjoy Gujarati food at Sakonis

Although the Green Street branch has closed, this chain of Gujarati vegetarian chaat houses (snack bars) is doing very well, having opened new branches in Leicester and Dubai. And deservedly so. Gujarati families often travel for miles to eat here; for many Gujarati housewives from neighbouring counties, a monthly food shopping trip to Wembley combined with a visit to Sakonis is a must. Buffets featuring Gujarati specialities are legendary. Make sure you try Sakonis's crispy bhajiya: wafer-thin potato slices fried in flavoursome chickpea-flour batter. The recipe is a well-guarded secret.
Sakonis *129 Ealing Road, Wembley, Middx HA0 4BP (8903 9601); 5-8 Dominion Parade, Station Road, Harrow, Middx HA1 2TR (8863 3399).*

455 Exchange potatoes at the Charity Potato Fair

Foodie trendification – as with gourmet burgers, say, or posh scotch eggs (*see p112*) – is all the rage. Surely the poor potato is ripe for rehabilitation? The organisers of London's Charity Potato Fair and Seed Exchange (www.potatofair.org) even reckon home-grown potatoes could be 'the new truffles'. This might be overstating the case a bit, but they have more than 100 varieties on offer at their annual January event (fourth Sunday of the month), held in Harris Girl's Academy (Homestall Road, SE22). They invite Londoners to come along, swap all kinds of flower, fruit and vegetable seeds (home-grown or shop-bought), meet fellow potato heads and get free gardening advice from experts. While the event is likely to appeal more to those who can tell their King Edwards from their Pink Firs, it's open to anyone keen to pick up tips on getting down and dirty in their back garden.

456

Learn savate fighting

The name is French for 'old shoe' – which is fitting as this aesthetic fighting art originated in the bars of 18th-century Marseilles. It's a combination of French 'foot-fencing' and boxing, and you can learn from British champion James Southwood (07950 456307), who holds classes on Thursday evenings (7.30pm) at Soho Gym, 11-15 Brad Street, SE1 8TG.

457 Look at one of the City's wilder buildings

The spectacular building at 3 Mincing Lane houses the London Underwriting Centre, which means the panoramic views and the circular atrium containing the world's tallest free-standing escalator system are off-limits to the public, but the glorious neo-Gothic roof is always worth a look. There's a great view of it heading north over Tower Bridge.

458-463

Visit Hawksmoor's six churches

St George Bloomsbury
Bloomsbury Way, WC1A 2HR (7242 1979/ www.stgeorgesbloomsbury.org.uk).

St Alfege Greenwich
Greenwich Church Street, SE10 9BJ (8853 0687/ www.st-alfege.org).

St Anne's Limehouse
5 Newell Street, E14 7HP.

St George in the East
Cannon Street Road, E1 0BH (7481 1345/ www.stgite.org.uk).

St Mary Woolnoth
Lombard Street, EC3V 9AN (7626 9701).

Christ Church Spitalfields
Commercial Street, E1 6LY (7377 2440/ www.christchurchspitalfields.org.uk).

464 Learn capoeira

A fusion of dance, martial arts and acrobatics, and resolutely non-contact, capoeira is beautiful to watch. Attacking moves are made acrobatic, in an exhilarating mix of handstands, cartwheels, springs and leaps, performed within a circle of dancers and to Afro-Brazilian music. There are two styles of capoeira: de Angola (a slower, sneakier form of the sport) and regional (a comparatively modern incarnation that's upright, flowing and acrobatic).

Just 20 years ago, capoeira was virtually unknown in Europe; now there are classes all over London. The main venue is the London School of Capoeira (Units 1&2, Leeds Place, Tollington Park, N4 3RF, 7281 2020, www.londonschoolofcapoeira.co.uk), but some other useful contacts are Greenwich Dance Agency (8293 9741, www.greenwichdance. org.uk), the Amazonas Capoeira Academy (0798 475 7689, www.amazonas.org.uk), East London Capoeira (Simon Atkinson, 07779 031273, www.capoeira-angola.co.uk), Association of Capoeira (Rodrigo Peres, 07050 073737, www.capoeiraworld.org) and international website www.capoeirista.com.

465 Attend the olde Strawberrie Fayre in Ely Place

An odd place – or Place – this little corner of Holborn is the site of St Etheldreda's Church (14 Ely Place, EC1N 6RY, 7405 1061, www.stetheldreda.com), commended in Shakespeare's *Richard III* for the strawberries grown in its gardens. In recognition of this, an annual Strawberrie Fayre is staged in late June (check the website for the exact date). There's plenty of traditional fun, games and strawberries, with all proceeds going to charity.

466 Cross the zebra crossing at Abbey Road

You *know* why. The recording studio itself is at 3 Abbey Road, NW8 9AY.

467 Ride the streets naked

From an embryonic – and brave – 58 people back in 2004, the World Naked Bike Ride (www.worldnakedbikeride.org) has grown exponentially (around 1,200 people participated in the London event in 2009). Simultaneously a protest against car culture and oil dependency as well as a celebration of the human body, it's like an eye-popping, show-stopping take on the Critical Mass cycle events that take place monthly in the city (*see p37*). The route encompasses Hyde Park, Piccadilly, Oxford Circus and both Westminster and Waterloo bridges. The only requirement for entry is nakedness – you don't even need a bike, roller skates will do.

468 Go night-fishing

Clapham's Eagle Pond (www.clapham angling.co.uk) and Lizard Lake in West Drayton are two of the many spots in London that offer night fishing facilities. For more, see the *Where To Go Fishing* guide published by the Environment Agency (0870 850 6506, www.environment-agency.gov.uk). It covers hundreds of night spots along the Thames; order a copy by phone or download it from the website. The Central Association of Provincial Angling Clubs (www.calpac.info) can also help with night fishing enquiries, and Dave Harper (www.warlingham-anglers.co.uk) offers lessons in London.

469 Learn Irish dance

Michael Flatley might have step(dance)ed out of the spotlight of mainstream media, but the Irish dance is still popular on the international stage. Try it for yourself at west London-based Delaney Academy of Irish Dance (www.delaneyacademy.com), which offers classes for adults and children aged four upwards at the Hammersmith Irish Centre (Blacks Road, W6 9DT).

470 *Read London novels in their settings*

Capital reads

*Tom Lamont **tours the capital with a bagful of the best London books.***

London has many literary landmarks, but it also lives a life between the pages of novels, many of which employ London almost as a character in its own right. What better place to read a novel than where it is set? The place where the hero is born, lives, dies; where love first catches, adulterers meet, feelings are formed, affection dies; where characters jostle, work, quip, fight.

In a reader survey by *Time Out* magazine, Martin Amis's *London Fields* was voted the capital's favourite London novel. Let's start with this – arguably the author's most unpleasant book, from an author whose speciality is unpleasantness – and pay a visit to a pub, perhaps the kind that inspired Amis to create the Black Cross. This pivotal, though fictional, spot is where the novel's four principal characters – Samson Young, Guy Clinch, Nicola Six and the loutish minor criminal Keith Talent – arrange their bizarre scheme for murder. The Black Cross is on Portobello Road, which actually boasts some rather nice pubs these

days. For comfort, sit down with a copy of the novel in the Sun in Splendour (7 Portobello Road, W11 3DA, 7792 0914); for an experience a little closer to the real thing, watch some of Keith Talent's beloved big screen sports in the Duke of Wellington (179 Portobello Road, W11 2ED, 7727 6727).

Like Amis, Ian McEwan and Julian Barnes employ London as a setting-cum-character throughout their oeuvre. McEwan's *Saturday*, is set in Fitzrovia on 15 February 2003, the day of the march against the war in Iraq. Read it near Henry Perowne's home, on a bench in Fitzroy Square. Christopher Lloyd, meanwhile, of Julian Barnes's first novel, *Metroland*, spends hours with his friend Toni mocking the posturing of bourgeois Londoners. Join them in the National Gallery (Trafalgar Square, WC2N 5DN, 7747 2885), people-watching: 'The gallery was fairly empty that afternoon, and the woman was quite at ease with the portrait. I had time to impart a few speculative biographical details. "Dorking? Bagshot? Forty-five, fifty. Shoppers' return.

Married, two children, doesn't let him fug her anymore. Surface happiness, deep discontent." ' For people-watching of a different kind, head to the Emirates Stadium (Ashburton Grove, N7 7AF) with a copy of Nick Hornby's *Fever Pitch*. Arsenal tickets cost £40 to over £100, and you might lose your place on the page if the on-field action hots up. Better to slip into one of the many nearby caffs.

Literature's great cads almost invariably live in London; there are so many opportunities for mischief. George MacDonald Fraser's Harry Flashman – Victorian soldier, bounder, coward and general shit – stars in 12 *Flashman* novels. He was a regular at the Horse Guards, so read of his villainous exploits and ill-gotten gains on Horse Guards Parade (Whitehall, SW1A 2NS). Kyril Bonfiglioli's Charlie Mortdecai – art dealer and rogue misogynist-in-chief of *The Mortdecai Trilogy* – lives on Upper Brook Street in Mayfair, but spends most of his time being beaten up in a police station on Half Moon Street in Green Park. Perhaps it would be

more fun to read the bawdy series in Indian restaurant Veeraswamy (Mezzanine Floor, Victory House, 99-101 Regent Street, W1B 4RS), where Mortdecai likes to eat when feeling dispirited. 'The splendidly dressed doorman gave me his usual splendidly military salute in exchange for the shiniest half crown I could find in my pocket. Cheap at the price. When depressed, go and find someone to salute you.'

Less caddish but equally unreliable was Iris Murdoch's Jake Donaghue, hero of her debut novel *Under the Net*. He gets all over London, mostly in pursuit of a girl, but also does a lot of sloping between the Charlotte Street newsagent owned by confidante, safe-keeper and all-round good egg Mrs Tinkenham and the pubs of Soho; pull up a seat in the Coach & Horses (29 Greek Street, W1D 5DH). Disillusioned World War I soldier Billy Prior, protagonist of Pat Barker's *Regeneration* trilogy, has more important issues to ponder (death, maiming, conscientious objection and the like). Join him as he takes 'an imaginary machine gun' and blasts the heads off the tulips by the Serpentine in Hyde Park.

The quick-talking Trinidadians of Sam Selvon's *Lonely Londoners* spend time in Hyde Park too – appraising women. 'They have a particular bench near Hyde Park Corner that they call the Play Around Section where you could go and sit with one of them… pretty piece of skin taking suntan.' Selvon's characters also ride on the 46 bus from Bayswater to Waterloo station, meeting immigrant arrivals and helping them settle in to the peculiarities of London life. 'Why they call it Bayswater? Is a bay? It have water?'

Richard Hannay, hero of John Buchan's *The Thirty-Nine Steps*, has just as much trouble adjusting to the capital after returning here from time in South Africa. He finds himself in direct contravention of Dr Johnson's law when he confesses that he is tired of London. 'I walked back to the flat I had hired near Portland Place. The crowd surged past me on the pavements, busy and chattering, and I envied the people for having something to do.' You have something to do, at least: sit down and read his subsequent adventure in the nearby RIBA Café (66 Portland Place, W1B 1AD, 7631 0467). A recurring character as famous as Hannay, if not as upstanding, is Raffles – the gentleman thief and amateur cracksman of EW Hornung's short stories. He plots his thefts from the Albany, a building off Piccadilly used for bachelor chambers as the 20th century got under way; conjure that bygone era by reading it nearby, in the splendour of the Wolseley (160 Piccadilly, W1J 9EB, 7499 6996).

Catching crooks less amiable than Raffles is Margery Allingham's Albert Campion. In *The Tiger in the Smoke* he must track knife-artist Jack Havoc through the grim network of London roads around fictional Crumb Street, where 'the fog sloped low over its sloped houses like a bucketful of cold soup over a row of dirty stoves'. Peter Ackroyd prefers to use real-life London in his novels; he is, after all, the city's unofficial biographer. In his work of fiction *Hawksmoor*, Christ Church Spitalfields is a key crime scene. If reading within a place of worship seems disrespectful, pop over to the Ten Bells (84 Commercial Street, E1 6LY, 7366 1721). Nab a stool by the window: much of the book's action takes place right

> '*Literature's great cads almost invariably live in London; there are so many opportunities for mischief.*'

outside. If detective stories appeal, there's always the Sherlock Holmes series. But would you really be unimaginative enough to read them in one of the themed cafés on Baker Street, or the Sherlock Holmes tribute pub (10 Northumberland Street, WC2N 5DB, 7930 2644)?

Michael Moorcock's *Mother London* is a virtual A-Z of London roads. We like reading the novel in the Star & Garter (4 Lower Richmond Road, SW15 1JN, 8788 0345), to which his characters repair after sessions of group therapy at a nearby NHS clinic. Drinking dens also play a key role in Patrick Hamilton's *Hangover Square*, although all of his are in Earl's Court. Try the Blackbird (209 Earl's Court Road, SW5 9AN, 7835 1855) or the Courtfield (187 Earl's Court Road, SW5 9AN, 7370 2626), renamed the Rockingham in the novel. Over on Fleet Street, the journalists in Michael Frayn's *Towards the End of Morning* drink away their lunch hours in El Vino (47 Fleet Street, EC4Y 1BJ, 7353 6786), while in Covent Garden the Lamb & Flag (33 Rose Street, WC2E 9EB, 7497 9504) is the agreed inspiration for George Orwell's prole pub, Moon Under Water, in *1984*.

Bowing to the inevitable a few years ago, King's Cross station installed a small tribute to the mythical platform that takes Harry Potter and his fellow child-wizards to Hogwarts: a plaque and a luggage cart, which is half-disappeared into the wall of the station annex that houses Platforms 10 and 11. Sharp-eyed readers might notice that the platform bears little resemblance to that described by

Rowling. That's because Rowling 'wrote about platform nine-and-three-quarters when I was living in Manchester, and I was actually thinking of Euston'. Less confusing are the bronze statue commemorating JM Barrie's greatest creation, Peter Pan, by the Long Water in Hyde Park, and the Paddington Bear statue in Paddington station.

In Angela Carter's *Wise Children* – not, of course, a children's book – the narrator occupies fictional 49 Bard Road in Brixton for the duration of her life. 'We've always lived on the left-hand side, the side the tourist rarely sees, the *bastard* side of Old Father Thames.' The improbable scene she describes from her Brixton window – 'There's Westminster Abbey, see? Flying St George's cross, today. St Paul's, the single breast. Big Ben, winking its golden eye' – is more likely to be seen from the Oxo Tower restaurant (8th floor, Oxo Tower Wharf, Barge House Street, SE1 9PH, 7803 3888). For a real Brixton atmosphere, curl up with the book in the Effra pub (38A Kellet Road, SW2 1EB, 7274 4180). Muriel Spark's *Ballad of Peckham Rye* is a homage to an area dear to the author. Dixie, her hero, lives at fictional 12 Rye Grove, but the characters take their walks in its two extant cemeteries near One Tree Hill, 'the Old one and the New'. Elizabeth Bowen's *The Heat of the Day*, meanwhile, begins at the Open Air Theatre in Regent's Park (*see p166*). 'The music could not travel far through the park – but hints of it that did escape were disturbing; from the mound, from the rose gardens, from the walks round the lakes people were being slowly drawn to the theatre by the sensation that they were missing something.'

While reading coming-of-age novel *Voyage in the Dark* by Jean Rhys, sit in Grosvenor Square, where Anna Morgan has her first fateful dinner with Mr Jeffries, or take tea in Selfridges (400 Oxford Street, W1A 1AB, 0800 123 400), where Anna meets her friend Maudie, flushed at the prospect of the marriage proposal. 'She was sure she could get him to marry her if she could smarten herself up a bit.' The youngsters of Colin MacInnes's *Absolute Beginners* have less definite aims. The unnamed narrator and his best friend 'the Wiz' take time out to appreciate the view over coffee and smoked salmon sandwiches from the top of a department store. 'The splendid outlook over London, the most

miraculous I know in the whole city, and quite unknown to other nuisance-values for our age, in fact, to everyone it seems, except these elderly female Chelsea peasants who come up there for their elevenses.' With all respect to its habitués, try the café atop John Lewis (278-306 Oxford Street, W1A 1EX, 7629 7711) – or move west to read the book on Wormwood Scrubs, 'a park with a name only Satan in all his splendour could have thought up'.

Graham Greene is the novelist of choice when hungry. Illicit dates between Maurice Bendrix and his friend's wife in *The End of the Affair* take place in Rules restaurant (35 Maiden Lane, WC2E 7LB, 7836 5314), while Colonel Daintry of *The Human Factor* is a big fan of the oysters at Overton's, now L'Oranger (5 St James's Street, SW1A 1EF, 7839 3774). Another fan of oysters – though not, one suspects, grown-up things like adultery – Bertram Wooster, lives with his trusty manservant on Berkeley Square. Pick one of PG Wodehouse's many and pull up a bench. Move to Fitzroy Square again if Jane Austen takes your fancy. It is here that *Pride and Prejudice*'s Bennett sisters stay on their forays away from country life for the London 'season'.

If that era's rural society belongs to Austen, Victorian London belongs to Charles Dickens. The city is as much a character in his novels as Pumblechook, Micawber and Fagin. Grab three of the man's most popular books and head to Garden Court, off Middle Temple, EC4, where Pip and Handel rent their rooms in *Great Expectations*; to 'Nancy Steps', adjoining Glaziers Hall (9 Montague Close, SE1 9DD) by London Bridge, where Nancy gets coshed by Bill Sikes in *Oliver Twist*; or to the Grapes pub in Limehouse (76 Narrow Street, E14 8BP, 7987 4396), the model for the Six Jolly Fellowship Porters in *Our Mutual Friend*.

Following Dickens's lead in keeping his favourite pub's name a secret, AP Herbert included Hammersmith boozer the Dove (19 Upper Mall, W6 9TA, 8748 5405) in *The Water Gypsies*, but disguised it as the Pigeons. Alan Bennett on the other hand – to the annoyance of local estate agents, we imagine, and heedless of driving down the value of his own pile – made no attempt to mask the location of his *Lady in the Van*: it was Gloucester Crescent in Camden.

471 Skiff out of town

Thames Skiff Hire (64 Carlton Road, Walton-on-Thames, KT12 2DG, 01932 232433, www.skiffhire.com) rents out lovely old clinkerbuilt double-skulling camping skiffs (complete with canvas canopy, camping equipment and sleeping mats) like the one Jerome K Jerome navigated upstream from London in his 1889 novel *Three Men in a Boat*.

472 Track down Eine's A to Z

Emma Howarth speaks to a graffiti artist who knows his alphabet.

Wear a fluorescent jacket and everyone thinks you're meant to be doing it,' says graffiti vandal and street artist Eine. 'It's only when they hear the rattle of a spray can that they call 999.'

Eine (aka Ben) is the artist responsible for the colourful giant letters painted on various shop shutters around east London. What started a couple of years ago with the notion that it would be pretty funny to paint two giant Es on Kingsland Road's Herbal club (before returning later to fill in the rest of his tag) has grown into something of a phenomenon, complete with numerous web pages devoted to tracking his whole alphabet down.

'I got the idea when I went back to paint the I and N,' says Ben. 'It looked so good. I thought why just keep on writing Eine everywhere? I've been doing it for years and it's so fucking boring. There are loads of shutters covered in tags and crap graffiti, loads of run-down shops that never even open. So I decided to do an entire alphabet but not tag it. Not telling anyone it was me made it more interesting.'

Ben painted five other letters on the shutters of closed-down shops before deciding that to get the project finished as fast as he wanted to he'd need to find a way to speed things up. What followed may well traumatise the angry hearts of 14-year-old taggers everywhere, but he simply knocked on a few doors and... well... asked. Most of the shop owners he spoke to had seen his work on shutters nearby and were happy to have him paint theirs too. They did, however, try to insist on choosing the letters themselves.

'Ruby Handbags asked for an R and an H, that sort of thing,' shrugs Ben. He tried to oblige, which left him with several repeats (he had to paint 35 letters to complete the alphabet) and a few rejects that no one wanted. 'The O was the last to go,' Ben recalls. 'I was painting a Q up on Kingsland Road and the shopkeeper next door asked if I'd do him a C. But I'd already done four of them.' So, in a return to vandal form, he agreed, then picked up his paintbrush and turned the C into an O when the owner knocked off for the night. 'Never saw him again after that,' he says.

Never mind the East End's graffiti-keen shopkeepers, the complete lack of concern from passers-by came as more of a surprise. Any notion of a masked artist skulking in the dark shadows of Hackney is entirely misplaced. Ben painted most of the letters in daylight, just as the shops shut for the evening, and not a single eyelid was batted. 'Like I said, a paintbrush means you're meant to be doing it,' he says.

He imagined the A-Z would get people interested, but is stumped by the 'hunt 'em down' obsession of some websites. A quick Google throws up several threads devoted to tracking down stray Zs and Js, and endless congratulatory backslapping among those who've found (and photographed) the lot.

Not sure where to start on your own spotting mission? Head for Hackney Road, Broadway Market, Kingsland Road and Brick Lane for starters. There are a couple on Redchurch Street too. You'll find that rogue O under Coco Shoes at 120 Kingsland Road, the Q next door. And the rest? Now, that would be cheating.

Keep your eyes peeled around town for new Eine alphabets too. Ben's got a new art-deco-style font ready to go and fancies 'doing a sinister message' on the shutters down Hackney Road. 'It'd be something you'd only ever see if you were travelling in a certain direction at 6am when all the shops are shut. A sinister message but in happy letters,' he laughs. 'Or I might do another A-Z in a different area of London so there's one in the north, one in the west and one in the south too.'

Signed Eine screenprints can fetch up to £175 and with his work perceived as street art rather than graffiti, even the east London Olympic clean-up seems to be leaving his alphabet unscathed. Locals love it, the shopkeepers are happy and other graffiti artists don't tend to tag over the top of it. A textbook case of tagger turned artist? 'Not really,' says Ben. 'I'd still rather vandalise stuff.'

473 Visit the Charles Dickens Museum...

It's easy to walk past the only surviving London house in which Dickens lived. You have to ring the doorbell to gain access to this unassuming townhouse with just a small plaque to mark it from the outside. Inside, there are four floors of Dickens material, from posters advertising his public speaking to rare editions of his work, in a house decorated as it would have been during Dickens's tenancy in the 1830s. Tickets are £6.

Charles Dickens Museum *48 Doughty Street, WC1N 2LX (7405 2127/www.dickensmuseum.com).*

474 ...or scale up and take in Dickens World. No, really

Incredibly, not an April fool's joke. In 2007, after investment of some £62 million, Dickens World (www.dickensworld.co.uk) opened as part of a regeneration scheme for the Medway town of Chatham, 35 miles south-east of London, and one of Dickens' many childhood homes. A shuttle bus from the train station whisks you to... well, a rather plastic-feeling shopping centre on the converted docks. Within, flickering lamps, dank water smells and impressively detailed theatre-set Dickensian architecture conjure some atmosphere, but it's hard to become totally immersed. The stand-out attraction is the single 'ride': the rather ponderous Great Expectations Boat Ride through the sewers and up over the roofs (yes, the roofs) of dismal Victorian London, complete with ghost train surprises. The Haunted House of 1859 is a great idea – ghostly characters materialise to recount their tales – but the technology is a little creaky for these CGI slick days. Even the '4D cinema show at Peggotty's Boathouse' (four dimensions? so that's time too) is half-baked: the 3D effect and glasses are cute, but the squared-off animation style irritating. Then there's the Six Jolly Fellowship Porters pub-restaurant, the shop (Dickens World fudge!), Fagin's Den soft play area (where's Fagin?) and a handful of slightly desperate actors in full Dickensian fig. One for connoisseurs of kitsch.

475-476 Drink sherry

Forget the annual glass of Bristol Cream at your granny's. Within bright, stylish surroundings Fino (33 Charlotte Street, W1T 1RR, 7813 8010, www.finorestaurant.com) offers a list of over 20 sherries and several dessert wines, by the glass or bottle, as well as a vast array of Spanish wines. Sherry styles cross the spectrum, from the light, tangy Puerto Fino, Solera Reserva, Lustau (£6.30 glass/£18 a bottle) through to intense fruity PX sherries such as the 1975 Don Pedro Ximenez, Gran Reserva (£8.30/£42).

Husband-and-wife team Sam and Sam Clark have done great things for tapas culture in this country at Moro (34-36 Exmouth Market, EC1R 4QE, 7833 8336, www.moro.co.uk) and they've been doing it for sherry too. Try old favourites such as Tio Pepe Fino (£4.20/£17.50) as well as ancient, age-dated sherries like Amontillado 1830 El Maestro Sierra (£80 a bottle).

477 Join the NFT

Like so many others, you might never actually use it, but at least membership of one of the great filmic institutions will make you feel all cultured. What's more, the NFT's refurbished South Bank site offers a gallery space, drop-in digital cinema and second café. Membership of the British Film Institute comes in three tiers and costs between £35 and £149, with those in the latter category also receiving four new BFI books or DVDs a year. Bog-standard membership gives you discounts at the NFT, where you can see some of world cinema's greatest features, priority booking to most screenings and invitations to exclusive members events.

BFI Southbank *Belvedere Road, SE1 8XT (7928 3232/www.bfi.org.uk).*

478 Shop for musical memorabilia at Dress Circle

A luvvies' paradise, Dress Circle (57-59 Monmouth Street, WC2H 9DG, 7240 2227, www.dresscircle.com) is the London authority on musical theatre, with a rich stock of original Broadway and West End cast recordings accompanied by a vast selection of books, souvenir programmes, libretti and sheet music. There's also a collection of British and American musical scores performed in foreign languages, plus musical karaoke backing tracks for those who can't resist a Gilbert & Sullivan sing-along.

Dress Circle

A few of my favourite

479-482

Ken Livingstone, former mayor of London

I've been eating in Vasco & Piero's Pavilion (15 Poland Street, W1F 8QE, 7437 8774, www.vascosfood.com) in Soho for donkeys' years. It's simple, Umbrian food with a good wine list. Not trendy but incredibly friendly and totally reliable.

I take as many opportunities as I can to visit London Zoo (Outer Circle, Regent's Park, NW1 4RY, 7722 3333, www.zsl.org, see p39 and p80) as I used to be the vice-president of the Zoological Society. The gorillas are magnificent and the giant galapagos tortoises (Dirk, Dolly and Dolores) are the latest new arrivals.

No matter how many times I go there I still cannot get over how much Trafalgar Square has improved since we ended its previous incarnation as a traffic-choked roundabout. The central staircase leading up to the north terrace and the National Gallery (Trafalgar Square, WC2N 5DN, 7747 2885, www.nationalgallery.org.uk) really opens it up.

The garden at El Parador (245 Eversholt Street, NW1 1BA, 7387 2789, www.el paradorlondon.com) is a great place to eat tapas outdoors in the summer. You'd never know you were near such busy streets. I did my very first *Esquire* restaurant review here.

Trafalgar Square hosts free events throughout the year including the Trafalgar Square Festival in August. For information about this and other events visit www.london.gov.uk.

483-490 *Admire London murals*

A depressing number have been knocked down, vandalised or obscured since their heyday in the 1980s, but London retains an impressive mural collection. Matt Brown visits the best.

The Spirit of Soho

This 1991 mural from the Free Form Arts Trust centres on St Anne, dedicatee of the local church. Her gaudy frock contains a veritable A-Z of Soho, with fruit and veg in the warp and local landmarks in the weft. A shifty looking crowd of (mostly male) local notables stands at her feet, hoping to gain a crafty upskirt vantage.
Corner of Carnaby Street and Broadwick Street, W1.

Cable Street mural

A winning combination of fascists, flags and fisticuffs. When Oswald Mosely decided to march his fascist blackshirts through the East End, the locals took umbrage – and various bits of plywood – and repulsed them. The Battle of Cable Street of 1936 is brilliantly remembered in this staggering mural from 1993. Superb.
Cable Street, E1, north of St George in the East burial ground.

Riders of the apocalypse

Warmongering world leaders, and Michael Heseltine, race around the Earth, Dr Strangelove-like, on cruise missiles that spew trails of cash. A karmic shield of peace symbols has been launched to engage them. Designed by über-muralist Brian Barnes in 1983.
Coldblow Lane, SE14, north end.

Kilburn murals

Two and a half murals for the price of one. Not that we're paying. Though if we had to spend a few coins on any of London's murals it would be these, created in 2004 by the Signal Project as the largest commissioned work of graffiti in the UK. Images of people leaving the city for the countryside, and vice versa, are accompanied by fanciful beasts and famous locals such as HG Wells. A splendid attention to detail, with many subtle references to local themes. The best in London.
Beneath Kilburn tube bridge, Kilburn High Road, NW6.

Brixton river mural

Brixton is home to several large murals, but this one (circa 1985) is my pick. A riverbank scene occupies the end of this semi-suburban terrace. At its heart, a watermill cunningly follows the building's angles. Ingeniously, one of the windows is real, allowing a glimpse into what's behind, and letting the occupants star in the mural. Definite touches of genius, even if it does need a good clean-up.
Corner of Strathleven and Glenelg Roads, SW2.

Stockwell mural

A potted history of Stockwell, again designed by Brian Barnes (1998). From famous residents such as Vincent van Gogh and, erm, Roger Moore, to the local war dead whose sacrificed lives are symbolised by hundreds of poppies. A portrait of Jean Charles de Menezes was added by Barnes, but later nixed by Lambeth Council.
Deep-level shelter walls on traffic island next to Stockwell tube, SW8.

Battersea in perspective

Another Barnes stormer, painted in 1988. This time, Battersea comes under his scrutiny, from an aerial perspective. The lofty view is well chosen – the plaque reveals just how many distinguished aviators came from the area.
Corner of Dagnall Road and Culvert Street, SW11.

Westbourne Park mural

Now here's something a little different. This pint-sized mural offers a distorted, Holbein-esque reflection of the Great Western Road. A crowd of cartoonish people waits at a bus stop as traffic moves away on the wrong side of the road (this being a mirror image). Yet, on the far left, the number 23 is not reversed. Stop screwing with our heads!
Junction of Fermoy Road and Great Western Road, W9.

491 Learn to love wine at Vinoteca

Vinoteca has 'wine lover' written all over it. Just one look at the list and you can tell it has been put together by folk who certainly know their La Chapelle from their Chapel Down. The venture was set up in autumn 2005 by a group of young, enthusiastic refugees from the wine and catering trades. In going from the frying pan to the fire, they created one of London's hottest wine bars. The 275-plus bin list champions the lesser-known and largely underrated wine regions of Spain (Txacolí, Calatayud, Cigales and Toro), France (Savoy, Gascony and Jura, plus sensible selections from Burgundy and Bordeaux) and Italy (Campania, Alto Adige, plus well-chosen bottles from Tuscany and Piedmont). Mark-ups are commendably low. By-the-glass selections (about £2.40-£8.85) might include a supple, lightly herbaceous Lagrein from northern Italy or a peppery, intense Estecillo Garnacha from Spain's Calatayud. The menu is an enticing read, with modish creations such as a oxtail crepinette accompanied with a cool scoop of horseradish cream, or a succulent roast guinea fowl with asaragus. If you fall in love with any of the bottles, take them home, as Vinoteca has a licence for off-trade sales too.

Vinoteca *7 St John Street, EC1M 4AA (7253 8786/www.vinoteca.co.uk).*

492 Let the kids take charge

At Coram's Fields, all adults have to be accompanied by a child to access (among other things) sandpits, a football pitch, a basketball court, climbing towers and a café. The assault-course pulley is very cool.
Coram's Fields *93 Guilford Street, WC1N 1DN (7837 6138/www.coramsfields.org).*

493 Run (or watch) the London Marathon

Late April; visit www.london-marathon.co.uk.

494-495 Buy a book in the RIBA bookshop, then read it in the RIBA Café

The Royal Institute of British Architects' listed 1930s building is well worth a few hours of anyone's time – for its lovely interior, its bookshop (there's a comprehensive collection of beautiful and technical architecture tomes) and finally its café which shares the first floor with exhibitions, pillars and a lot of space and light. With unobtrusive but stylish design (we love those semi-circular couches), smart and respectful service and generous spacing between tables, this is a serene and rather special place.
RIBA *66 Portland Place, W1B 1AD (7631 0467/www.riba.org).*

496 Have a romantic break in Ilford

Deep in the heart of Ilford and surrounded by extensive parkland is the recently restored Valentine's Mansion, built in 1698 for Lady Tillotson, the widow of the Archbishop of Canterbury. The gardens, complete with rococo grottoes, a dovecote and a walled kitchen garden are as pretty as a picture; inside you'll find artists' studios and temporary exhibitions of contemporary art.
Valentine's Mansion *Emerson Road, Ilford, Essex, IG1 4XA (8708 3370/www.valentinesmansion.com).*

497-499 Tour the capital's breweries

Fuller's brewery in Chiswick (Chiswick Lane South, 8996 2063, www.fullers.co.uk) is open for guided tours at £10 a pop. There are also a couple of bars with their own microbreweries: Zero Degrees (29-31 Montpelier Vale, SE3 0TJ, 8852 5619, www.zerodegrees.co.uk) in Blackheath and the Greenwich Union (56 Royal Hill, SE10 8RT, 8692 6258, www.greenwichunion.co.uk), the fine flagship of Meantime Brewery.

500

Take a load off in Cleaver Square...
Just off Kennington Park Road, SE11, this quiet residential square has been restored in recent years using money from the Lottery. It's a peaceful place for a game of boules (see p113) or to sup a beer.

501-516

...and assess the pick of London's other city squares

Albion Square, E8

This Italianate railed garden, right in the graffitied heart of Hackney, was completed by Islip Odell in 1849, when the area was undergoing a rapid transformation from rural to urban. The square still features a working fountain.

Bonnington Square, SW8

Incorporating a 'Pleasure Garden' designed by local residents, this bohemian pocket of south London is a communal hub, with a vegetarian restaurant operating a chef-rotation system and hosting weekly vegan nights. An inexplicable wooden rowing boat suspended above the entrance welcomes visitors into what is an overgrown jungle of a square.

Cabot Square, E14

Although Canada Square, with Ron Arad's impressive *Big Blue* sculpture as its centrepiece, has its advocates, we're more taken with neighbouring Cabot Square. Located to the west of Canary Wharf tower, it has a broad and calming fountain, as well as views over the docks on either side. If you get bored, wander south to the beautifully manicured Japanese-style garden by the Jubilee Line exit from Canary Wharf station.

Charterhouse Square, EC1

A square that isn't a square (it's actually more of a pentagon), Charterhouse was developed as a residential quarter in the 17th century, on the site of a plague pit – something we fancy the estate agents would have neglected to mention. The central area was enclosed in 1717.

Cloudesley Square, N1

Holy Trinity Church, which sits in the middle of this square, was built by Charles Barry in 1828 and is said to be an imitation of King's College

Chapel in Cambridge. The diminutive square (built in 1826) was the earliest of the Barnsbury squares, all of which boast late Georgian and early Victorian architecture – and command premium house prices.

Ebury Square, SW1

Jostling for prominence amid local heavyweight squares Sloane and Belgrave, Ebury is a tranquil and colourful square that has a fine central fountain. Once the location of the 11th-century Ebury farmhouse (it was part of the 430-acre Manor of Eia, as recorded in the Domesday Book), adjacent Ebury Street has been home to, among others, Mozart, Noel Coward and Vita Sackville-West.

Edwardes Square, W8

Built by Louis Changeur in the early 19th century, this square features a gardener's lodge that resembles a small temple, built in Greek Revival style.

Fitzroy Square, W1

Designed by Robert Adam in 1793, Fitzroy Square was built in two stages: the first, from 1793 to 1798, saw the construction of the east side (a unified Portland stone palazzo of individual houses); the second produced the stucco-fronted north and west sides. Former residents of the square include George Bernard Shaw, Virginia Woolf and Lord Salisbury.

Golden Square, W1

Formerly known as Gelding Square, Soho's Golden Square dates from the Regency period. It now houses many film production companies.

Gordon Square, WC1

A verdant alternative to the neighbouring Russell and Bloomsbury squares, this quiet space is frequented by students from the surrounding colleges intent on loafing but occasionally prevailed upon to exert themselves with some light Frisbee action. The location of an erstwhile residence of Virginia Woolf (the blue plaque is to be found at her more permanent address in nearby Fitzroy Square), Gordon Square was the epicentre of the Bloomsbury Group's literary activities.

Hanover Square, W1

Dominated by the art deco presence of Vogue House, this shady spot behind Oxford Street unites fashionistas, shoppers and workmen as an impromptu lunchtime picnic spot. St George's, an 18th-century church to the south of the square, was once the most fashionable place in town to exchange your vows: George Eliot and Teddy Roosevelt were married here, although not – we assure you – to each other.

Hoxton Square, N1

The square that spawned a thousand haircuts. This nocturnal green is well known for its fashionable bars, clubs and the White Cube art gallery. Lesser known is the fact that in 1598 playwright Ben Jonson killed actor Gabriel Spencer in a duel here, narrowly escaping a public hanging.

Lincoln's Inn Fields, WC2

This 17th-century square, laid out by Inigo Jones, is now a favourite spot for lunching lawyers from the Inns of Court. Sir John Soane's Museum faces on to the square.

Markham Square, SW3

Built on the site of an orchard, this attractive square was redesigned after World War II to look like a country garden; it features many unusual trees and colourful floral borders.

Tredegar Square, E3

A distinguished space that existed well before the east's gentrification, this spacious square has been dubbed 'the Eaton Square of the east'. It comes as a real surprise in down-at-heel Bow.

West Square, SE1

An unexpected patch behind the Imperial War Museum, this inviting residential square is a great spot for visitors looking for a green space in Southwark.

Golden Square

517 Get a decent meal in a museum café... honestly

Hurrah for Oliver Peyton (who also set up St James's Park restaurant Inn the Park, *see p293*) – and for the National Gallery for being brave enough to choose him to run their café over some corporate catering option. This is fine British food, in a modern (David Collins-designed) setting, at a reasonable price – especially in the café area, where a Cornish clotted cream tea will cost £5.50. On our last visit we ordered from the restaurant menu. Chilled cucumber and ginger soup came with subtle Dorset crab and a hint of melon; a chicken liver mousse was a one-note starter tuned to a pitch-perfect concerto. Mains were just as impressive: gently poached trout served with spring greens; and a wonderful melt-in-the-mouth ox cheek, braised with great patience, making a lovely match for a side of creamed spinach. The only shame is the limited opening times. We wish every museum café had the same commitment to good food.

National Dining Rooms *Sainsbury Wing, National Gallery, Trafalgar Square, WC2N 5DN (7747 2525/www.thenationaldiningrooms.co.uk).*

518-521 Spend a penny in London's best loos

Claridge's

For maximum luxury choose the Ladies to the right of the front entrance, which has pretty floral art deco tiling, carpets and trompe l'oeil murals depicting garden scenes and rose garlands. A polite, grandmotherly attendant in a smart navy suit fills an antique-style ceramic basin for you to wash and moisturise your hands with Floris toiletries. An adjoining room contains dark wood dressing tables with large mirrors at which you can sit to refresh your make-up, brush your hair or whatever.

Claridge's *55 Brook Street, W1K 4HR (7409 6307/www.claridges.co.uk).*

Crazy Bear

Once you've found these loos (in the basement bar, past the cigar cabinet and along a short, dark, wood-lined corridor) and worked out how to get in (by tentatively pushing the mirrored walls) you enter a dark, mirrored chamber with an ethereal purple glow – walls, doors and ceiling are mirrored, the floor is cracked metallic tiles and an ornate antique-style mirror adorns the wall in the Ladies. These lavs, designed by Crazy Bear's owner Jason Hunt, are far from tacky, although the lighting doesn't do any favours to girls (and guys) touching up their make-up.

Crazy Bear *26-28 Whitfield Street, W1T 2RG (7631 0088/www.crazybeargroup.co.uk).*

Saki

This Japanese bar and restaurant opposite Smithfield Market proudly boasted London's first public paperless toilet when it opened in 2006. Users control proceedings from a panel of buttons: sit and do the business, then push buttons to commence the cleansing jet of water and drying blast of air. Seats are cosily warm, and water and air temperature are adjustable. The Japanese have been using paperless toilets for some 40 years (approximately 90 per cent of Tokyo homes employ them), so why hasn't it caught on here? We say it's high time we all took the plunge.

Saki *4 West Smithfield, EC1A 9JX (7489 7033/www.saki-food.com).*

Sketch

Best of the lot here (*pictured*). A pair of sweeping staircases leading up from the circular bar below take you to an entire floor devoted to toilets. Eleven pods, designed by Noe Duchaufour Laurance, are arranged uniformly – a genuine 'wow' factor for a first-time visitor. Pods – each contains a loo – are white, floor, ceiling and walls are white, and there's the odd (yes, white) dining chair nestled against a wall. The overall effect, with its candy shades of pink and green light, is as though you've wandered on to a Kubrick film set. Our last visit saw an attendant dressed as a French maid locating vacant pods (all unisex) for anyone who seemed a bit confused by the whole thing.

Sketch *9 Conduit Street, W1S 2XZ (0870 777 4488/www.sketch.uk.com).*

Sketch

522 *Drink on the roof terrace at Gilgamesh*

This enormous space – surely the biggest bar/restaurant in London – was apparently inspired by the British Museum. It is variously panelled, decorated, bedecked and draped in intricately carved wood: scenes of mythic Babylonian battles, super-sized statuary, inlaid tables and friezes. Just when you think you've seen it all, a 40-foot glass ceiling opens up and you're suddenly on a roof terrace. The drinks list continues the Assyrian/Babylonian theme, so while you're up there you might sip on an Ishtar (made with Palma Mulata Rum, raspberries and champagne) or a Kutu (a concoction consisting of gin, chilli, mint and pink grapefruit).

Gilgamesh *Camden Stables Market, Chalk Farm Road, NW1 8AH (7482 5757/www. gilgameshbar.com).*

523 *Watch pro darts*

In pro darts, there are two tribes: the British Darts Organisation and Professional Darts Corporation each run their own World Darts Championship, but unless you fancy heading out to a leisure centre at Frimley Green (our thoughts exactly) the PDC is the one to follow. It was on 1 January 2007 at the Circus Tavern in Purfleet that the stuff of sporting legend occurred: Raymond 'Barney' van Barneveld beat the favourite Phil 'The Power' Taylor with a stunning comeback from three sets down, taking the championship on a sudden-death leg. The match was especially piquant since van Barneveld had defected from the BDO in February 2006 – with the express intention of taking on Taylor, the dominant force in PDC darts, and then with 13 World Championships to his name.

Since then the PDC World Championship has outgrown its cramped venue at the Circus (thanks largely to the great power struggle between these two darting heros) and now uses the considerably more spacious Alexandra Palace (and still people have trouble getting tickets). But the Hallowed Purfleet ground is still used as a darts venue (the inaugural Players Championship Finals and the final of the League of Legends Darts are held here). The place isn't for the faint-hearted. On our last visit, only one building showed signs of life, dim lights picking out a gravelly yard packed with haphazardly double-parked cars. Billboards outside advertised hen nights every Thursday, 'Extreme Fighting' and 'all the best *Sunday Sport* dancers'. Within, the all-day crowd (dress code: untucked shirts, cauliflower ears, broken noses) were still drinking as the evening session began at 7pm. Players emerged from the back of the room in a shroud of dry ice, surrounded by sinister Essex heavies. In addition to the contest, entertainment can be had at the Ladbrokes concession, where tenners, ponies and tons are flung chaotically on everything from the likely winner to the total number of 180s scored in the match. You could also join in the time-honoured pursuit of holding up self-penned slogans of support and shout-singing refrains about the personal appearance of one or other of the darters.

For more details, see www.pdc.tv.

524 *Enrol at the School of Life*

For a novel approach to education, we recommend a visit to the School of Life, set up by former Tate Modern curator Sophie Howarth. The School is about 'the practical application of philosophy on life's core subjects,' love, politics, work, family and play,' she explains. Each course (they range from short evening sessions to week-long retreats) has involved the input of well-known writers, artists, philosophers and journalists, including Alain de Botton, Geoff Dyer, Rosie Boycott and Martin Parr. It takes learning to unusual places: to furniture factories on Brick Lane, check-out tills in Waitrose, or excursions up the M1.

School of Life *70 Marchmont Street, WC1N 1AB (7833 1010/www.theschooloflife.com).*

525

Listen to the best steel drummers compete, a week before Notting Hill Carnival

Every year before Notting Hill Carnival, an enthusiastic crowd gather to watch the carnival's best-kept secret – Panorama. It has been a precursor to the festivities for 30-odd years, with the cream of UK talent battling it out for the coveted 'Champions of Steel' title. Incredible steel drumming is the highlight of the carnival for many: so do yourself a favour and avoid the crowds by heading instead to Hyde Park on the Saturday before Carnival to hear the best Calypso this side of Trinidad.

526-529

Watch football with fans of every nation

We can't list *every* nation, nor – since football is meant to bring the whole world together – are we going to encourage you to go where the fans of the easy teams gather. You know who we mean: the giddy samba stylists of Brazil, the Dutch total football fiends. Nope, those teams you can find for yourselves. We think it's time for you to embrace your inner German, clasp Croatia to your bosom, check out the Czechs (and Slovaks) and knuckle down for some serious Argentinian beef.

Argentina

This authentic *parrilla* in Hackney was the scene of much expat revelry during the 2006 World Cup – up until the quarter-finals, that is. Definitely the place to stand shoulder-to-shoulder with boys in sky-blue and white.
Buen Ayre *50 Broadway Market, E8 4QJ (7275 9900/www.buenayre.co.uk).*

Croatia

The manager of the Cadogan Arms has been welcoming Croatians (as well as Aussies: it's an unpopularity twofer) since the 2002 World Cup, after striking up a friendship with a Croatian student who was looking for a place to watch his national team play. Crazy strip, crazy guys.
Cadogan Arms *298 King's Road, SW3 5UG (7352 6500/www.cadoganarmsofchelsea.com).*

Czech Republic/Slovakia

The Czech and Slovak Club is a hospitable and welcoming den for Czechs and Slovaks living in London but it also extends a warm greeting to anyone who's up for sampling a fine selection of beers while clinging on for victory.
Czech and Slovak Club *74 West End Lane, NW6 2LX (7372 1193/www.czechandslovakclub.co.uk).*

Germany

The London branch of the German culture-promoting Goethe-Institut (50 Prince's Gate, Exhibition Road, SW7 2PH, 7596 4000) was fully booked for all of Germany's 2006 World Cup games, with the overspill heading to the Nanobyte (183-185 Wardour Street, W1F 82A, 7734 0037, www.nanobytebar.com). But down at the Octoberfest Pub everything, from beer to bar-snacks, comes straight from Munich – you can even watch German league matches.
Octoberfest Pub *678-680 Fulham Road, SW6 5SA (7736 5293/www.octoberfestpub.com).*

Old habits die hard, eh? Well fall back into your weak-willed Brazilophilia at *boteco* Barraco (10 Kingsgate Place, NW6 4TA, 7604 4664, www.barracocafe.co.uk) or Guanabara (Parker Street, Covent Garden, WC2B 5PW, 7242 8600, www.guanabara.co.uk), and indulge your orange self – while indulging in Oranjcboom – at famous old Dutch pub De Hems (11 Macclesfield Street, W1D 5BW, 7437 2494).

Things not to do

Stuart McGurk spends the worst day of his life in the capital – just so that you won't have to.

When a man is tired of London he is probably even more tired of hearing that quote. The truth is, any man would be tired of London if he spent any time on the hellish junction of Tottenham Court Road and Oxford Street, eating slices of the Black Death (mislabelled pizza) from street vendors, or shopping in those clothes stores that always claim to be on the brink of some apocalyptic closure with a final, last-ditch, end-of-the-century, there-really-will-be-no-more-of-these-sales sale.

Though never as vulnerable as the tourists, even the unwary Londoner can fall prey to such horrors. Who hasn't wandered past the steamy window of a Scotch-branded steakhouse and thought: could I? *could* I? So this is it. The definitive list of things to avoid in London.

1pm The 'Scottish' steakhouse

The ageing street whore of the London food world: they're on every corner, you can't imagine anyone could be mad enough to accept their hospitality, there's not quite enough meat on their bones… and it's mostly Americans taking up the offer.

'The best steaks in London' boasts the unaccredited quote on the menu. If you take away the first two words, it's completely accurate. Sitting down, my retinas burn from red-wavelength overload. The lights, the seats, the menu – everything except the meat in people's steaks. Unswayed, I order a 8oz sirloin for £13.50. After 15 minutes of ear abuse ('Baby Come Back' blares in misplaced optimism from the sound system) it arrives, complete with three limp lettuce leaves of 'accompanying salad'. More like a one-fingered vegetable salute.

The steak itself? It was surprisingly well-cooked, but had no taste. None. It was about as satisfying as eating the menu would have been.

I ask for the bill. 'You mean the check?', says the waiter, confused. It's clear: no Londoner has been here for at least two decades.

2pm *The east end of Oxford Street*

Post-steak, deciding that the best time to shop for clothes is at my fattest, I head to the Centre Point end of Oxford Street. Inside a shop whose name is indiscernible as the words 'Cheap! Leather! Coats!' covering the front, a wizened salesman tries his patter on an elderly lady in a pink bomber jacket (the kind of pink, I note, that could land planes). 'These jeans, only £10,' he says slowly. 'Yes? Yes?' Really turning the charm on, he pauses. 'Beautiful'. Pause. 'Look nice on you.'

Down the road, at the Outlet Store, I dodge the perma-sale racks (£5 rising to a hefty £8) and try on a baggy tracksuit outfit covered in gold dollar signs. An obese woman nods her approval, before browsing the 'Fuck Virgins, Do Me Instead' T-shirts. I feel ill. But extremely comfy.

3pm *The cardboard pizza slice*

Past Oxford Circus I decide to settle my stomach with something solid. Something reliable. Something basic. Something – it turns out – that seems to have been baked before the advent of the mobile telephone (examples of which are, conveniently, sold at the same stand). At least four servers stand in front of me – this one stand offers a quadruple threat, embracing the multiple strands of stomach evil that are pizza, kebab, fish 'n' chips and fried chicken. I go for a £1.50 slice of chicken pizza – reheated as I wait! – and it immediately sucks all moisture from my mouth. Close to vomiting, I buy a sorely marked-up can of Coke and back away slowly.

4pm *The Trocadero*

Heading to the Trocadero, I wonder if loud, constant, clashing noise is good for a dicky tummy. 'All the fun of the fair!' a placard outside insists. All the fun – without the candy floss, the rides, the atmosphere.

The noise – each arcade machine blaring an equal din – is almost indescribable. I try to think of a comparison, and come up with a group of manic psychotics in an echoey room. Shouting at each other. Shaking jars of trapped bees. And squeezing air-horns.

Essentially, the Trocadero is a place where moron teens of all ages can gather, threaten to slit your throat for a tube of change, and

still make it home in time for their *X-Factor* curfew. Young and old gasp at the penny falls, hoping to win the 30p jackpot, while others divide their time between driving sims and shoot-at-the-screen games that seem to the uninvolved observer worryingly like neo-con recruitment drives. I decide to get with the programme and play one of the latter; two small children openly laugh at me. Retreating to the comfortable nostalgia of *Street Fighter*, I play against a small Japanese boy who's managed to wear the imprint of his paw into the plastic. Without landing a punch, I leave – defeated and almost deaf.

5pm *The caricature*

I have never wanted a caricature done of me. Cameras put sufficient emphasis on my bad features as it is. But this is research: I stop just off Piccadilly Circus to be sketched by Roman, from the Ukraine. I am left with two things from the experience: a genuinely superb sketch, and trench foot. It took two hours of near-total stillness in the freezing London cold. I managed to pick the only perfectionist sketcher in London. Embarrassment is a huge factor. People walk past and stare at you as if you're a puppy waiting to be rehomed. Once the sketch takes shape, they stop and stare. Some people laugh. Several point. About an hour in, one spectator pointed out that the drawing was 'a bit better looking'. I had all the dignity of a circus freak, without even a share of the entrance fee.

7pm *The rickshaw*

I get to my feet – creakily – and stagger towards the tube station. Not to ride it, of course: taking the tube may be unpleasant, but every Londoner knows its importance. No. Today, I travel by rickshaw. It's February-cold and there are plenty of pedallers wishing they'd chosen a different season to work in London who bay for my attention and any excuse to get moving. I choose the least dangerous-looking, the one who looks like he might have passed some kind of test. As we zip over Waterloo Bridge – easily moving at *twice* the speed of pedestrians – I try not think how much it is costing me, and look forward to returning to normal life. To being a Londoner who knows exactly what things to avoid. Just as valuable, in its own way, as knowing the thousand things worth doing.

531

Enjoy the best Korean meal in town

Cah Chi is the most accessible Korean restaurant in London, particularly for newcomers to the cuisine. Staff are happy to explain the ins and outs of Korean cooking and the waitresses cut seamlessly from speaking Korean to Home Counties English. In terms of its interior, the venue feels more like a nursery school than a restaurant. Children's drawings adorn the walls, and menus are handwritten in chunky Korean script on coloured cards in thc window. The liberal use of varnished pine only adds to the kindergarten feel. But don't be deceived – the food is far from unsophisticated. We loved the variety of flavours and textures – the soft bite of the pork and vegetable dumplings, the slip and slide of the stir-fried glass noodles, the chilli zing of the spicy fried squid. The £18 menu is a bargain that includes four courses, plus Korean red rice and a huge spread of *panch'an* (including tangy sweet pickled radish and nutty soy beans in syrup). Delicious.
Cah Chi *34 Durham Road, SW20 0TW (8947 1081/www.cahchi.com).*

532 *Play footvolley*

Romário and Ronaldinho grew up playing footvolley on the golden sands of Brazil. It's basically beach volleyball, played to football rules: two versus two, over a net, with three touches per team and no consecutive kicks by the same player. Since the game works just as well on the more typical English surfaces of grass, gravel and mud, games have been spotted in several London parks (Hyde Park and Shoreditch Park for starters) and playgrounds. The UK Footvolley Association (www.footvolley.co.uk) is looking for players of both sexes to try out for the England team.

533 *Learn flower-arranging*

If to you flower-arranging means Women's Institute decorations in a suburban church nave, McQueens will be a bit of a surprise – their flowers occupy a world of Oscar ceremonies and *Vanity Fair* fashion shoots. The firm runs contemporary floral design workshops that range from one-day classes to five-week courses aimed at people who are thinking of becoming professional florists. All the workshops – which focus on everything from 'hand-tieds' (bouquets) through 'vases' to fruit and veg arrangement – teach theory and offer practical tips; you'll also be allowed to take whatever you create home at the end of the day. A one-day course costs £290, with a £29 deposit.
McQueens Floristry School *70-72 Old Street, EC1V 9AN (7251 5505/www.mcqueens.co.uk).*

534 *Tour Spencer House*

Designed by John Vardy, Spencer House was built between 1756 and 1766 for John Spencer, who became Earl Spencer the year before his house was completed. The building is one of the capital's finest examples of a Palladian mansion. The Spencers moved out just over a century ago and the lavishly restored property, now used chiefly as offices and for corporate entertaining, is open to the public on Sundays (guided tours only, closed January and August). The spectacular garden covering almost half an acre at the back of Green Park is sometimes also open for limited periods; phone to check times.
Spencer House *27 St James's Place, SW1A 1NR (7499 8620/www.spencerhouse.co.uk).*

535 *Sip sherry at a Sunday morning concert*

Classical music in opulent, Renaissance-style surroundings – with a pre-prandial tipple thrown in. Coffee is available too.
Wigmore Hall *34 Wigmore Street, W1U 2BP (7935 2141/www.wigmore-hall.org.uk).*

536-541

Drink in a pub with a real fire

Crooked Billet (*pictured*)
14-15 Crooked Billet, SW19 4RQ
(8946 4942/www.crookedbillet
wimbledon.com).

Earl Spencer
260-262 Merton Road, SW18 5JL
(8870 9244/www.theearlspencer.co.uk).

Fire Stables
27-29 Church Road, SW19 5DQ
(8946 3197/www.firestables
wimbledon.co.uk).

Grand Union
45 Woodfield Road, W9 2BA (7286 1886/
www.grandunionlondon.co.uk).

Holly Bush
22 Holly Mount, NW3 6SG (7435 2892/
www.hollybushpub.com).

Three Kings of Clerkenwell
7 Clerkenwell Close, EC1R 0DY
(7253 0483).

542 *Buy chocolate*

The city has various purveyors of the glorious stuff. First stop, for spectacular ganaches, truffles, mints and candied fruits, is L'Artisan du Chocolat (89 Lower Sloane Street, SW1W 8DA, 7824 8365, www.artisanduchocolat.com), London's most experimental independent chocolate shop. Irish-born proprietor Gerard Coleman, the Willy Wonka of home-grown chocolatiers, makes all of his trademark tobacco 'couture chocolate' (smoky, silky and intense) by hand. He has also created many other delicious innovations, among them the best-selling liquid salt caramels.

Sublime cocoa creations are also available at chocolatier Chantal Cody's charming Rococo (321 King's Road, SW3 5EP, 7352

plump, round, velvety truffles (banoffee, champagne or orange with lemon, perhaps), they make splendid gifts.

That said, Belgian chocolatiers continue to impress, and while chains such as Godiva (www.godiva.com) and Leonidas (www.leonidasbelgianchocolates.co.uk) beat a box of Thorntons any day, neither approach the finely honed flavours of Robert Linxe's Parisian Maison du Chocolat (45-46 Piccadilly, W1J 0DS, 7287 8500,www.lamaisonduchocolat.com), an independent shop that's a browser's paradise. Spacious and slick, with giant glass windows, the store sells seasonal individual cakes – perhaps a chocolate, mango and ginger Maiko in summer, or

Rococo

5857, www.rococochocolates.com). Longer established and less pioneering than L'Artisan, the company still shares a fondness for unusual flavours (cardamom, chilli pepper or orange and geranium bars, for example), but combines this with some nostalgic English rose and violet creams, plus fresh cream truffles.

Another British business that has long since proved that London could be up there with the chocolate masters of Brussels is Prestat (14 Princes Arcade, SW1Y 6DS, 7629 4838, www.prestat.co.uk). Its 'Appointment to the Queen' status is echoed in glorious packaging – pretty boxes in regal purples and ruby reds, embellished with gold crowns and elegant script. Filled with the store's strongest product, its

a Rigoletto caramel mousse-filled cake for winter. On a trip here the French for 'window shopping' – *lèche-vitrine* (literally meaning 'licking the window glass') – immediately becomes appropriate.

Elsewhere in town, try the Chocolate Society (36 Elizabeth Street, SW1W 9NZ, 7259 9222, www.chocolate.co.uk), selling connoisseur brands as well as own-label products; fun-orientated Montezuma's Chocolate (51 Brushfield Street, E1 6AA, 7539 9208, www.montezumas.co.uk) with giant chocolate buttons, animal shapes and dipped fruits, and Theobroma Cacao (43 Turnham Green Terrace, W4 1RG, 8996 0431, www.theobroma-cacao. co.uk), a friendly neighbourhood shop stocked with truffles and fondants.

543

Channel the spirits of Hendrix and Handel, simultaneously

It's one of those strange juxtapositions that the city seems to delight in, but baroque composer George Frideric Handel and psychedelic rock god Jimi Hendrix lived in the same Mayfair house. Not at the same time, more's the pity, although you could be forgiven for thinking that thanks to the efforts of the curators at the Handel House Museum. The beautifully restored house displays Handel's scores in the same room as photographs of Hendrix, and – if we remember right – in 2004 they organised a 'recital' in which jazz-punk tearaways Acoustic Ladyland (known for their reworkings of Hendrix) tore into some Handel. Details of tours of the younger H's flat are available by emailing your contact details to mail@handel house.org, but for the price of a £5 admission ticket you can feel the lingering presence of two incendiary musical talents in the main house. The Thursday recitals, more likely to feature tunes by the elder H, are a delight.
Handel House Museum *25 Brook Street, W1K 4HB (7495 1685/www.handelhouse.org).*

544

Put a foot in each Hemisphere at the Greenwich Meridian

545

Become a guerilla gardener

In late 2004 green-fingered radical and Elephant & Castle resident Richard Reynolds set up his own underground movement, giving himself the mission 'to fight the filth in public spaces with forks and flowers'. The idea is to overhaul neglected areas of greenery. So, in August 2006, an intolerably weedy bed near Manor House on Seven Sisters Road (sprinkled with the obligatory needles, cans, vomit and discarded weapons) was transformed into a luscious herb garden. More recently the unremitting concrete of Elephant and Castle has been liberally planted with cheery sunflowers. Check out www.guerillagardening.org to find out which digs are planned and suggest your own.

546

Let the kids cook dinner

Make the little blighters sweat through a shift at the Kids' Cookery School in Acton (107 Gunnersbury Lane, W3 8HQ, 8992 8882, www.thekidscookeryschool.co.uk), a totally inclusive project that is aimed at promoting culinary skills, healthy eating and food awareness among children of all ages and backgrounds. It's great fun and kids love the messy experience, picking up useful kitchen skills without realising they're learning.

Kids' Cookery School

547

Shop your way round London's most perfect high street

Just over the canal from Camden Town, leafy Primrose Hill is a world away from teenage goths, down-and-outs and cheap leather jackets. And in the picturesque curve of villagey Regent's Park Road, with its pretty cafés and mix of old-fashioned shops and stylish boutiques, it has a very fine 'high street' indeed.

Approaching from the bridge that connects the neighbourhood with Chalk Farm, at No.117 Regent's Park Road is the bijou beauty shop and studio Lost in Beauty (7586 4411, www.lostinbeauty.com), where art and vintage kit create a very pretty space. A further selection of footwear (by the likes of Camper and Paul Smith, as well as its own mid-priced label) can be found at Spice (No.162, 7722 2478, www.spiceshu.co.uk).

Unsurprisingly, given the A-list properties here, there's a good choice of upmarket homeware. Ian Mankin (No.109, 7722 0997, www.ianmankin.com) specialises in natural fabrics, from cotton gingham to luxury linens, while Richard Dare (No.93, 7722 9428, www.richarddare.com) is brimming with gleaming kitchen equipment and French country crockery. Graham & Green (No.164, 7586 2960, www.grahamandgreen.co.uk) offers an array of more affordable, globally sourced furniture.

For a spot of pampering, pop into the Studio Perfumery (No.170, 07762 119037), where luxury skincare products share shelf space with perfumes like vintage Gardenia from Isabey as well as more popular labels like Creed, Acqua di Parma and Serge Lutens. Or head down side street Erskine Road to Shengaia (No.2, 7722 2838), where locals come for massages and chemical-free skincare products. Next door at Press (No.3, 7449 0081), Primrose Hill chicks find their not-trying-too-hard designer chic (along with such luxuries as Golden Goose boots, made from 100 per cent leather and already worn in for you).

Back again on Regent's Park Road is another laid-back, lovely boutique called Studio 8 (No.83, 7449 0616), which showcases a global array of labels (for men and women) and Pauric Sweeny bags. Further along is mid-range and designer fashion favourite Anna (No.126, 7483 0411, www.shopatanna.co.uk). Yummy mummies are well served by Elias & Grace (No.158, 7449 0574, www.eliasandgrace.com), which has rails of super-cute kids' clothes upstairs, and chic maternity gear and designerwear (plus Gina shoes and Luella bags) downstairs.

Locals also have an excellent selection of independents to meet their daily needs. At No.156 is the brilliant hardware/homeware shop RJ Welsh (7722 5113) and when it comes to food there's Yeoman's (No.152, 7722 4281) for organic fruit and veg as well as Italian Anthony's Delicatessen (No.146, 7722 9246). Meanwhile at Primrose Hill Pets (No.132, 7483 2023, www.primrosehillpets.co.uk), with its lovely stained-glass shopfront, local pooches are kept as glossy and groomed as their well-maintained owners.

548

Catch the Bard on grass

The Open-Air Theatre in Regent's Park (0844 826 4242, www.openairtheatre.org) is perfect for summery Shakespeare romps. They tend to be popular, so book well in advance.

549 Appreciate London's 'renegade tiling'

The trouble with graffiti is its impermanence. No sooner have you heard about Banksy's latest coke-snorting policemen than the man himself has stepped in and had the paint scrubbed away (or sold it at auction – bricks and all – for thousands of pounds). Step forward 'renegade tiling', a slightly more durable form of street art – and one that chimes happily with the current London vogue for handicrafts. Look for Space Invader designs in pretty colours high on an alley wall beside the Dragon Bar (Leonard Street, EC2) and by St Anne's churchyard (Soho, W1), as well as a Johnny Rotten on Hanway Street, W1, and along Shoreditch High Street, E1.
www.space-invaders.com

550

Visit a capital windmill

They've survived lightning strikes, high winds and years of neglect, but London's remaining windmills hang on – albeit in a variety of conditions. The small, sailless wooden mill on Wandsworth Common looks forlorn; the run-down building on Mitcham Common is no more than a decrepit shell, and the brick base in Clerkenwell is really only for serious spotters. In Brixton, however, the restored Ashby's Mill in Windmill Gardens (Blenheim Gardens, SW2) has gained something approaching iconic status, and the windmill on Wimbledon Common (Windmill Road, SW19) has its own milling museum (8947 2825, www. wimbledonwindmillmuseum.org.uk).

Ashby's Mill

551
Pick up a bargain at the city's top car boot sales

Battersea
Battersea Tech College, Battersea Park Road (entrance in Dagnall Street), SW11 5AP (07941 383588).
Lively Sunday sale, from 1.30pm.

Cuffley
Junction of Cattlegate Road & Northaw Road, Herts EN6 (01707 873360).
Large Sunday sale (Apr-Sept), from 7am.

Holloway
Opposite Odeon Cinema, Holloway Road, N7 (01992 717198).
Small but popular sale that runs every Saturday from 8am and Sunday from 10am.

Kilburn
St Augustine's Church of England Primary School, Kilburn Park Road, NW6 5ST (8440 0170).
Saturday sale from 7.30am.

Wimbledon
Wimbledon Stadium, Plough Lane, SW17 0BL (01932 355538).
Great bargains on furniture and crockery at this Saturday sale from 7am; there's also a Wednesday sale at 10am.

Wood Green
New River Sports Centre, White Hart Lane, N22 5QW (01992 468619).
Friday sale from 6am.

552
Eat Indian street food at Imli

You don't have to travel to Chowpatty Beach to share the sensations millions of Indians enjoy every day; instead, go to Soho. At Imli, the spacious, contemporary – and considerably cheaper – offshoot of popular north Indian restaurant Tamarind in Mayfair, Indian 'tapas' is the hook. And it works: don't miss the seared slices of masala grilled beef, served atop mild cumin and turmeric mash with (a mouth-watering masterstroke) a coriander and avocado dip.
Imli *167-169 Wardour Street, W1F 8WR (7287 4243/www.imli.co.uk).*

553

Do the British Museum in your lunchbreak

Start at the main entrance at Great Russell Street and jog up the steps into Norman Foster's impressive glass-roofed Great Court. Don't dawdle. Swerve left into Ancient Civilisations (Gallery 8) – via the Reading Room to soak up the calm – and check out the Rosetta Stone. Next: the Elgin Marbles (Gallery 18), still causing rows between the British and Greek governments. Take a moment to reflect on our great nation's talent for plunder; humming the national anthem might help here.

Bound up the West Stairs to the Egyptian Galleries. Note the stunning Turkish and North African mosaics on the way. Forge ahead to Gallery 62 for a gander at the lavishly decorated coffins. Warning: you may need to use pointed elbows to fend off snotty-nosed schoolkids – there's no time to stand politely aside while they get their mummy-fix. Keep your eyes peeled for the turquoise shabtis tucked away in the corner of Gallery 63 – these figurines were buried with the deceased to do agricultural work in the afterlife. Before you jog on, look over the at-a-glance-guide to mummification by the door. Now press ahead to Gallery 56. First a breather in front of the Queen of the Night, a detailed relief of a Mesopotamian goddess, then sprint down the East Stairs, dominated by a 36-foot carved red cedar Canadian Totem.

Dash around the Enlightenment Gallery. If you've been keeping an eye on the clock, you should have enough time to visit the hands-on table to play with fossils, ancient pots or tiles. Try not to steal anything.

And that's it. Head for the exit, not forgetting to leave a donation in one of the boxes before you dash out of the door. Much is needed since the admission charge was scrapped in 2001.

British Museum *Great Russell Street, WC1B 3DG (7323 8000/www.thebritishmuseum.ac.uk).*

554 Participate in (or maybe just watch) the Tranny Olympics

Playing 'Pin the Cock on the Tranny' is, admittedly, not everyone's cup of tea – neither, we imagine, is doing a 100-yard-dash down Hoxton Street in size 11 patent leather heels very good for your posture – but them's the breaks if you want to be a tranny sporting champion. The third annual event was held here in August 2009.

British Museum

555 Have an old-fashioned knees up at the Palm Tree

East End boozers can be a little unwelcoming to those who haven't spent the last 50 years living in the area; local pubs for local people, in other words. The Palm Tree (Haverfield Road, E3 5BH, 8980 2918) is a little different. The welcome is usually warm at this Mile End boozer, and the decor in the timewarp front bar is little short of extraordinary. It's best approached on weekends, when a surprisingly swingin' jazz group set up in the corner and back a pro-am selection of local crooners as they belt their way through standards written before you were born.

556 Pay your respects to Grimaldi, the king of clowns

Clowns from all over the country head to London to take part in the service at All Saints Church (Livermere Road, E8) in early February. It's tempting to picture the pilgrimage in slapstick terms – lots of tiny cars puttering up to the steps of the church and then falling comically to pieces while the assembled throng throw custard pies at each other – but in fact the event has a serious purpose: reminding the world of the pioneering work done by a true theatre maverick. To learn more about Grimaldi, visit the Clowns International Gallery Museum (see p61).

557 Take the scenic route on the RV1

Sarah Guy pays her fare and hops aboard to ride the capital's star-studded bus route.

As an alternative to the better known sightseeing tours through town, the RV1 takes a lot of beating. It's not always fast, but it is fascinating – and it offers the chance to cross the river twice in a short space of time. Board the bus at the start of the route, opposite Tower Gateway DLR, and get off to a majestic start with the Tower of London on your right. St Katharine's Dock is on your left as you glide over Tower Bridge, heading towards City Hall and Shad Thames on the south side of the river. The bus turns right down Tooley Street, passing along the way Winston Churchill's Britain at War Experience (64-66 Tooley Street, SE1 2TF, 7403 3171, www.britainatwar.co.uk), the London Dungeon (28-34 Tooley Street, SE1 2SZ, 7403 7221, www.thedungeons.com), Hay's Galleria (Tooley Street, SE1, 7940 7770, www. haysgalleria.co.uk) and, just behind the Galleria, HMS *Belfast* (see p127), before curling round Southwark Cathedral and Borough Market. It then heads down Southwark Street and continues its run parallel to the Thames. If you haven't been tempted off the bus by the market and its myriad eating options – the likes of Tapas

Brindisa (18-20 Southwark Street, SE1 1TJ, 7357 8880), Roast (see p37) and Konditor & Cook (10 Stoney Street, SE1 9AD, 7407 5100, www.konditorandcook.co.uk) are open even when the stalls aren't – you may crack at the sight of the Table (see p186), a stylish and wallet-friendly café. Almost exactly opposite, hidden behind the main road (and less than two minutes away) is Tate Modern (see p190). The route continues to almost hug the river, giving you a glimpse of the water as it skirts Blackfriars Bridge, then whizzes along Upper Ground, past Gabriel's Wharf and the assorted cultural and culinary delights of the South Bank. The bus gets as far as the London Eye (see p132) before doubling its way back along York Road, round the London IMAX (see p214) and across Waterloo Bridge. Then it's just a short hop part way along the Aldwych, and left down Catherine Street before passengers are deposited in Covent Garden within sight of the piazza. OK, it isn't a Routemaster, but it is a charming route. Buses start at 6am, and the last one leaves Tower Gateway just after midnight (earlier on Sundays).

558

Meditate at the London Buddhist Centre
The building used to be a fire station, but chilled out considerably in 1978 when it was transformed into one of the largest urban Buddhist centres in Europe. The LBC (51 Roman Road, E2 0HU, 0845 458 4716, www.lbc.org.uk) offers daily meditation classes, organises retreats and works in the wider community through outreach projects.

559 Eat incredible Indian food at Painted Heron

Some Indian chefs chase Michelin stars; others are busy penning cookery books or being on the telly. Chef Yogesh Datta, on the other hand, has been quietly making culinary waves at this upmarket Chelsea restaurant. We've had some of our most thrilling Indian meals ever here. We almost swooned at the perfection of the butter chicken and the dun-coloured pilau rice was great too: fragrant with cardamom, cloves and cinnamon. More offbeat dishes, such as duck tikka with mint chutney, or the juicy tiger prawns in a lime pickle marinade, were perfectly balanced and presented and, on our last visit, even a dish as ubiquitous as kulfi was exemplary: served, as it was, as a lollipop but with a texture like butter. And with its stylishly stark decor of cream walls festooned with gorgeous monochrome contemporary art, Painted Heron is a seriously impressive venue.
Painted Heron *12 Cheyne Walk, SW10 0DJ (7351 5232/www.thepaintedheron.com).*

560 Drink martinis above Bermondsey Abbey

Designed, as they say, to resemble a Mediterranean market place, Dell'Aziz does a pretty good job of being all things to all men: pop in for deli fare, nibble tapas, pig out on mezze – or sip cocktails in the bar with a glass floor that looks down onto the 11th-century foundations of Bermondsey Abbey. Amen to that.
Dell Aziz *11 Bermondsey Squre, SE1 3UN (7407 2991/www.delaziz.co.uk).*

561 Take sample sips at the Great British Beer Festival

During this (not surprisingly) popular event, tens of thousands of visitors get to sample over 500 real ales plus 200 foreign beers as well as lager, cider and perry. Hiccups, belches and hangovers are guaranteed. The annual festival takes place at Earl's Court in early August; see www.camra.org.uk for exact dates.

562 Ride a recumbent in Dulwich Park

Ever heard of a recumbent? Essentially, it's a special type of bicycle that allows the cyclist to get around while putting his feet up. They're available for hire at Dulwich and Battersea Parks, for £10 per hour. So much more civilised than your average bike, the recumbent is perfect for Dulwich Park's car-free, road-lined flatness, and is a great way to see the park's azaleas, rhododendrons and rockery.

563 Visit the Notting Hill Coronet for cheap flicks on a Tuesday

One of London's finest cinemas, the Coronet was famously the last London cinema to allow smoking, and also appeared in the unwaveringly shmaltzy *Notting Hill*. It's also a great place to see cheap flicks, offering half-price admittance on Tuesdays, when all shows are a bargain £3.50.
Notting Hill Coronet *103 Notting Hill Gate, W11 3LB (7727 6705/www.coronet.org).*

564 Buy weird and wonderful fruit and veg at Queen's Market

Of all the markets in London, Upton Park's 100-year-old market has perhaps the most ethnically diverse produce for sale. Adjacent to Upton Park tube, and loomed over by an unprepossessing 1960s tower block, Borough Market it is not. But as a source of Asian and Caribbean ingredients – think everything from baskets of apples to raw fish bones – Queen's Market is superb. Bustling every weekday morning, the market traders and other locals recently successfully fought off the threat of redevelopment that had been looming over the market for a few years. Hurrah to that we say: it would have been a shame to lose a market that not only embraces the diversity that makes London what it is, but also lays it out, side by side, basket by basket.
Queen's Market *off the junction of Green Street and Queen's Street, E7 (www.friendsofqueens market.org.uk).*

565

Take in the view (with two feet on the ground) from Archway's 'suicide bridge'...

It mightn't sound nice, but the views from this infamous bridge across Archway Road, N19, are breathtaking. Go in a happy mood.

566 ...then cross London's other best bridges

Albert Bridge
SW3, SW11

Chelsea Bridge
SW1, SW8

Floral Street Bridge
Royal Ballet School, WC2

Green Bridge
Mile End Park, E3

Hungerford Bridge
WC2, SE1

Millennium Bridge
EC4, SE1

Pedestrian Bridge
Royal Victoria Dock, E16

Pier 6 Passenger Bridge
Gatwick Airport

Pontoon Bridge
East India Dock, E14

Rolling Bridge
Paddington Basin, W2

567 Learn to make sushi

Chefs from the Japan Centre's in-house restaurant Toku (212 Piccadilly, W1J 9HG, 7255 8255) lead small sushi- and sashimi-making classes every month. Priced from £140, the sessions last two-and-a-half hours and include a starter kit of Japanese ingredients to take home. Visit www.sushi-courses.co.uk for details.

568

Get stuffed (and enjoy London taxidermy)

Dover Street Market
17-18 Dover Street, W1S 4LT (www.dover-streetmarket.com).
Stuffed animals and birds are on display on five floors of this fashion store.

Florence Nightingale Museum
St Thomas' Hospital, 2 Lambeth Palace Road, SE1 7EW (7620 0374/www.florence-nightingale.co.uk).
Florence's beloved owl Athena, now stuffed, is on display at this museum (which will reopen in May 2010) dedicated to the great nurse.

Horniman Museum
100 London Road, SE23 3PQ (8699 1872/ www.horniman.ac.uk).
Look out for Edward Hart's fine collection of mounted birds (*see also p195*).

Natural History Museum
Cromwell Road, SW7 5BD (7942 5000/ www.nhm.ac.uk).
As well as its famous collection of dinosaur bones, the museum has a number of stuffed animals, including an enormous polar bear.

Les Trois Garçons
1 Club Row, E1 6JX (7613 1924/www.lestrois garcons.com).
Check out the striking giraffe's head at this stylish French restaurant. There's also a hyena, a tiger and a bulldog. In a tutu.

569
See signs of spring at the Isabella Plantation

In April or May this beautiful woodland garden in Richmond Park is heaven for flower lovers – this is when the azaleas and rhododendrons blossom. The sound of woodpeckers, and a meandering stream complete the wilderness feel. The plantation was begun more than 50 years ago and has been maintained organically for 15 years.

570
Get a collagen facial at Elemis

Busy city life is left behind as you walk down the narrow cobbled lane to this spa: a visit here is always an intensely relaxing experience. The excellent Pro-Collagen Quartz Lift facial (£115 for 75 minutes) will soften fine lines and leave your skin feeling cool and smooth. It all smells fabulous too.
Elemis Day Spa *2-3 Lancashire Court, W1S 1EX (7499 4995/www.elemis.com).*

571
Ponder the fourth plinth

Nowhere in London gives a better sense of Britain's long-departed imperial pomp than Trafalgar Square, dominated by the 185-foot column of Lord Nelson and three plinth-borne statues of 19th-century luminaries. Screw them: it's the fourth plinth, on the north-west corner, opposite the National Gallery's Sainsbury Wing, that's the interesting one. It was designed and built by Sir Charles Barry to display a statue of a horse, but no one stumped up the cash. It was then empty for 158 years until 1998 when some bright spark decided to plonk some modern art on it – in turn, sculptures by Mark Wallinger, Bill Woodrow and Rachel Whiteread. This led to the idea of the Fourth Plinth project, where the space is home to an ongoing series of temporary works of art from leading national and international artists. Marc Quinn, whose controversial *Alison Lapper Pregnant*, a 12-foot statue in glossy Carrara marble of a female artist born with no arms and shortened legs, argued the fourth plinth could be a symbol of London's respect for tradition that was simultaneously forward-looking, challenging itself through constant reinterpretation. We concur. As did many other Londoners in the summer of 2009 when they took to the plinth in their hundreds (one after another, for an hour each, over the course of 100 days) as part of Antony Gormley's *One and Other* project. Next up? Yinka Shonibare's scale replica of HMS Victory – in a giant glass bottle. We hope that local boy Nelson will approve. See www.fourthplinth.co.uk for more details.

572 Visit the Museum of Brands

Derek Hammond visits the heroic cavalcade of nostalgic products and their packaging.

Robert Opie's parents were celebrated collectors of children's lore and literature, and his brother, James, was already developing an expert's obsession with toy soldiers, so it probably didn't create too much of a stir when the pasty 16-year-old arrived home one day with a Munchies wrapper and declared his intention never to throw away anything ever again.

'It was like a blinding flash of light,' he says of that day in Inverness, 1963. 'It occurred to me that if I saved the wrapper from every product I bought, collectively they'd represent a social history of daily life in Britain. I grew up thinking that every house had its own museum.'

Ten thousand yoghurt pots later a tiny cross-section of Robert Opie's gigantic mountain of beautiful junk was opened to the public in 2005 on a quiet, stuccoed mews a couple of minutes off Portobello Road. To walk through the magnificently cluttered time tunnel of cartons and bottles, toys and advertising displays is to locate your own place in history. Time after time, you're sent mentally skittering back through the years, be it by a Hovis Coronation periscope, a '60s holiday brochure, a Bionic Crisis game or that packet of Country Store breakfast muesli that tasted like soggy wood chips.

As Opie has hinted, the Museum of Brands, Packaging and Advertising actually does far more than it says on the tin: 'My museum is not just about the history of packaging, it's about the story of Everyman.'

Archly arranged by Opie himself so as to stimulate the imagination as well as tug at the heartstrings, there are hundreds of subtle statements and bold question marks built into this far-from-random 120-year history of consumerism, culture, design, domestic life, fashion, folly and fate.

Why did certain brands dating back to Victorian or Edwardian times – Schweppes, Swan Vestas, Brasso, Bournville cocoa – manage to prosper, while others – Franklyn's Superfine Shagg, Lazenby's Jelly Crystals, HJ Simlick's London Improved Flaming Fuses – fell by the wayside? Did those bizarre hand-pumped vacuum cleaners really work? Is there still such a thing as a bile bean and, if so, does it still guarantee 'Radiant HEALTH and a Lovely FIGURE'? Whatever happened to the little bloke in the bowler hat who appeared on tins of Nesquik?

Out of the thousands of visitors who have taken the tour since the museum opened (admission £5.80, concessions £3.50), it's likely that every one went home with their own favourite impressions. Personally, I'd love to sample a sprinkling of Vencatachellum S Loganath Pavasal's catchy curry powder from the 1920s, and relished the cascading time-travel experience of watching brands such as HP Sauce and Johnson's Baby Powder subtly transmogrify over the years.

Museum of Brands, Packaging & Advertising *Colville Mews, Lonsdale Road, W11 2AR (7908 0880/www.museumof brands.com/www.robertopiecollection.com).*

ART FOR LESS

£5.50
WINSOR & NEWTON
COTMAN WATERCOLOUR
POCKETS SKETCHERS BOX
RRP £11.50

LESS THAN HALF PRICE

£8.95
WINSOR & NEWTON
WINTON OIL 200ML
TITANIUM WHITE
DOUBLE PACK
RRP £22

LESS THAN HALF PRICE

SPECIAL OFFER

£9.95
MOLESKINE
SKETCHBOOK
13X21CM
100 PAGES
RRP £12.95

£12.50
MOLESKINE
WATERCOLOUR
NOTEBOOK
9X14CM 200GSM
RRP £14.50

SPECIAL OFFER

HALF PRICE

£6.85
FABER CASTELL
9000 8B-2H
12 DRAWING PENCILS
RRP £13.75

£8.50
REEVES 16x12
TRIPLE PACK CANVAS
RRP £22.99

LESS THAN HALF PRICE

£12.95
CASS ART
HOG BRUSH PACK
SET OF 6
RRP £21.20

£3.95
DALER-ROWNEY OIL PASTEL
SET OF 24 RRP £10.45

LESS THAN HALF PRICE

SPECIAL OFFER

£6.95
SEAWHITE A5
CONCERTINA
SKETCHBOOK
70 PAGES 140GSM

£4.95
LETRASET PROMARKER 5 SETS
RRP £9.95

HALF PRICE

£10.50
WINSOR & NEWTON
HENRY & WILLIAM
COLLECTION INK
SET OF 8X14ML
RRP £22

LESS THAN HALF PRICE

CASS PROMISE – CREATIVITY AT THE LOWEST PRICES. WE'RE CONFIDENT OUR PRICES CAN'T BE BEATEN

FLAGSHIP STORE: 66-67 COLEBROOKE ROW
ISLINGTON N1, 5 MINS FROM ANGEL TUBE, 020 7354 2999

ALSO AT: 13 CHARING CROSS RD WC2 (NEXT TO THE NATIONAL GALLERY), 24 BERWICK ST W1
220 KENSINGTON HIGH ST W8. ALL STORES OPEN 7 DAYS WWW.CASSART.CO.UK

573 *Play bar billiards*

Providing an ideal, not too arduous, workout to accompany a pint, bar billiards involves sinking balls in holes of varying difficulty, without knocking down the skittles that protect the most high-scoring holes. A time limit is set on each game (eventually a bar drops inside the table preventing any more balls returning to be replayed), so – unlike billiards and snooker – even clueless novices know they won't be stuck at a game for hours. There are bar billiards at Pembury Tavern (90 Amhurst Road, E8 1JH, 8986 8597), Selkirk (60 Selkirk Road, SW17 0ES, 8672 6235, www.theselkirk.co.uk) and the Dog and Bell (116 Prince Street, Deptford, SE8 3JD, 8692 5664).

574 *Get instant karma in Holland Park*

Visit the beautiful Kyoto Gardens: the bridge at the foot of the waterfall is one of the city's most peaceful spots.

575

Sit by the Barbican lake

The Barbican lake sits in the middle of the Barbican Centre, and is worth remembering as an unlikely haven in an overwhelmingly concrete City. Take your coffee (from the rather corporate café) and sit at one of the outdoor tables and gaze out over the water, taking in the fountains, the waterfall (at the eastern end), St Giles's church (directly opposite the café) and the nature. Highlights include waterlilies in summer, mallards, moorhens and their offspring in season and the occasional heron. You can even pop out here during the interval – it's just as lovely at night.

576 *Get lost for words at the London International Mime Festival*

Mimefest was founded in 1977 and is now one of the world's most important visual theatre festivals. The event incorporates shows for children and adults, with performances by rising stars as well as a multitude of established names in the fields of circus arts, puppetry, physical theatre and live art. The festival takes place in venues across London (including the ICA, the South Bank Centre, the Barbican, the Clore Studio at the Royal Opera House and the cavernous Shunt vaults under London Bridge train station) for two weeks every January.

London International Mime Festival
*35 Little Russell Street, WC1A 2HH
(7637 5661/www.mimefest.co.uk).*

577 *Visit London's loveliest tube stations*

Everybody has their favourite tube station – and we don't mean the one you get off at to stumble home after a night on the sauce. For many people the beautiful architecture of St James's Park or Charles Holden's alien spacecraft Southgate station get them the nod. For some, the wonderful Eduardo Paolozzi mosaics are sufficient to raise Tottenham Court Road above its essential grottiness. For others the entrance to Temple wins for its oddly continental jauntiness. And that doesn't even touch on the stations we love for their cheeky quirks: Arsenal, because the tiling still clearly designates the station 'Gillespie Road' more than six decades since the name was changed; Bank, for the thrills of the Central Line's paradigmatic 'Mind the Gap' bend; even the ludicrous, tourist-baiting proximity of the Charing Cross/ Embankment and Leicester Square/Covent Garden pairs. But if we had to recommend just one station you have to see in all its architectural glory, it has to be this one: Canary Wharf. Sir Norman, we salute you.

Music is my radar

John Lewis **describes a rock 'n' roll journey through central London.**

Start at the King & Queen pub (1 Foley Street, W1W 6DL, 7636 5619), near what was Middlesex Hospital. This could be the unsung birthplace of British rock 'n' roll – the site of Bob Dylan's UK debut at a folk night organised by English folk legend Martin Carthy in December 1962. Ponder the extraordinary fact that this entire area was filled with squats until the early 1980s (Boy George squatted in several flats around Fitzrovia) as you get to Charlotte Street (the title of a Lloyd Cole song). Head south and turn left on to Goodge Street (the subject of Donovan's 1965 hymn to scoring dope, 'Sunny Goodge Street'). When you hit Tottenham Court Road, continue south and you'll reach the Odeon cinema at No.31, the basement of which once housed Pink Floyd's famous UFO (pronounced 'you-foe') nightclub, home to dozens of psychedelic happenings between 1966 and 1967. A few doors down, at the junction of Oxford Street and Tottenham Court Road, you'll happen upon the giant statue of Freddie Mercury that stands outside the

Dominion Theatre marking the entrance to the seemingly invincible musical that is Ben Elton's *We Will Rock You*. The theatre stands next to a site that, in its previous incarnation as a Horseshoe pub, housed some of London's finest bands between 1967 and 1982. Across the road is Hanway Street, a seedy, piss-stinking, late-night alleyway that's furnished with a quirky record shop (On The Beat, No.22), a specialist DJ equipment outlet (Westend DJ, Nos.10-12) and London's best vinyl jukebox (Bradley's Spanish Bar, Nos.42-44, *see p228*).

We're going to continue our journey south. As you cross over Oxford Street (immortalised in song by Everything But The Girl) and turn on to Charing Cross Road make sure you avert your tear moistened eyes from the former site of the legenary London Astoria (No.157). The giant art deco music hall hosted everyone from the Rolling Stones to Nirvana to the ever-popular Saturday nightclub G.A.Y. until it was forced out by the developers of Crossrail. Not to worry though, there's plenty more to see

nearby. On the left-hand side of Charing Cross Road you'll find Denmark Street, not only the home of the wonderfully intimate 12 Bar Club (22-23 Denmark Place), but also the hub of London's music industry for more than a century – both as the home of sheet-music publishing (it became Britain's answer to New York's 'Tin Pan Alley') and, later, as the home of dozens of tiny rehearsal studios (everyone from the Beatles to the Pistols played there). Now it's the place to go shopping for guitars. These music shops also creep out of Denmark Street: there are two fine folk instrument shops back in Rathbone Place, and others dotted along Charing Cross Road all the way down to Cambridge Circus.

Head westwards into Soho proper, passing the Borderline (in Orange Yard, off Manette Street) where Prince played a secret late-night gig, and you reach Greek Street. At No.49 you'll find what used to be the fabled Les Cousins, an all-night folk and blues venue that hosted the likes of Cat Stevens, Davey Graham, John

'The former Crosse & Blackwell pickle factory has hosted everyone from the Rolling Stones to Nirvana and was where Richey Edwards played his last ever gig with the Manic Street Preachers in 1994.'

Martyn, Bert Jansch and Paul Simon in the 1960s and early '70s. On neighbouring Frith Street is Ronnie Scott's (No.7, *see p288*), still Europe's best-known jazz venue and the site of Jimi Hendrix's last performance; he jammed onstage with Eric Burdon and War the night before he died in September 1970.

Walk south past the coffee bars on Old Compton Street (as documented by the Al Stewart song of the same name) and cross Shaftesbury Avenue into Chinatown to find the original Ronnie Scott's venue. There is now a Japanese restaurant at 39 Gerrard Street, but this is where all four Beatles went to watch Roland Kirk perform in 1963. A few doors down, No.48 used to be, until 2004, the Dive Bar, the gay pub under the King's Head that is namechecked in the Pet Shop Boys' song 'West End Girls'. At 13 Wardour Street you'll find an Irish pub that was the site of the Pogues' chaotic first stage appearance in 1981; ironically, it wasn't an Irish pub then, but a poncey New Romantic club called Cabaret Futura. A few doors down at No.33 was the Wag Club, above an Irish pub that used to be the Flamingo (where Billie Holiday played a secret gig in 1954). The Wag and the Flamingo were the joint cradle of London's R&B scene, where the likes of Georgie Fame, Geno Washington and Eric Clapton would play all-night gigs to Caribbean immigrants, US servicemen, prostitutes and hip young London soul boys and girls. The soul boy tradition continued until the late 1980s, when the Wag hosted legendary funk and rare groove nights.

Continue up Wardour Street (immortalised in the Jam's 'A-Bomb in Wardour Street'), back across Shaftesbury Avenue, and you'll get to a swanky Cuban-themed bar at No.90 called Floridita. This used to be the Marquee, the rock 'n' roll temple where the Stones, the Kinks and the Small Faces all played definitive shows. It also hosted Led Zeppelin's London debut as the New Yardbirds in October 1968. Just round the corner on the right is Trident Studios at 17 St Anne's Court, birthplace of the Beatles 'Hey Jude' and the studio where Queen, David Bowie, Elton John, Lou Reed and Marc Bolan had their most productive recording sessions in the 1970s.

Move westwards and you reach the market on parallel Berwick Street, Soho's record shop

'Heddon Street is the faceless mews where David Bowie posed for the front cover of Ziggy Stardust and the Spiders from Mars. Recreate Ziggy's posture by putting your foot up on a tea chest (you might want to bring one with you).'

heartland. It boasts several specialist dance, reggae and jazz outlets, including second-hand veteran Reckless Records (Nos.26 and 30) and Sister Ray (Nos.34-35), which, under its old name Selectadisc, adorned the cover of Oasis's 1995 album (*What's the Story) Morning Glory*. The excellent Sounds of the Universe is just around the corner at 7 Broadwick Street.

Travel further west on Broadwick Street and you reach Carnaby Street, the subject of a Jam song and once the mecca of British youth culture. To the north is the London Palladium (8 Argyll Street), the music hall that hosted era-defining gigs from the likes of Louis Armstrong, Duke Ellington, Frank Sinatra, the Beatles, Kate Bush and the Smiths – but continue west, crossing Regent Street, then head south on the far side. You'll shortly reach Heddon Street, the faceless mews where David Bowie posed for the front cover of *Ziggy Stardust and the Spiders from Mars*. Recreate Ziggy's posture by putting your foot up on a tea chest (we can't guarantee there'll be one, so you might want to bring your own) and enjoy a break.

579

Step in the studmarks of genius

With minor variations between clubs, the format of a football stadium tour is the same wherever it is conducted. First a stroll around the stands, then you're guided into the inner sanctum: the home dressing room (perhaps with a photo-op under the named and numbered shirt of your favourite imported utility midfielder), then a trot down the tunnel, imagining the sweaty palm of a club mascot clutched in your bling-ringed mitt and, at last, out on to the hallowed turf. Once you've paid homage to the home ground, head off for a whizzy tour of Wembley Stadium (www.wembleystadium.com, £15 adults, £8 children).

Arsenal

Emirates Stadium (Ashburton Grove, N7 7AF, 7704 4504, www.arsenal.com) is a 60,000-seat stunner. Standard tours (£12) include a visit to the museum. Dedicated fans might fancy the 'Legends' tour (£35), which includes a brief Q&A and signing session with a former player.

Charlton

Tours of the Valley (Floyd Road, SE7 8BL, 0871 226 1905, www.cafc.co.uk) normally cost £15 for adults and £10 for under-14s – the price includes lunch in Floyd's. Tours are sporadic, usually taking place in the summer holidays. Call 8333 4040 or email sales@cafc.co.uk to book.

Chelsea

The standard tour at Stamford Bridge stadium (Fulham Road, SW6 1HS, 0871 984 1955, www.chelseafc.com) costs £15; the 'Legends' option is £75.

Fulham

Craven Cottage tours (Stevenage Road, SW6 1HS, 0870 442 1234, www.fulhamfc.com) are conducted throughout the season (subject to home games) on Sundays (including lunch, £35 for adults, £17 children) and one Saturday a month (£9.50 adults, £6.50 under-12s. For more information or to book call 7384 4777.

Tottenham Hotspur

Tours of White Hart Lane (748 High Road, N17 0AP, www.tottenhamhotspur.com) run every non-match Saturday at 11am and 1pm, and cost £14.25 adults, £7.60 under-17s, free under-3s. Call 0844 844 0102 or email tours@tottenhamhotspur.com.

West Ham

Tours at Upton Park (Green Street, E13 9AZ, www.whufc.com) often happen during half-term; check the website for planned dates. They cost £10 adults, £6 children and include access to the museum. Call 0870 112 2700 to book.

580

Get lost over a cocktail in Lost Society

This two-storey bar and restaurant in Battersea is one hell of a place. Like the fantasy country-house party of your dreams, there's something of a roaring twenties feel to the Lost Society. On the ground floor there's a number of differently styled, but all equally decadent, bar areas, plus a little garden terrace – perfect for summer drinking. Upstairs, the pitched roof with exposed columns and beams is hung with an enormous chandelier, giving the space gloriously louche appearance. Deep-turquoise leather banquettes and cubes line bare brick walls decorated with painted peacocks (the live ones can preen themselves before the numerous mirrors). The drinks menu has a fine global choice of bottled beers, but it's the cocktails that demand special attention. On our last visit, an Amaretto Sour was a perfectly blended combo of Di Saronno shaken with lemon juice, sugar, bitters and egg white, while a vodka martini (Grey Goose, with a twist of lemon) was top-notch.

Lost Society *697 Wandsworth Road, SW8 3JF (7652 6526/www.lostsociety.co.uk).*

581 Order a lassi with your meal at the New Asian Tandoori Centre

This spot is favoured by Punjabi families as the number one venue for home-style cooking. Easy-wipe tables, functional decor and a lengthy takeaway counter don't lend romance, but boisterous bonhomie between staff and customers gives the café a cosy appeal. No one else churns out lassi as well as this: ice cold, sometimes flavoured with mango, sometimes left plain, these coolers make a marvellous meal when accompanied by puffed bhaturas (leavened deep-fried bread, like pooris but softer) and sweet-sour chickpeas.

New Asian Tandoori Centre *114-118 The Green, Southall, Middx UB2 4BQ (8574 2597).*

582 Take in a candlelit recital at St Martin-in-the-Fields

Very romantic. Show up on the night (Thur-Sat, 7.30pm) and nab unreservable tickets in the aisles for £8.

St Martin-in-the-Fields *Trafalgar Square, WC2N 4JJ (7766 1100/www.stmartin-in-the-fields.org).*

583 Enjoy a summer barbecue at the London Wetland Centre

A London 'secret' that everybody knows about but few people bother to visit, the London Wetland Centre is worth half-a-day of anybody's time. Forty hectares of nature reserve carved out of the south west London landscape, the Wetland Centre is home to numerous rare kinds of birds, and serves as both an introduction to ornithology and a great place to have an airy wander. It's open late on Thursday nights in the summer with half-price admission, musicians and a barbecue... though don't ask for chicken.

London Wetland Centre *The Wildfowl & Wetlands Trust, Queen Elizabeth's Walk, SW13 9WT (8409 4400/www.wwt.org.uk).*

584 Get eye-to-eye with four London corpses

Ginger

You'll find this red-haired cadaver in Room 64 of the British Museum (Great Russell Street, WC1B 3DG, 7323 8000, www.the britishmuseum.ac.uk). A naturally preserved Predynastic mummy, 'Ginger' (check out the hair) is surrounded by burial goods, including pottery vessels that were filled with food to accompany him to the afterlife.

Lindow Man

Stay in the British Museum to meet this dried-out individual. His 2,000-year-old body was discovered near Manchester in 1984 and is now exhibited in a quiet spot in Gallery 50.

Jeremy Bentham

The moral philosopher (1748-1832) eccentrically requested in his will that his body be preserved and stored in a cabinet at University College London (Gower Street, WC1E 6BT, 7679 2000). It attends official functions so that Bentham's presence can live on. The body currently has a wax head; the real one was replaced because too many of those pesky students were mucking about with it.

Minnie

Once you've found the atmospheric Petrie Museum of Egyptian Archaeology (University College London, Malet Place, WC1E 6BT, 7679 2884, www.petrie.ucl.ac.uk, *see p52*), trot along to Gallery 2 to say hello to Minnie. That's the name given by staff to the coiffured head of a mummy, whose eyebrows and lashes are still divertingly intact. The gloomy surroundings make it all wonderfully spooky.

585 *See spirals at a Japanese restaurant*

Noodle bars seem more common than fish 'n' chip shops in London these days, but it's a lot harder to find anywhere serving okonomiyaki – a kind of savoury pancake made from cabbage, dough, pieces of tempura batter, and a choice of vegetables, meat or fish. At both Abeno (47 Museum Street, WC1A 1LY, 7405 3211, www.abeno. co.uk), situated conveniently close to the British Museum, and Abeno Too (17-18 Great Newport Street, WC2H 7JE, 7379 1160), just as handy for Covent Garden, raw ingredients are cooked on a hot metal plate (teppan) in the middle of your table. Our favourite moment is when the palm-sized patties are deftly decorated with first a spiral of pale mayonnaise and then another of lustrous brown Worcestershire-style sauce squirted from hand-held bottles. Then just sit back and watch the sprinkled bonito fish flakes that waft gently as your pancake cooks through.

586

Play a mean pinball

Forget computer games and un-winnable electronic quizzes. Head for these London boozers and have a flipping good time. Wizard!

Hole in the Wall
5 Mepham Street, SE1 8SQ (7928 6196).
'Medieval Madness' machine.

Royal George
Goslett Yard, 133 Charing Cross Road, WC2H 0EA (7734 8837).
'Playboy' machine.

White Hart
69 Stoke Newington High Street, N16 8EL (7254 6626).
'Dr Who' machine.

587

Learn about ice-cream in, um, a canal museum

The London Canal Museum (12-13 New Wharf Road, N1 9RT, 7713 0836, www.canalmuseum. org.uk) is housed in a former 19th-century ice warehouse used by Carlo Gatti for his famous ice-cream, and it includes an exhibit on the history of the ice trade and ice-cream. This is the most interesting part of the exhibition as the collection looking at the history of the waterways is rather sparse. Still, everybody loves ice-cream, right? Admission £3.

588 Read in the shadow of the King George collection

This towering black storage facility in the British Library houses its priciest tomes. What to read? Our trawl through London's best books (*see p140*) might help.
British Library *96 Euston Road, NW1 2DB (0843 208 1144/www.bl.uk).*

589 Shop for posh stationery at Smythson

An old-fashioned, discreet trader – there are no price-tags! – Smythson (40 New Bond Street, W1S 2DE, 7629 8558, www.smythson.com) has been selling posh stationery to the upper-crust since 1887. These days royals, Hollywood stars, and anyone else who can afford it browse the rows of pistachio-green mock-croc writing folders, calfskin manuscript books (we're not making this up) and, the shop's trademark, pale blue featherweight paper bound in leather. There may be better-value stationery shops in London, but none match Smythson for its sheer elite-luring audaciousness. Well worth a browse; staff, it should be noted, are courteous and helpful to paupers as well as princes.

590

Lunch at the Table

The Table (83 Southwark Street, SE1 0HX, 7401 2760, www.thetablecafe.com) is a gem of a café inhabiting an architect-designed space on an otherwise grim stretch of Southwark Street. It features raw concrete walls, chunky wooden tables and benches, an outdoor courtyard, an open kitchen and plate-glass windows. A long table by the front window displays sandwiches and a superb, Mediterranean-inspired salad bar. Selections such as baby shrimp pasta salad or roast pumpkin with spinach leaves, are charged by weight and change weekly. Dishes such as chargrilled sea bream or minute steak are cooked to order at a different counter then supplemented with your choice of Italian garnishes. Wonderful.

591 Play floodlit tennis in Battersea Park

The mammoth riverside Battersea Park offers an impressive 19 flood-lit courts attached to the Millennium Arena (Albert Bridge Road, SW11 4NJ, 8871 7537). Courts cost £6.75 per hour during peak time, £6.30 off-peak, and must be booked in person.

592 *Join in with the family fun at London's galleries*

Camden Arts Centre

Offers a programme of courses – including drawing and pottery classes – every Saturday and Sunday throughout the year and also on weekdays during school holidays.

Camden Arts Centre *Arkwright Road, NW3 6DG (7472 5500/www.camdenartscentre.org).*

Dulwich Picture Gallery

Hosts kids' workshops run by art experts during school holidays, teaching them artistic basics like colour and dimension. After-school art courses include things like portrait painting and papier-mâché.

Dulwich Picture Gallery *Gallery Road, SE21 7AD (8693 5254/www.dulwichpicture gallery.org.uk).*

National Gallery

Storytelling sessions for the under-5s, creative workshops for 5-11s and practical art lessons for 12-17s will keep your kids occupied during the school holidays. The gallery also runs free artist-led family drawing sessions on the second weekend of every month. Family talks focused on viewing the paintings take place every weekend.

National Gallery *Trafalgar Square, WC2N 5DN (7747 2885/www.nationalgallery.org.uk).*

National Portrait Gallery

A varied programme of children's workshops take place every third Saturday of the month during term time and on week days during the school holidays. Kids can learn to make everything from foil jewellery to clay shoes while getting to know the gallery's collection.

National Portrait Gallery *St Martin's Place, WC2H 0HE (7306 0055/www.npg.org.uk).*

Pump House Gallery

Family workshops take place throughout the year. See the website for further specific details of artist-led sessions for children, focused around current exhibitions.

Pump House Gallery *Battersea Park, SW11 4NJ (7350 0523/www.pumphousegallery.org.uk).*

Southbank Centre

The arts complex made up of the Royal Festival Hall, Queen Elizabeth Hall and the Hayward Gallery holds frequent events (an annual literature festival, storytelling sessions hosted by eminent authors and family music days) as well as popular outdoor summer installations.

Southbank Centre *South Bank, SE1 8XX (7960 5226/www.southbankcentre.co.uk/family).*

Tate Britain

Major exhibitions are always accompanied by special activities for children, particularly during the school holidays. An 'art trolley', packed full of paints, crayons and other messy goodies, is available at weekends.

Tate Britain *Millbank, SW1P 4RG (7887 8888/www.tate.org.uk).*

Tate Modern

There's plenty here to keep children occupied, with activity trails and jazzy multimedia guides (£4) available from the information desk. Drop-in 'Start' sessions with educational games are held on Saturdays, Sundays and school holidays, and a permanent 'family zone' is open during gallery hours.

Tate Modern *Bankside, SE1 9TG (7887 8008/www.tate.org.uk).*

National Gallery

593

Dip into Hummus Bros

A small, stylish Soho fast food café that doesn't take life too seriously – and is seriously dedicated to houmous. The chickpea and tahini purée is given main-event status by being served in shallow bowls with a hollow in the middle. This is filled with such extras as chicken in tomato sauce, chunks of stewed beef, fava beans, guacamole or a mushroom mix – to be scooped up with warm white or brown pitta bread. Excellent side dishes like tabouleh, roasted aubergine and vegetable salads (plus Innocent smoothies, herbal teas and a handful of desserts) complete the success story. And a success the brothers have been, recently opening a second branch near Holborn station. At both venues, lunchtime diners pack in to sit at the long shared tables and benches. It's great-value food – no main course costs more than £8 – and diners are treated impeccably. Where else will a server bring over a glass of steaming mint tea unbidden, or a little malabi dessert, off the cuff and on the house? An excellent operation; may it continue to grow.

Hummus Bros *www.hbros.co.uk; 88 Wardour Street, W1F 0TH (7734 1311); Victoria House, 37-63 Southampton Row, WC1B 4DA (7404 7079).*

594

Experience the avant-garde at the Horse Hospital

Since 1993 the Horse Hospital has been staging a variety of esoteric arts events ranging from the screening of rare films to concerts, left-field theatre productions and art exhibitions. Recent events have included Blood Exhibition, an exploration by film makers, designers and dancers of the mysterious liquid that keeps us all going, as well as numerous indy film screenings such as *Dust and Illusions*, a history of the Burning Man music festival in Texas.

The Horse Hospital *Colonnade, WC1N 1HX (7833 3644/www.thehorsehospital.com).*

595 *Spot London weather vanes*

The Beaver
60-64 Bishopsgate, EC2
Beaver weather vane: sounds like a potential Googlewhack. But London does possess one, atop this tower on Bishopsgate. The golden rodent is a reminder of the Hudson Bay Company, purveyors of beaver pelts and other furs since 1668. They quit the spot in 1970, and stopped trading scooped-out animals in 1989.

The Chelsea Footballer
Chelsea FC, Stamford Bridge, Fulham Road, SW6
Modelled on George 'Gatling Gun' Hilsdon, who scored five goals on his Chelsea debut in 1906.

The Cricketer
Lord's Grandstand, St John's Wood Road, NW8
A treasured cricketing icon, gifted to the MCC by architect Sir Herbert Baker in 1926. The cast iron frame depicts a stooped Father Time, fiddling with his wicket.

The Dragon
St Mary-le-Bow, Cheapside, EC2
A winged dragon built by Robert Bird in 1674 sits on a Wren steeple. It's said that every one of Wren's post-fire churches featured a different weather vane design. None is finer than this nine foot-long monster, high above Cheapside. A more recent near-replica can be found on St James Bermondsey.

Gresham's grasshopper
Royal Exchange, EC2
This spindly-legged, gilded-bronze insect has sat on successive iterations of the Royal Exchange since before the great fire. The grasshopper is the symbol of Thomas Gresham, the Tudor who founded both the Royal Exchange and Gresham College.

The Mayflower
Liberty, Great Marlborough Street, W1
It's only right that this dotty shopping institution should have a maritime bauble. Its mock Tudor frontage was assembled from the timbers of two ships, HMS *Hindustan* and HMS *Impregnable* (the latter was once the largest wooden ship in the world). The weather vane was designed by EP Roberts in the 1920s and represents the Pilgrim Fathers' *Mayflower*.

A few of my favourite things

596-602

Suggs, musician and DJ

One of the places that I really love in London is the Inner Circle in Regent's Park (NW1 4NR, 7486 7905). In the spring and summer it has a wonderful rose garden – it's like something out of a fairy story, every type of rose that you could think of. The open air theatre (0844 826 4242, www.openairtheatre.org, *see p166*) is also a fantastic way to spend an afternoon. You can't rely on the weather, but it has some great shows on the programme. **When it comes to pubs, I love the Dublin Castle (94 Parkway, NW1 7AN, 7485 1773, www.dublincastle.co.uk). It's a great live music venue; Madness basically started their career there. It's still run by the same family that ran it all those years ago, and they really encourage new talent.** One of my favourite shops is James Lock & Co (6 St James's Street, SW1A 1EF, 7930 8874, www.lockhatters.co.uk). It's the only place that Nelson and Wellington ever met, as they both bought their hats there. **For lunch I love the tapas at Barrafina (54 Frith Street, W1D 4SL, 7440 1463, see p193). A lovely family own it and they only serve proper, traditional tapas – much better than a stodgy sandwich.** Whenever I'm in central London I stop in at Soho's Bar Italia (22 Frith Street, W1D 4RP, 7437 4520, *see p289*) for a coffee. It's a great place to sit and watch the vibrancy of the city. **If you're looking for the best Guinness in London, the place to go is the Toucan (19 Carlisle Street, W1D 3BY, 7437 4123, www.thetoucan.co.uk). Always full of funny old characters.** I regularly go out for dinner to St John's (91 Junction Road, N19 5QU, 7272 1587). There's always such a jolly atmosphere about it, and the standard of food and the selection of wine are fabulous. I'd recommend the Venezuelan brandy!

603

Scare yourself stupid
in Tate Modern

If you press your face to the glass on the fifth floor of the gallery (Bankside, SE1 9TG, 7887 8888, www.tate.org.uk) you can look right down into the Turbine Hall. It's a long way down.

604-612

Attend a free public lecture

British Academy
Organising public lectures for over a century, the British Academy persuades intellectuals public figures to impart their wisdom. The ticketless talks normally start at 5.30pm. Timothy Garton Ash and Lauri Taylor are recent speakers.
10 Carlton House Terrace, SW1Y 5AH (7969 5246/www.britac.ac.uk/events).

Conway Hall
The Ethical Society has encouraged freedom in moral and spiritual life through events at Conway Hall since 1929, and the venue continues to be a hub for progressive thought. Its Sunday lectures take place at 11am.
25 Red Lion Square, WC1R 4RL (7242 8032/ www.conwayhall.org.uk).

Dana Centre
This state-of-the-art (licensed) centre – affiliated to the Science Museum – encourages adults to take part in innovative evening debates about contemporary science, technology and culture. Topics such as how society's attitudes to drugs and climate change are likely to develop in the future are covered in entertaining and interactive ways. For tickets, phone the Centre or email tickets@danacentre.org.uk.
165 Queen's Gate, SW7 5HD (7942 4040/ www.danacentre.org.uk/events).

Gresham College
Gresham College was set up 400 years ago to provide free lectures. Mathematician John D. Barrow is among the eight lecturers who talk about anything from 'Danish Fairytales' to 'The maths of race fixing and money laundering'.
Barnard's Inn Hall, EC1N 2HH (7831 0575/ www.gresham.ac.uk).

National Gallery
The National Gallery runs several series of well-respected and informative talks. These include lunchtime lectures (1pm Tue-Fri), ten-minute talks (4pm Mon-Fri), 'Painting of the Month' discussions, and the 'Points of View' series (6.30pm Fri) where experts from other fields bring their non-art historical approach to bear on the collection.
Trafalgar Square, WC2N 5DN (7747 2885/www. nationalgallery.org.uk/what/events/free_events.htm).

New London Architecture
The first permanent exhibition space to be dedicated to London's architecture runs a programme of talks that highlights whatever's new in architecture and planning in the capital. The Breakfast Talk Series offers breakfast at 8am, followed by an 8.30am lecture; recent talks have covered the issues such as the impact and opportunities presented by CrossRail and 'London's Learning', a discussion of new school architecture. For tickets register on the website.
Building Centre, 26 Store Street, WC1E 7BT (7636 4044/www.newlondonarchitecture.org/talks.php).

Royal Institution of Great Britain
The popular Christmas Lectures series, which is held in December each year, is the Royal Institution's flagship event. The series was started in 1825 to present complex scientific and mathematical issues to young people in an entertaining manner – perhaps using demonstrations with animals or with magic tricks – and are always presented by top international scientists. 'The 300 million years war' lecture in 2009 will discuss the battle for supremacy between plants and animals.
21 Albemarle Street, W1S 4BS (7409 2992/ www.rigb.org).

Royal Society of Arts
The RSA runs free lectures on a wide variety of subjects. Recent talks have included 'Party conferences: who needs them?' and 'The Economic Consequences of Mr Brown'.
8 John Adam Street, WC2N 6EZ (7930 5115/ www.thersa.org/events).

University College London (UCL)
Ingest your sandwich and get some intellectual nutrition at the same time at UCL's 40-minute lunchtime lectures, intended to offer an insight into research carried out at the university. Lectures start at 1.15pm (Tue and Thur).
Darwin Lecture Theatre, Gower Street, WC1E 6BT (7679 9719/www.ucl.ac.uk/news/events).

613 *Order tapas at Barrafina*

There is just one L-shaped, marble-topped counter running around the periphery of Barrafina's small room. From your perch on a high stool you can sip a glass of dry sherry, chat to the cheery, engaging staff, and watch the steel hotplate in action as the simple and traditional tapas are prepared. The seafood is beautifully simple: sardines (crisp and meaty) a la plancha, octopus served with capers and tender, fresh prawns in garlicky butter; and the other dishes work well too, especially the roast quail, morcilla with piquillo peppers and, of course, the jamon. But care is taken over everything: our tortilla with ham and spinach was tested by no less than three members of staff to check that it both firm and juicy, the dessert was a most delicate, deconstructed crumble, and the food is accompanied by some top-notch wine (31 varieties plus seven sherries).

Sure, Barrafina is tiny (there are only 23 seats at the dining counter), doesn't take bookings and is often packed. But if you can get a stool, you'll be served some of the best tapas in the capital. And if you don't think the experience here is very Spanish, you've probably been hanging around too many back street bars in Seville

Barrafina *54 Frith Street, W1D 4SL (7440 1463/ www.barrafina.co.uk).*

Barrafina

614 *Visit the Bolan shrine*

The sycamore that Marc Bolan's car hit – on Queen's Ride in Barnes Common – has become something of a memorial site. His fans have formed a group called the T-Rex Action Group (www.marc-bolan.org), fitted a caliper to the tree to stop it from toppling and installed a bronze bust of Bolan, along with plaques for the other now-deceased members of T-Rex. Rumour has it that on 16 September, the anniversary of Bolan's death, there's an annual memorial party by the tree. Only one way to find out…

615 Stop for a coffee at the Café at Foyles

This easy going café (Foyles, 113-119 Charing Cross Road, WC2H 0EB, 7440 3207, www.foyles. co.uk) shares floorspace with Ray's Jazz, one of London's best-curated jazz collections – modern, avant-garde, soul, world and blues are all covered – so it figures that it should serve correspondingly tasteful fodder (sandwiches, cakes, juices and the like). Bench seating along the windows is perfect for solo snacking and also for watching – perhaps a little smugly – the punters come and go from the blander Borders opposite.

616 Write a script

They used to say everybody had a novel in them, but there's no money in books any more (unless you're Dan Brown – or Jordan) so the smart cookies have turned to scriptwriting. There are a number of places offering courses of various degrees of seriousness in London (see www.britfilms.com/training/shortcourses for the rundown), but one of the best is at the Script Factory (www.scriptfactory.co.uk), a body that has been developing new scriptwriters since 1996. Whether you're interested in a full-length course or a one-off masterclass presented by an established writer, the Script Factory is on hand; it also offers advice and support to those in the middle of their masterpiece.

617 Dance alfresco

You want to dance? During the daytime? Outdoors? Well, crazyhead, Dance Alfresco is for you. Organised by the co-director of Kensington Dance Studio, Kele Baker, Dance Alfresco (www.dancealfresco.org) takes place throughout the spring and summer on the Broadwalk in the middle of Regent's Park, allowing couples to learn to ballroom dance or tango in the open air. And if you are the proud possessor of two left feet, then just go along and watch – it's quite a sight, we assure you.

618 Play fives

In Britain, fives (or handball) is firmly associated with the public schools. Not surprising, really, as the three variations on the sport emerged from Eton, Rugby and Winchester. The independent educational sector is still its main focus: the principal courts in London are in smart schools. That doesn't mean fives is elitist: it is played by men and women of all ages and backgrounds, and public courts at Westway Sports Centre (1 Crowthorne Road, W10 6RP, 07790 736 719, www.westwaysportscentre.org.uk) are helping to extend participation.

619 Become more Chilean than beans

'Más chilena que los porotos' – it's a Chilean expression, all right? With an estimated 3,000 expats living in London, enjoy your own little bit of Chile in Borough at El Vergel (8 Lant Street, SE1 1QR, 7357 0057, www.elvergel. co.uk). For the perfect lunch here, arrive late – when most of the local office workers have moved on. Armed with a magazine or book, indulge in a tortilla crammed with refried beans, spring onion, coriander and guacamole. If you want a larger lunch, try a chicken or lamb stew, or the Chilean signature dish, sweet and creamy pastel de choclo (a corn pie).

620 Take it easy at May Fair

The slick Eastern-themed spa in the May Fair Hotel has a wonderful aromatic steam room. After spending some time in there, you can cool down by stepping into a fountain of crushed ice or a gentler mist (or monsoon), choose from six different massage options and then retire to a heated marble recliner in the serene relaxation room for fruit, sorbet and herbal teas.

May Fair Spa *May Fair Hotel, 1 Stratton Street, W1A 2AN (7915 2826/www.mayfairspa.com).*

621

Visit the wonderful Horniman Museum

Tea trader Frederick J Horniman assembled a great number of curiosities in this culturally active art nouveau museum (100 London Road, SE23 3PQ, 8699 1872, www.horniman.ac.uk), left to the people of London in 1901.

The main collection is divided into several sections. The Natural History Gallery contains skeletons, pickled animals, stuffed birds and insect models in glass cases, presided over since the collection opened by a plump stuffed walrus measuring 12 feet tall. The African Worlds Gallery has Egyptian mummies, ceremonial masks and a huge Ijele masquerade costume; be sure to check out the papier-mâché model of Kali dancing on Shiva, purchased by Horniman himself on a visit to Calcutta in 1894. The Centenary Gallery celebrates a century of collecting, with puppets and more masks, models and icons. In the Music Gallery, the walls are hung with hundreds of instruments of every type, with touch screens on tables for you to hear their sound and a 'Hands On' room for visitors to bash away at world instruments, such as Thai croaking toads and a bodhrán from Ireland.

A must-see is the Apostle clock on the gallery above the Natural History collection; when it chimes four o'clock, 11 apostles come out and bow to the central Jesus, while the 12th, Judas, turns away. All this is complemented by a brand new aquarium (*see p 79*) plus a regular programme of films, concerts, talks and children's workshops. The gardens, with their animal enclosure and conservatory, are also lovely, and the spacious café provides a welcome pit stop.

622

Wander through Highgate Cemetery...

With dramatic tombs topped by towering angels, shrouded urns and broken columns, Highgate exudes a Romantic atmosphere of ivy-covered neglect. The original 1839 West Cemetery (which can only be visited as part of an official tour; book ahead at weekends) is breathtaking: long pathways wind through gloomy catacombs and the graves of notables such as Christina Rossetti and chemist Michael Faraday. Prize sites include the tombs lining Egyptian Avenue (pharaonic styling being all the rage in the late 1830s) and the ring of neo-classical tombs known as the Lebanon Circle. Not quite as atmospheric, the East Cemetery – added just 15 years later – allows you to wander freely as you seek the memorials to Marx and George Eliot. The cemetery closes during burials, so call ahead.

Highgate Cemetery *Swains Lane, N6 6PJ (8340 1834/www.highgate-cemetery.org).*

623 ...then the rest of the 'magnificent seven'

Abney Park Cemetery
Stoke Newington High Street, N16 0LN (7275 7557/www.abney-park.org.uk).

Brompton Cemetery
South Lodge, Fulham Road, SW10 9UG (7351 9936/www.brompton-cemetery.org).

Kensal Green Cemetery
Harrow Road, W10 4RA (8969 0152/ www.kensalgreen.co.uk).

Nunhead Cemetery
Linden Road, SE15 3LP (7732 8396).

Tower Hamlets Cemetery
Southern Grove, E3 4PX (8983 1277).

West Norwood Cemetery
Norwood Road, SE27 9JU (7926 7900).

A few of my favourite things

624-631

Roxy Beaujolais, restaurateur

I really enjoy checking out different genres of restaurant. Before I opened the Bountiful Cow (51 Eagle Street, WC1R 4AP, 7404 0200) I did a lot of homework about steakhouses. One of the best-known places I tried was an Argentine restaurant called Buen Ayre (50 Broadway Market, E8 4QJ, 7275 9900, www.buenayre.co.uk).

I buy all the meat for my pubs from a wonderful butcher called McKanna Meats (21 Theobald's Road, WC1X 8SL, 7242 7740). I'd say they're the best in London: a proper, old-fashioned butcher shop. They do good wholesale prices, or you can just pop in for a great pork pie.

I love looking at modern architecture, for example the new portico of the National Gallery (Trafalgar Square, WC2N 5DN, 7747 2885, www.nationalgallery.org.uk). There's now an excellent view as you walk down the steps.

I love going to see arty films and productions at the Tricycle Theatre (269 Kilburn High Road, NW6 7JR, 7328 1000, www.tricycle.co.uk). It's a local community theatre with a cinema and a playhouse.

Wigmore Hall (36 Wigmore Street, W1U 2BP, 7935 2141, www.wigmore-hall.org.uk) is a very important part of London's music scene. I love chamber music, so my husband and I go regularly.

If people in London want the perfect dry martini, then they should come to the Seven Stars (53 Carey Street, WC2A 2JB, 7242 8521). I keep the gin in the freezer all the time, so it doesn't dilute. I say our martini is like a woman's breast: one is not enough, and three is too many.

The Royal Courts of Justice (Strand, WC2A 2LL, 7947 6000, www.hmcourts-service.gov.uk), which is next to the Seven Stars, is a great place for gossip. They get all the excitement.

632

Dance to swing-era American tunes

Learn your steps at the Jive Nation boot camp (www.jivemation.co.uk), then head to the Jive Party at the Rivoli Ballroom (350 Brockley Road, SE4 2BY, 8946 2664, www.london rivoliballroom.co.uk) or swing at the 100 Club's Stompin' (100 Oxford Street, W1D 1LL, 7636 0933, www.swingdanceuk.com). It's like punk never actually happened.

Rice work

You no longer have to take off to Tokyo to sample the subtleties of saké. Time Out *magazine's food editor Guy Dimond tastes the rice wine's rich range of styles right here in the capital.*

I'm picking at a sea bream, seated on the floor with my long legs tucked beneath me like badly folded origami, wearing a samurai hat made out of newspaper. In this undignified pose, the fine distinctions between junmai ginjo, dai-ginjo and lesser sakés are being explained to me. 'Kampai!' says my host, as yet another flask of premium saké is poured into my cup. I can see it's going to be a long night.

It used to be that saké scholars would have to travel to Japan, in my case the Iinuma Honke saké brewery in the Chiba Prefecture, in order to further their appreciation of the drink. Ten years ago, Londoners might have been able to find expense account sakés in the sort of Japanese restaurants frequented by oriental businessmen, or warmed-up, low-grade saké in Japanese cafés. Now several London restaurants have gone as far as installing 'saké sommeliers' to guide interested customers through ever-expanding selections.

Sayaka Watanabe (*pictured*), a trained expert from Tokyo, was London's first saké sommelier when she started work at Zuma restaurant in March 2003. Zuma (5 Raphael Street, SW7 1DL, 7584 1010, www.zumarestaurant.com) is one of a wave of Japanese restaurants that takes its saké seriously, and stocks over 40 different types. Although, like many Japanese people, she uses the term 'rice wine' to describe saké, the refined rice is in fact brewed in a process more akin to beer-making. 'It's not wine, because the brewing process is quite different, but it's the simplest way of explaining it to customers. In alcoholic strength (typically 14%-16%) it's closest to wine, and the subtleties of flavour are similar.' Having a saké sommelier was clearly a success, as Watanabe was joined by an assistant, Satomi Okubo, in 2005; Okubo is also a trained saké expert. Over the course of a week, the two of them will help nearly a third of customers choose saké to go with their meal; most of the rest still order wine. 'When I started two years ago, I found that most non-Japanese customers didn't even know what saké was. But things have really changed over those two years; I even get customers coming in asking for specific brands or styles.'

Saké comes in many guises. Saké styles range from light and refreshing to aged and slightly oxidised, and there are unpasteurised sakés that are milky in appearance. In general the most popular sakés are delicately aromatic and resemble white wines, but with a different spectrum of aromas, broadly similar to lighter sauvignon blancs. Sakés also vary from slightly sweet to very dry.

'Scholars used to travel to Japan to further their appreciation of saké; now several London restaurants have saké sommeliers.'

Watanabe trained in Japan, but the majority of London's saké sommeliers are French wine waiters who have discovered saké appreciation through wine. 'The style and character of wine and saké are similar,' says Matthieu Garros, wine sommelier turned saké sage at Umu (14-16 Bruton Place, W1J 6LX, 7499 8881, www.umurestaurant.com, *see p223*). 'We even use the same words to describe them: punchy, dry, fruity, lively. If you understand wine, you can understand saké.'

As I learnt at the Iinuma Honke brewery, the quality of saké depends on many factors, but the main one is how 'polished' the rice is – that is, how much of the coarse outer layer of the uncooked rice is mechanically ground off before the rice is steamed. Cheap saké (futsu shu) has only a quarter of the outer grain taken off; premium sakés (which tend to have the phrase 'ginjo' somewhere in the name) have as much as three-quarters; these typically cost about the same as a good bottle of wine. In Japan, saké is drunk in a great variety of shapes and designs of cup, chosen for their looks, but to get the full benefit of the aroma it is best to use a Western-style tulip-shaped wine glass, which concentrates the aromas around the rim.

Though most gaijin (non-Japanese) are used to drinking saké warm, to appreciate the complex flavours of a premium saké it is best served cold, ideally 12°C (rather like the difference between drinking mulled and chilled wine). 'Warm sakés tend to be the poorer grades,' says Morgan Selva, manager of Japanese restaurant Sumosan (26B Albemarle Street, W1S 4HY, 7495 5999, www.sumosan.com). 'We serve two warm sakés and even flavoured sakés [an innovation too far for most purists, and usually made in London rather than Japan] because there is such demand for them, but our saké sommelier, Jean-Louis Naveilhan, tries to encourage people towards the better quality chilled sakés, served in proper wine-tasting glasses. We have around 30 of these, and people tend to pay the same amount as they might for a great bottle of wine: typically £22-£50 per bottle.'

Though saké is typically paired only with Japanese dishes, pan-oriental restaurant Gilgamesh is also exploring the trend. The restaurant uses a lot of the strong South-east Asian flavours not found in Japanese food, but stocks 32 sakés, typically selling 20 or 30 bottles a week. How successful a pairing it makes is debatable as saké has a very delicate flavour, which can be destroyed by strong flavours such as chilli.

Why the surge of interest in saké? It could be the boom in Japanese food (if a food becomes popular, the drink usually follows), helped by a successful marketing campaign by new British saké importer iSake (which has created its own saké labels as well as importing other brands) making the drink seem more accessible.

Although saké drinking is on the increase in London, sales in Japan are in steady decline, because Japanese-brewed lager is seen as more 'modern' and the vodka-like Japanese spirit shochu is preferred as a 'cool' drink among young Japanese. Maybe they just don't like wearing paper samurai hats.

634

Spend a night in a swish hotel

It sounds so simple, but it's actually rather rare for Londoners to check into a plush hotel in their own city. Why do we leave these treats to the tourists? For the best stay money can buy, you'll be able to find suites at Claridge's that tip the £5,000 a night mark. But excess doesn't have to be about the green folding stuff. Room 16, for instance, at the far more modestly priced Portobello Hotel (22 Stanley Gardens, W11 2NG, 7727 2777, www.portobello-hotel.co.uk), has a round bed and a Victorian clawfoot bath in the middle of the room that Johnny Depp allegedly filled with champagne for Kate Moss.

If sharing a mattress with a screen icon (years after they slept on it) pushes your buttons, the Covent Garden Hotel (10 Monmouth Street, WC2H 9LF, 7806 1000, www.firmdale.com) is where Scarlett Johansson was resident for several months during the filming of *Match Point*. The most luscious room is the Loft Suite (from £1150), which has a mezzanine bed space – it's where Liv Tyler always stays. We also like room 110, which has windows on facing walls and so gets flooded with natural light during the day. The Gore (190 Queen's Gate, SW7 5EX, 7584 6601, www.gorehotel.com) offers the chance to sleep in Judy Garland's old bed – adding to the campery, the suite's bathroom has original hand-painted tiles depicting a chariot pulled by winged horses.

Hazlitt's (6 Frith Street, W1D 3JA, 7434 1771, www.hazlittshotel.com) has a wonderful period piece in the form of its stately Baron Willoughby suite (£300), where the sitting room is graced by the original 18th-century Jacobean panelling. We prefer the attic rooms, however, with their sloping ceilings (and floors!) and Mary Poppins views across the rooftops of Soho. There are more wonderful rooftop views from myhotel bloomsbury's myplace (11-13 Bayley Street, WC1B 3HD, 7667 6000, www.myhotels.co.uk), which is a beautiful studio apartment (£500) that has its own private roof terrace.

If size matters, the royal suites at Brown's (33 Albemarle Street, W1S 4BP, 7493 6020, www.brownshotel.com) have bedrooms and adjacent reception rooms that even past guests such as Napoleon III must have looked at with envy. The bathtubs are big enough to accommodate several soapy bodies at a time and, a nice touch this, the showers are designed for sharing, with two independent shower heads (two heads, of course, always being better than one).

Undergoing a much-anticipated £100 million restoration programme at the time of writing, the Savoy's (Strand, WC2R 0EU, 7836 4343, www.savoy-group.co.uk) beds will probably be London's hottest once the famous hotel on the Strand opens its doors again in early 2010. Keeping an essentially art deco vibe, the refurb highlights are expected to include a rooftop pool and an opulent new Royal Suite (prices currently unavailable but undoubtedly astronomical).

635

Check off London artworks at Tate Britain

The Thames above Waterloo Bridge
JMW Turner, 1830-35, Room 18.

The Pool of London
André Derain, 1906, Room 18.

State Britain
Mark Wallinger, 2007, Duveen Galleries.

Shelterers in the Tube
Henry Moore, 1941, Room 8.

Piccadilly Circus
Charles Ginner, 1912, Room 19.

Horse Sale at the Barbican
Robert Bevan, 1912, Room 19.

Camden Girls
James Boswell, 1947, passageway before Room 17.

Kensington Gravel Pits
John Constable, 1811-12, Room 11.

A Bank on Hampstead Heath
John Constable, 1820-22, Room 11.

636-645
Go deco!

Art deco is a difficult style to pin down, tipping over at its various extremities into modernism, art nouveau, Cubism and Futurism. Indeed, it wasn't until 1966 that it was formally named. Certain things can, however, be said with some authority. It is a decorative style, celebrating the innovations and preoccupations of the times (plastics, chrome, aluminium, jazz, skyscrapers), and it embraces anything from pared-down geometric forms to flamboyant Egyptian iconography. Its hallmarks include fan motifs, zigzags and careful streamlining. Maybe you think you can come up with a more workable description? Check out these essential architectural examples and have a bash.

Apollo Victoria
This Grade II-listed building, designed by Ernest Wamsley Lewis and WE Trent, opened in 1930. The exterior has two matching openings with pronounced horizontal banding and deco lettering inset in the concrete. Most of the original interior is gone, but there are various maritime motifs and typically deco railings.
17 Wilton Road, SW1V 1LL.

Battersea Power Station
Battersea Power Station's dramatic profile of fluted chimneys on stepped bases of vertically textured bricks was called a 'futurist icon' and a 'new cathedral' when it was completed in 1934. The Grade II-listed building, derelict for more than two decades, has been the focus of much-protracted planning debate. Latest estimates put the site's reopening (as a commercial and residential centre) back to 2020.
Kirtling Street, SW8 5BW.

BBC Broadcasting House
The Portland stone exterior of Broadcasting House has been compared to a ship, due to its curved and accentuated front section, clock tower and aerial mast. Designed by Val Myer and opened in 1932, the building is adorned with deco sculptural elements by Eric Gill and has a terrific foyer.
Portland Place, W1A 1AA.

Carreras Cigarette Factory
The Carreras Cigarette Factory (*pictured above*) was built to a design prepared by ME and OH Collins and opened back in 1928, its architecture inspired by Tutankhamun's Tomb. Recent refurbishment as office space restored many of the original features, including (above the entrance) two eight-foot black cats that had been removed in the 1960s. Greater London House, as the place is now known, isn't open to the public, but can be appreciated from the road.
Hampstead Road, NW1 7AD.

Daily Express Building
The modernist façade of this 1932 building – designed for the *Daily Express* newspaper by Sir Owen Williams with Ellis, Clarke & Atkinson – has a classic streamlined form, clad in shiny black Vitrolite and clear glass, with rounded corners. Robert Atkinson designed the striking interior – despite being closed to the public (it is now occupied by Goldman Sachs), the impressive entrance lobby can be seen from the street.
133 Fleet Street, EC4 2BH.

Daily Telegraph Building

With its imposing frontage, 120 Fleet Street originally housed the editorial offices and printing plant of both the *Daily* and *Sunday Telegraph*. It was designed by Elcock and Sutcliffe in 1928, with Thomas Tait – a Scot who had previously studied under Charles Rennie Mackintosh – as a consultant. Goldman Sachs, evidently great fans of Fleet Street deco, have offices in this building too.
120 Fleet Street, EC4.

Hoover Building

Apart from residents of Perivale, not many Londoners trek out here. But it's well worth the effort to see this piece of architecture – possibly the finest art deco structure in Britain. Built in 1932, the principal building is a low-lying, two-storey white structure with its front divided into 15 bays by massive Egyptian-style pillars. It also has an outstanding central doorway that is framed by a huge sun-ray design. The rear part of the building was sensitively converted into a Tesco supermarket in 1989, and the place has been celebrated in song (Elvis Costello's 'Hoover Factory').
Western Avenue, Middx UB6 8BW.

Ideal House National Radiator Company

Now Palladium House, it was designed by Gordon Jeeves and Raymond Hood and opened in 1928. Described as the 'Moor of Argyll Street', it has a polished black granite façade topped by gold Moorish- and Persian-inspired enamel-on-bronze bordering around a stepped roof.
Corner of Argyll Street & Great Marlborough Street, W1.

Isokon Building

Designed by Canadian architect Well Coates under commission from design firm Isokon, this Grade I-listed concrete block of flats (*pictured below*) was something of an experiment in communal living. Famous residents have included Agatha Christie and Bauhaus founder Walter Gropius. The building was refurbished in 2003 for the Notting Hill Housing Association.
Lawn Road, NW3 2XD.

Oxo Tower

The distinctive window design that spells out 'OXO' was an effective contrivance by Albert Moore in 1928 to get round advertising restrictions (rooftop windows were OK but rooftop advertising was not). Oxo Tower now houses shops, restaurants and flats.
Tower Wharf, Bargehouse Street, SE1 9PH.

646

Drool over the food halls in Harrods

You could admire the Mohammad Al Fayed waxwork in menswear or worship at the Dodi and Diana shrine in the basement. You could check out the ten-foot-tall gold pharoah in the Egyptian Room or try to eat and drink your way round all of the 26 (count 'em) in-store restaurants and bars. But when we're at Harrods (85-135 Brompton Road, SW1X 7XL, 7730 1234, www.harrods.com) and feeling the need for full-bore, over-the-top opulence, there's only one destination: the legendary food halls. Nor do they disappoint – chandeliers drip with ornamental grapes in fruit and veg, while the meat and game room retains its original Edwardian Royal Doulton tiling. You could even buy something to eat.

647 Laugh out loud in the Cartoon Museum

The global furore sparked by the publication of cartoons of the Prophet Mohammed in a Danish newspaper in 2006 highlighted the power and influence of the comic artform. The Cartoon Museum, which reopened in Bloomsbury in March 2006, reinforces the significance of cartoon art but also serves as a powerful reminder that cartooning is fun – you're actually encouraged to laugh out loud.

'Britain has a wonderful history of political satire,' enthuses Oliver Preston, the Cartoon Museum's chairman. 'This museum is about celebrating and promoting the very best in British cartoon art.' Opposite well-known World War II political cartoons by Low and Vicky hang gems by Thelwell – whose playful countryside images always bring a smile to the face – and Giles, whose work reveals much about what people wore, thought and did in the middle of the 20th century.

On the ground floor of this transformed former dairy, the cartoons are displayed in chronological order, starting with the early 18th century, when high-society types back from the Grand Tour introduced the Italian practice of *caricatura* to polite company. From Hogarth it moves through the much parodied *Plum Pudding* by James Gillray, plus works by John Bull and George Cruikshank (who was born around the corner from the museum) – British cartooning's 'Golden Age' (1770-1830). While 'Modern Times' may not be a label those under 50 would choose for the dates 1914 to 1961, in that section are interesting wartime cartoons and social commentary. The 'New Satire' – works published from 1961 onwards – includes Ralph Steadman, Steve Bell, Dave Brown, Matt and others on topics from Brown and Blair to mad cow disease. It is perhaps indicative of the gallery's bent that while downstairs the artists' names are immediately recognisable, upstairs – where comic strip art drawn from *2000AD*, the *Dandy*, the *Beano* and other favourites of our youth is displayed – is much more about the characters portrayed: from Rupert to Dan Dare and Judge Dredd.

Cartoon Museum *35 Little Russell Street, WC1A 2HH (7580 8155/www.cartooncentre.com).*

648 Immerse yourself in orchids at Kew

Kew's orchid festival, which runs for a month from the beginning of February each year, is a great opportunity to enjoy these most exotic of tropical flowers. Exhibits in the past have included fallen trees draped in epiphytic orchids, while the 30,000 tropical plants in the Princess of Wales Conservatory were enhanced with orchids placed among the tropical climbers on the building's support columns. If you can't make the festival itself, Kew has permanent Orchid Zones that display rare orchids throughout the year.

Royal Botanic Gardens (Kew Gardens)
Kew, Richmond, Surrey TW9 3AB (8332 5655/ information 8940 1171/www.kew.org).

649

Eye up haute fashion over lunch at Obika

As you might expect from the eaterie occupying space opposite Gucci in the Superbrands section of Selfridges, glass-and-steel Obika (400 Oxford Street, W1A 1AB, 7318 3620, www.obika.co.uk) is something of a looker. Classified as an Italian 'mozzarella bar', with two regional varieties assembled with such delicacies as wild boar salami and smoked swordfish, it serves fine food – and wine that comes care of Liberty Wines, one of the top Italian wine importers to the UK. Perhaps more crucially, one of the 'bars' overlooks the catwalk of shoppers, providing some pleasurably fashionable entertainment for solitary lunchers.

650 Buy a brand new skin at Brown's Hotel

A combination of dry skin buffing, filing, clipping and scrubbing, with a soothing foot and leg massage, nail conditioning and polishing. Pure luxury for £60. Pedicure heaven.

Brown's Hotel *33 Albemarle Street, W1S 4BP (7493 6020/www.brownshotel.com).*

651

Get acquainted with Vyner Street

Martin Coomer *takes you on a guided tour up and down London's artiest alley.*

Vyner Street is the ideal gallery strip. Hugging Regent's Canal, the semi-industrial cobbled street is located in a gallery-rich area of the East End, pioneered decades ago by the likes of Maureen Paley. What kept the art world away for so long? The answer's simple: economics. Seven or so years ago when the street was better known for its post-private view hangout (the Victory pub) than its burgeoning galleries, there was no boom in contemporary art sales. Back then, Nylon and Mobile Home set up shop here, each showing young international artists to critical acclaim. But the galleries couldn't stay the course, which pinpoints just how much the art world has changed in that short space of time. These days, the market for contemporary art is considerably hotter and London hustles to be at its centre. Started in 2003, the Frieze Art Fair attracts major collectors from around the world to the capital every October. Fringe events such as the Zoo Art Fair for younger galleries benefit from the trickle-down effect.

One person who has hung around is VINEspace director Della Gooden. Over ten years ago when most of these buildings were occupied by the rag trade, Gooden worked here as an artist. Now her gallery space at No.25A shows a stable of emerging artists and Vyner Street has the highest concentration of galleries in the East End. Gooden's space is most readily identified by its fluorescent green 'Open/Nope' neon – a piece by gallery artist Richard Box.

'The new Cork Street' was how, half-jokingly, gallerist David Risley described the street when he opened here in 2005, having had a peripatetic career as a curator and dealer (he was instrumental in setting up Zoo Art Fair in 2004). Synonymous with blue-chip galleries and, until the early 1990s, London's major art thoroughfare, Cork Street in Mayfair now languishes in relative obscurity. Risley's gallery, which represents rising stars like Masakatsu Kondo, is the product of a very different system, as are his neighbours. Until his recent move to Copenhagen, he shared the building at No.45 with two galleries: Fred and One in the Other. A stalwart of the scene, having founded the non-profit space Milch, then gone on to co-direct Rhodes + Mann, Fred Mann started this solo venture in 2005 and shows a cross-generational range of artists including painter Peter Jones (who paints slightly malevolent-looking toy monkeys), German duo Abetz/Drescher and Turner Prize nominee Cathy de Monchaux. Mann continues to branch out. In 2006 he opened a project space in Leipzig and formed a record label, Fred (Label), which has so far released music by artists as diverse as New York art rocker Guy Richards Smit and English soprano Catherine Bott. Chris Noraika's One in the Other also comes with a good pedigree. Overlooking the canal, his basement space is a handsome platform for the likes of photographer Anna Mossman and video artist Karen Russo.

The arrival in 2007 of the Wilkinson Gallery, at Nos. 50-58, confirmed Vyner Street's rise to prominence in the art world. Moving from around the corner on Cambridge Heath Road to a new 6,500-square-foot space, shows here have included work by US conceptualist Joan Jonas, Leipzig painters Tilo Baumgartel and Matthias Weischer as well as haunting landscape pieces by Elizabeth Magill.

However, the real pleasure is that, for the moment at least, the street has not become too off-puttingly spiffy. The big guns have not scarred off interesting smaller spaces like Ibid Projects at No.21, notable for painters like Christopher Orr and Anj Smith, and the not-for-profit Alma Enterprises at No.1, home to the curatorial group LAND. They are both essential components of a healthily diverse scene.

652 Watch a military re-enactment

The Royal Gunpowder Mills were involved in the making of explosives for more than three centuries. Gunpowder production began here back in the 1660s; later, the manufacture of guncotton, nitro-glycerine, cordite paste and the highly explosive tetryl was undertaken; then, after World War II, the mills became a research centre for non-nuclear explosives and propellants. Few of the more than 20 historic buildings on the 175-acre site have been renovated, in a deliberate attempt to convey their long and complex past. The costumed battle re-enactments are popular and usually involve some kind of live firing. Charge! Admission £7.20, concessions £6.20.
Royal Gunpowder Mills *Beaulieu Drive, Waltham Abbey, Essex EN9 1JY (01992 707370/www.royalgunpowdermills.com).*

653 Walk in peace

A slow, silent, meditative walk in peace, for peace, this gathering takes place on the first Sunday of every month, starting from the café at Speakers' Corner in Hyde Park, W1. For more details, check online at www.walkinpeace.org.

654 Discover dogs at Discover Dogs

Far less formal than Crufts, Discover Dogs is an annual canine extravaganza that continues to go from strength to strength. Held at Earl's Court in mid November (check the website www.discoverdogs.org.uk for exact dates), you can meet more than 180 dogs, discuss pedigrees with breeders and gather info on all matters of the mutt. There are also competitions in categories such as 'dog that looks most like a celebrity' and 'OAP' (for dogs over seven years old). The Good Citizen Dog Scheme offers discipline and agility courses, and you can meet husky teams and watch police-dog agility demonstrations.

655-659 Tick off London's best comedy clubs

Banana Cabaret
The Bedford, 77 Bedford Hill, Balham, SW12 9HD (8682 8940/www.bananacabaret.co.uk).
Banana Cabaret has four or five stand-ups per show, usually of good quality – Mark Thomas warmed up for his politically charged television shows here, and Omid Djalili has also graced the stage. Tuesday is the night for new acts, but Saturdays get the highest recommendation.

Comedy Café
66-68 Rivington Street, Shoreditch, EC2A 3AY (7739 5706/www.comedycafe.co.uk).
This purpose-built Shoreditch venue usually features three or four stand-ups on Thursday, Friday and Saturday – expect the likes of caustic comic Zoe Lyons. Wednesday is open mic night.

Comedy Store
1A Oxendon Street, Soho, SW1Y 4EE (Ticketmaster 0844 847 1728/www.thecomedystore.co.uk).
The place every comic wants to play. This venue is purpose-built for serious punters, with a gladiatorial semicircle of seats, and generally favours trad stand-up. Go on Tuesdays for the topical 'Cutting Edge' shows, on Wednesdays for top improv outfit the Comedy Store Players.

Downstairs at the King's Head
2 Crouch End Hill, Crouch End, N8 8AA (8340 1028/www.downstairsatthekingshead.com).
This Crouch Ender started up in 1981, when the alternative comedy scene was just beginning. It's a favourite with many big-name comedians for trying out new material, but has always showcased new talent too: the long-running Thursday 'try out night' – up to 16 new acts take the mic – kick-started the careers of Mark Lamarr and Eddie Izzard. Saturday night's Comedy Cabaret pulls in a big crowd.

Hampstead Comedy Club
The Pembroke Castle, 150 Gloucester Avenue, NW1 8JA (7633 9539/www.hampsteadcomedy.co.uk).
A long-established pub club in a new venue offering stand-ups and assorted others on a Saturday night from 9pm, all held together by resident host Ivor Dembina.

660

Shape up, military style

If you like the idea of getting fit without the aid of music, machines or lycra, join other 'recruits' at British Military Fitness (7751 9742, www.brit milfit.com) for a workout in the park. A typical session will involve running relays, team games and circuit-training exercises, graded according to ability. The monthly fee is £35 for one class a week or, if you're really keen, £46 for unlimited classes.

661
Marvel at the elaborate Arab Hall of Leighton House

Located on the the edge of swanky Holland Park, Leighton House is one of the capital's most singular pieces of Victorian architecture, largely due to its exquisite Arab Hall. Inspired by a Moorish palace in Sicily, 19th-century artist Lord Frederic Leighton conceived the hall as a showcase for his exquisite collection of 16th- and 17th-century Damascus tiles – the resulting intricacies, and blue and gold hues, are magical. The newly refurbished house, which also displays some of Leighton's painting collection, reopens in Spring 2010.
Leighton House *12 Holland Park Road, W14 8LZ (7602 3316/www.rbkc.gov.uk/leightonhousemuseum).*

662
Journey to Forbidden Planet

Nerds unite at London's premier shop for sci-fi and fantasy gubbins. Forbidden Planet (179 Shaftesbury Avenue, WC2H 8JR, 7420 3666, www.forbiddenplanet.com) is the HMV for *Star Wars*, Tolkien and Buffy fans. The colossal selection of books in the megastore's basement covers the spectrum from science fiction and ufology to crime, graphic novels and political or anarchist titles. Manga and anime books and comics are also stocked, and there's a huge range of merchandise and paraphernalia. Christopher Lee has been known to pop in for the odd book signing.

663
Moonwalk

Moonwalk is a charity walk, held each May in aid of breast cancer research. What's so special about that? First off, it takes place at midnight. Second and best, each of the event's more than 15,000 participants (men included) wears a lavishly decorated bra and little else to power-walk the 26.2-mile route. Many have underestimated the challenge – it may be a walk but it is also a marathon, and a sleep-deprived one. Places sell out fast; visit the website (www.walkthewalk.org) to book.

664
Celebrate the hot cross bun

Every year the proprietors of Bromley-by-Bow's 'Bun House', a pub more formally known as the Widow's Son Inn (Devons Road, E3 3PJ, 7515 9072), hold an Easter ceremony that involves hanging a single, fresh, hot cross bun from the ceiling on Good Friday. As the story goes, it's all to do with the practice of a mourning mother 200 years ago. She would attach a new bun to her pile each year for her only son – a sailor who never returned from the sea. The site of her home is now the pub, and the owners take the ceremony seriously. Very seriously: last year DJs, bands, free beer and some television cameras were on hand to mark the moment.

665
Experience Dame Edna as an impressionist

The Dame Edna Experience features the best impressionist on the scene today. Before taking to the stage at the Royal Vauxhall Tavern (372 Kennington Lane, SE11 5HY, 7820 1222) as the all-singing, all-mimicking Dame Edna Experience, Jonathan Paul Hellyer worked with children in care. 'Can you imagine?' he laughs. 'Me, working in a home! This big camp thing doing all these voices! The poor kids didn't know who they were dealing with half the time.' They're not the only ones. The great thing about Hellyer's act is that you never quite know who you're dealing with. He may come on looking like Edna, the great Aussie female impersonator. But you never know what's going to pop out of his mouth. One minute it's the voice of Nat King Cole, the next it's Patsy Cline. He even does the BBC version of 'Perfect Day', complete with all the voices, in perfect pitch. It's an act that has brought him great acclaim on the gay scene through his weekly residency at the Sunday afternoon S.L.A.G.S. session at the RVT. 'I'd agreed to do four weeks, until they found someone more permanent,' he recalls. Nearly ten years later, he's still there, holding court and being foul (as he puts it, 'I couldn't go on stage and get away with the same blue murder if I wasn't wearing a dress'). The show begins at 5.30pm and costs £7.

666 *Get to know the goths*

The ludicrous Intrepid Fox may have relocated to St Giles High Street, but our goth heart still remains in Soho, staked in a cellar shots bar. Garlic & Shots (14 Frith Street, W1D 4RD, 7734 9505) is genius. The concept is straightforward: it serves just about anything, so long as it comes with garlic. Skip the food in the upstairs restaurant and head downstairs to try the 'blood shot' – a tomato, garlic and chilli vodka shot – followed by a garlic beer chaser with garlic chips on the side. OK, it might pong a bit inside, but there's always the very nice yard out the back.

667 *Attend an American Thanksgiving Day Service*

Few Brits really know what Thanksgiving is for, but it's easy enough to find out. Just head to the annual service at St Paul's Cathedral. Held at 11am on the fourth Thursday of November, the service is mainly attended by London's resident Yanks, but is open to anyone. If you can't get to St Paul's, join the American church congregation that meets in the Whitfield Memorial Church (79A Tottenham Court Road, W1T 4TD) – or simply make friends with one of London's 45,000 Americans.

668 *Take in a blockbuster at the IMAX cinema*

Squatting like a great glass barrel on a sunken roundabout near Waterloo, the BFI London IMAX Cinema (1 Charlie Chaplin Walk, SE1 8XR, 0870 787 2525, www.bfi.org.uk/imax) offers a gloriously lowbrow counterpoint to the nearby National Film Theatre. While it still earns its bread and butter showing educational shorts aimed at a kiddie audience, the IMAX is also increasingly showing proper Hollywood blockbusters such as the latest *Harry Potter* and *The Dark Knight*. The giant screen and incredible sound can lead to sensory overload, but it beats watching a documentary about Everest, three-dimensional or not. Tickets are £8.75-£15.

669 *Row on the Serpentine*

London's finest boating lake, Hyde Park's Serpentine, was once the River Westbourne. The river used to feed 11 ponds across the park but it was dammed in 1730 and now runs largely underground. Hiring a rowing boat on a summer's day is an essential London experience: pay the man a fiver, row out into the middle of the lake and let yourself drift. You'll feel like you're in an Evelyn Waugh novel. The lake at Regent's Park also has boats for hire, but doesn't quite match the elegance of the Serpentine.

670

Release the tensions of city life with yoga

Contrary to popular belief, you don't need to be all that flexible to start doing yoga. Originating in India more than 4,000 years ago as part of a spiritual and ascetic belief system, yoga offers an approach to health and well-being that makes you feel better physically but also benefits the mind. The incredible growth in popularity of the discipline – some regard London as the European capital of yoga – means that Londoners are thoroughly spoiled for choice when it comes to finding themselves a yoga class that suits their needs.

The degree of emphasis a class places on the spiritual side of the discipline depends on the style of yoga you go for and, of course, on the person who is teaching you. So, before you choose a class, it is important to decide why you want to do yoga. If your aim is to relax and de-stress, you'll need a calm, meditative style. If you want something active that keeps you fit, you should seek out a more cardio-vascular practice. Even if you have back problems or other health concerns, there will be an appropriate style. The most common yoga styles are astanga, bikram, iyengar, hatha, shadow, kundalini, sivananda and therapeutic.

Be aware that gyms and health clubs often send their fitness trainers on nothing more intensive than a weekend yoga teaching course, so we recommend seeking out a specialist centre if you're interested in beginning yoga. These include the Yoga Place in Bethnal Green (1st floor, 449-453 Bethnal Green Road, E2 9QH, 7739 5195, www.yogaplace.co.uk), the Life Centre in Notting Hill (5 Edge Street, W8 7PN, 7221 4602, www.thelifecentre.com) and Triyoga in Primrose Hill (6 Erskine Road, NW3 3AJ, 7483 3344, www.triyoga.co.uk).

A good starting point is to contact the British Wheel of Yoga (25 Jermyn Street, Sleaford, Lincs NG34 7RU, 01529 306851, www.bwy.org.uk), which runs teacher-training courses and is recognised by Sport England.

671-682 *Enjoy a hotel tea*

If you're seeking the quintessential English experience, head to one of London's posh hotels to indulge in the ritual of a formal afternoon tea. It can be an expensive business, and you'll have to dress up smart, but when everything is as it should be – fresh and interesting sandwiches, piping hot crumpets, extravagant cakes and rivers of refreshing teas – this is a great way to spend an afternoon. These teas are always popular, so book well in advance.

The Bentley
27-33 Harrington Gardens, SW7 4JX (7244 5555/ www.thebentley-hotel.com).
Tea served 3-6pm daily, £21-£30.

The Berkeley
Wilton Place, SW1X 7RL (7235 6000/ www.the-berkeley.co.uk).
Tea served 2-6pm daily, £35-£49.

The Capital
22-24 Basil Street, SW3 1AT (7589 5171/ 7591 1202/www.capitalhotel.co.uk).
Tea served 3-5pm daily, £18.50.

Claridge's
55 Brook Street, W1K 4HA (7409 6307/ www.claridges.co.uk).
Tea served 3-5.30pm daily, £33-£40.

The Connaught
16 Carlos Place, W1K 2AL (7499 7070/ www.theconnaught.com).
Tea served 3-5.30pm daily, £28-£38.

The Dorchester
53 Park Lane, W1K 1QA (7629 8888/ www.thedorchester.com).
Tea served 2.30-4.45pm daily. Set tea £33.50-£42.50; £48.50 high tea.

Fortnum & Mason
181 Piccadilly, W1A 1ER (7734 8040/ www.fortnumandmason.co.uk).
Tea served 2-6.45pm daily. Set tea £33.75-£42.75; £36-£45 high tea.

The Landmark
222 Marylebone Road, NW1 6JQ (7631 8000/ www.landmarklondon.co.uk).

Tea served 3-6pm daily. Set tea £30, £35-38 including glass of champagne.

The Lanesborough
1 Lanesborough Place, SW1X 7TA (7259 5599/ www.lanesborough.com).
Tea served 4-6pm daily, £31-£39.

The Ritz
150 Piccadilly, W1J 9BR (7493 8181/ www.theritzhotel.co.uk).
Tea served (reserved sittings) 11.30am, 1.30pm, 3.30pm, 5.30pm, 7.30pm daily, £37 (for 7.30pm sitting the price includes a glass of champagne).

Threadneedles
5 Threadneedle Street, EC2R 8AY (7657 8080/ www.theetoncollection.com).
Tea served 3-5pm Mon-Fri, £16.50.

Claridge's

683 Munch on a Maid of Honour

These ladylike puff-pastry tarts, filled with a lemon-scented almond and curd cheese mixture, have an impressive London history: no less a person than Henry VIII is said to have had a hand in the naming. One tale is that, while still with his first wife, Catherine of Aragon, he discovered Anne Boleyn and the other ladies-in-waiting of Hampton Court eating the delicious tarts, and named them in their honour. As a chat-up technique it clearly worked, since the rest really is history.

Once the recipe escaped the kitchens of Hampton Court (some say it was kept under lock and key), commercial production began in Hill Street, Richmond, in 1750; that shop closed in 1957. The Original Maids of Honour shop (288 Kew Road, TW9 3DU, 8940 2752, www.theoriginalmaidsofhonour.co.uk) opened in 1867 and was the third outlet of the Newens family business – the same family runs it to this day. The Maids of Honour are produced in a bakehouse behind the shop and adjacent chintzy tearoom that are a familiar sight to anyone who drives past Kew Gardens. The tarts cost £1.55 and they're delicious.

684 Slurp your way through the White Horse's beer list

It's going to take more than a single sitting to sample the entire range of beers at this admirable Parsons Green pub – there are some 20 on draught, including the first-rate Harveys Sussex Best Bitter and Adnams Broadside, plus another 150 in bottles, many of them hailing from overseas. An alphabetical approach is a possibility, in which case start with Australia and Coopers Extra Strong Vintage Ale, before moving on to the Belgian brews. The pub is also known as the Sloaney Pony, attracting, as it does, a fair few Hoorays. In summer their braying is dissipated if you sit in the large beer garden. Barbecues (in the warmer months) and ambitious, mostly British, cooking are on the menu – with beer- or wine-pairing suggestions.

White Horse *1-3 Parsons Green, SW6 4UL (7736 2115/www.whitehorsesw6.com).*

685 Pay your respects to the London Stone

Every day hordes of City workers rush past a stone set in a glass case in the front of the Sportec sports shop opposite Cannon Street station, with no inkling that it is one of the oldest, most mysterious and possibly most historic relics in London. Supposedly once marking the centre point of London, in 1742 it was deemed an obstacle to traffic on Cannon Street and relocated to the wall of St Swithin's Church across the road. It was the sole relic to survive after the German bombing of the church in 1941 – perhaps a sign that it does possess mystical powers, perhaps due to the fact that it's, uh, a big stone.

Shrouded in legend, the stone has been argued to date back as many as 3,000 years, possibly even to the Druids. These days, though, the stone is unnoticed by the public and scorned by museums. Brushed off as an impenetrable mystery, the British Museum says there is no way to date it to before its first written record and the Museum of London scathingly calls it 'an uninteresting lump of stone'. Despite being thus scorned by the academics, it remained an icon for a millennium, its past all the more alluring for the speculation that continues to surround it.

686 Come over druidic in Lewisham

OK, the Dome was a bad idea from the get-go, but one millennium project always had our support... that's right, the stone circle in Lewisham's Hilly Fields. It isn't quite Stonehenge – the largest of the circle's dozen stones doesn't reach much over hobbit height – but it's certainly more impressive than a birdbath-cum-sundial. There's even an elegant pair of taller stones, dedicated to St Norbert, that forms a kind of gateway into the ring of granite boulders. There's little by way of sacrificial virgins or dancing naked in floral garlands here – upsets the parents at the children's playground, you see – but the stone circle does form the focal point of the Brockley Society fair each summer.

687

Play table football – but absolutely no spinning

There's always an enjoyably boisterous atmosphere at London's original table football bar, Café Kick (43 Exmouth Market, EC1R 4QL, 7837 8077, www.cafekick.co.uk). You get your kicks on the three René Pierre babyfoot tables at the front but, when things get too heated, there's always refreshment in the shape of fine bottled beers (Portuguese Sagres, Brazilian Bravara) served from the bar at the back. Forget half-time oranges and go for sharing platters of meat and cheese instead.

Sister establishment Bar Kick in Shoreditch (127 Shoreditch High Street, E1 6JE, 7739 8700, www.cafekick.co.uk) has serious retro appeal (think 1950s Italian decor and plenty of formica) – and some serious fussball players. The latter meet on Thursday evenings and table football tournaments take place on the last Thursday of the month. Beginner sessions have been introduced, though, so there's no need to be shy. Just make sure you never, ever spin. It's *so* declassé.

688

Watch the pros on dance machines

The mix of Japanese tourists, techno-savvy kids and delinquent youths hanging around the dance machines at the Trocadero Centre at Piccadilly Circus (www.londontrocadero.com) all have one thing in common: they can bust a groove for high scores most of us can only dream of. There are similar machines in the South Bank's Namco Station (www.namcostation.co.uk) and downstairs at Hamley's on Regent Street.

689 Ride a Routie

Remember when you could risk life and limb by jumping on and off buses while they were still moving? Remember the shenanigans of trying to dodge the conductor? Well, we hope you do – it's half a decade since the last of the regular Routemaster buses, the 159, rolled into Streatham Garage for the final time.

For over 50 years the conductor-operated Routemaster bus served London both as a uniquely practical means of travel and an international symbol of the capital. At the start of 2006 the red double-decker headed a list of the nation's most popular icons, along with Stonehenge and the FA Cup. It was withdrawn from service, despite prior assurance from ex-Mayor Ken Livingstone that this would not happen (to wit: 'only a ghastly dehumanised moron would want to get rid of the Routemaster'), but Transport for London announced soon afterwards that the bus would live on along two 'heritage' routes. Beautifully refurbished Routies now run through the central London sections of routes 9 and 15, 1960s vehicles lovingly repainted in their original colour scheme, complete with a cream-coloured horizontal stripe.

The buses run daily every 15 minutes from 9.30am to 6.30pm and supplement the normal bus services. Route 9 takes in the Royal Albert Hall (westbound service only), Aldwych, the Strand, Trafalgar Square and Piccadilly Circus; route 15 runs from Trafalgar Square to Tower Hill and allows passengers to glimpse the Strand, Fleet Street and St Paul's Cathedral. Note that conductors now only check tickets rather than selling them – buy one before you board.

Talking of buying, the extreme Routemaster fan could actually do just that: Routies can be picked up second-hand for as little as £5,000, with the best starting place being the Routemaster Association website (www.routemaster.org.uk). Pick up a must-have 'My other car is a Routemaster' sticker for 50p.

690 Get a walk-in backrub

For a quick stress-busting session, drop in on one of the quick-stop massage stations run by Walk-In Backrub (www.walkinbackrub.co.uk). The convenience factor is high: you don't need to take your clothes off or even to lie down, as the treatments take place on ergonomic leather chairs. You'll find branches pretty much wherever serious shopping gets done: Covent Garden (14 Neal's Yard, WC2H 9DP); Fitzrovia (11 Charlotte Place, W1T 1SJ); Carnaby Street (2nd floor, Kingly Court, W1B 5PW); Selfridges (4th floor, 400 Oxford Street, W1A 1AB); and Kensington High Street (Whole Foods Market Store, 63-97 Kensington High Street, W8 5SE).

691
Stop in at the Shop at Bluebird

Where can you find a pair of pristine post-war Lady armchairs designed by Marco Zanuso, Dosa silk pyjamas, Rupert Sanderson heels, a facsimile of Sylvia Plath's *Ariel* manuscript and a mini Rolleiflex camera under one roof? Part lifestyle boutique, part design gallery, the Shop at Bluebird is making the King's Road rock again. Occupying the ground floor of the art deco garage where racing driver Sir Malcolm Campbell's Bluebird cars are thought to have been assembled in the late 1920s, it recently joined Terence Conran's Bluebird restaurant/café/deli complex (350 King's Road, SW3 5UU, 7351 3873, www.theshopatbluebird. com). The 10,000-square-foot space is a shifting showcase of clothing (for men, women and children), lingerie, accessories, shoes, furniture, books and gadgets.

Staff have been vetted for friendliness and the constantly changing displays have a sense of fun. The book section is illuminated by a ceiling installation of over 1,000 lightbulbs; art T-shirts and niche denim sit in disembowelled TVs; and jewellery, from an international roster of independent designers, is 'modelled' by a stuffed fox and owl. Fashion-wise the house style is more understated than edgy and embraces a huge variety of non-ubiquitous labels from Europe and America. A music section, with hand-picked selections by industry insider Nigel Templeton, is manned by guest DJs at weekends.

692
Watch American football

The most popular spectator sport in the US, American football has had mixed fortunes here since the London Ravens began training sessions in Hyde Park in 1983. At its peak in 1987 there were 165 teams registered in Britain – now there are fewer than 50 playing in the British American Football League (www.bafl.org.uk). There are two London teams playing BAFL Division 1: the Finsbury Park-based Blitz and the Cobras from Boston Manor. The season runs from May to September; see the BAFL website for details of upcoming games.

693-698
Celebrate Burns Night

A handful of Scottish outposts in the capital see to it their nation's expats can honour Scotland's favourite poet with a night of haggis, whisky, poetry and general roaring drunkenness. The Rob Roy (8-9 Sale Place, W2 1PH, 7262 6403) is London's most committed Scottish pub; it serves the excellent Deuchars IPA and provides reasonable food (try the stovies). For something more refined, contemporary Scottish bar and restaurant Albannach (66 Trafalgar Square, WC2N 5DS, 7930 0066, www.albannach.co.uk) offers an annual set Burns supper, as do Scottish restaurant Boisdale (Swedeland Court, 202 Bishopsgate, EC2M 4NR, 7283 1763, www.boisdale.co.uk) and Mayfair joint Patterson's (4 Mill Street, W1S 2AX, 7499 1308, www.pattersonsrestaurant.com). Haggis, of course, is served at them all.

If you need to dance, the Ceilidh Club (www. ceilidhclub.com) hosts events in different venues each year and a less likely celebration occurs at the Hackney LCC Burns Night Supper & Dance. Held at Sir Thomas Abney School (Fairolt Road, N16), it's the biggest event in the London Cycling Campaign calendar. For a fully ceremonial supper (including haggis, neeps, tatties, whisky *and* dancing) tickets are just £15; booking is essential (www.hackney-cyclists.org.uk).

Television centre

Is there any patch of London Gabriel Tate failed to visit in his quest to bring you the city's best TV locations?

Wherever you are in London, you're walking on a TV set; you're probably also being watched by someone on the box, given the growth of the surveillance society. And if you're going to be a TV star, it might as well be where some TV history was made.

What Percy Thrower would have given for CCTV in the *Blue Peter* garden back in 1983 when former footballer Les Ferdinand helped 'a few people over the fence' during a now-infamous night-time break-in? Despite rumours to the contrary, the garden isn't to be replaced with a virtual replica which means you can still (until at least 2011 anyway) visit on a guided tour of Television Centre (Wood Lane, W12 7RJ, 0870 603 0304). It'll be more enjoyable than trying to find the non-existent pillar box at 221B Baker Street (*DangerMouse*), even if it's less worthy than picking up litter on Wimbledon Common (*The Wombles*).

While we're on the subject of kids' TV, you've a wealth of options if you're hunting the school from *Grange Hill*. The series was as peripatetic

as a supply teacher, starting in Kingsbury High School (Princes Avenue, NW9 9JR), moving to Willesden High School (Doyle Gardens, NW10 3ST), then settling in South Thames College (now Fulham Prep, Greyhound Road, W14 9RY) for the imperial era of Tucker Jenkins and 'Just Say No'. The surroundings are rather gentrified, but get your angles right and you'll be spotting Zammos and Ro-lands before you know it.

Almost as synonymous with 1980s television is *Only Fools and Horses*, which used a tower block in west London as the Trotters' home: Harlech Tower (Park Road, W3) stood in as Nelson Mandela House until 1989, when filming moved to Bristol. If you own a Reliant Regal (in fact, any vehicle will do), try hurtling through Rotherhithe Tunnel, SE16 – adhering to the 20mph speed limit, of course. You'll be in the tyre tracks of Patrick McGoohan's Lotus Seven, as seen in the title sequence of *The Prisoner*.

Don't crash. You might end up having to get a replacement from a modern-day Arthur Daley – whose *Minder* car lot can be found at

the junction of Augustine Road and Dewhurst Road in Hammersmith. It's been built over now.

West London was fertile territory for *The Sweeney*. An alleyway beside the Warrington Hotel in Maida Vale (93 Warrington Crescent, W9 1EH), for example, played host to one of Carter's many kickings. It's part of the Gordon Ramsay empire now, so pop in for a pint of corn-fed organic prawns, you slaaaags.

Before you get too bogged down in a world of flock wallpaper and casual misogyny, visit the settings of some more modern metropolitan comedies. *Spaced*'s 23 Meteor Street is, in fact, Carleton Road in Tufnell Park, N7, where the odd skateboarding slacker and TA obsessive might still lurk. The exterior of Collinge & Clark, on Leigh Street, WC1, was the site of foul-mouthed, dipsomaniac misanthropy in *Black Books*, while Croydon's Zodiac Court (165 London Road) was the exterior used for Mark and Jez's much-abused flat in *Peep Show*.

A rather more widely viewed lynchpin of Channel 4's schedule over the past few years has been *Big Brother*. The more recent series have been filmed at Elstree Studios (Shenley Road, Borehamwood, Herts WD6 1JG), while the house Nasty Nick and chums lived in was beside a rather charming park in Bow, by Three Mills Studios (Three Mill Lane, E3 3DU). Not far away, by Old Ford Lock, is Lock Keeper's Cottage (E3 2NN), home of C4's tarnished jewel in the crown, *The Big Breakfast*. You'd need a hanglider to recreate the opening credits' swoop towards the house but, even if you managed that, you probably wouldn't fit through the letterbox. Just as well: it's now a private house.

Another lock played host to one of British television comedy's finest moments: in the course of the fish-slapping dance from *Monty Python's Flying Circus* Michael Palin is pitched into Teddington Lock, TW11, by John Cleese with a halibut. Once you've dried off, strut down to Thorpebank Road in Hammersmith, where the 'Ministry of Silly Walks' begins.

Keeping with the water theme, the Grand Union Canal – make that 'Walford Canal' –

West London was fertile territory for The Sweeney. An alleyway beside the Warrington Hotel played host to one of Carter's many kickings. Gordon Ramsay has now turned the place into a gastropub, so pop in for a pint of corn-fed organic prawns, you slaaaags.

in Alperton, NW10, saw the first demise of Den Watts, in one of *EastEnders'* rare ventures out of its fictional E20 set (in Elstree).

Shooting up the class ladder from Walford, Belgravia's 65 Eaton Place, SW1, was home to the Bellamys of *Upstairs Downstairs*. (The '1' was painted on for the show, nitpickers might like to know.) Neo-Palladian country house Wrotham Park in Barnet, EN5, is scarcely less posh, and was twice the scene of toffee-nosed revelry: it was Lord Kessler's house in *The Line of Beauty*, Brinkley Court in *Jeeves and Wooster* and, plummeting swiftly back down the ladder again, the place where Ashley Cole and Cheryl Tweedy had their wedding blessed. Perhaps they were fans of the shows.

More harrowing melodrama? Ken Loach's epochal Wednesday Play *Cathy Come Home* was one of the first TV dramas to be largely shot on location, documentary-style. The easiest location to find is Liverpool Street station, where Cathy's children are snatched by social services. Actress Carol White's shrieks of anguish still echo around the concourse.

The London Underground has, of course, provided settings for TV drama upon TV drama. *The Bill*, for example, makes much use of the abandoned station at Aldwych, while Chancery Lane tube and *This Life* are inseparable in viewers' minds (the exterior of their house on 'Benjamin Street' is actually on Southwark Bridge Road, SE1, between the river and Southwark Street). But for heart-in-the-right-place political activism, you can't go far wrong with Wolfie Smith, determinedly striding out of Tooting Broadway station, SW17, to convert more unsuspecting souls in *Citizen Smith*. 'Power to the people!'

Giving power to the people to pitch their ideas, then swiftly stealing it back while cutting their ideas to shreds are the business 'dragons' of BBC's *Dragons' Den*. The Tarantino-style shot of them walking down a red-brick road was filmed in Backchurch Lane, E1, outside Wool House where the show is filmed. Other Beeb success stories that made good use of the capital include *Spooks* (the exterior of Thames House is actually Freemason's Hall on Great Queen Street, WC2) and *Extras* (the stage debut of Andy Millman, played by Ricky Gervais, takes place at the New Wimbledon Theatre on the Broadway, SW19 1QG).

All this will, with any luck, have stirred up some feelings about TV, whether warmly nostalgic about how it used to be or angrily relevant to the way it is now. So why not pay a visit to 22 Frith Street in Soho? Here, in 1926, John Logie Baird first demonstrated his new invention: it's the birthplace of television.

...or be part of a studio audience

It's easier than you might think to get on telly, albeit not necessarily in a starring role. To apply for free tickets to be part of a TV audience in the capital, visit www.bbc.co.uk/tickets for the BBC; www.itv.com/tickets for ITV; and www.channel4.com/tickets for Channel 4. The majority of their studio audience shows are filmed in London.

729 *Blow the budget at Umu*

Umu is an authentic slice of metropolitan Japan in central Mayfair, from the understated entrance to the sleek wood panelling to the unstinting detail paid to the serving plates and all that goes on them. There's no denying that all this comes at a price – two of you could easily spend more than £300 – but the food is impeccably sourced (many ingredients are imported from Japan) and artfully prepared (the salmon was beautifully cut and watching a sushi chef wielding his knives is almost as much of a treat as eating the finished product). Unless you're a millionaire, Umu is special-occasion territory, but for Japanophiles it's a must-try.
Umu *14-16 Bruton Place, W1J 6LX (7499 8881/ www.umurestaurant.com).*

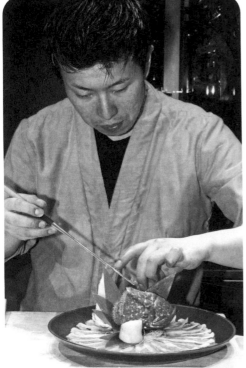

730 *Visit the Wellcome Collection*

This £30 million venture on the Euston Road explores the connections between medicine and art through experimental exhibitions and the collection of pharmacist Sir Henry Wellcome. Housing at least 1,500 exhibits, including a 14th-century Peruvian mummy and Napoleon's toothbrush, the collection has three sections: Medicine Man (objects from Sir Henry Wellcome's vast collection), Medicine Now (exhibits focused on contemporary medical science) and a space for temporary exhibitions. *www.wellcomecollection.org.*

731 *Find love in London's galleries*

The Loving Company (7193 3738, www. lovingcompany.com) specialises in events for (gay and straight) singletons based on their interests – 'Loving art' being an enduringly popular theme among others such as 'Loving music' and 'Loving travel'. Previous nights have been held at the Hayward Gallery, the V&A, Tate Modern and the Wallace Collection and they are usually attended by around 150 hopeful souls.

732-737

Drink in an old gin palace

'All is light and brilliancy.' So said Charles Dickens of a London gin palace in *Sketches by Boz*. These 'splendid mansions', he went on, were filled with 'stone balustrades, rosewood fittings, immense lamps, and illuminated clocks.'

Only a handful still exist, but they're well worth a visit (even if pints and Kettle Chips have replaced gin as the main seller). Starting centrally, the Princess Louise (208-209 High Holborn, WC1V 7EP, 7405 8816), built in 1872, is missing only its original partitions – the gin palaces were each split into bar, saloon and numerous other drinking areas. What remains is a magnificent horseshoe-shaped wooden bar (complete with clock), a moulded ceiling and intricately carved woodwork, all reflected in tall engraved mirrors. The patrons are slightly crusty, but the interior is like a pub cathedral. In Soho, the Argyll Arms (18 Argyll Street, W1F 7TP, 7734 6117) is where shoppers head to admit defeat over half-pints and pub pies. The real reason to come here is for the rich endowment of Victorian etched mirrors, snob screens and mahogany; the original layout is intact, too – a corridor leads to the large back saloon past three small snug bars. For knockout Victoriana, the Albert (52 Victoria Street, SW1H 0NP, 7222 5577) is a fabulous confection of hand-cut glass, carved dark wood and old gas light fittings, built in the 1860s to honour the Empress's departed prince. Ignore the tourist-bait T-shirts relating to MPs who have drunk here, and enjoy sitting back in an ornate cocoon.

In the City, where many old-timers of the London pub world are still standing, is the 1869 Viaduct Tavern (126 Newgate Street, EC1 7AA, 7600 1863), just across the road from the Old Bailey court. Take in the busts of 16 Victorian hanging judges and vow to keep your nose clean. Up in north London is the Island Queen (87 Noel Road, N1 8HD, 7354 8741). Swathed in wood and etched glass, it celebrates nautical glory with a wave-damaged wooden figurehead, palm leaves and prints of ships; a vast island bar presides over the middle of the lofty single room.

Best of the lot, though, is the Prince Alfred (5A Formosa Street, W9 1EE, 7286 3287). The beautiful old tiling and exquisitely curved frosted glass frontage barely prepare you for the architectural delights within: a complex series of snugs with a fabulously ornate half-moon dark-wood bar as centrepiece. The snugs (free to hire!) once kept the proles from the posh, and stand now as fascinating testimony to the British class system.

738 Check in on the Chelsea Pensioners

The Royal Hospital in Chelsea is not your average old folks' home, but then the Chelsea Pensioners are not your average old folks. About 350 of them live here, all of them ex-soldiers. They have their own club room, amenity centre, billiards room, library, bowling green and gardens. Some work in the museum, which gives a detailed account of the life of a pensioner from the 17th century to the present day. Free to enter, the museum has a mock-up of an in-pensioner's room, designed by Wren, and there are paintings, ceremonial arms, medals bequeathed by former residents and uniforms on display.

The familiar scarlet coat and tricorn hat that the old soldiers wear for ceremonial duties (including visits to Stamford Bridge) date back to the 18th century, but these aren't in evidence when you visit the hospital on an ordinary day: dark trousers and pale blue shirts are the standard mufti for relaxing at home.

Royal Hospital Chelsea *Royal Hospital Road, SW3 4SR (7881 5200/www.chelsea-pensioners.co.uk).*

739 Visit London's last sewer lamp

On Carting Lane, a gloomy side street off the Strand between the Savoy and the ShellMex building, find London's last remaining sewer-powered gas lamp, still giving out its queasy yellow glow around the clock, thanks to a hollow iron column that allows sewer vapours to travel to its flame. Lit by the capital's slurry since the 1880s, this Patent Sewer Ventilating Lamp represents Victorian ingenuity at its best. Unlike the lamp, we're not taking the piss.

740-745 *Skateboard*

London's many skaters are blessed with an increasing number of designated skateparks in which to practise their tricks. The graffitied stretch of the South Bank beneath the Royal Festival Hall remains the beating heart of the London skate scene; the powers that be, after spending years trying to get rid of the skaters, recently gave up and installed a number of purpose-built grind boxes. Other options include: Cantelowes skatepark (Cantelowes Gardens, Camden Road, NW1, www. cantelowesskatepark.co.uk), which reopened in May 2006 as part of a £1.5 million redevelopment; the eccentric concrete bowl in Finsbury Park, N4; the Stockwell Skatepark (Stockwell Park Road, SW9, www.stockwellskatepark.com); the imaginatively designed White's Grounds underneath the railway arches off Tooley Street next to Tower Bridge; and the varied apocalyptic sprawl of BaySixty6 (Bay 65-66, Acklam Road, W10 5YU, 8969 4669, www.baysixty6.com).

746 Drink bubble tea in Chinatown

Bubble teas, aka pearl teas, are fruit juice and tea 'cocktails' that are a big culinary trend in Hong Kong. The 'pearls' are balls of starch made from tapioca, sago, or even more unusual ingredients such as sweet potato. You suck these up through an oversized straw. Jen Café (4-8 Newport Place, WC2H 7JP, no phone) is one of several Chinatown cafés that serve them. We recommend honeydew melon flavour.

747 Get inside the Houses of Parliament

Given how few Londoners get to see inside Parliament, it's strange that the regular summer tours of the building seem to be left to tourists. Big mistake: the tours of the main ceremonial rooms, including Westminster Hall (one of the finest medieval buildings in Europe) and the two Houses are superb. Available from July to October, they cost £11.70 (£7.80-£5 concessions). Oh, and if you write to your MP with a request, they *have* to give you a tour of the building.
Houses of Parliament *Parliament Square, SW1 (0844 847 1672/www.parliament.uk).*

748 Be a groundling at the Globe

Hugely popular with American tourists – who cling to the fond myth that all Brits are entirely literate in the works of Shakespeare and attend the theatre on a daily basis – the Globe is often dismissed by locals as a Shakespeare theme park. Although that attitude is understandable with the volume of visitors the theatre receives, it's completely wrong. The productions are often exceptional and the atmosphere unique. Embrace the real experience and stand through an entire five-acter: not only can you wander around and get different views of the stage, but it also keeps you alert. Cheats should get in early so they can lean against a wall.
Shakespeare's Globe *21 New Globe Walk, SE1 9DT (7902 1900/www.shakespeare-globe.org).*

749 Breakfast at E Pellicci

Caffs don't come more pukka than E Pellicci. It was the Kray brothers' favourite greasy spoon and has been in the same family for nigh-on a century (its art deco interior is now Grade II listed). Service is friendly, and there's a neighbourly feel to the place. After brekkie, there are salads, grills, chops and sarnies to keep you here through the rest of the day – and mugs of tea, of course.
E Pellicci *332 Bethnal Green Road, E2 0AG (7739 4873).*

750 Go for broke on the horses

Never mind Ascot, London has its own racing alternative in the shape of down-to-earth Kempton Park (Staines Road East, Sunbury-on-Thames, Middx TW16 5AQ, 01932 782292, www.kempton.co.uk). It might not have the same glamour, but with the combination of a booze, a flutter and the aroma of upturned earth, who needs airs and graces? Meetings take place year-round and are well attended. For an even less refined atmosphere, you could head to the Flower Pot pub (128 Wood Street, E17 3HX, 8520 3600) in Walthamstow for a wager on one of its regular race nights.

751 Powerpram!

Liz Stuart set up Powerpramming (www.power pramming.com) after giving birth, inviting the local mother and baby group to get fit with her. Exercises, taught by a qualified post-natal instructor, revolve around the use of a pram. 'The older babies find it fascinating and hilarious, watching carefully as mum works out,' says Stuart. 'The younger ones tend to find the movement makes them sleepy.'

752 Risk your teeth on old-fashioned sweets at Hope & Greenwood

'It's 1955 in my sweetshop, young man,' announced Miss Hope to an impudent Radio 4 journalist during one of many features on her centre of sweetie excellence, which opened in East Dulwich in 2004. Miss Hope, who runs the shop with Mr Greenwood (no vulgar Christian names here, thank you), had always played sweetshops as a little girl, and this jar-lined retail confection is the realisation of her dreams. It is indeed a shop of dreams, both for children and for those adults who rue the passing of rosy apples, sherbert pips, chewing nuts and cola cubes from the confectionery canon. Hope and Greenwood have proved that the sweets of 20 years ago are still out there, you just have to be a special sort of sweetshop to stock them all. It's not just nostalgic adults with mouthfuls of fillings who crowd into this most beautiful of shops – children bundle in here daily after school for a fix of liquorice whips and pineapple chunks.

If the stock sounds a mite too synthetic be assured that Hope & Greenwood also sells handmade chocolates and quality brands, such as Lindt and Suchard. To make the shop pay – you can't run a business based on a stream of kids asking for 'two ounces' of Tom Thumb drops – the proprietors also sell a fine range of sweetie-related goods, such as retro tins and jars, gift wrap, bunting and boxes.

Parting is such sweet sorrow – but you know full well you'll be coming back again sooner than your dentist would wish.

Hope & Greenwood *20 North Cross Road, SE22 9EU and 1 Russell Street, WC2B 5JD (www.hopeandgreenwood.co.uk).*

753-775

Pop a coin in the capital's best jukeboxes

Approach Tavern
47 Approach Road, E2 9LY (8980 2321).
TV sports plays silently in this charming Bethnal Green boozer, all the better to hear the jukebox uninterrupted. £1 will buy 5 plays.

Barrio North
45 Essex Road, N1 2SF (7688 2882/ www.barrionorth.com).
Super-cool tunes at this trendy Islington bar, from DFA, Talking Heads and, naturally, Chas 'n' Dave.

Boogaloo
312 Archway Road, N6 5AT (8340 2928/ www.theboogaloo.org).
Probably the most famous jukebox in London. David Bowie and Dusty Springfield tunes are among the regular spins.

Bradley's Spanish Bar
44 Hanway Street, W1T 1UT (7636 0359).
Probably London's best vinyl juke; £1 will buy you three plays.

Crobar
17 Manette Street, W1D 4AS (7439 0831).
£1 buys three tracks from the likes of Lynyrd Surely no juke in the UK has more Iron Maiden?

Ed's Easy Diner
12 Moor Street, W1D 5NG (7434 4439).
If kitsch is your thing, pump 20p pieces into a personal mini-jukebox for classic 1950s tracks.

Endurance
90 Berwick Street, W1F 0QB (7437 2944).
You can choose from a selection of 100 tunes at this Berwick Street landmark.

The Good Mixer
30 Inverness Street, NW1 7HJ (7916 6176).
There's a predictably decent indy collection on the box at this temple to 1990s Brit Pop.

Half Moon
93 Lower Richmond Road, SW15 1EU (8780 9383/www.halfmoon.co.uk).
An excellent array of rock and pop classics.

Hawley Arms
2 Castlehaven Road, NW1 8QU (7428 5979).
£1 buys five songs; this juke also carries tracks by unsigned bands.

Hobgoblin
272 New Cross Road, SE14 6AA (8692 3193).
Indie and glam rock, in keeping with the student vibe at this New Cross haunt.

Hope & Anchor
207 Upper Street, N1 1RL (7354 1312).
There are two jukeboxes at this grizzled rock pub, both of them most often pitched somewhere between Pixies and Joy Division. Always with the volume on full-whack.

King Charles I
55-57 Northdown Street, N1 9BL (7837 7758).
Covers all corners from Bowie to country.

Mucky Pup
39 Queen's Head Street, N1 8NQ (7226 2572/).
A juke that's well stocked, rock-heavy and free.

Prince George
40 Parkholme Road, E8 3AG (7254 6060).
Three tracks for £1 from a choice of about 80 CDs.

Three Kings
7 Clerkenwell Close, EC1R 0DY (7253 0483).
There's a selection of 80 vinyl seven-inches that changes every week; at £1 for seven songs, it's also a bargain.

Shakespeare
57 Allen Road, N16 8RY (7254 4190).
It's £1 for 5 tracks here and it's loaded with Morrissey. Need we say more?

The Social
5 Little Portland Street, W1W 7JD (7636 4992).
The bar staff often give free tokens; usually it's £1 for seven plays.

The Swimmer at the Grafton Arms
13 Eburne Road, N7 6AR (7281 4632).
Over 800 CD tracks that rotate every couple of months; five songs for £1.

776 *Drink in a German beer garden*

You fancy having a little lederhosen-slapping fun and happen to be visiting Richmond? No problem. Stroll along beside the river past Richmond Bridge and you'll find yourself at Stein's (Richmond Towpath, Richmond, Surrey TW10 6UX, 8948 8189, www.stein-s.com). Little more than a kiosk and some outdoor tables with heaters, Stein's sells Bavarian dishes to families from the German school in nearby Petersham. It's a real German snack bar, serving various styles of bratwurst (pork sausage), weisswurst (white veal sausage), side orders of tangy sauerkraut and potato salads, and, of course, apple strudel and Black Forest gateau. There's even Erdinger wheat beer on tap. The location, right beside the river, just couldn't be better. Wunderbar. Shame it's open only in summer.

777 *Try your hand at rugby netball*

So what do prop forwards and hookers do when the rugby season ends? Play rugby netball, of course. This intriguing hybrid has been unique to Clapham Common since 1903, with a midweek evening league running from May to July. See www.netrugby.com for details of how to join in the fun.

778-779 *Savour absinthe*

The wormwood-based 'green fairy' spirit raised its head above the bars of a few outré establishments back in the mid-1990s amid much chatter of prohibition laws having been repealed (an ingenious marketing gimmick-turned-urban legend, for the drink was never banned in this country). Detroit Bar (32 Earlham Street, WC2H 9LD, 7240 2662, www.detroit-bar.com) is still serving a mean 'overproof' cocktail but London's prime absinthe peddlar must surely be Gerry's Wines and Spirits (74 Old Compton Street, W1D 4UW, 7734 2053, www.gerrys.uk.com) who keep the fairies coming with their 15 different varieties.

A few of my favourite things

780-783
Cerys Matthews, musician

Any excuse to go on an open-topped bus, I'm there. Especially when the sun's out; you just sit there, burn in the sun and learn the potted history of the city. Last time I had a guide with really terrible microphone technique but we managed to get a lot of information from him nevertheless. **Portobello Road is absolutely the best place for people-watching, as well as buying fresh fruit and hotdogs. I'd hang around in a nice Italian restaurant just off it called Osteria Basilico (29 Kensington Park Road, W11 2EU, 7727 9957). It does a good carpaccio of beef and serves some excellent wine.** There's also a Spanish restaurant called Galicia (323 Portobello Road, W10 5SY, 8969 3539). Being there is like visiting Spain without having to do the journey. **Football at Highbury and Stamford Bridge. I love it. Any football match, to be honest, mainly for the singing and the chanting and the general abuse. It's like going to a gig – it's the power of the crowd more than the magic of the players. I just love the sound.**

784-785 *Sky-dive*

What better way to heighten the pleasure of life than a near-death experience? Both the London Parachute School (The Byre, Woods Farm, East Hampstead Road, Wokingham, Berks RG40 3LE, www.londonparachuteschool.com) and the North London Parachute Centre (Block Fen Drive, Wimblington, nr March, Cambs PE15 0FB, 01449 616613, www.ukskydiving.com) run day courses that suit novices, and both are just a short train journey out of the capital. Course fees start from £155.

786

Visit the Thames Barrier

The key player in London's flood defence system and an arresting piece of modern architecture. Time your visit to see the barrier in action: each autumn there's a full-scale testing and there's also a partial test closure once a month. Call 8305 4188 for dates.

787

Chuckle at old playthings in Pollock's Toy Museum

Housed in a wonderfully creaky Georgian townhouse, Pollock's museum is named after Benjamin Pollock, who was the last of the Victorian toy theatre printers. The nostalgic value of old board games, clockwork trains and Robertson's gollies can hardly be overestimated for adults. For young children, however, the displays can seem a bit static and irrelevant; what they seem to enjoy most are the shop and the regular free puppet shows (generally held on Saturdays).

Pollock's Toy Museum *1 Scala Street (entrance on Whitfield Street), W1T 2HL (7636 3452/ www.pollockstoymuseum.com).*

788

Shiver at old medical instruments in the Old Operating Theatre

The tower that houses this salutary revelation of antique surgical practice used to be part of the chapel of St Thomas's Hospital, founded on this site in the 12th century. When the hospital was moved to Lambeth in the 1860s most of the buildings were torn down to make way for London Bridge station and it was not until 1956 that the atmospheric old operating herb garret was discovered in the loft of the church. Visitors enter via a vertiginous wooden spiral staircase to view the medicinal herbs on display. Further in is the centrepiece: a Victorian operating theatre with tiered viewing seats for students. Just as disturbing are the displays of operating tools that look like torture implements. Other display cases hold strangulated hernias, leech jars and amputation knives. The museum has a shop full of tricks and stocking fillers, but also real educational aids such as mini-skeletons. Check the website for events (such as demonstrations of Victorian surgery) and on-site lectures.

Old Operating Theatre, Museum & Herb Garret *9A St Thomas's Street, SE1 9RY (7188 2679/ www.thegarret.org.uk).*

789 *Tour Twickenham Stadium*

Tickets for rugby internationals are hard to come by, but the little museum in Twickenham Stadium offers some compensation. Tours take in the home dressing room, the players' tunnel and the Royal Box. A permanent collection of memorabilia, chosen from the museum's 10,000-piece collection, charts the game's development from the late 19th century, including England's World Cup victory in 2003. You'll also find the oldest surviving international rugby jersey and the Calcutta Cup, now safe in English hands until 2008 (it's awarded annually to the winners of the England–Scotland match). Video snippets recall classic matches; a simulated scrum machine tests your strength.

Twickenham Rugby Stadium *Rugby Road, Twickenham, Middx TW1 1DZ (8892 8877/ www.rfu.com).*

790 *Play golf in the streets at the Shoreditch Open*

This increasingly popular event in late May takes the concept of 'urban golf' to its logical conclusion: players negotiate an 18-hole, par 72 course through the streets of Shoreditch, along back streets, between buildings and through car parks, using a leather golf ball stuffed with goose feathers (to prevent window breakages), a mat to play off and fire hydrant covers for holes. This being Shoreditch, the ironic donning of pastel-coloured Pringle sweaters and brogues is encouraged. Apply online (www.sgcgolf.com) to be one of the 60-odd participants.

791

Listen to the choir at Westminster Cathedral

Some of the best choristers in the world sing daily at morning mass (10.30am) and evening prayers (5.30pm).

Westminster Cathedral *Victoria Street, SW1P 1QW (7798 9055/www.westminstercathedral.org.uk).*

792
Dine at the chef's table

Just as reality TV series now require an element of jeopardy to keep the viewers' attention, fine dining seeks to lure customers by inviting them into the kitchen to see the temper tantrums and pot-boiler dramas. The 'chef's table' originated overseas (probably first in the US, then in Australia), where it meant a table inside the kitchen where diners could watch the chefs in action while having their meal. However, the term is now used very loosely for any booth or table with a view of the kitchen – available often at a premium price, and usually seating a group of between four and 12 people.

The Gordon Ramsay group of restaurants (www.gordonramsay.com) has been the most enthusiastic supporter of the concept here, as you might expect from a company that is never slow in promoting its chefs as performers and celebrities. And the concept is proving popular, especially for corporate entertaining. Restaurants currently offering chef's tables include Maze (London Marriott, 13 Grosvenor Square, W1K 6JP, 7107 0000), Gordon Ramsay at Claridge's (55 Brook Street, W1K 4HR, 7499 0099), Marcus Wareing at the Berkeley (The Berkeley, Wilton Place, SW1X 7RL, 7235 1200), and, as of Spring 2010, a reborn Pétrus (1 Kinnerton Street, SW1X 8EA).

Don't forget, however, that countless other restaurants – Turkish grills, sushi bars and gastropubs, for example – afford you a fine view of the chefs at work for a fraction of the price you'll be paying for a seat at one of Mr Ramsay's hallowed tables.

793
Watch a horse being blessed

Continuing a tradition started in 1968, when the stables in Hyde Park were threatened with closure, Horseman's Sunday sees the vicar of St John's Church (Hyde Park Crescent, W2 2QD, 262 1732, www.stjohnshydepark.com/horsemans) bless a cavalcade of 100 horses. It's quite a sight. The midday blessing takes place once a year in mid September.

794
Hire your own rickshaw

Though certainly an eco-friendly way to see the city, hiring a rickshaw to travel around London isn't cheap, and can also be a little embarrassing (no one delivers withering looks of contempt quite like the native Londoner). Nevertheless, Ecochariots Rickshaw Hire (2 Addington Street, SE1 7RY, 7207 3435, www.ecochariots.com) rents out sleek, modern-looking rickshaws (what they like to describe as the 'limo of the rickshaw world') that seat up to three people. Hire cost is £180-£300 per day depending on how far you intend to go and how hard you intend to work your driver.

795-799
Drink champagne

The elegant art deco bar at Claridge's Hotel (55 Brook Street, W1K 4HA, 7629 8860) boasts a champagne selection that's among the best in the world. Prices start at £14.50 for a glass of Laurent-Perrier and run all the way through to the thousands for rare vintage bottles from the likes of Veuve Clicquot, Krug and Louis Roederer. Staff are extremely knowledgeable and the detailed, extensive list is updated regularly.

If you visit on the right night, the blood-red champagne and oyster bar at Boisdale of Bishopsgate (Swedeland Court, 202 Bishopsgate, EC2M 4NR, 7283 1763, www.boisdale.co.uk) is dead sexy. Sit at the marble-topped bar and sip one of 30 champagnes, starting at £9.75 for a glass of house fizz through to £320 for a bottle of Louis Roederer Cristal 2002, alongside a dish of great seafood. The whisky list is also extensive. Other good places to sip a glass of bubbly are Vertigo 42 (Tower 42, 25 Old Broad Street, EC2N 1HQ, 7877 7842, www.vertigo42.co.uk), with its panoramic view (see p12), the cool and calm Texture (34 Portman Square, W1H 7BY, 7224 0028, www.texture-restaurant.co.uk) and, of course, all 95.8 metres of the Champagne Bar at St Pancras Station (St Pancras International, Pancras Road, NW1 2QP, 7843 4250, www.searcys.co.uk/stpancrasgrand).

800

Watch a dragon boat race

Based at the London Regatta Centre at Royal Albert Dock, E16, the Thames Dragons (www. thamesdragons.com) crew a 20-seat boat with an ornately carved head in lung-bursting 500-metre races, occasionally longer distances such as the 22-mile Great River Race (*see p123*). Dragon boat racing is an unusual, sociable sport, with training every Thursday and Tuesday from 7pm, and events around the country on most summer weekends. The Dragons are among the UK's top clubs but still need more paddlers, including beginners. Forget the Oxbridge boat race – real fun on the river comes in the shape of a dragon.

801-811
Support your local bookshop

Happily, the current London vogue for smaller, independently owned shops extends to local bookshops. Sure, they can't compete with the super-chains on price, but they often provide a better informed service and more select titles, reintroducing casual shoppers to the pleasure of browsing a curated collection of books that shows the personality of the selector. From the Review bookshop (131 Bellenden Road, SE15 4QY, 7639 7400), Bookseller Crow on the Hill (50 Westow Street, SE19 3AF, 8771 8831, www.booksellercrow.com) and John Sandoe (10 Blacklands Terrace, SW3 2SR, 7589 9473, www.johnsandoe.com) to the Owl Bookshop (209 Kentish Town Road, NW5 2JU, 7485 7793) and Primrose Hill Books (134 Regent's Park Road, NW1 8XL, 7586 2022, www.primrose hillbooks.co.uk), many small bookshops do their best to integrate into their communities

by organising regular events and showing commitment to promoting local authors. Support them!

In Waterloo, Crockatt & Powell (119-120 Lower Marsh, SE1 7AE, 7928 0234, www.crockattandpowell.com) runs a book club and regular readings, while Hackney's Broadway Books (6 Broadway Market, E8 4QJ, 7241 1626) has cemented an enthusiastically loyal clientele simply by its responsiveness to local readers' preferences. Shops like Big Green Bookshop (Unit 1, Brampton Park Road, N22 6BG, 8881 6767, www.biggreenbookshop.com) and Village Books (1D Calton Avenue, SE21 7DE, 8693 2808) have focused on creating spaces that people enjoy spending time in, while other independents have worked hard to develop specialisms that suit their particular locale: Kilburn Bookshop (8 Kilburn Bridge, Kilburn High Road, NW6 6HT, 7328 7071) is good for Irish and Caribbean literature, for example, whereas Bolingbroke Bookshop (147 Northcote Road, SW11 6QB, 7223 9344) in family-friendly Clapham is strong on children's fiction.

812 Shop for art materials at L Cornelissen & Son

This delightful art materials shop – which recently celebrated its 150th year of trading – is one of the loveliest in London. The window displays are fascinating, showing off traditional flat-topped, glass-stoppered regent jars filled with rainbow-coloured pigments (vermilion, azurite, verdigris, malachite, lapis lazuli) that are sold by the bag. These sit alongside wooden cases full of coloured pastels and pencils, while the shelves in the interior heave under a fine array of brushes, tools for restoration work and gilding, waxes and gums, as well as equipment for calligraphers.

L Cornelissen & Son *105 Great Russell Street, WC1B 3RY (7636 1045/www.cornelissen.com).*

813 Watch the remote-controlled aeroplanes on Wormwood Scrubs

814 *Birdwatch*

Despite what you may think, birdwatching can be surprisingly productive in this built-up capital of ours. All you need is a pair of binoculars (8x or 10x magnification's best and RSPB or Opticron models sell for under £100), clothes to match the habitat (green, grey, beige, brown or muted blue are fine) and a good field guide, with illustrations rather than photos: best for most purposes is probably the *Collins Pocket Guide to Birds of Britain and Europe* by Heinzel, Fitter and Parslow. Thereafter, it's about using your eyes, ears (it's usually easiest to discern the presence and identity of birds by calls or song) and common sense.

What can you find in London, and where? You can see cormorants from Waterloo Bridge, herons along the Thames towpaths, and sparrowhawks and kestrels in West End squares. You'll find more wherever there's a lot of vegetation: pay a visit to the London Wetland Centre (Queen Elizabeth's Walk, SW13 9WT, 8409 4400, www.wwt.org.uk) or Leg O'Mutton Reservoir (Lonsdale Road, SW13), a hidden, half-mile-long, 90-foot-wide waterway 20 minutes' walk along the river from Richmond, accessed via a towpath on Lonsdale Road. Elsewhere, try Hampstead Heath, Richmond Park, Brent's Welsh Harp Reservoir, Sydenham Hill Wood or Dagenham Chase. If you just want to see the exotic ring-necked parakeets that have steadily colonised the south-east over the last few decades, check out the avenue of trees just north of Hyde Park's Albert Memorial: listen for loud squawks, look up and wait for them to take flight.

815

Learn the secrets of Westminster Bridge Road

First look at No.100, a block of posh flats now inhabited by bankers, Japanese businessmen and Kevin Spacey. It used to be the headquarters of MI6 and is alleged to have secret prison cells and a secret passage to nearby Lambeth North tube station. Then head a few yards north on the other side of the road. Nestled between a Spar and a Chicken Palace, No.121 has a terracotta, mildly Gothic frontage that shields the remains of one of London's strangest railway stations – the Waterloo terminus of the Necropolis Railway, which took coffins from London to a Surrey graveyard. The brainchild of the London Necropolis Company, from 1885 'the stiffs express' would take corpses daily to their final resting place in Brookwood Cemetery, 30 miles south-west of London.

816 Visit Battersea Park Children's Zoo

London Zoo may have all the headline-grabbing exotic animals, but there's a lower-profile zoo south of the river with creatures waiting to make your offspring's aquaintance. The new owners have pitched this zoo just right for the toddlers, with residents like playful otters, talking mynah birds, cuddlesome sheep and wide-eyed monkeys. There are also Shetland ponies, goats and a multi-storey mouse house. The shop is strong on pocket-money toys and there's space for you to picnic if you don't fancy the on-site Lemon Tree Café.

Battersea Park Children's Zoo *Battersea Park, SW11 4NJ (7924 5826/www.batterseaparkzoo.co.uk).*

817 Visit Battersea Dogs & Cats Home

Not many people seem to know this sanctuary is open to casual visitors. There's a souvenir and accessories shop, a café and a collection of tributes to dogs and their owners. If you're thinking of picking up a new pet, you should bear it in mind that the adoption process can take several visits. Every year in September the 'Annual Reunion' takes place (in Battersea Park), an event that brings together some of the families who have rehomed Battersea dogs over the years. It's a big ol' knees up that involves a fancy-dress parade (fancy dress for the dogs, of course) and plenty of activities. Any dog is welcome to take part.

Battersea Dogs & Cats Home *4 Battersea Park Road, SW8 4AA (7622 3626/www.battersea.org.uk).*

818 Step into Churchill's war room

Churchill's war room is preserved exactly as it would have been during a Cabinet meeting in World War II. An extension explores his childhood and career, with his stirring speeches played over speakers and a 50-foot-long computerised timeline that shows you what Churchill was doing and saying – and what political events were unfolding – at any point during his life. Look out, too, for the great man's half-smoked cigars.

Cabinet War Rooms & Churchill Museum *Clive Steps, King Charles Street, SW1A 2AQ (7930 6961/www.iwm.org.uk).*

819-828
Eat out with the kids

Banners

Free popcorn, colouring books and toys turn an afternoon at Banners into a free-for-all for kids. This is where hungry Crouch Enders come throughout the day, for portions of food as generous as the welcome. The 'world food' encompasses Mexican, Greek, Thai and particularly Caribbean cuisines (jerk is a favourite sauce).

Banners *21 Park Road, N8 8TE (8292 0001).*

Benihana

This global teppanyaki chain, which was founded in 1964 by ex-Olympic wrestler Rocky Aoki, has three London branches. Working on a 'food as event' basis, don't be surpirsed to see your meals prepared and cooked before your eyes on a hot plate by red-toqued chefs who arrive like gunslingers, except that their low-riding belts hold knives instead of six-shooters. They're performance artists as much as chefs, and conversation around the table stops as they get to work with a flamenco rat-a-tat of metal on metal.

Benihana *www.benihana.co.uk*
100 Avenue Road, NW3 3HF (7586 9508);
37 Sackville Street, W1S 3DQ (7494 2525);
77 King's Road, SW3 4NX (7376 7799).

Bodean's

This is what they call good eatin' down South (the US, not Portsmouth), which means it isn't a place for vegetarians, smokey barbecued meat being the main point. A rack of baby back ribs is chewy meaty perfection; the children's menu lists a mini-version, alongside chicken or turkey or ham, with ice-cream to follow.

Bodean's *www.bodeansbbq.com*
10 Poland Street, W1F 8PZ (7287 7575); 4 Broadway Chambers, Fulham Broadway, SW6 1EP (7610 0440); 169 Clapham High Street, SW4 7SS (7622 4248).

Brilliant Kids Café

Sitting next to the kids' clothing and equipment store of the same name, this mummy-magnet offers a wholesome menu and has a lovely garden. Savoury dishes might include tomato and mozzarella quiche or balsamic chicken with lentils; own-made elderflower cordial could complete a virtuous, good-value, light lunch.

Brilliant Kids Café *8 Station Terrace, NW10 5RT (8964 4120/www.brilliantkids.co.uk).*

Chapters All Day Dining

Families with children in tow are gently directed to the first floor at this universally popular Blackheath Brasserie. The all-day dining strapline translates to a menu that spans eggs bendict and cream teas as well as hearty traditional roasts, subtle fish dishes and kids' staples such as macaroni cheese, sausages and mash or fish and chips.

Blue Kangaroo *555 King's Road, SW6 2EB (7371 7622/www.thebluekangaroo.co.uk).*

Crumpet

Bright, airy and uncluttered, this place is all about children: ample space for buggies, plenty of high chairs, a special play den at the back and a serious focus on simple, healthy fare. A tempting assortment of old-fashioned cakes is on display, and the menu offers a good range of sandwiches, salads, snacks and smoothies.

Crumpet *66 Northcote Road, SW11 6QL (7924 1117/www.crumpet.biz).*

Crumpet

Gracelands

Frizzante@City Farm

This delightful Italian café within Hackney City Farm chalks up a different menu every day. Sensitive souls may hesitate to order the grilled chicken skewers out of respect for the bantams pecking around outside, but be assured they are delicious (the skewers, that is).

Frizzante@City Farm *Hackney City Farm, 1A Goldsmith's Row, E2 8QA (7739 2266/ www.frizzanteltd.co.uk).*

Gracelands

For local parents, Gracelands is almost too good to be true. Children can entertain themselves in a designated play corner while their parents drink coffee and take advantage of the wireless internet connection to work on their laptops. There's a friendly local feel, highlighted by a noticeboard on which people give away outgrown baby stuff, advertise local yoga classes and get childcare. Creative quiches (goat's cheese and sweet potato is a favourite) and salads show a loving touch in the kitchen.

Gracelands *118 College Road, NW10 3QE (8964 9161).*

Marine Ices

More than 70 years old and run by descendants of the original owner, this popular ice-cream parlour and restaurant has a *famiglia* ambience. There always seem to be excited children inside, usually with their sights fixed firmly on the traditional gelateria at the back, whose fantastic ice-cream menu is famed far and wide.

Marine Ices *8 Haverstock Hill, NW3 2BL (7482 9003/www.marineices.co.uk).*

Masala Zone

With six London branches, this is the top zone for curry-loving families: a share-worthy menu, low prices and lots of room for family groups to let their hair down. The children's menu delivers accessible dishes in portions small and delicate enough to encourage even the most reluctant palates.

Masala Zone *www.realindianfood.com. 9 Marshall Street, W1F 7ER (7287 9966); 80 Upper Street, N1 0NU (7359 3399); 147 Earl's Court Road, SW5 9RQ (7373 0220); 25 Parkway, NW1 7PG (7267 4422); 48 Floral Street, WC2E 2DA (7379 0101); 75 Bishop's Bridge Road, W2 6BG (7221 0055).*

829

Climb the Monument

When London was being rebuilt after the Great Fire of London, Charles II decided to leave a monument dedicated to the event. Up (and up) went the Monument, Wren's tribute to the blaze – and it's just been reopened again following a £4.5 million refurbishment. Clamber up the 311 steps, and you'll be rewarded with a giddying view across London. What's more, with it being exactly the same height (201 feet) as the distance from the bakery where the great fire started, you can freak yourself out by staring at exactly where you'd land if it suddenly toppled over.

The Monument *Monument Street, EC3R 8AH (7626 2717/www.the monument.info).*

830
Attend a concert in the Square Mile

In recent years the respected City of London Festival (7583 3585, www.colf.org) has played on the theme 'Trading Places', forging links between London and other cities. In 2009 it based these links around latitude 60° north, other recent years have seen creative links between the capital and India, France and Switzerland. Concerts take place from late June to early July in some of the finest buildings in the City. The programme comprises traditional classical music, such as concerts from the London Symphony Orchestra, as well as more unusual offerings from the worlds of jazz, dance, visual art, literature and theatre. There are outdoor and free events.

831-832
Get domestic

The Museum of Domestic Design & Architecture (Middlesex University, Cat Hill, Herts EN4 8HT, 8411 5244, www.moda.mdx.ac.uk) takes an intriguing look at the changing aesthetics and ideals of the home. A permanent exhibition explores the trends in the early 19th-century home, displaying fabrics, wallpaper and catalogues. The museum's Domestic Design archive contains some 4,000 books, magazines and trade catalogues relating to design for the home and household management. There are regular temporary exhibitions; these have already included a display of outrageous wallpaper designs and a study of how Underground posters illustrate the relationship between city and suburbs. Across London, the Sewing Machine Museum (292-312 Balham High Road, SW17 7AA, 8767 4724, www.sewantique. com) also pays tribute to domestic life. Dedicated to Thomas Albert Rushton, founder of the Wimbledon Sewing Machine Company, it contains antique sewing machines, dating from the 1850s to the 1950s. A replica of the original Wimbledon Sewing Machine Shop, which was built in Merton Road, can also be visited.

833
Horse around Hyde Park

Few people know there are stables and a riding school in the park. Lessons are £59-£95 an hour.

Hyde Park & Kensington Stables *63 Bathurst Mews, W2 2SB (7723 2813/www. hydeparkstables.com).*

All keyed up

The founders of two London blogs, diamond geezer and Malcolm Eggs, describe the genesis of their online odes to the capital, while Matt Haynes argues the case for his printed London 'zine.

diamond geezer

I like to think that I've been to places you haven't, but might be interested in visiting after you've read about them. I've tracked the complete length of the long-lost River Fleet, and followed in John Betjeman's footsteps across suburban Metro-land. I've taken in the view from Richmond Hill, Beckton Alp and even the top of the Gherkin. I've been to museums that get ten visitors a day, and to stations long abandoned by any visitors at all. Wherever you turn in London, I've discovered that there's always a good story to tell.

It was never meant to be a blog about London. In fact, it still isn't, not entirely, but I guess writing a lot about London is inevitable when you live here. I moved to the capital about ten years ago from a small Suffolk village where high culture meant the annual tea-towel exhibition in the church hall. London, thankfully, is very different from a small Suffolk village.

I've been writing my blog, diamond geezer, daily since 2002. Sometimes I stumble across something worth writing about whilst I'm out in town. A particularly grim commute on the tube, for example, or turning up in Trafalgar Square at the same time as the lady with the hawk whose job it is to scare away all the pigeons. But most of the time I go out and look deliberately. I like to discover the London beneath the surface, be it in a particular geographical location or at a point in history (or both). The blog gives me a perfect excuse to go there and experience it for myself, then come back and write about it all afterwards.

As an East Ender, I have the dubious honour of living within a mile of the new Olympic Stadium. I've taken a particular interest in London's progress towards winning, and now delivering, the 2012 Games, and I'm keeping a close eye on the vanishing landscape of the Lower Lea Valley. They'll not get away with anything down there over the next few years without me noticing.

Writing about life in the capital means I get a lot of feedback from London-based readers, sometimes even the local media. But I get emails from across the country, and have regular readers all around the world. People everywhere care about London, so it seems. It's a fascinating city on so many levels (in much the same way that my old village wasn't), and so people will always want to discover more about it. Me, I'm more than happy to oblige.

diamond geezer *diamondgeezer.blogspot.com/ www.lndn.blogspot.com*

Malcolm Eggs

Starting a blog is one of the easiest things you can do. It's definitely easier than boiling an egg – and only slightly harder than eating one. You go to a website, enter some details, think of a name and you're off. Perhaps they should make it more difficult: I just did a snap poll of my girlfriend's living room and found that everyone present had at least one blog (and somebody had three).

London Review of Breakfasts was inspired by the tepid beans, gloomy egg and half-arsed bacon I was served in a designer gastro-bar. This joy-sapping 'meal' was delivered by a sulky waiter in combats and cost £8.50. It was an all too common tragedy. Who was holding these cynical egg-sucking profiteers accountable? Could *we* hold them accountable? An online repository of London breakfast reviews, manned by a shadowy cabal of critics, each with hidden identities: it seemed so obvious.

It took three idle minutes on a Saturday morning to set it all up. I adopted the pen name Malcolm Eggs and was soon joined by Herby Banger, Hashley Brown and Dr Sigmund Fried. We took our notebooks to American bars in Clerkenwell and Turkish caffs in Hackney, to a Wetherspoons pub in an airport (not bad), a McDonald's on a High Street (awful) and an IKEA in a retail park (surprisingly good). Where there was breakfast, we sampled, discussed and described it. More contributors volunteered. Then the London blog Londonist.com wrote about us and we were suddenly flooded with readers, not just from London but from Zambia, China, Newcastle. The *Sunday Times* came to take a picture of me with a bacon sandwich in front of my face. Buoyed with confidence, our writers started to find their muse: baked beans were compared to armies and teabags to bulldog testicles. It was fun; it still is.

I think that what success the LRB has had (our daily readership could fill, say, Bethnal Green Working Men's Club, but not the Rivoli Ballroom) comes down to the fact that it has a very specific subject matter. The best London blogs have a specific niche, something that makes them easy to explain over loud music in a crowded pub.

I've no idea what the future holds for the LRB. Perhaps we'll try and get a book published, or launch a range of crockery. Then again, what's that tightness on the left side of my chest?

London Review of Breakfasts
www.londonreviewofbreakfasts.blogspot.com

Matt Haynes

What paper does best is substance. Sure, webzines cost nothing and you can endlessly re-edit, but a two-grand printing bill focuses the mind wonderfully. And being fixed in immovable type means each issue is complete, unique, the same all over the world and throughout all of time. The first issue of *Smoke* may be imperfect, but the British Library's got a copy of it in a large shed somewhere in Yorkshire; future academics will be able to debate the significance of the unusually dark backgrounds on page 12 till the Thames runs dry.

I've convinced you? Want to start your own? Some tips. Before sending anything off to the printer, put it aside, have a week in Margate, then peruse it again with refreshed eyes and brain. Admittedly, in practice, guilt at having lied to your printer so often, anxiety about missed launch dates, and proof reading sessions that last until 4am *might* tempt you to shove it all in a jiffy-bag just to be done with it. But when the proofs arrive, the first thing you'll notice is the mispelling of horseradish in 30-pt bold font on the cover. (The second thing you'll notice is that you've got an article about radish-based condiments in a magazine about London). The moral? Don't scrimp on proofing time. You'll need it.

Don't scrimp on printing either. I spent years convinced there were extended syllabi of exams you needed to fail in order to become a printer, so multifarious were the misdeeds of those I'd worked with. So find a magazine that's similar to what you want to produce, and get its printer's number. You could, of course, use the old fanzine method of collating and stapling loose A4 sheets, but shops like professionalism. They also like barcodes, but that's no hassle: unlike ISBNs, an ISSN is free from the British Library (www.bl.uk).

Taking it round said shops is a terrible, soul-destroying business, during which you'll encounter snobbery, indifference and maddening resistance (bookshop in Kew: 'There's not enough about Kew in it'). To start a new magazine, though, it's the only way. Once you've done all the hard work and reached your physical limit (5,000 copies of *Smoke* is all I can shift by bus and tube), you might consider giving half your profits to a distributor. Staff in most shops, especially the chains, actually like dealing direct with distributors; I suspect because it makes them feel cool.

No one will like dealing with you in the run-up to Christmas, so don't publish in October, November or December. Or January and February for that matter, because shops are suffering post-Christmas tristesse. March and September are for new Spring/Autumn lists, so avoid those too. And forget May through to August, as everyone's on holiday. April is good; you can combine your launch party with my birthday.

Smoke: A London Peculiar
www.smokelondon.co.uk. To subscribe, email smoke@smokelondon.co.uk or call 7582 2877.

Tap into more London blogs
Belle de Jour
www.belledejour-uk.blogspot.com
Once infamous, now famous (that means book and TV spin-offs), 'diary of a London call-girl'.
Egg, Bacon, Chips and Beans
www.eggbaconchipsandbeans.com
Another homage to the London caff, written by 'spoon aficionado Russell Davies.
All in a Day's Work
www.londoncabby.blogspot.com
An insightful portal into the mind of a black cab driver.
Pigeon Blog *http://pigeonblog.wordpress.com*
The pigeon's eye view of our capital.
Random Acts of Reality
www.randomreality.blogware.com
A London ambulance driver on his working life.

835 *Learn jeet kune do*

Jeet kune do is a simple, direct martial art. Why bother stamping on an attacker's foot, grabbing their hand and subduing them with an arm bar when a simple strike to the throat would do the job far more quickly? The Bob Breen Academy (www.bobbreen.co.uk) now based at SPACe (31 Falkirk Street, N1 6HF) runs sporadic courses (see website for details). Best avoid the pubs for a while, though.

836 *Take Moroccan tea at Mô*

The sweet smell of sheesha pipes and mint dominates proceedings at Mô, where they take their Moroccan stylings seriously. Decor is pretty much flawless in this respect: tables, couches, stools, low-hanging lamps and drapes run along either side of the thin room, so the place feels as though it's all clutter and colour, leaving it a mite claustrophobic. Momo, the famed Moroccan restaurant next door, is virtually inaccessible if you haven't booked, and its spill-over makes this affiliate bar busy as well. Still, if you arrive early enough, you'll find that the Tea Room is a lovely little nook in which to spend an evening.

Mô Tea Room *25 Heddon Street, W1B 4BH (7434 4040/www.momoresto.com).*

837 *Dine in the dark*

The pitch-black dining room at Dans Le Noir (30-31 Clerkenwell Green, EC1R 0DU, 7253 1100, www.danslenoir.com/london) has patrons literally left in the dark, guessing what their surroundings – and dishes – look like. It's a remarkably disconcerting feeling but also a potentially uplifting experience as you begin to empathise with your blind waiting staff. Menus are colour coded (blue for fish dishes, red for meat lovers, green for vegetarians and white for 'chef's surprise'). Napkin up: you'll leave with plenty of dropped food down your front.

A few of my favourite things

838-842
Julie Myerson, author

I love to go to Borough Market on a Saturday morning with my husband and our Border Collie (she's hoping to get thrown whole sausages by the stallholders). **I love visiting Spitalfields Market on a Saturday afternoon with my children. They usually make straight for Rokit (101-107 Brick Lane, E1 65E, 7375 3864, www.rokit.co.uk) and Beyond Retro (110-112 Cheshire Street, E2 6EJ, 7613 3636, www.beyondretro.com), for a rummage around.** I have to be alone whenever I go to Columbia Road Flower Market on a Sunday. This is not a place where you want to be hurried. **The Old Operating Theatre & Herb Garret (9A St Thomas's Street, SE1 9RY, 7188 2679, www.thegarret. org.uk, *see p232*) is magic – and strange. You go up a secret winding staircase at the side of St Thomas's Church all the way to the attic, and you're swept back a hundred years.** No one seems to have realised, but the Walworth Road where I live has two fabulous restaurants. Dragon Castle (114 Walworth Road, SE17 1JL, 7277 3388, www.dragoncastle.co.uk) is a deliciously opulent Chinese with real carp sploshing about in a pond in the entrance hall. La Luna (380 Walworth Road, SE17 2NG, 7277 1991), a friendly neighbourhood Italian with wonderful food, is where my husband and I go when we're tired, to escape the kids and comfort ourselves with the linguine gamberone.

843

Remember 7/7

The 52 stainless steel pillars of this memorial in Hyde Park (www.royalparks.org.uk) represent the 52 people who died in the terrorist attacks on 7 July 2005.

7 JULY 2005
08:50
ALDGATE

844 *Eat at the River Café*

Only Londoners would happily pay through the nose for Italian peasant food… and it's all too easy to scoff at restaurants run by celebrity chefs. But the food at Rose Gray and Ruth Rogers's River Café (Thames Wharf, Rainville Road, W6 9HA, 7386 4200, www.rivercafe. co.uk) seems to improve with age. Ingredients are impeccably sourced, dishes are simply prepared – and priced according to the former rather than the latter. High summer is the best time to visit; it's easier to get a table and that table is likely to be in the courtyard, amid trailing raspberry bushes and squash plants. Many customers look vaguely as though they must be in the public eye, but celebrity or not, all first-timers should opt for the deservedly famous 'Nemesis' dessert. Chocolate heaven.

845 *Play women's football...*

Women's football has really taken off over the past decade and there are now dozens of local teams looking for players. If you are interested in joining in, either contact the London County Football Association (11 Hurlingham Business Park, Sulivan Road, SW6 3DU, 0870 774 3010, www.londonfa.com) or visit the Football Association website (www.thefa.com) to find a club that's convenient for you.

846 *...or just watch*

Professional women's football in England is now at a seriously high standard. Even better, at £5 to watch the FA Women's Premier League, it's cheaper than even non-league football. With the national team having qualified for September 2007's World Cup in China, interest in the women's game is expected to grow. Most of London's pro clubs also have a women's team, with Arsenal and Charlton probably the best. See www.thefa.com/Leagues/WomensPremier League for fixtures.

847 *Tour Lord's*

The wearers of the famous egg-and-bacon tie (orange and yellow stripes) have come to love the NatWest Media Centre, the stunning raised pod that dominates Lord's, the self-proclaimed home of cricket. The centre joins the portrait-bedecked Long Room on the guided tour (you'll need to book), along with the expected range of battered bats, photos and blazers. There's plenty of WG Grace ephemera and, of course, the Ashes urn. Since England's Ashes victory in 2009, it's gratifying to know that (for once) both the replica – which usually resides in Australia these days – *and* the original are currently in place here.

Lord's Tour & MCC Museum
Marylebone Cricket Club, Lord's, St John's Wood Road, NW8 8QN (7616 8595/www.lords.org).

Lord's

848 *Find a busker when you want one*

Find them at Carling-associated 'licensed busking' spots in Angel, Bank, Bond Street, Canary Wharf, Charing Cross, Euston, Green Park, King's Cross St Pancras, Leicester Square, London Bridge, Oxford Circus, Piccadilly Circus, South Kensington, Tottenham Court Road, Victoria, Waterloo and Westminster tube stations. Below, busker Helmut Scholz explains why he loves to perform.

I started busking in Munich and Frankfurt in 1977 or 1976, and came to London in 1984, where I played in a shopping arcade in Kensington; London was an easier place to busk. But I first came to London in the 1960s as a young student. I was just fascinated by this system under the earth, like a labyrinth. But even before that a schoolfriend of mine visited London and he told me about the Underground, where he had heard a violinist playing Bach and some of that stuck in my brain and that's what I'm doing now!

To get my pitch on the Underground I had to have an audition, which was a very nasty experience. I was nervous. I know people who didn't get their licence because they were too nervous. I don't remember what I played in my audition. I think one was too slow for them, but they liked another. What funny people!

I don't know why they audition at all because if buskers aren't good enough nobody cares and you go home again so it's completely unnecessary torture! I think everyone should be allowed to play as long as they don't come back if they aren't good enough and nobody gives them any money.

My favourite pitch is Bank One (there are four pitches at Bank), which is definitely not the best one for money, but it's a place where

people can stand and listen for a while. If you are ignored for an hour and a half, it affects you; if you feel a response from the audience, it affects you. It's like football.

My favourite time of day to play is between 10am and noon. The day is still a bit fresh, you don't get the drunks that you get in the evening. You can play for the situation and the audience, like the Fool in Shakespeare. Peak times don't work for me. Everyone is just rushing past and nobody cares. I have never had people ask for requests. Sometimes they ask what I am playing. I was asked by two policemen once at Green Park and I told them it was one of my own compositions, so they were quite impressed. People dancing is an everyday thing. Children especially. That is part of my job, to make people dance. You don't get trouble on the Underground if people are dancing.

When I busk I have a repertoire of two hours, but I also improvise. The most intense things happened the day after the bombing. I was at Bank and I didn't know what to play, so I played things I don't normally play like Bach's *St Matthew Passion*. I was crying when I played. Those people had died around the corner in the tunnel. They were like my audience and playing those songs was my way of saying goodbye.

849 Take a peek at Strand Lane's 'Roman Bath'

Neither Roman nor really a bath, this splendid little curio at 5 Strand Lane, WC2, can be glimpsed through a murky barred window down a cruddy side alley off Surrey Street, which is behind King's College. The red-brick plunge pool is first mentioned in records towards the end of the 18th century and Dickens wrote about it in *David Copperfield*, but archaeologists have found no evidence to confirm it has Roman origins. It's a fascinating oddity, nevertheless.

850

Get your hands on 1,000 years of history at the National Archives

The National Archives is an extraordinary collection of documents, located by the river in Kew. You can order anything up from the vaults, whether it's the files on a famous spy, your great grandfather's Boer War record or a plan of the sewers in Lagos, Nigeria (this last is the heaviest document in the archive). Part of the fascination of a visit to the Archives lies in the fact that – even though the records are all meticulously catalogued by title – there are 100 miles of shelving, which means that an individual file might not get read from one century to the next. No one can tell you exactly what's inside and hence any number of secrets might be filed away along those seemingly endless shelves.

Much of the archive is available online – you can search for files, pay for them to be scanned and emailed to you – but the allure of this place is entwined with the desire to actually get your hands on the physical documents. There's something intensely romantic about peeking into the daily routines of spooks and mandarins who once invested so much effort into staying out of sight. You will need to show your ID and decant your possessions into a plastic bag or lockers to gain entry.

National Archives *Ruskin Avenue, TW9 4DU (8876 3444/www.nationalarchives.gov.uk).*

851

Appreciate everyday heroes at Postman's Park

Something of a secret oasis in the less than verdurous surroundings of the City, Postman's Park – off Aldersgate Street, EC1, and named after the post office that once stood on its southern side – is a delightful retreat. Conceived by socialist George Watts in the late 19th century, its main feature is the touching 'Heroes Wall', a display of 34 Victorian ceramic plaques commemorating fatal acts of bravery, such as that of John Cranmer of Cambridge, 'a clerk in the London County Council who was drowned near Ostend while saving the life of a stranger and a foreigner (1901)'. There's been a resurgence of interest in the park in recent years, and it was a key location in Patrick Marber's London-based play *Closer*, later made into a film (*see p63*).

852 Take in a cowbell show over dinner at the Tiroler Hut

With the rest of Westbourne Grove giving itself over to multimillion-pound residential conversions and lots of minimalist spas and hair salons, the Tiroler Hut provides some much-needed kitsch. Situated below street level, this family-run Austrian bar-restaurant has been trading since 1967 under the same management – the accordion-playing Joseph and his wife Christine. On any given night you might find Joseph, dressed in traditional Alpine garb, yodelling, playing the accordion or tinkling his Tyrolean cowbells, while boisterous diners in the restaurant tuck into cheese fondue or a plate of bratwurst. Be prepared to sing along to a tune or two from *The Sound of Music*.

Tiroler Hut *27 Westbourne Grove, W2 4UA (7727 3981/www.tirolerhut.co.uk).*

853

The focus at the Shochu Lounge (Roka, 37 Charlotte Street, W1T 1RR, 7580 9666, www.shochulounge.com) is on Japan's vodka-like spirit shochu, here tinctured with things like cinnamon ('for joy of life') or lemon ('for virility'), served neat or in cocktails. Set in the basement, the wooden vats and rustic bar counter, low tables and plush, boxy red seats in enclaves, make for a setting that's half style bar, half film set for Zatoichi.

854

Have dinner at the dogs

An illustrious past that included visits from Winston Churchill and Lana Turner, and Brad Pitt and David Beckham (who worked here as a teenager) sadly didn't stop the glorious Walthamstow Greyhound Stadium being closed in August 2008 to make way for housing. Which leaves London – once home to 30 dog tracks – with just one (plus two on its outskirts at Crayford and Romford). At Wimbledon Stadium (Plough Lane, SW17 0BL, 8946 8000, www.lovethedogs.co.uk), restaurant Star Attraction offers long rows of benches overlooking the finish line, while the TVs in the more intimate Bistro restaurant mean you needn't miss any of the action.

855

Climb One Tree Hill

From Honor Oak Park in SE23, clamber through pretty woodland to the lofty summit of One Tree Hill, known as such because it is rumoured that Queen Elizabeth I picnicked here beside a single oak tree. There's no shortage of trees on the hill now and the original oak is long gone, but a replacement stands in its place. Well worth the climb for spectacular city sunsets and, in spring, to see one of London's few populations of woodpeckers hammering away.

856 Learn to make your own chocolate

At Hannah Saxton's fun and informative My Chocolate courses, held every Sunday in Farringdon, participants make fudge, truffles and pralines, and learn to dip their own hand-made chocolates. There are recipes to take away and, of course, chocolate – see if you can make it home before you scoff the lot. The course costs £55; phone (7269 5760) or check the website (www.mychocolate.co.uk) for dates.

857

View art by youngsters

Struggling to get the bairns to appreciate the merits of the National Gallery? Took 'em to Carsten Höller's slides in Tate Modern and they said they preferred the ones in the park? You might have better luck with a visit to the London International Gallery of Children's Art (Waterlow Park Centre, Dartmouth Park Hill, N19 5JF, 7281 1111, www.ligca.org), which celebrates the creativity of children from around the world. Far-reaching exhibitions have ranged from the showcase of young talent that is Tokyo's Artscape competition to photographs taken by children from London's ethnic minorities. Art and story telling workshops that cater for five- to 12-year-olds are held on Saturday mornings and cost £5.

858

Tour the State Apartments at Buckingham Palace

It's getting on for 20 years since the Queen started to open her home to the great unwashed during the summer months, but Londoners have been reluctant to take up her annual invitation. It could be the entry charge that puts people off: £16.50 is pretty steep, even if it doesn't go into the Queen's hot little hand – rather to the upkeep of the Royal Collection, which includes paintings by Canaletto and Rubens, with work displayed on a rotating basis in the Queen's Gallery. If you do decide to visit (and, really, it's worth it just to see displays of Lizzie's bling), allow about two hours and don't forgo the audio guide. You'll hear from, among others, the chap whose job it is to oversee the laying of the table in the State Dining Room. Enthralling.
Buckingham Palace *Buckingham Palace Road, SW1A 1AA (7766 7300/www.royal.gov.uk).*

859

Take an Original London Walk

In the words of the lovely and arthritic Judy, a tour guide with London Walks (7624 3978, www.walks.com), we may owe some of our greatest works of literature to a bit of a temperature and a runny nose. Charles Dickens, you see, nearly became an actor before he took to writing, but suffered a terrible head cold on the day of his first audition and didn't show up.

It's appropriate that the name of Dickens comes up, as back in the 1860s he had already cottoned on to one of the greatest joys that London has to offer: 'Whenever I think I deserve particularly well of myself, and have earned the right to enjoy a little treat, I stroll from Covent Garden into the City of London and roam about its deserted nooks and corners.' Unlike New York or Paris, London has never been subjected to logical planning, but has grown organically out of a thick mulch of story and experience. What better way to explore, then, than as part of a guided walking tour led by a local expert, who showers his or her charges with historical detail, trivia and anecdote at every concealed alley and hidden courtyard. Judy leads a 'Shakespeare's & Dickens' London' walk, one of over 100 walks the company runs each week, from 'Ghosts of the Old City' to 'The Beatles "In My Life" Walk'.

Other notable walking companies include Citisights (8806 4325, www.chr.org.uk), Performing London (01234 404774, www.performinglondon.co.uk) and Silvercane Tours (07720 715295, www.silvercanetours.com), which also does movie location walks including the 'Big Knickers Tour' (*Bridget Jones's Diary*) and a *Da Vinci Code* walk.

860 Sit between Churchill and Roosevelt

The wartime big-hitters are preserved in jocular conversation on a sturdy bench in Bond Street, created by American sculptor Lawrence Holofcener. What price a Bush/Blair sculpture depicting enthroned king and palm-flapping lackey?

861 Eat at Sketch without blowing the budget

If Sketch is famous for one thing, that's the outrageous price of dining. But fear not: if you can't manage the infamous Lecture Room and mid-range Gallery, you can still opt for the relatively proletarian pricing of Glade. There you can taste the imaginative and inventive flavour combinations of Pierre Gagnaire, the celebrated chef who oversees the kitchen from his HQ in, er, Paris, at prices that are fair for this level of quality. Glade is fun, quirky and amusingly pretentious. Of course, no trip to Sketch would be complete without a visit to the fabulous loos (*see p154*).
Sketch: The Glade *9 Conduit Street, W1S 2XG (7659 4500/www.sketch.uk.com).*

862 Get your cart marked

The principal method of getting yourself and your chattels round the capital in the fourteenth century, carts are now pretty much obsolete, thanks to black cabs, red buses and white vans. Nonetheless, every June the Guildhall hosts a Cart Marking Ceremony for the Worshipful Company of Carmen (www.thecarmen.co.uk). The owners of around forty 'carts', ranging from horse-drawn carriages to steam wagons and even Transport for London buses, come to the event to have their vehicle branded (and therefore 'licensed to carry goods at a fair price') by the Lord Mayor.

863 Learn to flamenco dance

Often improvised and incredibly dramatic, flamenco deals with the grand themes of death, anguish, despair and religious doubt. To learn the dance, you'll need a pair of hard-soled shoes with a heel. Peña Flamenca de Londres is a flamenco club that meets on the second Sunday of every month except August at St Aloysius Social Club (20 Phoenix Road, NW1 1TA). The club's website (www.flamenco-london.org.uk) has links to many other teachers and schools.

864 Laugh like a horse

Malcolm Hay meets the founders of the Laughing Horse, a cottage industry fast becoming a mini empire.

Back in 1999 Alex Petty was involved with running a weekly comedy night at the Black Horse in Richmond. Kevin McCarron was a regular on the bill. 'Kevin has always been a prolific writer,' Petty declares. 'He'd do a new routine every week. At that time he wasn't a particularly good compère. But he could talk for hours and keep the audience in a good mood. When our resident compère left, Kevin took his place.'

Petty had no ambitions to become a performer. But two other comedians had worked with him on the club. One was Rob Lee. 'Rob got married, gave up comedy and moved to Brighton.' The other was Fenton McCoot. 'Fenton was a barber before he became a comic. He gave it up because handling scissors got dangerous when he had the shakes.' Fenton was responsible for booking acts. Then one night he vanished. 'Literally. He didn't turn up. Suddenly he wasn't there.' McCarron and Petty were left in charge. 'That was in 2000,' they explain. 'We've not heard from him since.'

At that point their only ambition was to run this regular weekly club. 'We'd called it the Laughing Horse because the venue was called the Black Horse and it sounds like "laughing hoarse". Yes, it's an excruciating pun. As unfunny then as it is now.' But the partnership blossomed. Their influence increased. 'There's no masterplan,' McCarron and Petty claim. 'It seems to grow organically. Managers at other venues come to our shows, like what they see and approach us. It's taken on a life of its own.'

The Laughing Horse empire now consists of eight London clubs, as well as regular nights all over the country. They take shows to the south of France and Monaco. They run a nationwide Laughing Horse New Act of the Year competition with a prize fund of £2,500 and the guarantee for the winner of paid work in Laughing Horse clubs.

Remarkably, McCarron and Petty have achieved all this while holding down 'normal' day jobs. McCarron lectures in English Literature at Roehampton University, where he's introduced comedy courses as part of the Creative Writing programme. Petty works in IT for a bank. 'Sadly, there's no synergy with comedy there,' he says. 'But both our jobs are quite flexible. We also have a lot of comics who run the actual nights for us – people like Aggie Elsdon, Nigel Taylor, Sion James, Jay Sodagar, Kevin Shepherd and Lewis Bryan, to name just a few!'

Petty does the bookings, promotion and PR. McCarron helps out with this and hosts many of the shows. They share an identical philosophy and the same dislikes: 'Comics who become promoters to give themselves stage time. Small nights where it's all about the comics and the audience is disregarded. Gong shows – they're bloodthirsty gladiatorial events and degrading for the performers.'

Above all, they take a realistic view of what's needed. 'With our knowledge of acts playing the circuit, we can book comics into each club who suit the size of room, budget, location and so on.' More often than not, this doesn't involve 'big' names. 'We'd noticed there was a large number of acts who couldn't get a paid slot at, say, Banana Cabaret, but could perfectly well headline one of our smaller places.' But there's a growing ambition too. One long-term plan is to run venues and produce shows at the festivals in Brighton, Leicester, Glasgow and Kilkenny. And Adelaide.

Laughing Horse *www.laughinghorse.co.uk.* **Brixton** *The Dogstar, 389 Coldharbour Lane, SW9 8LQ (7733 7515);* **Camden** *Camden Head, 100 Camden High Street, NW1 0LU (7485 4019);* **Earl's Court** *344 Old Brompton Road, SW5 9JU (7370 2449).* **Kingston** *20 Fairfield South, Kingston, KT1 2UL (8296 0479);* **Piccadilly** *The Goat Tavern, 3 Stafford Street, W1S 4RP (7629 0966);* **Richmond** *The Hope of Richmond 155-177 Kew Road, TW9 2PN (8940 5465);* **Soho** *Coach & Horses, 1 Great Marlborough Street, W1F 7HG (7437 3285);* **Twickenham** *Heatham House Youth Centre, Whitton Road, TW1 1BH (8288 0950).*

865-867 *Shop for cheese*

Neal's Yard Dairy (17 Shorts Gardens, WC2H 9UP, 7240 5700, www.nealsyarddairy.co.uk) is the best place in London to introduce your taste buds to the bounty of cheeses produced in Ireland and the British Isles. In business for over 25 years, the Dairy began by selling just the cheeses it had made, but then started buying them from small artisan cheesemakers across the country. The cheeses are matured in the cellars beneath the shop, which means they are always sold in peak condition. Customers are given generous tastings – and their feedback is actively sought. Knowledgeable, passionate staff are on hand to advise on care and storage. Over 50 seasonal varieties will be on sale at any given time, some of the more unusual being ardrahan (a creamy, pungent Irish cow's milk cheese), crockhamdale (a sweet, sharp sheep's cheese from Kent) and harbourne (a crumbly goat's cheese from Devon).

Cheese fans should also seek out iconic cheese boutique La Fromagerie (2-6 Moxon Street, W1U 4EW, 7935 0341, www.lafromagerie. co.uk). Its owner travels extensively around Britain and the Continent, selecting artisanal cheeses. The result is unusual selections, such as lingot de la monastère, a thyme-scented goat's cheese from the Dalmeyrie monastery, or Venetian cheeses like vezzena. There's also a tiny tasting café with a roster of cheesy events.

Then there's Paxton & Whitfield (93 Jermyn Street, SW1Y 6JE, 7930 0259, www.paxtonand whitfield.co.uk); according to Winston Churchill, 'a gentleman only buys his cheeses' from here. Since it opened on this site in 1797 (it began as a stall in Aldwych market back in 1742), Britain's oldest cheesemonger has been awarded innumerable royal warrants, and little has changed in the shop's appearance – it's still an old-fashioned emporium of brass railings and fresh flowers.

Neal's Yard Dairy

868-869
Celebrate Shakespeare's birthday

When 23 April comes, Shakespeare's Globe (21 New Globe Walk, SE1 9DT, 7902 1500, www.shakespeares-globe.org) throws open its doors to celebrate the birth of the Bard, offering a range of free activities, including training from the theatre's actors on how to perform lines in front of a packed auditorium (if you're lucky you might even get a go on the stage). Past events have included lessons on how to wear a toga and in gladiatorial fighting, as well as a 'best theatrical death' competition.

Meanwhile, over at Southwark Cathedral (SE1 9DA, 7367 6700, www.dswark.org/cathedral) there's an annual humorous talk and a concert (featuring comedians such as Arthur Smith and musician Rick Jones) to mark the occasion. See the cathedral's website for details.

870
Choose Juice at Ranoush

The original Ranoush Juice Bar (43 Edgware Road, W2 2JR, 7723 5929) vibrates to the buzz of the Edgware Road Middle Eastern enclave, remaining the favourite local fast food joint right up to its 3am closing. An array of fruit is piled behind the counter; choose a combination and it will be squeezed for you. Ranoush's shawarma (lamb) kebabs shouldn't be missed either – they could well be London's best – and there's a wide choice of fresh salads and warm meze too. Takeaway is the norm, although a handful of tables are crammed inside.

871
Walk under the Thames

Yes, it's a bit dank and smelly, but how often do you get the chance to walk under a river? The Thames foot tunnel at Greenwich is open to the public, connecting Island Gardens at the southerly tip of the Isle of Dogs to Greenwich, near the *Cutty Sark*. The echoes are impressive, the surroundings rather spooky.

872
Take a punt on High Stakes bookshop

Tomes such as *How to Win the Pools* and *The Racing Retirement Plan* sit beside less ambitious titles like *Discovering Backgammon* in this small and welcoming shop. Dedicated to gambling books, this is the only enterprise of its kind in the UK. As well as betting strategy and gambling, stock includes books on the concept of 'chance', the history of gambling and sports almanacs.

High Stakes *21 Great Ormond Street, WC1N 3JB (7430 1021/www.highstakes.co.uk).*

873
Learn about seafood at Billingsgate Market

Billingsgate Market, which moved out to West India Dock near Poplar in 1982, was previously in the City (off present-day Lower Thames Street) where it had traded for some 900 years. Its name is still synonymous with fish, and over the past few years, a Seafood Training School on the first floor of the market (Office 30, Billingsgate Market, Trafalgar Way, E14 5ST, 7517 3548, www.seafoodtraining.org) has been teaching children, prospective fishmongers and intrigued members of the public all about fish and seafood preparation and cookery. The 'Shellfish Workshop' course (costing £195 including breakfast and a big bag of fish to take home) entails guidance on such matters as cleaning squid, butterflying prawns and buying the freshest specimens. Those aiming to enter the trade receive free tuition.

874
Buy bits of the Beatles

Four London Beatles Days (01902 766733, 07801 564622, www.beatlesdays.com) are held each year, on a Sunday in Bloomsbury's Park Inn Hotel (92 Southampton Row, WC1B 4BH). Fab Four fans flock to these fairs to buy all sorts of Beatles memorabilia. A vast range of stock is up for grabs, from original LPs to recently licensed new merchandise. An 18-inch John Lennon action figure for £40, anyone?

875 *Do the weekly shop at Damas Gate*

Famous foodies such as Joanna Blythman and Nigella Lawson are fans of Damas Gate (81-85 Uxbridge Road, W12 7NR, 8743 5116), an enormous, bustling, inexpensive Middle Eastern supermarket that is central to life in Shepherd's Bush. There's a vast display of fresh vegetables, fruit and herbs outside; inside, a butcher's counter offers halal meat, and a fast food section sells own-made falafels, kebabs and shawarma sandwiches to take away. Long aisles are stacked with aromatic spices, flatbreads, olives, Lebanese pastries, soft drinks and wines. Blocks of feta and fresh pickles are laid out in buckets, and there's an enormous selection of high-quality nuts, including bright green sliced pistachios.

Urban explorers

For author Nick Royle, *London's abandoned buildings have always been fascinating. He describes his compulsion to find a way inside the ruins that most of us only see from the outside. Meanwhile, photographers* Alexander Shields *and* William Eckersley *spent a year recording the city's derelict spaces. Their stunning images, recently collected in a book, reveal that there can be incredible beauty in decay.*

Despite the extraordinary concentration of London's population, both itinerant and fixed, it's often thought to be rather easy to feel very alone in the capital. The sheer numbers of people only serve to make the already isolated feel even more cut off from humanity. Everybody is in a rush; no one has time for anybody else. A cliché. And like most clichés, there's some truth in it. But it's also possible to feel that there are too many people in London, too many people in any one building, for you ever to feel truly alone. It can be a good thing, in the right circumstances, to feel alone, to experience a little solitude.

I have been breaking into London's abandoned buildings for more than 20 years. Part of the attraction, certainly, is this very particular sense of solitude. But it is only part

of it. Sometimes, indeed, I have not been alone. As a resident of Shepherd's Bush through the mid to late 1990s, I developed a fascination for the great white arched building between the Central Line station and the Holland Park roundabout. Above the flyposted glass doors was the name of an insurance company, but almost a century earlier the building had been the main entrance to the Franco-British Exhibition Halls. I had tried and failed to find my own way in and so visited those great empty halls in the company of a representative from the developers who would eventually knock the buildings down.

At the other end of what would later become the Westfield Shopping Centre, I had a look inside the then disused Wood Lane tube station, accompanied by an employee of London

Underground. The tour was interesting, but it was only later, when I climbed back in over the wall on my own to conduct further, clandestine explorations, that my heart started to beat faster.

My first taste of abandoned buildings came in the mid 1980s when a summer job at Pizza on the Park provided me with an opportunity to enter St George's Hospital, now the Lanesborough Hotel, which had been lying empty for a couple of years. Not quite empty, though. White coats draped over swivel chairs and boxes of photographic slides scattered across laboratory work benches gave the hospital the air of a place abandoned in a hurry: a gift to a writer of fiction.

The City of London Maternity Hospital on Hanley Road, Hornsey, was in the process of being knocked down, having closed in 1983, when I wandered in three or four years later. The West London Hospital in Hammersmith was facing demolition when, in October 1998, I spotted a door at the rear of the building that was hanging off its hinges. That's the thing: you don't actually have to commit violence to property to explore London's abandoned buildings, and I never do. Nor do I take anything from them, apart from photographs, digital video and inspiration for stories. Disused spaces, particularly institutional or industrial buildings, have a unique atmosphere, a blend of the poignant with the sinister, melancholy with loneliness. You imagine the thousands of lives that have undoubtedly left some trace in the crumbling plaster, the blistered paintwork.

And your mind – well, my mind – works overtime conjuring various fictional possibilities. What could happen here is as interesting to me as what might have already taken place.

I have occasionally taken risks when entering buildings. St George's Hospital could only be reached by jumping across a gap between two ledges. The gap was narrow but the drop was deep. More than 20 years later, trying to find a way into a much-fancied former cinema in Shepherd's Bush, I climbed a drainpipe to reach an open toilet window one floor up, but the window would not open any wider. I had been inside the building while it was still in business as the Mecca Bingo Hall, so why was I so intent on gaining entrance once it had been boarded up?

It's not just the thrill of being somewhere you're not supposed to be. I am a self-confessed coward and look forward to confrontation with security guards with as little relish as I anticipate encounters with territorial squatters. It's more to do with having a relationship with the building itself and experiencing at first hand the unmistakeable atmosphere of a space that has been abandoned.

Every day for several years, whether by road or rail, I would pass the creamy-tiled Paddington Maintenance Depot, which stood hard by the Westway close to the mainline station. Some admirers have likened the building to an ocean liner or battleship for its bold curvaceous lines; I would agree only insofar as to ascribe female gender to the

structure, designed in 1965 by Bicknall & Hamilton architects. For me, the building was a woman. I admired her; she was inaccessible; I desired her. I would gaze at her longingly from the Hammersmith & City Line. When driving into town on the Westway I would hug the inside lane so as to be nearer to her. In order to get closer still, I would negotiate the slip roads and roundabouts that had been draped around her like so many silk scarves.

Then, one lucky day, I saw that someone had left a window open. Perhaps one of the many graffiti writers who had been all over her, both inside and out. Known, Fume, Tube, Demo, NIG. Heart pounding, I entered the building. To be inside after so long, to have the run of the place, from the shadow-festooned depths of the lower floors to the wraparound views from the upper storeys, quite literally took my breath away.

In 2001 the building became the head office of a high-street fashion chain. The Monsoon Building, as it is now known, still has many admirers, among them Philip Davies of English Heritage, who has said that 'the long-term interest of such a landmark building is best served by its remaining in use'. It may seem perverse to disagree with a remark born of such obvious good sense, yet I know if I were to be invited back to view the restored stairway mosaics and the double-height open-plan office on the ground floor, I would miss the scrunch of broken glass underfoot. I would pine for the smells of rot and damp. And I would have to imagine I could still taste, in the back of my throat, the loneliness, the desolation and the sheer gut-wrenching excitement of being in an abandoned building.

Nicholas Royle's latest book *Mortality* is published by Serpent's Tail. Alexander Shields and William Eckersley's book *Left London* can be purchased for £25 from www.leftlondon.co.uk and bookshops including the ICA, Design Museum, Tate Modern, Photographers' Gallery, Ian Shipley and Borders.

877-878
Eat Turkish in the small hours

In a country of tiresomely early closing times, the Turkish eateries that line Green Lanes provide much-needed quality late-night nosh. Pick of the bunch is Sedale (2 Salisbury Promenade, N8 0RX, 8800 1636), which serves until 2am. From low-priced meze to main meals (lamb and chicken kebab skewers, plus some brilliant quail kebabs) or smaller takeaways like lacun (full-size minced lamb and onion pizzas, only £1.50 to go), the food is consistently impressive.

Over on Kingsland High Street, local Turkish café Sömine (No.131, E8 2PB, 7254 7384) serves food right around the clock. Try the flatbread stuffed with spinach and potato, one of the astonishingly cheap stews or comforting mani (a serving of meat and dumplings done in the central Turkish style, which means lots of little dumplings stuffed with lamb, covered in thick yoghurt, with spicy, sour red seasoning sprinkled on top).

879
Buy Time Out magazine

If we still haven't given you enough to do…

880
Visit Britain's oldest wine merchant

Berry Bros & Rudd (3 St James's Street, SW1A 1EG, 7396 9600, www.bbr.com) has been trading here since 1698 and everything from the evocative shopfront to the panelled tasting rooms and vaulted Georgian cellars is dripping with heritage. In line with its lofty location on St James's Street, this is a pompous kind of place, but the pedigree isn't the only draw – the staff are knowledgeable and, though the 2005 Château Haut-Brion might set you back £500, the house wines come in at under a fiver and it also stocks some of the finest New World wines ever to wash up on these shores.

881
Enjoy the arts outdoors in east London

Taking place in June each year, the Greenwich+ Docklands International Festival (8305 1818, www.festival.org) is an exciting mix of free theatrical, musical and site-specific outdoor events at various venues across east and south-east London, many in the vicinity of Canary Wharf. Past spectaculars have included aerial percussionists, 30-foot-diameter wheels of colour rolling through Bow and some impressively inventive pyrotechnics.

882
Converse, mobile-free, at the Nag's Head

You're best off arriving at the Nag's Head (53 Kinnerton Street, SW1X 8ED, 7235 1135) stone cold sober: the layout of this tiny little pub, originally stables, is mind-bending enough without alcohol to exaggerate the effect. The floor in the main bar is at least a foot lower behind the bar than it is in front of it, rendering the staff in curious miniature as they pour perfect pints of Adnams. But our favourite bit? The well-enforced mobile phone ban: no beeping, no ringing, no barked voicemails – just the hum of real conversation.

883
See something modern at the Laban theatre

By all means stroll in for the contemporary dance performances within, but also allow yourself time to stand outside and admire the incredible Herzog & de Meuron building. **Laban** *Creekside, SE8 3DZ (8691 8600/ www.laban.org).*

884

Give the Museum of London a second chance

*Jack Lohman tells **Peter Watts** there are plenty of exciting new developments at a repository that is reinventing itself for the 21st century.*

Not many museum directors are like Professor Jack Lohman. Not many are the son of Polish refugees who settled in London after spending World War II in concentration camps. Not many conduct tours of their museum in any one of 12 languages, and hope to learn a few more before the 2012 Olympics. Not many are trained architects overseeing a thorough and expensive redesign of the museum. Not many worked for Solidarity under communism, or in Berlin before the Wall came down, or made TV programmes with Simon Wiesenthal.

Lohman, now 48 years old, has been director of the museum since 2002. While he may have taken an unorthodox journey to the position, it's one that makes sense for a man who has always loved London and museums. 'My parents settled in West Kensington, which was a very Polish area,' he says. 'They were always passionate about London. My mother is over 80 and there isn't an exhibition she hasn't seen. We saw London as a country in itself. We didn't go to Stratford or Bath or Bristol because we had London – and something of that mentality has stayed with me. If I'm leaving London, I'm leaving by air – I'd sooner do that than go and visit some place in Kent.'

Lohman is keen to expand knowledge of London geographically as well as historically. 'A lot of people fixate on central London; they forget we have this necklace of important places – Haringey, Tower Hamlets, Wembley, Streatham – they're all part of the story.'

To challenge this, Lohman has organised a link between London's smaller museums, the London Museums Hub, a joint venture with 'the Horniman, the Geffrye, the London Transport Museum and ourselves to create a galaxy of museums working together across London.

'We want to raise the profile of all the smaller non-national museums because the nationals take all the limelight and we don't know enough about the small museums. We've so much choice: everything from the Croydon Clocktower, university collections, private collections, local authority collections – there are something like 238 museums in this city and I've been to most of them!'

Lohman is also committed to completely renovating the museum itself. The Roman and medieval galleries have already been dealt with and the lower ground floor – everything from the Great Fire – has also been revamped. Due for completion in 2010, complete with a new and much more welcoming glass entrance on London Wall, the project has cost over £18 million: £11.5 million coming from the Heritage Lottery Fund (HLF), the rest raised through schemes such as the 'Sale of London's History', which allows donors to sponsor years of historic significance on a museum timeline.

'We've been on this journey of change, attempting to upgrade all the displays, partly because the archaeologists have changed our understanding of London,' says Lohman. 'The medieval gallery presented a view of London that was 30 years out of date.'

As well as using archaeologists to improve our understanding of the past – 'we know so much but there's more out there, and the more we find the more complicated it gets' – Lohman wants to ensure the museum does not miss out on those contemporary artefacts that will help future Londoners appreciate their city. 'We've got to make sure we collect material from the Olympics, and we're interested in things like the remembrance books from the July bombings. We want to remember people here – there's no single memorial to the Blitz in London, or to slavery, but we can do that here. You don't need a flame for everything, but you can acknowledge it as part of your history.'

Museum of London
150 London Wall, EC2Y 5HN (7001 9844/ www.museumoflondon.org.uk).

885

Fly a kite

You can fly a kite pretty much wherever
there's enough space, with Blackheath and
Hampstead Heath particularly popular spots.
Blackheath also hosts an annual kite-flying
festival (www.thekitesociety.org.uk), a riot
of aerial colour and bravado. Those wanting
to get more serious with their flying should
look to the British Kite Flying Association
(www.bkfa.org.uk).

886

Watch the Ceremony of the Keys

Dating back 700 years, this is the ceremony during which the Yeoman Warders lock the entrances to the Tower of London (Tower Hill, EC3N 4AB, 0844 482 7777, www.hrp.org.uk) at precisely 9.53pm each evening. The ticketed public assembles at the West Gate at 9pm, and when it's all over at about 10pm the Last Post sounds. Apply for tickets (well in advance) on the website.

887

Learn wing chun with a Shaolin monk

Wing chun is one of the major schools of kung fu, one studied by Bruce Lee. The techniques help practitioners to flow with the opponent's energy rather than attempting to challenge it. Ordained Shaolin monk Sam Dyson (07830 358637, www.fightschool.co.uk), who trained in Thailand, Japan and China, offers home tuition in wing chun and Shaolin kung fu in central and west London.

888 *Hide away with a bottle in Gordon's*

A crumbling, candlelit warren of a wine bar, Gordon's is the kind of hideaway in which Laurence Olivier might have wooed Vivien Leigh – it still feels like a cellar of naughty Londoners getting frisky away from the stern torch of the ARP warden. Fine wines, costing from £3.85 a glass and £13.95 a bottle, are detailed on a huge menu, and there are also barrels of fino, amontillado and oloroso, port and Madeira. A special place.

Gordon's *47 Villier's Street, WC2N 6NE (7930 1408/www.gordonswinebar.com).*

Gordon's

889
Visit the Animals in War Memorial

One of the silliest of London's thousands of statues, plaques and memorials, the Animals in War Memorial sits on the edge of Hyde Park and commemorates the horses, dogs, elephants, pigeons and glow worms that saved the world from destruction in two world wars. As if this wasn't surreal enough, it was partly inspired by a book by bonkbusteress Jilly Cooper. Designed by David Backhouse, the memorial takes the form of a 60-foot Portland stone wall with bas-reliefs of the animals, and bronzes of two mules, a horse and a dog.

890
Discover Discover

There's not much in the way of greenery or playspaces for kids in Stratford, so community-driven story centre Discover (1 Bridge Terrace, E15 4BG, 8536 5555, www.discover.org.uk) is an unexpected delight for parents and their little 'uns. Developed from a piece of wasteland in collaboration with local children, artists and musicians, Discover is an interactive 'story trail' that encourages under-eights to give their imagination free rein. There's a handsomely designed playground, as well as many low, softly lit 'caves' that contain machines that allow you to hear your own echo, manipulate puppets or appear almost instantaneously on screen, starring in a film that was shot in the garden. Entry to the garden is free; the 'story trail' costs £4.50, or £4 for concessions.

891
Learn to pole dance in your own home

Pole-dancing school and networking club Pole Addicts (www.poleaddicts.com) is yet another manifestation of the diverse scene at the Bethnal Green Working Men's Club (see p295). It runs lessons in risqué twirling in your own home: one of the school's teachers will drive round in a neatly branded Transit van and set the pole up in your house. Call 07727 116356 for a quote for pole hire and lesson.

892-893
Get out of the cinema and into film clubbing

Cinema and clubbing are not generally thought to be the closest bedfellows: one requires an asymmetric haircut and copious intoxicants, the other demands a darkened room and two hours of unbroken silence. However, all that changed in 2007 when the team behind Secret Cinema (www.secretcinema.org) started their unique movement of guerrilla cinema going, which has since then become one of the capital's worst-kept secrets. About once a month, up to a thousand cinema lovers turn up for a night of film and fancy dress – with no idea of what movie they are about to watch.

To get into the inner sanctum, you'll need to sign up on the website and await further instructions. The location (which in the past has included a disused railway tunnel, the Hackney Empire and Dulwich College) only gets revealed a couple of days before the event, with further tantilising dress code instructions to give a flavour of what's going to be screened. 'Rock Gods, Shady Promoters, Metal Heads and Old School Rockers' turned out not to be *Spinal Tap* (as well all thought) but the premiere of a new documentary, called *Anvil*, about a down and out rock group. 'Bring a torch – it might be dark' was the clue for the *Ghostbusters* night held at the Royal Horticultural Halls. Further props and decorations, live bands and actors make sure the evening's escapism is felt on and off the screen throughout the night.

For a more low-key cinephile experience head to The Roxy Bar & Screen (128-132 Borough High Street, SE1 1LB, 7407 4057). London's only dedicated movie bar opened its doors in August 2006, and houses a 13-foot screen, floor-to-ceiling velvet curtains and a clutch of intimate candlelit tables. It regularly screens classics, shorts and art house films, and you can grab a beer, a cocktail or some food while you're at it. 'Live cinema' – in old money, rescoring films – is another evolving trend at the Roxy; the programme has already included rescored screenings of Sylvain Chomet's animated masterpiece *Belleville Rendez-vous* and Fritz Lang's *Metropolis*.

894

Picnic at a Kenwood House concert

The quaintly titled and long-running 'Music on a Summer Evening' concert series at Kenwood House (Hampstead Heath, NW3 7JR, 0870 333 1181, www.picnicconcerts.com), a glorious stately home on the edge of Hampstead Heath, is one of London's great summer pleasures. Spectators set up camp on the lawn armed with a picnic to listen to music from the likes of Art Garfunkel, Jools Holland or members of the Buena Vista Social Club. Carluccio's (www.carluccios.com) will render your evening still more relaxing by preparing a hamper (£45 for two people) that you can pick up on the night. While you're here, be sure to check out the wooden 'bridge' near Kenwood House: it can't be crossed as it isn't a bridge at all, merely a folly designed to make the place look nice. Most hospitable.

895

Shop for an umbrella (you can't have too many in rainy old London)

Generally known to Londoners as 'that lovely old umbrella shop', James Smith & Sons has been in business for an impressive 176 years – something that says as much about the quality and variety of brollies on offer as it does about London's weather. In addition to every possible size, shape and shade of brolly, this is the place to pick up a shoe horn, hip flask, walking stick or – in case you happen to be a millionaire tycoon – a jewel-topped cane. Despite the shop's impressive history (Gladstone was a customer), staff are friendly rather than frosty and are more than happy to let tourists gawp at their array of stock. The precise nature of the closing time – 5.25pm on the dot – dates back to the habits of the original James Smith, who had to leave at that time to catch his train home. Truly, a London institution.
James Smith & Sons *53 New Oxford Street, WC1A 1BL (7836 4731/www.james-smith.co.uk).*

896

Learn stonemasonry

Matt Caines, the stonemason-in-residence at Abney Park Cemetery (North Lodge, Stoke Newington High Street, N16 0LN, 7275 7557, www.abney-park.org.uk), runs weekly drop-in classes in stone carving on Tuesday mornings and Thursday afternoons. The participants are helped to create sculptures from limestone, slate, sandstone or marble, using a process that works from original clay maquettes up to the final carving and polishing. Thursday classes begin with an introduction to stone conservation and voluntary work around the cemetery. Tools and materials are provided and classes cost £10, £8 concessions.

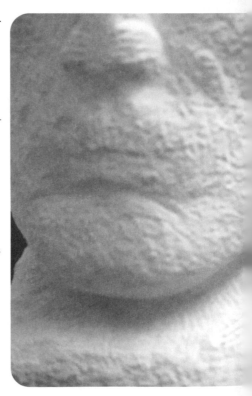

897 Watch sentence being handed down at the Old Bailey

Old Bailey – the name is synonymous with crime in London. Shame it's known as the Central Criminal Court these days. Founded in 1539 as a session house for Newgate Gaol, the court has hosted thousands of famous defendants, from American colonist William Penn to Oscar Wilde (he gave his lauded 'love that dare not speak its name' speech here in 1895) and East End gangsters the Kray brothers. Members of the public are welcome to visit the courthouse – built by Edward Mountford in 1907 and topped by the statue of blind (signifying impartial) Justice – and you can watch British justice in action; a notice by the front door details forthcoming trials. Note that bags, cameras, dictaphones, mobile phones and food are prohibited and no storage facilities are provided.

Central Criminal Court *Corner of Newgate Street & Old Bailey, EC4M 7EH (7248 3277/ www.hmcourts-service.gov.uk).*

898 Get an Indian head massage

This highly versatile massage is carried out on the head and shoulders of a fully clothed person, which makes it perfect for anyone who is uncomfortable with the notion of undressing in front of a complete stranger. Indian head masseurs employ a range of deep thumb and finger pressure, friction and soothing effleurage to the upper back, shoulders, upper arms, neck, scalp and face. The massage can reduce muscular and nervous tension, and improve circulation of the lymphatic fluids that oxygenate the cells, flushing out toxins. Indian head massage can help with headaches, and often gives the client an all-round feeling of relaxation.

Narendra Mehta, blind from the age of one, is the man who is credited with bringing this therapy to the UK; in 1995 he established the London Centre of Indian Champissage (136 Holloway Road, N7 8DD, 7609 3590, www. indianchampissage.com), where a 30-minute head massage costs £25.

899 Sample the pasta at Locanda Locatelli

It's notoriously difficult to get a seat at this fashionable and expensive restaurant, although you might be successful if you try to book for the new Sunday lunchtime slot. Once ensconced, read the menu carefully – the pasta dishes are among the best in town. The menu changes frequently, but choices include beautifully simple classics such as ricotta and spinach parcels coated in butter and sage and richer options like linguine with lobster, garlic and chilli. Main courses such as mondeghili (meatballs) with saffron rice and roast sea bream won't disappoint either. The interior is dark, with wood veneer, convex mirrors and expansive tan leather loungers: bring light to the darkness by indulging in one of the exquisite selection of ice-creams and sorbets.

Locanda Locatelli *8 Seymour Street, W1H 7JZ (7935 9088/www.locandalocatelli.com).*

900

The capital has two towering pagodas: one in Kew Gardens (pictured), completed in 1762, and one in Battersea Park, built in 1985. The perfect spots in which to sit back and do some serious thinking.

901 Pass the time at the Clockmakers' Museum

The eternally punctual won't mind taking time out to survey the hundreds of ticking and chiming clocks, watches and horological masterpieces at the Clockmakers' Museum, which opened to the public in 1874. Overseen by the Worshipful Clockmakers' Company, one of the few official guilds still functioning in the capital, this is the oldest collection of clocks in existence. Among the celebrity timepieces is the watch Sir Edmund Hillary carried to the top of Everest in 1953. Admission is free.

Clockmakers' Museum *Guildhall Library, EC2V 7HH (7332 1868/www.clockmakers.org).*

902 Shoot some hoops in Covent Garden

There are full-size basketball courts in leisure centres all around the capital, but little known is an outdoor half court in the garden of St Giles-in-the-Fields Church (St Giles High Street, WC2H 8LG). Anyone can show up and play.

903 Learn the secrets of the Masons (sort of)

No longer the secretive organisation beloved by conspiracy theorists, the Freemasons are happy to invite anybody – even Catholics! – into their massive art deco headquarters, (60 Great Queen Street, WC2B 5AZ, 7831 9811). Built between 1927 and 1933, Freemason's Hall is the largest Grand Lodge in the country and houses the (free) Library and Museum of Freemasonry, one of the biggest collections of Masonic material in the world. The hall also does regular tours of its extraordinary interior, every hour on weekdays from 11am to 4pm. The central Grand Temple is a sight to behold – two one-and-a-quarter-tonne bronze doors open on to a chamber seating 1,700 and are decorated with mosaics and stained glass depicting figures and symbols from Masonic ritual. The handshakes are still a secret, though.

904-905 Take a Turkish bath

There used to be around 100 Victorian Turkish baths in London, but now only a handful remain (none of which are actually Victorian). The bath on Ironmonger Row (1-11 Ironmonger Row, EC1V 3QF, 7253 4011, www.aquaterra.org) was built in the 1930s, has a pleasant, informal air as well as a hot room, a steam room and a pool, and costs a bargain £8 on weekday mornings for non-members (£13.30 weekends and afternoons). Dating from around the same time is the gorgeous art deco Turkish bath at the Porchester Centre (Queensway, W2 5HS, 7792 2919, www.courtneys.co.uk), which features two Russian steam rooms, three Turkish hot rooms, a Fin log sauna and an ice-cold plunge pool. It'll set you back a bit more, at £22.10 for non-members, but the overall feel is less like a municipal swimming baths.

906 Cycle around an empty London on Christmas Day

Aside from England's World Cup matches, Christmas Day is the only time of year when this heaving city feels empty of people. Southwark Cyclists take advantage with their annual Christmas Day bike ride. Rather funkily titled the '2512 Cycle Ride', it involves a leisurely tour around the silent city while everybody else is indoors opening their presents. You can glide out when you feel you've had enough, or stay the course for a late lunch on Edgware Road and a pub visit at the very end. The group meets at Cutty Sark Gardens, SE10, next to the *Cutty Sark* on Christmas morning; see the website (www.southwarkcyclists.org.uk) for details.

907

Call in on the old police box on St Martins le Grand, EC1

One of the last of its kind. Fans of *Doctor Who* will love it.

908

Sit down for a Chelsea brunch at Tom's Kitchen

Tom Aikens opened this concertedly straightforward but modish brasserie at the end of 2006. Located just a block away from the King's Road, it's well sited for a leisurely weekend brunch before or after a shopping adventure. Food is rootsy Anglo-French in style. As well as typical brunch foods like waffles, you'll find the likes of moules marinière with cider, tarragon and calvados, steak sandwich with big chips, rocket and parmesan salad, and fish pie with salmon and cod. An army of smartly dressed staff provides the service. There's a bar on the first floor. **Tom's Kitchen** *27 Cale Street, SW3 3QP (7349 0202/www.tomskitchen.co.uk).*

909-913

Order an early pint

And by early, we don't mean a quick half straight after work – we mean a quick half with your breakfast. The pubs round Smithfield (try the Cock Tavern, East Poultry Avenue, EC1A 9LH, the Hope, 94 Cowcross Street, EC1M 6BH, or New Market, 26 Smithfield Street, EC1A 9LB) open early to satisfy the post-work cravings of the workers at Smithfield meat market. The banter can be a trifle on the rough side, but that's only to be expected. These men have been heaving carcasses all night. Over in Borough Market, the Market Porter (9 Stoney Street, SE1 9AA, 7407 2495) opens at 6am; on Fleet Street, venerable old Victorian boozer the Punch Tavern (99 Fleet Street, EC4Y 1DE, 7353 6658) starts serving at 7.30am. It seems the old-time journos were no less prone to a liquid breakfast than the market workers.

914

People-watch at Zuma

Situated at the front of one of the hippest, slickest restaurants in London, this contemporary bar attracts A-listers like bees to honey. The drinks list features more than 40 types of sake, shochu and cocktails made from fresh fruit and Japanese spirits, and the decor is the last word in pared-down chic. Natually, such an experience is neither cheap (a mere bottle of water will set you back £4.50) nor casual (seats can require a week or two's wait). So, is it worth it? We think so. The *Flintstones*-chic interior is a hoot, the new-style sushi and sashimi are as good as ever, and observing the super-fashionable at play, well, priceless.

Zuma *5 Raphael Street, SW7 1DL (7584 1010/ www.zumarestaurant.com).*

915

Shop for a ukulele

*Emma Howarth **visits east London's Duke of Uke for a browse and a strum.***

Forget George Formby, the humble ukulele has come of age. The last couple of years have seen a monthly ukulele night at Bethnal Green Working Men's Club (www.workers playtime.net) find not so much a new audience for the instrument as a hungry mob desperate to get in on the act. Meanwhile, easy living periodical the *Idler* started up the Idler Ukulele Orchestra, combining pints with practice sessions at the Three Kings pub in Clerkenwell. Cybill Shepherd even appeared on the *Kumars at No 42* in July 2006 with a uke as her mid-interview party piece.

At the front line of the ukulele revolution is Matthew Reynolds, founder of the Duke of Uke ukelele shop on Hanbury Street, just off Brick Lane. Reynolds set up shop in March 2006 after receiving what at first seemed a disappointing birthday present; he wanted a mandolin, he got a cheap uke. Previously a guitar player, he found himself fast seduced by the ukulele's relaxed, easy charm, a sentiment shared by his customer base: grungy teens, East End locals and serious musicians contemplating the pricier models before heading for the shop's downstairs recording studio. Rock stars, too, have been known to cast away their guitars and angsty snarls for a strum. The Duke has had Bob Geldof tap dancing in delight in the doorway, while Pete Doherty missed the point entirely when he shambled in for a harmonica.

Despite the dubious patronage of Doherty, cast aside notions of east London trendiness; the chirpy uke allows little scope for moody posing. It's jaunty cheer all the way at the Duke of Uke, with a host of workshops, events and gigs on the schedule. The ukulele is also a very inclusive instrument: cheap, small, easily portable, with basics that are simple to learn.

Sold? Reynolds other half, Ane Larson, who combines working at the shop with running ukulele tuition at schools in east London, offers a few tips for splashing out on your first uke. 'If you can stretch to an £80 model, rather than a cheaper £30 one, you'll appreciate the better sound quality,' she says. 'There are four sizes to choose from. Soprano is the smallest, and sounds great alongside other instruments. A concert uke, which has a longer neck and larger body, is better for regaling friends with tuneful solo melodies. Larger still are tenor and baritone ukes, the latter strung like a guitar.'

If you're keen to get strumming, the Duke of Uke can organise private tuition. Or you could simply join one of its weekly beginners' workshops; check the website or drop in to the shop for more details.

'Make the most of its current popularity,' says Larson. 'Trawl the web for new songs, orchestras, gigs and events.' Uke players have never had it so good.

Duke of Uke *22 Hanbury Street, E1 6QR (7247 7924/www.dukeofuke.co.uk).*

916 *Doff your hat to the women of World War II*

Just south from the Cenotaph on Whitehall stands the distinctive Memorial to the Women of World War II. Unveiled by the Queen on 9 July 2005, as part of the commemorations marking the 60th anniversary of the end of the war, the bronze monument features women's work clothes hanging on pegs. It was designed by sculptor John Mills, inspired by the advice given in 1945 to the seven million or so women who had contributed to the war effort to 'hang up your uniforms and overalls and go home – the job is done'. A welcome addition to the sober environs of the country's corridor of power.

917 Learn the gory secrets of St Bart's

After a short video explaining the history of Bart's and its founding in 1123, the Museum of St Bart's Hospital (St Bartholomew's Hospital, West Smithfield, EC1A 7BE, 7601 8152, www.bartsandthelondon.nhs.uk) offers a crash course in the changing face of London hospitals. Displays explain how Bart's developed, while offering plenty of mean-looking instruments and bottles marked 'poison' to gawp at. There are also two Hogarth memorials to admire, plus a great book full of illustrations of injuries, ruptures, lesions and pus. Admission is free.

918

Admire Wellington's loot (and death mask) at Apsley House

This Robert Adam-designed house, on Hyde Park Corner (www.english-heritage.org.uk/apsleyhouse), is crammed with artworks plundered by or presented to Wellington during his career, including impressive candelabras and a giant neo-classical statue of Napoleon. It also, creepily enough, houses his death mask. There's not a huge amount in the way of biographical detail about the man himself, but you'll pick up plenty while trying to reach the complementary Wellington Arch via a tortuous underpass enlivened by informative mosaics. The Arch itself has viewing platforms and a permanent display about other London arches.

919 Rollerski

Cross-country skiing without the snow – you wear skis with wheels on them – is not only ideal preparation for the slopes, it's also a fun, low-impact workout and good cross-training. The Rollerski Company (07968 286129, www.rollerski.co.uk) holds beginners' sessions in Hyde Park every Saturday at 11.30am; two-hour sessions cost £20, including ski hire.

920 Drink tea at Yauatcha

Yauatcha is best known as Alan Yau's all-day dim sum restaurant, but that's just the basement. The ground floor is an exquisitely chic tea room and pâtisserie serving rare Chinese and exotic Taiwanese varieties of tea during the day. Blue-glass walls, chill-out music and low seating lend an air of classy serenity. The beautifully presented cakes and pastries, although inspired by French tradition, are given an oriental twist.
Yauatcha *15-17 Broadwick Street, W1F 0DL (7494 8888).*

921 Get up early for Dawn Chorus Day

The first public Dawn Chorus Day event in the UK was held in Birmingham in 1984, but London bird lovers have taken the celebration up keenly over the past two decades. If you know your tweet from your twitter, go it alone in your local park or your back garden, then feed your findings back via the official website (www.idcd.info). Otherwise, set the alarm early on the designated Sunday in early May (see the website for the exact date) and head for one of the organised events. The London Wetland Centre is a prime location – and the gathering here normally includes a group breakfast. In the past, events have also taken place at Tower Hamlets Cemetery and Roundshaw Downs Local Nature Reserve. So grab your binoculars and head for the birds in the bushes – you can always go back to bed afterwards.

922 Fuel up before a hike on the heath

Thirty years after it opened, the Hampstead Crêperie still draws queues every day, come rain or shine. The stall serves dozens of delicious sweet and savoury crêpes and gallettes, but be warned, they make for a messy snack – and there are no tables and chairs.
Hampstead Crêperie *77 Hampstead High Street, NW3 1RE (www.hampsteadcreperie.com).*

923 *Go adventure racing*

Looking for a new challenge? Turn running into an adventure, suggests Jessica Eveleigh.

Lasting five hours or five days (and sometimes even longer), adventure races are multidisciplinary events that test competitors on every level. Each one of these races is an emotional, mental and physical journey that demands fitness, technical skills, endurance, strength, speed and teamwork.

Most races take you off road and into the great outdoors; others are urban adventures that utilise the city environment. Running, mountain biking, kayaking and navigating are integral to most, but there is always a strong element of surprise. You won't know the course details until shortly before the start and, along the way, you may have to scale slippery climbing walls, shimmy under cargo nets, try parkour or learn survival skills.

'AR involves a range of different disciplines, which improves strength and cardiovascular fitness and reduces the risk of injury,' says top London personal trainer

Jamie Baird. 'You get outdoors and work in a team – this gives you that competitive edge and makes you work harder. You'll get a better workout than you'll ever achieve in a gym.'

There are a number of AR events near London that are open to beginners. Dynamic Adventure (01425 674326, www.dynamic adventureracing.co.uk) holds a one-day series for beginners and more experienced racers in the South and London regions. Meanwhile, for those who feel more comfortable on the streets, Rat Race Urban Adventure (0845 009 4365, www.rat raceadventure.com) confines the sport to a city. It has previously organised courses in Manchester and Bristol and runs annual events in London in September – check the website for updates.

To find out more about AR, look at www.sleepmonsters.com, which has a calendar of UK and global events, training tips and a lively forum.

924 Fly a plane at the Royal Air Force Museum

There's been an airfield at Hendon since 1910, hence its claim to be the birthplace of aviation in Britain. These days the Aerodrome houses more than 80 historic aircraft – among them World War I Fokkers, World War II Spitfires and a state-of-the-art Eurofighter Typhoon – in World War I hangars and a listed aircraft factory building. Longing to fly yourself? In the interactive Aeronauts Gallery you can take a pilot aptitude test to see if you've got 'the right stuff' (and whether you'd be able to keep your lunch down). **Royal Air Force Museum Hendon** *Grahame Park Way, NW9 5LL (8205 2266/www.rafmuseum.org).*

925 Order fish at J Sheekey – but leave room for dessert

London's most renowned fish restaurant remains a winner, its star quality relatively undimmed by the passing years, or recession – in fact, it has recently added an oyster bar in adjoining premises. Once ushered inside by the top-hatted doorman and led to your table in one of several immaculately maintained restaurant rooms (if there are no tables, there's often room at the very handsome bar), you'll be confronted with a pleasingly plain-speaking and unflashy menu, egalitarian enough to sit beluga caviar alongside (admittedly poshed-up) jellied eels. Sheekey's seldom turns out a dud; the cooking is competent and quality-controlled (good basic grills, classic sides) and sometimes knocks your socks off (the famous fishcake, for example, or grilled cuttlefish with cockles and romero pepper). Save room for the near-legendary honeycomb ice-cream, one of the capital's must-scoff desserts. This place isn't just about the food – it's a destination restaurant. **J Sheekey** *28-32 St Martin's Court, WC2N 4AL (7240 2565/www.caprice-holdings.co.uk).*

926 Play unicycle hockey

You read that right. Played on a basketball-sized court using ice-hockey sticks and a tennis ball that has lost its bounce, this is one of the capital's more esoteric activities. The London Unicycle Hockey Club (07976 732723) meets every week at the Westway Sports Centre and welcomes anyone who wants to look daft to join. They're nicknamed the Lunis, so phobics of wackiness should probably steer clear.

927 Drink vermouth at the Bar at the Dorchester

A flight (intended for sharing) is a fine way to get yourself acquainted with the impressive vermouth collection – said to be the largest in the UK – at the Bar at the Dorchester. It highlights the distinct flavours of the fortified wine, from light and dry to intensely sweet and herbal. As part of its refurbishment, the Bar was redesigned by French architect Thierry Despont. The new look – with its plush banquettes and red glass spikes fringing the room like extraterrestrial bulrushes – is a little Eurotrashy, but fun and luxurious all the same. **The Bar at the Dorchester** *53 Park Lane, W1K 1QA (7629 8888/www.thedorchester.com).*

928 Go back to Futurism at the Estorick Collection

Assembled by American political scientist, writer and art collector Eric Estorick, this collection of modern Italian art focuses on Futurism – the artistic movement founded in Italy in the early 20th century that despised all things old and loved speed, technology and nationalism. Highlights include paintings by artists including Giacomo Balla, Umberto Boccioni, Luigi Russolo and Carlo Garra. The collection is housed in Northumberland Lodge, a Grade II-listed Georgian house just a stone's throw from Highbury Corner. Admission free. **Estorick Collection of Modern Italian Art** *39A Canonbury Square, N1 2AN (7704 9522/ www.estorickcollection.com).*

929 *Celebrate Chinese New Year*

Even if the festivities around Trafalgar Square mainly revolve around the sale of pricey noodles to tourists, it's still worth braving the crowds to see Chinatown come to life for Chinese New Year in mid February, also known as Spring Festival. Celebrations begin at 11am with a children's parade from Leicester Square gardens to Trafalgar Square, where the lion and dragon dance teams perform traditional dances. Expect about 50,000 people, a sea of red lanterns, fireworks (at lunchtime and at 5pm) and – yes – mountains of noodles.

930

Order a cup of whelks at Tubby Isaacs

Standing outside the Aldgate Exchange pub on the corner of Goulston Street and Middlesex Street, E1, a few yards from the hustle and bustle of Petticoat Lane, Tubby Isaacs seafood stall has been trading since 1910. Currently owned by Paul – thick-set, friendly-faced grandson of Tubby himself – the seafood is top quality. Eels, whelks, cockles, crabs… they've got the lot. Whelks cost £2, and are served in a polystyrene cup. Take instruction from Paul and do it properly: flavour the whelks with a slosh of vinegar, chilli vinegar if you're feeling adventurous (the handwritten label on the bottle says: 'Hold at arms length – very, very hot'), and some salt and pepper. How do they taste? Like the sea, of course. A bit rubbery, though not at all slimey. A cheap, charming sliver of London's seafood heritage. The stall is open on Petticoat Lane Market trading days.

931

Check out the remains of a dodo at the Grant Museum

If you're not fazed by the skeletons of, say, a walrus, a baboon or a giant iguanadon, you'll find the animal specimens here fascinating. Part of University College London, this free museum might first appear chaotically cluttered, but specimens are carefully categorised into evolutionary groups. The dodo bones are stored in a box and laid out in specially cut-out padding for protection. Because we really wouldn't want to lose them too.
Grant Museum of Zoology *Darwin Building, University College London, Gower Street, WC1E 6BT (7679 2647/www.grant.museum.ucl.ac.uk).*

932 *Play mini-golf in Broomfield Park*

Crazy golf enthusiasts insist that Broomfield Park's 18-hole felt putting course (Broomfield Park, Aldermans Hill, N14, 8882 1899) is the best in the London area. There might not be any windmills to negotiate, but the putting surface is fast and true and houses an imaginative array of obstacles to putt round or through. Games cost £3.50, £2.50 children.

933-934

Watch a puppet show

Islington's celebrated Little Angel Theatre (14 Dagmar Passage, off Cross Street, N1 2DN, 7226 1787, www.littleangeltheatre.com) is the only permanent puppet theatre in London. Its Saturday Puppet Club runs over nine weeks (£80, concessions £55) and culminates in a show for friends and families. Across town, take in a puppet performance at the picturesque Puppet Theatre Barge. It's moored by Buccleuch Gardens, just upstream from Richmond Bridge.

Little Angel Theatre

935

Marvel at how an enormous machine was 'lost' for decades

The purpose-built space that is the Kirkaldy Testing Museum houses a massive 19th-century hydraulic machine, designed to measure the strength of industrial materials. Amazingly, it was discovered by chance in 1974, by civil engineer Dr Denis Smith, having been 'lost' for decades. Realising its historical significance, Smith managed to secure the four-storey building as the HQ of the Greater London Industrial Society.

The machine itself was designed in 1866 by Scotsman David Kirkaldy and was one of only two such devices ever made (the other disappeared in Belgium). It could be used to test the strength of everything, from bricks and concrete to aluminium and steel. It can be temperamental, but if you're lucky, you may see it in operation. The museum is open on the first Sunday of every month.
Kirkaldy Testing Museum *99 Southwark Street, SE1 0JF (01372 722989).*

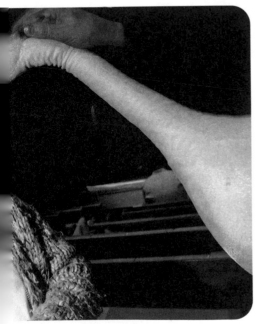

936 *Watch an ice hockey game*

As the old joke goes, 'I went to see a fight, then a game of ice hockey broke out'. London has never taken kindly to American sports and, despite the fast, violent entertainment it offers, ice hockey is no exception. The old London Knights spluttered to a halt a few years ago, to be replaced by the London Racers, who also eventually disbanded. That left London with Lee Valley Lions, Haringey Greyhounds and Streatham Redskins, all of whom play in the amateur third-tier English National League. One division up, you'll find the outer-capital likes of Bracknell Bees, Guildford Flames, Romford Raiders and Slough Jets. For details of fixtures and venues, visit www.eiha.co.uk.

937 *Listen to the Longplayer... in your own time*

No need to hurry in getting along to this aural art exhibition, as it runs until, er, 2999. Longplayer (www.longplayer.org), developed by musician Jem Finer with the support of artistic collective Artangel, has been running at the lighthouse at Trinity Buoy Wharf, E14 since New Year's Day 2000. A 'musical sound loop', Longplayer can also be heard in Nottinghamshire, Egypt and Brisbane. Something that has to be seen – or rather, heard – for yourself, the exhibit is open 11am-5pm at weekends. Admission free.

938 *Attend the London Design Festival*

First held in 2003, the annual, mid September London Design Festival (www.londondesign festival.com) showcases the extraordinarily creative nature of the capital's design scene. Events are held at various locations all over London, but the festival centres around the Truman Brewery on Brick Lane. Among the events are talks, artist showcases and installations; they are attended by most of the UK's leading designers. Like a ten-day browse at the Conran Shop.

Free Kicks

*Paul Murphy **takes his place on the sidelines for the weekend drama of the amateur leagues.***

'How much do you want it? How much do you *really* want it?' screams a track-suited man, dancing wildly on the touchline, veins in his forehead bulging. His arms swing wildly as another misplaced pass is intercepted and quickly fed out wide to the dreadlocked winger on the rival team. The ball zings into the box, but the striker loses his footing and the ball bounces harmlessly into the goalkeeper's arms. Another man and his crop-haired dog stand watching dispassionately as 22 mud-splattered men of wildly varying degrees of agility and fitness punt a football up and down the lush green pitch under the watchful eye of a referee, pristine in his black shirt and shorts.

All around them similar scenes are acted out on more football pitches than you can imagine. Hackney Marsh South is a huge field, liberally dotted with goalposts, corner flags and white pitch markings. Just over a small footbridge and a short stretch of the River

Lee are the further 11 pitches that make up Hackney Marsh East; along with the bigger South Marsh and the east tip of Victoria Park, they comprise Hackney Marshes' staggering 80-plus full-size pitches. On almost every Sunday during the season, you'll be lucky to spot a single empty one. There should be a neon sign up: 'Welcome to Hackney Marshes, London's home of amateur football.'

The Marshes' footballing days really date back to World War II. Hackney, and the East End in general, suffered badly from bombing, and rubble from East End buildings destroyed in the Blitz was dumped here; as a result, the pitches enjoy excellent drainage, despite the proximity of the River Lee. From the outer edges of the pitches you can hear the rumble of Sunday morning traffic on the concrete Eastway and in the distance you can see the blocks of flats that surround the Marshes.

The decision to tarmac over one part of the East Marshes and turn it into a temporary car park for the London Olympics met with a great deal of opposition from users. As well as the likely impact on local wildlife (there are dedicated bird hides just a little further north, for example), few habitués of the Marshes believed the land would really be restored to recreational use after the Games. Rather than the promised improvements to facilities, they expected the land to be sold off for extremely profitable redevelopment. However, the Olympic Delivery Authority has provided a written guarantee that the land will eventually be handed back, and there are plans for improved facilities aimed partly at compensating for the loss.

There are many leagues at the Marshes playing both Sunday morning and afternoon fixtures, including a women's league, a Turkish league and an Asian league. The most prestigious of them all is the Hackney and Leyton Football League,

which has been at the Marshes since the end of the war. Made up of five divisions and 51 teams, the league is one of the most highly regarded around and the games are very competitive. Matches kick off on Sundays at 11am for league games and 10.30am for cup games. Most matches draw a couple of dozen very vocal and enthusiastic spectators, equally divided between men and women. The crazy mix of players adds to the fascination of a few hours spent strolling between games – Hackney Marshes offers a snapshot of the grass-roots complexity of the only truly global team sport.

For anyone interested in taking part in the insanity, the best advice would be to spend a Sunday checking out the teams that are playing and then have a chat with them after the game. The Hackney and Leyton Football League has an up-to-date and excellent website, which has details of fixtures, teams and pitch directions

'There should be a neon sign up: Welcome to Hackney Marshes, London's home of amateur football.'

(www.hackneyandleytonfootballleague.co.uk). The average cost for anyone playing with one of the teams in the league would be around £5 per game, which includes the cost of pitch hire as well as public liability insurance. Pitches can be booked by phone on 8985 8206 or 8986 8615.

But, of course, those who are happy to experience the madness of multiple-pitch football without pulling on a pair of shinguards can appreciate the spectacle for free. And it's not just footballers and football spectators who enjoy the Marshes: any weekend you'll find joggers, walkers, bird watchers and even kite fliers too.

940

Make a call from London's first red phone box

Take two steps off Piccadilly into the imposing courtyard arch of the Royal Academy and swing open the doors of telephonic history. This sheltered red kiosk is a Grade II-listed building – not just the first ever vermillion-red telephone box in the whole world, but its wooden prototype. Dial H for history!

941 *Land-board*

Kite land-boarding is as similar to kite-flying as a moonlit walk is to walking on the moon. Basically, you're strapped to an oversized skateboard and dragged along by a kite the size of a parachute. It's fast, frenetic and, surprisingly, possible in London. Kitevibe (7870 7700, www.kitevibe.com) uses the great expanse of Richmond Park for teaching. Lessons cost around £55 but are dependant on experience.

942 *Discover Burmese food*

Mandalay (444 Edgware Road, W2 1EG, 7258 3696, www.mandalayway.com) is London's only Burmese restaurant, but would hold its own against much pricier oriental venues. Take no heed of the drab Edgware Road surroundings and head into the small, family-run establishment. Sharing influences with Thailand, India and China, Burmese cuisine celebrates contrasting flavours to great effect. Expect plenty of fish and seafood, fragrant bowls of rice and noodles, and light aromatic curries. Staff are passionate about their craft and happy to take curious customers on a guided tour of the menu.

943 *Work out, outdoors*

Who needs to spend time under artificial lights in a sweaty gym when you can lug kettlebells about in the great outdoors? Outdoor Kettlebells (07595 303295/www.outdoorkettlebells.com) replaces the tedium of the gym with outdoor workouts. These take place on Highbury Fields and aim to improve mobility, balance, strength, endurance, flexibility and posture, bringing all the muscles of the body into play – not just those used on a pec deck or leg press. Outdoor Extremes (7731 3133/www.outdoor extreme.com) also gets you out in the fresh air at Highbury, Battersea Park or Wandsworth Common – again with an emphasis on all-round fitness through kettleball training. A six-week course with either outfit costs £70 for one class each week and £120 for two.

944 *Watch the London Triathlon*

It can seem like sadism to watch athletes putting themselves through such torture. The London Triathlon involves a swimming, bike and running race, with events taking place over three distances: the Super Sprint (400m swim, 10km bike, 2.5km run), the Sprint (750m swim, 20km bike, 5km run), and the Olympic (1.5km swim, 40km bike, 10km run). The races are important fundraisers for charity and, in the past, have taken place on the first weekend of August at the London Excel Centre (1 Western Gateway, Royal Victoria Dock, E16 1XL, 7069 5000). Check the website (www.thelondon triathlon.com) for exact dates.

945

Stand through a performance at the Royal Opera House

Non-seated tickets cost £5 to £15 each. Bargain. **Royal Opera House** *Bow Street, WC2E 9DD, (7304 4000/www.royaloperahouse.org).*

946

The ultimate Frisbee craze began on college campuses in the '60s and is best described as netball with a flying disc. Teams of seven try to pass the disc up the pitch (as in netball, you can't run with it) and into the American football-style 'end zone'. Drop it or miss it, and possession passes to the opposition. The scene in London is based around Clapham and Wandsworth commons. The former is home to European champions Clapham United, but there are plenty of teams springing up all over the capital. The London Ultimate Association website (www.londonultimate.com) has a directory of teams.

947 *Get back into Ronnie Scott's*

Does life begin at 40? Theatrical impresario Sally Greene hopes so. That said, it's not as if Ronnie Scott's has had a quiet first four decades. Arguably the most famous music venue in Europe, the dimly lit Soho hangout has hosted a veritable A-to-Z of jazz greats since saxophonist Scott and business partner Pete King moved it to 47 Frith Street from its original Gerrard Street location in 1965. Few jazz joints can match it for history.

However, since Scott's death in 1996, the club's past has increasingly looked like overtaking its present. When King finally sold the place to Greene in 2005, he handed over a club that can scarcely have been redecorated since it opened. Whoozy on whisky, head fugged by a billion cigs, with hard-earned character emanating from every tear in the tablecloths, Ronnie Scott's was a club that was literally decades out of time.

Greene soon shut the place for a subtle yet character-altering renovation. The tables are no longer held together with gum and duct tape. The lights are a little brighter. The food and drinks menu has received a total overhaul. And, of course, smoking is banned these days. The club hasn't quite been reborn, but it's had a heart transplant.

Of course, someone has to pay for all this, and it's the customers. Ticket prices have risen under the new regime, with the added irritation that seats are guaranteed only to diners. The food has improved – there's now an a la carte menu – but drinks are still on expensive side, with half a lager costing £3.50.

Yet, from the monochrome photos on the wall to the heart-of-Soho location, the place retains its mystique. Purists grumble about the cheesification of the music programme, which reached a nadir when fabulous New York pianist Benny Green was bumped from headliner to support act in order to make room for the Blues Brothers Band. But the booking policy under the old management had long since lost its spark, hamstrung by an insistence on weekly residencies and a reliance on a handful of bankable acts.

In much the same way that the new decor pays tribute to the club's history while unsentimentally looking to the future, Greene and her team have broadened the programming remit. There's still room for long-time favourites such as Georgie Fame, but the intimate space has also welcomed the likes of Wynton Marsalis and Christian McBride. Sure, it's not the club it once was. But had nothing changed then it's likely that rather than writing this eulogy, we'd be penning an obituary.

Ronnie Scott's *47 Frith Street, W1D 4HT (7439 0747/www.ronniescotts.co.uk).*

948

Stop for a sip at Green & Blue

Part wine shop, part wine bar, Green & Blue
has more than one way to please south London
oenophiles. Proprietor Kate Thal is a champion
of small-scale, high-quality wineries. Many of
those on the list are family-run and many are
organic or biodynamic operations. The list
is broad ranging, with fine pickings from
all around the world, from Lugana in Italy
to Swartland in Thal's native South Africa.
These are hand-selected wines, a far cry
from the sort of bottles found in supermarkets.
You can buy a wine to take home or you can
drink it on the premises for a modest mark-up.
In the room at the back (which doubles as a
tasting room) you'll find some cracking wines
by the glass, such as a fresh summery rosé
from Pic-St-Loup in France and a crisp, vibrant
Frankland Estate Rocky Gully riesling from
Australia. To eat, there's a selection of
antipasti, meats and cheeses (on our last visit,
a 'superior' pork pie was exactly that). G&B
also runs regular tasting evenings; check the
website for details.
Green & Blue *36 Lordship Lane, SE22 8HJ (8693
9250/www.greenandbluewines.com).*

Bar Italia

949 *People-watch from Bar Italia*

In honesty, neither the bitter coffee, nor the
pre-prepared ciabatta sandwiches, nor the
unexciting pizzas here are that special: what
Bar Italia (22 Frith Street, W1D 4RP, 7437
4520) oozes is aged, authentic character. The
red leather stools, ancient till and enormous
Rocky Marciano poster behind the counter are
the stuff of Soho legend, unchanged for decades.
Prices are too high (about £6 for a parma ham
and mozzarella ciabatta) but are about justified
if you nab an outdoor seat: there are few better
people-watching spots in London.

950

Cross Waterloo Bridge at night
From the stunningly lit
exterior of Somerset House
to the lights along Victoria
Embankment, the glowing
Houses of Parliament to the
illuminated London Eye.
Try telling us you could
live anywhere else.

951

Visit the best address in London

Forget about dropping the bonus on a personalised number plate, how about stumping up for the city's most prestigious address? Sadly, English Heritage got there first: Apsley House (149 Piccadilly, W1J 7NT, 7499 5676, www.english-heritage.org.uk) was known as No.1 London back when Kensington was still a village, since it was the first building you reached on your journey into the city. Fortunately, you don't need an office in Docklands to be able to afford to look around: £5.70 is enough for a peek at the Duke of Wellington's residence, although the parts of the building still occupied by his descendants are strictly out of bounds. Lucky devils.

952

See the pet cemetery in Hyde Park

Like something out of a Stephen King novel, the macabre Hyde Park Pet Cemetery is hidden behind railings at Victoria Gate on the Bayswater Road. It appeared in the 1880s, when Cherry, a Maltese terrier, was buried here. By 1893 there were 33 gravestones for departed cats and dogs, with the last burial taking place in 1967. George Orwell described it as 'perhaps the most horrible spectacle in Britain'. The cemetery is closed to the public, but you can peer through the railings at this mawkish sight. What more encouragement do you need?

953 Take an open-bus tour at night

OK, so you might think there's something horribly naff and touristy about going on an open-bus tour of London, but trust us, it's an experience you'll enjoy more than you might think. Put a fresh twist on the expedition and tour with London By Night (www.london-by-night.net), a company that offers two-hour tours from £15 (£11 online) per person. It'll be dark, so no one will spot your blushes.

954 Enjoy soup and a sandwich at Paul Rothe & Son

This store dates back to around 1900 and wears it well, making Marylebone Lane's charming grocer an architectural as well as a foodie curiosity. Two soups – one meat, one vegetarian – are offered daily and these are made by Paul Rothe himself. Sandwich fillings are also made on site, and include Austrian liptauer, made with cream cheese, anchovy paste and capers; and kummelkase, a blend of Stilton, caraway and cream cheese. These can be used to fill bagels, ciabattas, baps, baguettes, bloomer bread or Ukranian rye bread. What would the Earl of Sandwich have thought?
Paul Rothe & Son *35 Marylebone Lane, W1U 2NN (7935 6783).*

955

Pay your respects to those who lost their heads at the Tower

The world's most famous prison, the Tower of London (Tower Hill, EC3N 4AB, 0844 482 7777, www.hrp.org.uk) has held thousands of notables during their periods of incarceration over the years. But while many were imprisoned here, only a select few – the most sensitive cases – were offed by an axeman in the Tower itself; most heads and shoulders parted company on nearby Tower Hill.

A memorial to those executed on Tower Green was unveiled in late 2006. Designed by artist Brian Catling, it commemorates just ten, including unlucky royal wife Anne Boleyn and one-time favourite of Elizabeth I, the Earl of Essex. 'It's a focal point for visitors to contemplate, reflect and remember all those prisoners executed at the Tower of London over the centuries,' says the Tower's Natasha Woollard. And it does a pretty good job – following the inscription round its circumference, you also take in the Tudor houses across the way, the iconic White Tower bearing down, the leaves rustling in the breeze, and you shiver slightly at the thought that these would have been the last things those engraved names saw.

956 Attend the V&A village fête

Held in the museum's John Madejski courtyard garden, this annual fête is a great tradition. Tongue-in-cheek games and activities at stalls in previous years have included etch-a-sketch with Simon Kinnear, body-painting with Thomas Matthews and ping-pong with People Will Always Need Plates. The big lure, though, is always the tombola, which, instead of the usual tat, has prizes you might actually want. Winners in the past have taken away a Favela chair by the Campana Brothers and a signed Convex mirror designed by Sebastian Wong. The fête takes place over a Friday and Saturday and in late July and admission is £1.
Victoria & Albert Museum *Cromwell Road, SW7 2RL (7942 2000/www.vam.ac.uk).*

957 Get a table by the lake at Inn The Park

This is one of the best-located restaurants in London – and it's a looker too. The modern wooden structure fits perfectly into a lakeside slot in St James's Park, with every table having a water view. We've a real soft spot for this place – good for families (staff are charming with young diners), it's also a romantic night-time haunt, and whatever the occasion, it's affordable. Breakfasts might be a full english or a bowl of granola with yoghurt and pomegranate; at lunch there's a choice of sandwiches or a full meal. On our last visit, we made fast work of treacle tart with clotted cream, but special mention has to go to the British cheese plate: £8.50 bought goat's cheese, stilton and cheddar, a shiny apple, chutney and plenty of biscuits. All this is buttressed by a global wine list and fine cocktails. A park café par excellence. Owner Oliver Peyton is also behind the National Dining Rooms (*see p154*).
Inn The Park *St James's Park, SW1A 2BJ (7451 9999/www.innthepark.co.uk).*

958 Learn to make hats

Regarded by *Vogue* as the 'milliners' milliner', Rose Cory (Rose Cory Millinery, Shrewsbury House, Bushmoor Crescent, SE18 3EG, 8856 9190, www.rosecory.co.uk) has been making hats for more than 40 years, and counted the Queen Mother among her many clients. Cory teaches classes to all levels of experience for a very reasonable £35 a day. Many of her students have gone on to become successful milliners in their own right.

959 Watch films al fresco

Despite the unpredictability of London's weather, a trend has emerged in the past few years for outdoor film screenings during the summer months. Events and locations change year by year, but the Serpentine Gallery, Somerset House, the Scoop (the ampitheatre beside City Hall near Tower Bridge) and the National Theatre have emerged as popular venues for moonlit screenings. In summer 2009 the Scoop's offerings included *La Vie en Rose* and *Oh Brother Where Art Thou?*, while Somerset House's programme included *West Side Story* and *Slumdog Millionaire*. It's worth checking *Time Out* magazine's weekly listings for these events between June and September each year.

960 See the Pearly Kings and Queens on show

London's Pearlies – button-wearing costermongers – are an institution, originally elected from among their fellow costermongers to safeguard their rights, but now concentrated on charitable activities. They can be hard to track down, but to cop an eyeful, head to the Harvest Festival at the Pearlies' adopted church, St Paul's in Covent Garden, in early October, when the top faces in the Pearly community gather for a special service. See www.pearlysociety.co.uk for exact dates.

961 *Munch a macaroon at Ladurée*

Bringing Parisian café culture bang up to date, the London branch of Ladurée, inside Harrods, boasts a wealth of delicate dainties for shoppers with sweetly indulgent tastes. Right at the cutting edge of food fashion, this elegant café borrows from the Parisian trend of launching pâtisserie collections in much the same way as clothes designers showcase a new season's line. We're talking the likes of liquorice macaroons, orange blossom creams and Arabica coffee mousses. The decor is as ornate as the wares on offer: weighty chandeliers, pastel-shaded pâtisserie boxes and streams of colourful ribbons complement rows of perfectly executed pâtisserie, lush chocolates and a magnificent choice of macaroons. Bag a table in the light and airy café area for the closest seats to the impressive display counter. The religieuse – choux pastry, crowned with a swathe of rose-scented rosettes of cream – is an outstanding version. Traditionalists can take their pick from éclairs, millefeuilles and elegant meringues. If you've time for just one quick bite, make it a macaroon – they're to die for.
Ladurée *Harrods, entrance on Hans Road, SW1X 7XL (7893 8293/www.laduree.com).*

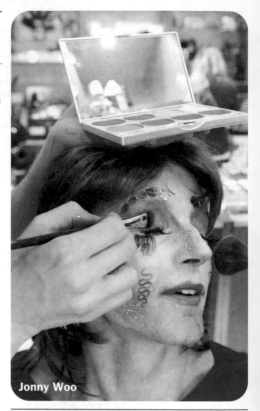

Jonny Woo

962

Watch Doggett's Coat and Badge, the oldest race in London

The Boat Race might get all the publicity – probably thanks to all the Oxbridge grads incumbent in the media – but the oldest boat race in London is the Doggett's Coat and Badge race. Held every year since 1715, the race between London Bridge and Chelsea was instigated by Thomas Doggett, an Irish theatre impresario, after he was rescued from drowning by a Thames waterman. These days the now-extinct London ferrymen have been replaced by amateur rowers. After the race, retire to Putney's Coat and Badge pub (8 Lacy Road, SW15 1NL, 8788 4900) for refreshment.

963

Keep your eyes down for gay bingo

Anarchic nights of gay bingo have hit that usually serious home of culture, the ICA (the Mall, SW1Y 5AH, 7930 0493, www.ica.org.uk). Drag performance legend Jonny Woo is your host, aided by Ma Butcher on the number cruncher and DJ Sizzle on the decks. Sporting his fabulous 'gutter couture' Jonny presides over some outrageous cabaret – as well as those all-important numbers. Makes a change from bingo in the church hall. Entry is free with an ICA admission ticket, but expect crowds. Takes place occasionally; phone ahead to check exact dates.

964

Check out the goings-on at Bethnal Green Working Men's Club

Retro nights out are still going strong at this east End bolt-hole, says Time Out *magazine's Simone Baird.*

Clubland's a funny thing. It wasn't that long ago that wearing a cravat and brogues or vintage tea dress and pearls would have had you laughed out the door of most cool underground clubs (jeans and Converse rule, yeah?). But for the last half of the naughties, grandparents' wardrobes and charity shops the city over have been raided as club kids step back in time – way back – revelling in all things cabaret, burlesque and vintage wax. And is was the Bethnal Green Working Men's Club that provides the centre for this unlikely fad that shows no signs of abating.

Down a sidestreet and then down another you'll find this temple to retro. Chances are you'll walk past the nondescript Victorian building (no eye-watering neon signs or burly security guards here, thank you very much), although the queue snaking around the corner at 8pm might be a giveaway.

Downstairs remains the stronghold of the original members; it's in the school hall-styled room on the ground floor that all the club fun happens. The brown formica walls and heavy red velvet curtains were in fashion in the early 1970s, but the bar prices are also happily retro. The stage is framed by a giant heart made of red lights, most of which work, and the dancefloor is surrounded by wobbly tables and sticky carpet.

The genius was opening the club's doors to creative young promoters who transformed it into a dress-up-and-dance paradise featuring all things vintage and off-the-wall. You can now shimmy to an endless array of old sounds of every genre on club nights. On other nights would-be cabaret acts – some great, some cringeworthy – vie for attention next to burlesque starlets trying a trick or two with balloons, hula hoops or an evil-looking chainsaw and recent themed nights have included the hugely popular Cream Revue, the club's version of a 1950s prom.

It's the kind of place that welcomes everyone and encourages tomfoolery, playfulness and good times. Just like a working men's club should.

Bethnal Green Working Men's Club
42-46 Pollards Row, E2 6NB (7739 7170/ www.workersplaytime.net).

965 *Visit the grandfather of all gastropubs*

What went wrong with the democratically priced gastropub? When the Eagle pub in Clerkenwell installed an open kitchen, a blackboard menu and Mediterranean cuisine back in 1991, the aim of founders Michael Belben and (chef) David Eyre was that their pub should be an affordable, casual, fun place to eat; somewhere you can seamlessly make the transition from pint to polenta, and back again. Others saw what the Eagle had done, and a whole generation of chefs wanting their own place became pub landlords. Now there's barely a London neighbourhood without its own gastropub – or several.

In recent years, the gastropub has gone upmarket, with much investment in smart interiors, menus boasting increasingly complex dishes, and – the coup de grâce for the gastropub concept – dining areas segregated from the bar. Prices have crept up, too, in many cases exceeding the cost of an equivalent meal in a restaurant – leaving only a clutch of worthy gastropubs offering good meals at a good price.

The Eagle remains one such establishment. The place buzzes with energy (and noise – if you want a quiet chat, come here during the day), and the chefs manning the tiny kitchen area behind the bar are kept busy. A short blackboard menu lists hob- and grill-based Med dishes such as napoli sausages with white beans and salsa verde and yellowfin tuna with sauce romesco. Add to this a good beer selection, lots of decent wines by the glass and bottle, plus the laid-back but civilised vibe, and the enduring popularity makes perfect sense.

'A gastropub should be a real pub,' Michael Belben once said. 'Keep it real.' Here, they've kept it real.

The Eagle *159 Farringdon Road, EC1R 3AL (7837 1353).*

966 *Get a tarot reading over coffee*

At mystical and magical-themed café Twelfth House (35 Pembridge Road, W11 3HG, 7727 9620, www.twelfth-house.co.uk) you can order astrological chart sessions alongside your coffee with owner Priscilla for £30. You can also just have your basic chart printed for £5, or select a 'tarot card of the day' for £3.

967

Shop for accordions

Emilio Allodi's Lewisham shop was founded in 1953 and its racks heave with every type of accordion: 1940s, Gestapo-car-style accordions, white jewelled wonders that recall Elvis in a Nudie suit, and tiny little ones for toddlers. Squeezeboxes aren't the only things to look at: Allodi also gets some wonderfully weird customers. There was the Geoff Capes-sized man-mountain who bought a baby's accordion to play in the bath, a tone-deaf Elvis impersonator, and a lady who matches her hair colour to her accordions.

Allodi Accordions *143-145 Lee High Road, SE13 5PF (8244 3771/ www.accordions.co.uk).*

968 *Climb the Henry VIII mound*

One of London's best, yet least-known, views can be had from the highest point in Pembroke Lodge, within Richmond Park – the Henry VIII mound. On a clear day, you can look through a special gap in the hedge and see as far as St Paul's, ten miles to the east – a view that has been enjoyed for nearly 300 years, and is now fiercely protected. The mound may date back to the Bronze Age; Henry VIII is rumoured to have stood here to watch for a signal from the Tower of London announcing the beheading of Anne Boleyn.

969 *Lunch at Sweetings*

In business since 1830 and occupying its current premises for more than 100 years, Sweetings can rightly claim to be a City institution. Open only for lunch, it's exceedingly popular with Square Mile suits (mainly male), so arrive early or late if you don't want to have to wait – you can't book. The slightly shabby interior, with its mosaic floor and cricketing prints, is a charmer. Seating is mainly on stools at high counters covered in white linen, behind which the amiable serving staff (trapped for the duration) dole out plates of potted shrimps and dressed crab, followed by fish pie or whole fish grilled, poached or fried. Buttered brown bread plugs any gaps. Drinks include Pimms, draught Guinness and bitter (served in pint or half-pint silver tankards) and lashings of white wine and champagne. Cooking can be plain – witness whole smoked haddock, of good quality but unadorned save for a poached egg balanced on top. And there's more than an air of public-school dinners about the watery spinach and defiantly retro puddings such as spotted dick and steamed syrup sponge. But we wouldn't have it any other way: may Sweetings last another 100 years.

Sweetings *39 Queen Victoria Street, EC4N 4SA (7248 3062).*

970 *Shop at Dover Street Market*

Comme des Garçons designer Rei Kawakubo's ground-breaking six-storey space (17-18 Dover Street, W1S 4LT, 7518 0680, www.doverstreet market.com) combines the edgy energy of London's indoor markets – concrete floors, tills housed in corrugated-iron shacks, Portaloo dressing rooms – with rarefied labels. Theatrical displays, combined with such conversation pieces as Victorian taxidermy and vintage porn, make for a fascinating browse, even if you can't afford the goods – although there are less expensive items (a vintage seed packet in the Labour and Wait concession, for example, is £2). Once you've taken it all in, have a sit-down in the Rose Bakery on the top floor.

Dover Street Market

Under the gavel

*Stuart Husband **shows you how to view world-class works of art in a civilised, crowd-free environment.***

Love art but coming increasingly to dread the gloves-off gladiatorial combat of overcrowded, over-regulated, over-curated museums? There is an alternative, when you want to see great works in the capital, that's quieter, gentler and – best of all – absolutely free.

Auction houses enjoyed an unprecedented boom while the City paid out ever-larger bonuses and London consolidated its reputation as European capital for oligarchs. And the economic downturn has failed to quell its vitality. And one of the welcome boons is the wealth of art going on show at the likes of Sotheby's and Christie's before going under the hammer; true, only one lucky person can walk off with a Warhol fright-wig self-portrait (for anything up to £2 million at today's torrid prices) but, in the days before a major sale, anyone can wander in and view the lots, courtesy of the museum-worthy displays in the auction houses' galleries – a trickle-down effect that's unusually genuine and (albeit briefly) truly democratic.

According to Helen Perkins, a deputy director at Sotheby's, there's never been a better time to come and view the covetable wares in its seven well-appointed galleries. 'For the first time, London is replacing New York as the main sale-site for front-rank painting and sculpture,' she says. 'London is a magnet for the Russians, South-east Asians and, increasingly, the Chinese, and they're particularly keen on Impressionist and contemporary art. So a lot of extremely good pieces are coming on to the market as a consequence.'

In 2007, Sotheby's biggest-ever sale of Impressionist and contemporary art was chock-full of blue-chip names – Cézanne, Renoir, Van Gogh, Gauguin, Klimt, Magritte, Duchamp, Soutine, Bacon, Warhol, Richter, Basquiat. It brought in close to £200 million. 'Shows like that one give us the chance to mount a display that can compete with anything at the National or the Tate,' says Perkins. 'And a lot of the paintings and sculptures we get have been in private collections, so they sometimes haven't been seen in public for decades. It's a great chance for people to view these unfamiliar works by artists they like, before – in some cases – they disappear again.'

Yet the auction houses are the first to concede that they have a bit of an image problem. With their hushed, carpeted entrances presided over by liveried doormen, and their Savile-Row-and-Swarovski habitués, they can seem a little… 'intimidating?' says Mitzi Mina of Sotheby's. 'I think we have been guilty of that in the past. But now we're looking to actively encourage more casual visits. We want to make it clear that you don't have to have an interest in bidding to come and enjoy the exhibits.'

Sotheby's outreach programme includes its foyer café (which offers pre-gallery croissant-and-coffee fortification or prime lunchtime people-watching opportunities) and, for the February show in 2007, the debut of a huge marquee in nearby Hanover Square to show some of the more cutting-edge works from the contemporary sale and to offer the kind of white-wall-wooden-floor-groovy vibe you'd expect at the Frieze Art Fair (though with a higher Lobb footfall than would ever be seen in Regent's Park). 'It's a tribute to the increasing depth and breadth of our shows, and it's a more relaxed and accessible way of presenting them,' says Helen Perkins.

Displays are generally mounted in the five or six days that lead up to a major sale, with opening hours running from 9am to 3pm or perhaps 4pm (noon to 5pm at weekends). They exemplify the saleroom/museum divide. At 10am the airy, spacious galleries are usually virtually empty. There are no groups of sulky schoolkids or shrieking students hunkered down in front of the pictures, and your contemplation is further enhanced by the lack of velvet ropes (you can look an Egon Schiele waif or a Cindy Sherman clown right in the eyes), hawk-like attendants and – the worst of the lot – the infuriating hiss of audio guides. If you want the artists' 'motivation' or art-historical back-story, you can pore through the lavishly illustrated sale catalogues that hang in every room; the wall-labels concentrate on how much each painting is expected to fetch, providing a much more piquant *Antiques*

Roadshow-style frisson ('Ooh! One and a half million for a Peter Doig!'). While the 'star' lots are highlighted, the salon-style hang of the rest of the show emphasises the law of the marketplace rather than any curatorial bias or reverence; thus, small but perfectly formed works by Gauguin and Van Gogh face off in what amounts to a hallway, while a wealth of offerings from artists long considered second-tier – Maurice de Vlaminck, Raoul Dufy, Kees van Dongen – makes its case for reassessment (or not – picking out the wheat from the chaff is part of the fun). No wonder Brian Sewell – hater of crowds and castigator of curators – now writes as many reviews of salerooms as he does of museums.

The survival of the art market amid the collapse of the financial markets has been down to the continued presence of buyers. In September 2008 Damien Hirst made £95.7 million for a two-day sale of his work at Sotheby's, against a

'There are no groups of sulky schoolkids or shrieking students hunkered down in front of the pictures, and your contemplation is further enhanced by the lack of velvet ropes.'

background of financial market meltdown. The sale brought praise for Sotheby's policy of mining new markets in Russia, the Middle East, India and China – countries where there are wealthy buyers looking to collect well-known artists. Sotheby's 2009 contemporary art show is to include an Arab and Iranian section for the first time, alongside the likes of Andy Warhol, Damien Hirst, Antony Gormley and Anish Kapoor. Meanwhile, Chinese art is making its presence felt on the contemporary scene, and Sotheby's holds regular auctions of Russian paintings, often featuring Impressionist works.

With the auction houses still piled high with Old, Current and Future Masters, the 'Saleroom Circuit' could come to rival, if not supplant, the museums. There is one area where the latter still trumps the former, however; you can't yet buy souvenir postcards of the houses' star lots. But given the marketing savvy of Sotheby's, Christie's et al, that's one gap in the market that won't be left unplugged for much longer.

The Impressionist and Contemporary Art sales are generally held twice a year; check the websites at www.sothebys.com and www.christies.com for precise dates and exhibition opening times.

972-974

Explore Somerset House, then enjoy the art in its Courtauld and Embankment galleries.

The first Somerset House on this site was a Tudor mansion commissioned by the Duke of Somerset, demolished in 1775 to make way for an entirely new building – effectively the first purpose-built office block in the world. Architect Sir William Chambers spent 20 years working on the imposing neo-classical edifice overlooking the Thames. Various government offices took up residence here, including the Inland Revenue. The Revenue is still here but the rest of the building – which now houses the Courthauld and Embankment galleries – is now open to the public. Children never tire of running through the choreographed fountains in summer; in winter the grand courtyard is covered by an ice rink. The Dusk Bar, on the river terrace, has an innovative design by Tom Dixon. Its blue panels are made of Rodeca, a translucent polycarbonate construction material; they glow blue when lit up at night.

The Courtauld Institute of Art Gallery (7848 2526, www.courtauld.ac.uk/gallery) has one of the country's best collections of paintings – diverse and eclectic, yet on a more manageable scale than, say, the National. Although there are some works from earlier periods, the collection's strongest suit is its Impressionist and Post-Impressionist paintings. Famous works include Manet's astonishing *A Bar at the Folies-Bergère*, as well as plenty of superb Monet's and Cézannes, important Gaugins (including *Nevermore*), and some excellent Van Goghs and Seurats. On the top floor you get to the 20th century and a selection of gorgeous Fauvist works, a lovely room of Kandinskys and plenty more besides.

The new Embankment Galleries house interesting temporary exhibitions in the fields of art, architecture, fashion and design and there is also a permanent display downstairs, with a ceremonial barge and information boards describing the place's history, to the accompaniment of Handel's water music.

Admission to the Courthauld and Embankment Galleries is £5 for each space. But the Courtauld is free to all between 10am and 2pm on Mondays.

Somerset House *Strand, WC2R 1LA (7845 4600/ www.somerset-house.org.uk).*

975

Attend the London Tattoo Convention

An astonishing 15,000 sailors, heavy metal fans and hell's angels attended the first London Tattoo Convention (www.thelondontattooconvention.com) in 2005, so it's no surprise that this has become an annual event. Around 150 different artists attend the event in Brick Lane, each exhibiting a different take on the art of inflicting ink and pain on the human body with needles. Don't go along drunk because heaven knows what you'll come back sporting.

976

Take a gander at swan upping

All the swans on the River Thames belong either to the Queen or the Vintners' or Dyers' livery companies. Every year in the third week of July, a bizarre ritual takes place along the river, starting at Sunbury on the Monday (departing from Sunbury Lock at about 9am), and finishing at Abingdon in Oxfordshire. Herdsmen paddle about trying to count and mark the cygnets. The Dyers' swans are marked with a nick on one side of the beak; the Vintners' swans receive a nick on both sides whereas the Queen's are left unmarked, though occasionally a prime specimen is bagged for a state banquet. The Queen's Swan Marker duly produces a report on the results of the census. Pure Monty Python. Check the web (www.thamesweb.co.uk/windsor/windsor1999/upping.html) for more details.

977 *Go windsurfing*

The basics of windsurfing are relatively easy to grasp, though the first few attempts generally involve a good deal of time in the water or falling into it. Mastering the sport takes determination, but with a bit of practice you should be skimming along in no time. The Royal Yachting Association (0845 345 0400, www.rya.org.uk) is responsible for official courses and holds a list of London clubs.

982 *Learn traditional dancing*

For more than a century, the English Folk Song & Dance Society (Cecil Sharp House, 2 Regent's Park Road, NW1 7AY, 7485 2206, www.efdss.org) has helped preserve and promote the traditional songs and dances of England. However, the displays and courses hosted by the society's HQ range much more widely afield, encompassing ceilidhs, Caribbean quadrilles, salsa and jive, as well as clog dancing and more Cotswold morris dancing than you can shake a stick at. Musicians often play at the venue too (*see p39*).

978-980
Play pub chess

Strange and oxymoronic as it may sound – chess being a game of tactical, logical reasoning and your average boozer being the location of anything but – the capital actually hosts a number of chess lovers' pubs with boards for all stashed behind the bar. Try the Harrison (28 Harrison Street, WC1H 8JF, 7278 3966, www.harrisonbar.co.uk), the Brixton Bar & Grill (15 Atlantic Road, SW9 8HX, 7737 6777, www.brixtonbarandgrill.co.uk) or the Wargrave Arms (40-42 Brendon Street, W1H5HE (7723 0559) on a Tuesday or Wednesday night.

981 *Pay homage to the camp Christmas Tree at the V&A*

On display in December at the V&A in South Kensington. This is one full-on, highly decorated tree. And it beats the lovely – if spindly – one in Trafalgar Square.

983-984
Eat vegetarian haute cuisine

In the world of high-end dining, vegetarian dishes can often seem like an afterthought. Not so at top-notch French restaurant Morgan M (489 Liverpool Road, N7 8NS, 7609 3560, www.morganm.com), an ambitious venture renowned for its superb vegetarian food. Hits include intensely flavoured chilled gazpacho with a solitary croûton on top, served with gorgeously flavoured tomator and olive oil sorbet, or perhaps the verdant, 'just picked' flavour of steamed English asparagus capped with shaved truffles, served in a pool of sprightly, dense broad bean velouté.

Another fave for vegetarians at the swanky end of the market is French restaurant Roussillon (16 St Barnabas Street, SW1W 8PE, 7730 5550, www.roussillon.co.uk), which boasts a whole menu full of beautifully presented dishes. You might find the likes of spring vegetables in tempura with herb salad, black truffle risotto with parmesan and brown butter, or green ricotta quenelles with sautéed girolles and crispy sage.

985
Experience martini theatre at Duke's

What's the secret of a good martini? The bar at Duke's Hotel (35 St James's Place, SW1A 1NY, 7491 4840, www.dukeshotel.co.uk), known worldwide for mixing the best martinis in London, can give you a few pointers. Duke's uses only Tanqueray or Bombay Sapphire gin and Cristal or Smirnoff Black vodka, freezes them for 24 hours, and serves in a cocktail glass that's been frozen before use. Little wonder that the relaxing, comfortable bar of this elegant, privately owned hotel is popular with American visitors. Worth it for the theatricality as much as the sip you get at the end of it.

986
Find serenity in Westminster

College Garden, in the grounds of Westminster Abbey, has been under continuous cultivation for more than 900 years. Today, you can still see the 14th-century stone precinct walls at the far end of the garden, and five tall plane trees, planted in 1850. Much of the garden, though, is laid to grass; charity fundraising events take place here in the summer.

College Garden *Westminster Abbey, SW1P 3PA (7222 5152/www.westminster-abbey.org/visit-us college-garden).*

987
Take a trip on Hammerton's Ferry

The quickest – and most charming – way to get across the Thames. Set up in 1908 by one Walter Hammerton, this tiny wooden boat, with room for 12 passengers, operates daily from Marble Hill House to Ham House (and vice versa) from mid February to the end of October. It's the sole survivor of the numerous ferries that plied this stretch of the river for hundreds of years. Times have changed: the boat has an electric motor these days, and the fare – a penny when it started – is now £1 for adults, 50p for children (though you don't pay extra for bikes).

College Garden

988 Get into London's private gardens

Thanks to its popularity over the ten years it's been running, the annual Open Garden Squares Weekend event – held in mid June – has grown to include 190 gardens, with several recent additions, including the gardens of Goring Hotel near Victoria, the British Museum's India Landscape and Fann Street's wildlife garden. Undoubtably one of the major attractions of the weekend is the chance to sample the delights of the very posh squares that are closed to the public for the rest of the year, such as Belgrave Square in Knightsbridge. This enormous garden, four and a half acres in total, boasts a children's play area, a tennis court, a 'quiet garden' and an enviable collection of statuary. For a full list and exact dates, see www.opensquares.org.

989

Order from the set menu at Arbutus

Providing great cooking at very reasonable prices is no easy trick. But Arbutus pulls it off with aplomb. The set lunch is a steal for cooking of this imagination and flair at £15.50 for three courses, as is the pre-theatre menu (5-7pm) at £17.50 for three courses. Wine prices, too, are almost shockingly diner-friendly, especially the choice by 250ml carafe – over 60 are available in this way. A sense of balance and proportion pervades the cooking, and there is nothing superfluous, but no stinting on what matters either. Squid and mackerel, combined in a 'burger' is a trademark starter. Other dishes might be salt cod brandade or a gaillette of pork. A floating island often crops up on the set menu, though other delicate but rewarding desserts might include roast peach with lemon thyme and salted caramel ice-cream or panna cotta.

Arbutus *63-64 Frith Street, W1D 3JW (7734 4545/ www.arbutusrestaurant.co.uk).*

A few of my favourite things

990-995

Christian O' Connell, radio DJ

One of our family treats is to go to the Charlotte Street Hotel (15-17 Charlotte Street, W1T 1RJ, 7806 2000, www.charlottestreet hotel.com) for a posh breakfast every couple of months. Charlotte Street is a lovely place; I started my stag do at the gorgeous tapas bar Navarro's (67 Charlotte Street, W1T 4PH, 7637 7713, www.navarros.co.uk). **Shopping wise, I love the fantastic Italian shirt shop Eterno (19 Conduit Street, W1S 2QR, 7493 5603, www.eternolondon. co.uk). The shirts are so beautifully made – it's a treat to go there for an annual buy.** Every Saturday and Sunday at 8am I walk to Richmond Deer Park (Holly Lodge, Richmond Park, TW10 5HS, 8948 3209, *see p53*). It's so beautiful. We have picnics by the lakes there in the summer and watch the deer feeding. **On a Saturday I love going to the library with my dad. The British Library (96 Euston Road, NW1 2DB, 7412 7332, www.bl.uk) has such a unique aura: there's something very special about the atmosphere. You can feel the knowledge surrounding you. One of the few places in London that's calm and peaceful. This is a noisy city and the British Library is a haven from it.** My daughter is transfixed by the Thames – the sheer size of it. We're going on a boat trip this summer – a good one that goes from Kingston, past Putney and on to Westminster (Westminster Passenger Services, 7930 2062, www.wpsa.co.uk).

The Christian O'Connell Breakfast Show is on Virgin Radio every weekday 6am-10am.

996 *Learn circus skills at Circus Space*

You get a lot of clowns in Hoxton, not all of them unintentional. Circus Space has been teaching circus skills from its Coronet Street base since 1990, offering courses that vary from one-off taster days and evening classes to the UK's only degree-level education in the circus arts. The £99 introduction to circus skills day is definitely the best way to get started: learn to balance on the tight wire, stilt walking, both the flying and the static trapeze, juggling and diabolo. It's all good fun and great exercise. It also offers a Western skills day, during which you can learn lassooing and other cowboy arts. Yahoo!

Circus Space *Coronet Street, N1 6HD (7729 9522/www.thecircusspace.co.uk).*

997

Visit the wonderful Sir John Soane Museum

Where too much is never enough. A leading architect in his day – he was responsible for the building that houses the Bank of England (*see p77*) – Sir John Soane obsessively collected art, furniture and architectural ornamentation, partly for enjoyment and partly for research. In the early 19th century he turned his house into a museum to which 'amateurs and students' should have access.

Much of the museum's appeal derives from its domestic setting. Rooms are modestly sized but modified by Soane with ingenious devices to channel and direct natural daylight and to expand available space, including walls that open out like cabinets to display some of his many paintings (works by Canaletto, Turner and two series by Hogarth). The Breakfast Room has a beautiful and much-imitated domed ceiling inset with convex mirrors, but the real wow is the Monument Court, a multi-storey affair stuffed with an array of sculpted stone detailing that had been removed from ancient and medieval buildings.

At the lowest level of the court is a sarcophagus of alabaster that's so thin it's almost translucent. It was discovered in a tomb in Egypt's Valley of the Kings, before being removed by 19th-century treasure hunters. Soane bought it after the British Museum declined the opportunity; he was so elated, he partied for three days. With this kind of passion, no wonder his curios are such a treat.

Sir John Soane Museum *13 Lincoln's Inn Fields, WC2A 3BP (7405 2107/www.soane.org).*

998

Listen to the bells of St Clement

St Clement Danes Church is said to have given rise to the nursery rhyme 'Oranges and Lemons' (though others, including St Clement Eastcheap, claim the same distinction). The bells ring out the tune at 9am, noon, 3pm and 6pm daily.

St Clement Danes *The Strand, WC2R 1DH (7242 8282).*

999

Sleep somewhere extraordinary

It would be some people's worst nightmare, but for us it's a dream: a sleepover with the mummies in the British Museum (Great Russell Street, WC1B 3DG, 7323 8195, www.thebritish museum.ac.uk). Sure, the preliminaries are a bit mundane: you need to be (or be responsible for) an 8- to 15-year-old who is a Young Friend of the museum (£20 per year; see the 'join in' section on the website for details). You're then eligible for one of the much-coveted 250-plus places on any of four sleepovers held each year. The £27.50 ticket pays for loads of activities, including storytelling and crafts workshops (perhaps making a Greek vase or a mosaic), and gives you the chance to explore the museum well after everyone else has been booted out. Book well in advance.

The British Museum isn't the only one of London's attractions to offer such events. Similar sleepovers are hosted once a month at the Science Museum (Exhibition Road, SW7 2DD, 0870 870 4868, www.sciencemuseum. org.uk) and, if you can get together a group of 20-40 children, on board the *Golden Hinde* (St Mary Overie Dock, Cathedral Street, SE1 9DE, 0870 011 8700, www.goldenhinde.com), a reproduction of Sir Francis Drake's galleon.

1000

Stop. Catch your breath. Sit down. You've earned it.

In a deckchair in Green Park, perhaps. With a cup of Monmouth Coffee Company coffee. Maybe on the top floor of Tower 42, or astride a Trafalgar Square lion. We'll leave the last choice up to you. It shouldn't be difficult. That's the magic of London. There are more than a thousand things to do.

A-Z index

Thematic index

Note: number refers to page, not list entry.

A

aeroplane spotting
Heathrow Airport — 29
RAF Museum — 278
remote-controlled — 235
anarchic London
Critical Mass — 37, 107
flash mobs — 85
guerilla gardening — 165
graffiti — 145
Speakers' Corner — 68
animals
aquariums — 79
bat walks — 44
deer park — 53, 307
dog show — 209
dogs & cats home — 237
insects — 135, 157
war memorial — 267
see also birdwatching; zoos
antiques
auctions — 104
Church Street — 108
archaeology
mudlarking — 44
museums — 52, 184, 264
architecture & buildings
art deco — 115, 204-205
derelict buildings — 258-262
exhibitions — 149
lectures — 192
modern — 138, 197, 263
Open House London — 126
stations — 178-179
art
auctions — 300-302
aural — 281
depicting London — 203
graffiti — 145
lectures — 192
life modelling — 84
materials — 235
murals — 148
open studios — 52
'renegade tiling' — 166
sculpture — 174, 253
'Secret' fundraiser — 32
street art — 46
see also galleries
arts venues (mixed media)
Horse Hospital — 188
Roundhouse — 49
Scoop — 130-131
auctions
antiques — 104
art — 300-302

B

bars *see* pubs & bars
baths
'Roman' — 249
Turkish — 272
see also swimming
beauty & grooming
barbers — 29
facials — 174
pedicures — 207
spas — 174, 194
tattoos — 304
beer
breweries — 149
festival — 172
German — 159, 229
quality ales — 68, 119, 216
birdwatching
areas & equipment — 236
dawn chorus — 276
swan-upping ceremony — 304
Wetland Centre — 184
woodpeckers — 252
blogs — 242-243
boats & boat trips
boating lakes — 214
canal trips — 137
dragon boats — 234
ferry — 306
historic ships — 127, 309
puppet theatre barge — 280
races — 123, 234, 294
as regular transport — 92
river tours — 49, 307
speedboats — 61
skiff hire — 144
Tate to Tate service — 12
bookshops — 77, 219, 235
café — 194
children's — 46
cookery — 88
gambling — 256
local — 234-235
sci-fi & fantasy — 212
travel & maps — 26, 73
breakfast
blog reviews — 243-244
greasy spoon — 226
hotel — 307
market — 37
park — 293
bridges
best — 104, 173
views from — 10-11, 173, 290
buses
night tours — 292
open-top — 229, 292
Routemaster — 65, 218
RV1 — 169

C

cafés
astrology & tarot — 297
bohemian — 77, 132
bookshop — 194
Cabman's Shelters — 85
classic — 64, 226, 289
crêperie — 276
good coffee — 119
good for lunch — 186, 188
historic — 216
juice bar — 256
Parisian — 294
RIBA — 149
see also pubs & bars; restaurants; teas
cakes
American — 134
Chelsea Buns — 123
Maids of Honour — 216
canal
museum — 186
walks & boat trips — 137
cars
banger races — 99
boot sales — 167
veteran rally — 13
cemeteries
best — 197
nature reserve — 118
pets — 292
children's attractions
aquariums — 79
brass rubbing — 133
butterflies — 157
city farms — 19
Coram's Fields — 149
diving courses — 61
dodgems — 37
Duck Tours — 49
Easy Peasy Skate — 124
galleries — 187, 252
kite flying — 265
literary characters — 142-143
mini-golf — 280
puppet shows — 280
sleepovers — 309
steam railway — 115
story trails — 267
theatre — 46
see also parks; zoos
chocolate
making your own — 252
shops — 164, 227
Christmas
bike ride — 272
Frost Fair — 128
lectures — 192
Peter Pan Cup Swim — 23
show — 55
tree — 305

Advertisers' index

Please refer to relevant sections for addresses and/or telephone numbers

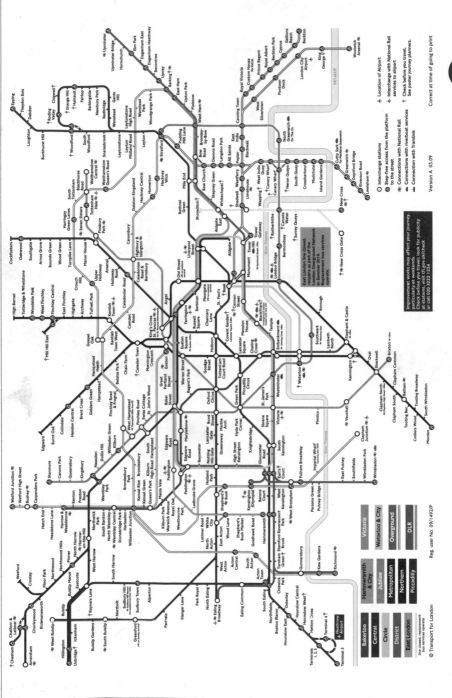

Time Out

1000

things to do in London

timeout.com

Time Out Guides Ltd
Universal House
251 Tottenham Court Road
London W1T 7AB
United Kingdom
Tel: +44 (0)20 7813 3000
Fax: +44 (0)20 7813 6001
Email: guides@timeout.com
www.timeout.com

Published by Time Out Guides Ltd, a wholly owned subsidiary of Time Out Group Ltd.
Time Out and the Time Out logo are trademarks of Time Out Group Ltd.

© **Time Out Group Ltd 2010**

10 9 8 7 6 5 4 3 2 1

This edition first published in Great Britain in 2010 by Ebury Publishing.
A Random House Group Company
20 Vauxhall Bridge Road, London SW1V 2SA

Random House Australia Pty Ltd 20 Alfred Street, Milsons Point, Sydney, New South Wales 2061, Australia

Random House New Zealand Ltd 18 Poland Road, Glenfield, Auckland 10, New Zealand

Random House South Africa (Pty) Ltd Isle of Houghton, Corner Boundary Road & Carse O'Gowrie, Houghton 2198, South Africa

Random House UK Limited Reg. No. 954009

Distributed in USA by Publishers Group West
1700 Fourth Street, Berkeley, California 94710

Distributed in Canada by Publishers Group Canada
250A Carlton Street, Toronto, Ontario M5A 2L1

For further distribution details, see www.timeout.com.

ISBN: 978-1-84670-176-4

A CIP catalogue record for this book is available from the British Library.

Printed and bound by Firmengruppe APPL, aprinta druck, Wemding, Germany.

The Random House Group Limited supports The Forest Stewardship Council (FSC), the leading international forest certification organisation. All our titles that are printed on Greenpeace approved FSC certified paper carry the FSC logo. Our paper procurement policy can be found at http://www.rbooks.co.uk/environment.

Time Out carbon-offsets its flights with Trees for Cities (www.treesforcities.org).